I0760122

Hitler's War Against the Partisans during Operation Barbarossa

DEDICATION

This book is dedicated to the victims of military aggression.

Hitler's War Against the Partisans during Operation Barbarossa

June 1941 to the Spring of 1942

Dr Antonio J. Muñoz

AN IMPRINT OF PEN & SWORD BOOKS LTD
YORKSHIRE – PHILADELPHIA

First published in Great Britain in 2025 by
FRONTLINE BOOKS
an imprint of Pen & Sword Books Ltd
Yorkshire – Philadelphia

ISBN 9 781 03612 149 5

A CIP catalogue record for this book is available from the British Library.

Typeset by Concept, Huddersfield, West Yorkshire, HD4 5JL
Printed on paper from a sustainable source by
CPI Group (UK) Ltd, Croydon CR0 4YY

The Publisher's authorised representative in the EU for product safety is Authorised Rep Compliance Ltd., Ground Floor, 71 Lower Baggot Street, Dublin D02 P593, Ireland.
www.arccompliance.com

For a complete list of Pen & Sword titles please contact
PEN & SWORD BOOKS LTD
47 Church Street, Barnsley, South Yorkshire, S70 2AS, England
E-mail: enquiries@pen-and-sword.co.uk
Website: www.pen-and-sword.co.uk
or
PEN & SWORD BOOKS
1950 Lawrence Rd, Havertown, PA 19083, USA
E-mail: uspen-and-sword@casematepublishers.com
Website: www.penandswordbooks.com

Contents

List of plates vi
List of figures, tables and maps vii
Author's note x
Introduction 1
1. German preparations for invading and occupying the USSR 15
2. The *Ostland* (Baltic) and Belarus regions 31
3. The SS command in the Baltic States and North Russia and the employment of locally raised volunteers 61
4. Controlling the rear areas of Army Group North 91
5. The start of the war behind the lines 107
6. Collaboration in Belarus and central Russia, 1941–1942 113
7. The war against the Jews and the partisans resurgent 123
8. Rear area security in Ukraine and southern Russia 151
9. German security divisions in Ukraine and southern Russia 173
Conclusions 185
Appendix: Russian volunteer formations in the East, 1941–1942 191
Glossary of German military and political terms 193
Notes 203
Bibliography 221
Index of Persons 239
Index of Formations 243

List of plates

1. German guards and their canine companions.
2. German tracker dogs and their handlers.
3. A German armoured train and its guards.
4. A German armoured train somewhere in Ukraine, 1943.
5. An improvised armoured train, 1942.
6. German police parade, 1940.
7. A police commander and his staff.
8. German police in the field.
9. An armoured car of the German police in Russia, 1942.
10. General Bronislav Kaminski, 1944.
11. SS Lieutenant General and Lieutenant General of the Police Erich von dem Bach Zelewski.
12. Hanging suspected partisans.
13. Member of the Schutzmannschaft in action.
14. Schutzmannschaft in battle.
15. A Schutzmannschaft inspects a suspect.
16. A new Schutzmannschaft volunteer.
17. Rifle practice for the Schutzmannschaft.
18. Soviet partisans in the summer of 1941.
19. Training new partisan recruits.
20. The results of a partisan attack.

List of figures, tables and maps

Figures

3.1. The SS and police command structure in the Baltic States 74
8.1. Field commands and local commands under Army Group South, March 1942 160
9.1. The 444th Security Division on 15 May 1941 173
9.2. The 454th Security Division on 15 May 1941 175
9.3. The 454th Security Division in August 1941 176
9.4. The 444th Security Division in March 1942 177

Tables

1.1. German losses on the Eastern Front and replacements 22
2.1. SS and police units available for employment in the USSR in the summer of 1941 38
2.2. German security divisions in Belarus and central Russia, 1941 56
3.1. Forces available to the Command Staff of the National Leader of the SS 64
3.2. Command Staff unit strengths, June 1941 65
3.3. Command Staff unit strengths, April 1942 66
3.4. Latvian police forces in Riga, August 1941 68
3.5. Regular Order Police units employed in North Russia 70
3.6. German Police Losses, December–March 1942 71
3.7. Police battalions assigned to security divisions, June 1942 76
3.8. German and foreign *Ordnungspolizei* and SD personnel, 1 October 1942 77
3.9. Distribution of Estonian Auxiliary Police Companies, summer 1941 81
3.10. Distribution of self-defence battalions, late 1942 81
3.11. The Estonian Self-Defence Organization, summer 1941 82
3.12. Estonian units created by the German Order Police in 1941 83
3.13. Other Estonian units raised by the German Army in 1941 84

3.14. Eastern troop strengths for Army Group North, February–July 1943 . . . 85
4.1. Guerrillas and civilian suspects captured or shot by security divisions operating behind the lines of Army Group North, 30 September–29 October 1941 . . . 97
4.2. Location of the staff for the Chief of the Secret Field Police, Army Group North . . . 104
4.3. Location of the units under the Secret Field Police Chief, Army Group North . . . 104
4.4. External commands created by the 713th Secret Field Police Group . . . 105
4.5. Partisans killed or captured by secret field police units, 1941–1942 . . . 106
6.1. Belarusian Auxiliary Police recruits in Baranovichi, 1941–1944 . . 118
7.1. Numbers of Jews killed in the Baltic States, 1941–1944 . . . 126
7.2. Estimated numbers of victims killed by the Nazis in the East, 1939–1945 . . . 133
7.3. Arms supplied to the White Russian Partisans in 1942 . . . 135
7.4. Police losses in front-line combat, December 1941–March 1942 . 136
7.5. Partisan brigades in Belarus, February 1942 . . . 137
7.6. Extermination of the Jewish population in the Baltic States and Belarus, June–December 1941 . . . 141
7.7. Murders linked specifically to certain SS, police and secret field police units, June 1941–January 1942 . . . 146
7.8. Belarusian partisan weapons, autumn 1941 . . . 148

Maps

1. The German occupation zones bordering the Baltic states, Belarus, East Prussia (Germany) and the so-called Generalgouvernement (occupied Poland) . . . 28
2. The various borders of Belarus, 1939–1944 . . . 33
3. Partisan concentrations in Belarus, 1941 . . . 58
4. The Baltic States in 1941 . . . 67
5. Communications network for the SS in the East in the summer of 1941 . . . 72
6. Principal rail lines in northern and central Russia . . . 93
7. Soviet partisan activity in the region of Army Group North, autumn 1941 . . . 99

8. Partisans in the area of Army Group North, December 1941 101
9. Cholm and the surrounding area, 18 January 1942 134
10. The military situation in Cholm on 21 January 1942 135
11. Ukraine, southern Russia and the northern Caucasus Mountains, showing the areas of partisan activity by the autumn of 1941 153
12. German security divisions in western Ukraine, 10 September 1941 166
13. Anti-partisan drive in Novo Moskov-Pavlograd, December 1941 to January 1942 170

Author's Note

A regime, of whatever kind, collapses only under the weight of defeat.

[Benito Mussolini]

History is cyclical

John Gray was one of only a few academics in the world who anticipated, and warned of, the coming economic collapse of 2008. He claims that economic boom periods in the market can be deceptive, given that history is cyclical. The key word we should take note of is 'cyclical', meaning that history is never progressive but recurring. In simple terms, history repeats itself. With regard to history repeating itself, I have observed numerous parallels between Adolf Hitler and Vladimir Putin, proving Dr Gray's analysis of repeating cycles. Back in the 1930s and 1940s it was expansionist dictatorships that threatened the world. Although Benito Mussolini and the Empire of Japan represented a threat to peace, Adolf Hitler and Nazism were the greater dangers. Today Xi Jinping is pushing communist China into a more aggressive stance with regard to the South China Sea and the issue of Taiwan.

Yet it is Vladimir Putin of the Russian Federation who is now the larger danger to world peace. During the past ten years, our world has seen the rise of autocrats all over the planet. Many nations are now run by authoritarian regimes. Examples that immediately come to mind are Kim Jong-un of North Korea, Bashar al-Assad of Syria, Viktor Orbán of Hungary, Recep Tayyip Erdoğan of Turkey, Daniel Ortega of Nicaragua, Nicolas Maduro of Venezuela, Miguel Diaz-Canel of Cuba, Aleksander Lukashenko of Belarus, Ramzan Kadirov of Chechnya and, of course, Vladimir Putin of the Russian Federation. The list of autocrats is much longer. In fact, in the past 17 years there has been a decline in democracy around the world. Only twenty-five nations have seen improvements in human rights and advances in liberal reforms, while a whopping sixty nations have slipped into authoritarianism.[1]

That is more than double the number of nations who have come closer to democracy. If twentieth-century history is our guide, and if this trend continues, then the twenty-first century will likely see more conflicts brought on by men calling themselves 'General Secretary', 'Chairman', 'Supreme Leader' or even 'President for Life'. In particular, Vladimir Putin has been active in exporting his despotism beyond the borders of the Russian Federation. That is what sets him apart from other despots. While most authoritarian leaders today are content with oppressing their own people, Vladimir Putin has begun 'exporting' his dictatorship to other nations. Of course, I'm referring to the current invasion of Ukraine. The parallels between Hitler and Putin, as we shall see, are there for anyone to observe if they care to notice.

Waiting in the wings, much like Benito Mussolini did from 1939 to 1940, Xi Jinping of China is looking to see if Putin gets away with carving up Ukraine. Like Putin, Xi Jinping has an eye on conquering land outside the current borders of mainland China. In addition to building artificial islands in the South China Sea, then claiming 'territorial waters' around them, the Chinese communist government in Beijing has always claimed that Taiwan is a 'breakaway' province that rightfully belongs to mainland China. Taiwan was established on the island of Formosa after General Chiang Kai Shek and the Nationalist forces lost the Chinese civil war in 1949. If Putin succeeds in taking Ukraine, the Chinese communist leader may feel emboldened to make a similar attempt to grab Taiwan by force, sooner rather than later.

The long Russian authoritarian winter

In 1960 Gerald Reitlinger published a groundbreaking study titled *The House built on Sand: The Conflicts of German Policy in Russia, 1941–1945*. Dr Reitlinger explained how the German attempt at empire-building in the East failed, given the absurd and counterproductive Nazi policies towards the very people whom they wished to rule. This work was released around the height of the Cold War. It was timely then because it showed, among other things, that many of the people who inhabited the Soviet Union had been, and continued to be, unhappy with the communist system. The establishment of the 'Iron Curtain', as Winston Churchill described it in 1946, imprisoned not only those peoples living within the borders of the Union of Soviet Socialist Republics (USSR), but all of eastern Europe as well. The population in these areas chafed at the lack of freedom and inaccessibility to even basic consumer goods that were needed for everyday life. The Soviet system stifled individuality and offered only repression, deprivation and harshness to its citizens.

Vladimir Lenin's Bolshevik state was not that dissimilar to the Czar's rule when it came to repression. In fact, Lenin's government proved to be harsher than the Czars had ever been. Joseph Stalin's rule (1924–1953) was even more severe. Current estimates by Russian scholars as to the number of people who perished as a result of Stalin's regime stand at around 20 million. The only one to beat that record is Adolf Hitler. The communist state that followed under Nikita Khrushchev (beginning in 1953) and Leonid Brezhnev (in 1964) was, in many ways, not as repressive as the Stalinist period, but the system had not altered substantially enough for the population of the Soviet Union to enjoy the benefits that come from living in a free society. In that communist 'utopia', individuals could not question or criticize the state. Doing so was to risk ostracism, alienation or even imprisonment. People also lived in fear that someone would inform on them if they were overheard complaining about the state or said the 'wrong thing'.

Free travel was not permitted and individuals could not enjoy the benefits that come from economic independence, except for high party officials who received rewards that the common Soviet citizen could only dream of. In essence, the autocracy of the Czars and the dictatorship of the Leninist and Stalinist period gave way to the oligarchy of the old guard in the Central Committee of the Communist Party. Throughout the communist period, citizens of the USSR would spend hours standing in bread lines or queueing at the local department store, hoping to be able to purchase provisions or scarce consumer goods. This was because most of the nation's GDP was going to the production of military hardware.

Why did Russia end up as a kleptocracy?

When Brezhnev died in 1982, Yuri Andropov, another old-timer from the Central Committee, was elected General Secretary of the Communist Party. Andropov died in 1984, serving less than two years, at which point another old-timer, Konstantine Chernenko, was elected. Chernenko lasted an even shorter time than Andropov, dying in 1985, not even a year after assuming office. Members of the Central Committee thereupon chose a candidate who was significantly younger than most of the old guard who had served up until then. The hope was that this new General Secretary would not have to be replaced in a couple of years. This turned out to be Mikhail Gorbachev, born in 1931 of a Russian father and Ukrainian mother. Employing what he called *Glasnost* (openness) and *Perestroika* (restructuring), Gorbachev set about trying to reorganize the Soviet economic and political system. The job seemed insurmountable, but Gorbachev began to make slow progress.

However, the changes that he was implementing seemed so progressive and democratic that in 1991 the hardliners in the Communist Party attempted a coup against Gorbachev. The coup ultimately failed, and that failure led directly to the collapse of the USSR and the formation of the Russian Federation under Boris Yeltsin. The establishment of the Russian Federation in 1991 seemed to bring hope that perhaps the long Russian 'authoritarian winter' might break, and democracy could finally take hold. Unfortunately, two things occurred which quickly halted the swing towards democracy. First, instead of trying to support the newly created democratic institutions in Russia, the United States (US) declared victory in the Cold War and set about establishing itself as the sole superpower in the world. Secondly, the appointment of Vladimir Putin as president of the Russian Federation in 1999 eventually condemned Russia's newly born democracy to a slow death.

Putin, a KGB hardliner and a true believer in the Soviet communist system, worked slowly at first, crippling and undermining the newly created democratic institutions in Russia. In this he adopted the old Benito Mussolini adage: 'If you pluck a chicken one feather at a time, no one will notice.' So, following this method, Putin usurped the democratic checks and balances in the country and slowly created the kleptocracy that exists in Russia today. Putin was not alone in this. He had help from people who felt as he did. The Weimar Republic was likewise undermined by officials who resented democracy and longed for a return to the rule of the *Kaiser*. Still others wished for a new authoritarian leader to emerge. These men worked against the republic from within, subverting the government. The parallels here between the failed Weimar Republic and the failed attempt to bring true democracy to Russia are obvious.

Where was the United States?

Following the collapse of the USSR, the US involved itself in several conflicts, some of which were not of its making, like Saddam Hussein's invasion of Kuwait in 1991 and the 2001 attack on America by Al Qaeda. But in 2003 the US elected to invade Iraq. This was a war of choice that ultimately proved to be costly and debilitating to the US in terms of lives lost, the huge financial expense of the conflict, and the loss of political capital around the world. George Bush Jr opted for a pre-emptive policy that said the US would act if it saw a threat in the making. This unnecessary conflict also helped to destabilize the delicate political balance in the Middle East. While it was true that Al Qaeda was responsible for attacking the US on 11 September 2001, its presence was in Afghanistan, not Iraq. In order to justify the invasion of Iraq, the US government accused Saddam Hussein of having weapons of mass destruction. Hussein was also blamed for conspiring with Al Qaeda, even though those in the US government knew very well that Hussein was a secular tyrant, who would not have allowed a fundamentalist theocratic movement like Al Qaeda into his country.

By 2003 Saddam Hussein was no longer a threat to the US or even to his Arab or Persian neighbours. After his defeat in 1991, he had been content to remain within the borders of Iraq and butcher his own people. However, the neo-conservatives in the George Bush Jr administration saw an opportunity for regime change, under the twin guises of the pre-emptive policy and of fighting Al Qaeda. They felt this change could occur at the point of a gun, and that ousting Hussein would alter the political landscape of the Middle East in favour of the US. The political situation in the Middle East did change after the invasion of Iraq, but it was not the change for which the neo-conservatives had hoped. The nation that in the end benefited most from Saddam Hussein's fall was the Islamic Republic of Iran. Today Iraq has close relations and partners with Iran, while the US has lukewarm relations with Iraq. At great cost in human life and financial expense, the US has inadvertently aided a sworn enemy (Iran).

Hubris, it seemed, had taken the US to a place where it was completely invested in what would become the longest conflict it had ever fought. Initially in Afghanistan, only limited US forces were employed, backed up by local warlords whose allegiance was not guaranteed. The US had used few forces at the start of the Afghan war because it was saving the bulk of the troops for the invasion of Iraq. As a result, the one chance to capture Osama bin Laden early, at Tora Bora, was lost because one of the Afghan 'allies' was bought off and turned a blind eye while Osama bin Laden and his cohorts slipped away. Mistakes were also made in Iraq once the country was occupied.

The first mistake was placing a minority Shiite leader to head the new Iraqi government. After a lifetime of being abused by the Sunni majority, the Shiites were dying for payback. Nouri al-Maliki began to favour the Shiites, while the Sunni were marginalized. Another mistake was the United States government's decision to disband the entire Iraqi Army, using the Coalition Provisional Authority. The Iraqi Army employed hundreds of thousands of Sunnis. The consequences of demobilizing so many Sunni men would prove to be detrimental. These decisions, and others, led directly to further alienation and resentment among the Sunni population. Many former Iraqi soldiers, now out of work and seeing their country led by a Shiite leader bent on weakening the power of the Sunni majority, were easily radicalized. These ex-Iraqi Army soldiers became ready recruits for a new terrorist organization: ISIS. Slowly but steadily, attacks against US troops in Iraq began to increase.

The demise of the fledgling Russian democracy

While the US was distracted with its Iraqi adventure, Russia was struggling to establish its democratic institutions. The period from 1991 to 1999, I would venture to say, was very similar to the period of the Weimar Republic from 1921 to 1933. A nation that was only accustomed to one form of authoritarianism or another (Germany in 1921 and Russia in 1991) was asked to accept democratic institutions and to embrace them willingly. As stated earlier, as in the Weimar Republic, there were people in the new Russian government who opposed democracy. The principal opponent in Russia's bid for liberalism was Vladimir Putin. When he was appointed President of the Russian Federation (after Boris Yeltsin retired), he was in a perfect position to attack that nascent Russian democracy from within. Just as Putin was given the position of President of the Russian Federation in 1999, Hitler was given the position of Chancellor of Germany in 1933, and just like Putin, he began to undermine the Weimar Republic until he obtained the dictatorship that he wanted. Again, the parallels between both men are obvious.

Putin was a child of the communist system and was wholly indoctrinated in the principles that had kept the USSR together. Using patience and the dirty tricks of his former KGB trade, he employed bribery, coercion and blackmail, and even worked with the Russian and Chechen mafia to eliminate or intimidate politicians, industrialists and reporters, forcing them to bend to his will. Those who refused to be subverted were killed. Those critics whom Putin could not reach because they were living outside the Russian Federation were eventually killed as well. It became quite common for Russian dissidents to be poisoned with Polonium-210 by agents of the Russian Federation's Federal Security Service (FSB), many of whom were former KGB members. For example, Russian dissident Alexander Litvinenko was poisoned in 2006. In 2015 another dissident, Boris Nemtsov, was assassinated while taking a walk near the Kremlin. Those who are in the know claim that it was the Chechen mafia who killed Nemtsov, yet the person who benefited most from his murder was Vladimir Putin. While living in the United Kingdom, Sergei Skripal and his daughter were poisoned using Novichok in 2018. In 2020 Alexei Navalny, a brave critic of Putin, was poisoned. He survived, only to be charged with false corruption charges that sent him to jail for 13 years. Navalny died on 16 February 2024. He was only 47 years old. Many people had warned Navalny not to return to Russia, for fear of what would happen. Nevertheless, this courageous critic of Putin refused to be cowed. Like so many before him, he paid the ultimate price for defending democracy in Russia. Since the start of the Second Chechen War (in 2000), more than 200 Russian politicians and reporters from television and print media have been assassinated in Russia, a number that parallels the number of moderate and left-leaning German politicians and newspaper editors who were killed by right-wing assassins during the period of the Weimar Republic. Slowly, Putin has destroyed or usurped the new democratic institutions in Russia, including a free press. Adolf Hitler did the same thing.

The Russian parliament has become simply a rubber stamp for Putin's wishes and desires in much the same way that members of the *Reichstag* became a rubber stamp for Hitler. Newspaper and TV reporters in Russia must toe the line and only present to the Russian people the version of history and events that Putin wants to show them. This is yet another parallel with Hitler's Third Reich. Once he was certain that his position as President of the Russian Federation was secure for another twenty years, Putin lamented openly that the collapse of the Soviet Union was the greatest calamity to befall the world in the twentieth century. We hear today, as the Russian invasion of Ukraine continues to wreak destruction, pain, misery and death, that the majority of Russians support Putin's war and his version of events. The ludicrous and spurious accusation by Putin that he is eliminating Nazis from the Ukrainian government is simply an excuse for aggression.

Unfortunately, he is believed by the majority of Russians. It's not merely the *babushkas* who believe him, but middle-aged people and even young adults. This is because Vladimir Putin has turned what were independent and impartial Russian news outlets into the political mouthpiece of his regime. Those who are not fooled do not dare to speak openly. The situation has not been helped by the fact that the majority of the Russian people have not experienced true democracy and its advantages for any serious amount of time. Not knowing any better, perhaps some Russians actually prefer the harshness and repression of a police state, simply because it is familiar to them.

Professor Jeffrey Herff, an expert on the history of the Weimar Republic, remarked in 1986 that the Weimar Republic 'was a republic without republicans'. This was echoed by Sebastian Ullrich in a work that was released in 2009.[2] Both claimed that the German people at the time were only accustomed to authoritarian rule, and therefore were less inclined to support a democratic government when it was offered to them, especially when there were anti-democratic agents working from within to undermine that very democracy. This is the same scenario that Russia has experienced since 1999. It is also another reason why democracy was not firmly embedded in Russian society. Granted, there were some in Russia who tried to defend the newly created independent institutions, like a free press. Many who did so were targeted and paid the ultimate price. Putin and his cronies made sure of that, and that democracy would not flower in Russia. Taking all of this into account, we can say that the parallels between the history of the Weimar Republic and the Russian Federation are undeniable.

A forgotten lesson from the past

While the US was spending much human capital and economic effort being the sole superpower of the world, fighting a war of consequence and a war of choice, it should have been supporting Russia's young democracy by all means. Frankly, the Americans dropped the ball, forgetting their own history. Back in 1918, when the First World War ended, President Woodrow Wilson wished to aid the newly established democracies of Europe that had been created from the ashes of four former empires. He wanted to do this by sending both money and experts to those new democratic nations in Europe. Two things put a stop to this. First, Wilson had a stroke towards the end of his second term that incapacitated him for about a year. Second, US Congress refused to allocate any funds towards supporting the new democracies of Europe. Instead, the US became isolationist and ignored Europe altogether.

Within 20 years (by 1938), the only true democracy left in central Europe was Czechoslovakia.[3] In that same year Adolf Hitler's threats yielded appeasement from the West yet again.[4] At Munich, Adolf Hitler was able to acquire the Sudetenland from Czechoslovakia, after he promised Neville Chamberlain and Édouard Daladier that he would make no further territorial demands. The Sudetenland was a stretch of frontier border between Germany and Czechoslovakia that contained a sizeable *volksdeutsch* (ethnic German) population. The Sudetenland also happened to contain the principal mountain defences for Czechoslovakia. At Munich, Édouard Daladier of France and Neville Chamberlain of the United Kingdom didn't even bother inviting the Czechs to the negotiating table. Benito Mussolini, who really had nothing to do with the problem, showed up at the meeting uninvited, but was given a seat, while the Czechs, whose future was being decided, were left out.

When the Germans acquired the Sudetenland, they effectively stripped the country of its defensive fortifications along the Czech-German border. Months later, in March 1939, Hitler's armies quietly marched in and took over what was left of the Czechoslovakian nation. Hitler's troops entered Prague during a heavy snowstorm, which ironically intimated the dark period ahead for the Czech people. Had the US supported the new democracies of Europe after the First World War, events might have had a different outcome. In 1991, instead of declaring victory in the Cold War, the US should have assured that victory over the USSR by supporting democracy in Russia by any and all means possible.

Edmund Burke was right

We can speculate that matters might have been different if the United States in 1991 had concentrated on making sure that democracy would take a firm hold in Russia. Today the nation of Ukraine, and indeed all peaceful nations of the world, are suffering from Russian aggression, directly or indirectly, either at the point of a gun or through rising food and fuel prices, all because for years many nations turned a blind eye to Russia's bullying. Ukrainians are dying by the thousands and people around the world are starving because the war is affecting grain shipments. The world had to suffer the Second World War because Adolf Hitler was appeased from 1934 until 1938, as he became stronger and more dangerous. Vladimir Putin has been emboldened by the apathy and lethargy of the West. Europe in particular has had a large dependence on Russian oil and natural gas. This has led the nations of Europe to ignore Russia's growing belligerence in exchange for a steady energy supply. The Russian Army, long known for its brutality and heartlessness, devastated Grozny, the capital of Chechnya, in 1994. The Russian Army did terrible things in Georgia, when Russian-backed separatists in the South Ossetian *Oblast* declared their independence from Georgia in 2008 and sought Russian 'protection'.[5]

The heinous tactic of targeting civilians, as seen in Ukraine, was perfected by the Russian Army during the Syrian civil war in 2016. Entire cities in Syria were levelled by Russian artillery and air strikes. In particular, hospitals and schools were targeted as a way of demoralizing their opponents. In the twisted logic of tyrants, killing the children of your enemy limits the rise of future soldiers who will oppose you. Even chemical weapons were used against the Syrian civilian population. Although President Obama warned Bashar al-Assad of Syria that employing chemical weapons was a line he should not cross, Assad, who benefited from the protection of the Russian Army, employed those chemical weapons to horrific effect.

The US and others condemned this barbaric act, but in the end nothing was done by any Western leader, just as nothing had been done when the Russians committed war crimes in Chechnya and in Georgia. Employing terror and targeting the civilian population have become part of the *modus operandi* of the Russian Army. That sounds awfully familiar if we think back on the Nazi period with its politicized army, which committed untold war crimes. During the Second World War the Third Reich kidnapped tens of thousands of Nordic-looking children from all across Europe. They did so in order to raise them as Nazis. Today, Putin's regime has admitted to stealing as many as 700,000 Ukrainian children, under the guise of protecting them from the war. The woman in charge of coordinating this massive effort is Maria Lvova-Belova, one of Putin's stooges. Stories are now filtering out of Russia that indicate Putin has ordered the indoctrination of these Ukrainian children in order to raise them as Russians. Again, the parallels between what the Nazis did and what Putin is doing are there for anyone to see.

Empty promises

In 1991, when the Soviet Union collapsed, both the newly created Russian Federation and the US made a promise to Ukraine that if it would give up its nuclear arsenal (there were nuclear missiles stationed in Ukraine), the United States and the Russian Federation would guarantee and protect the territorial integrity of its borders. In February 2014 Vladimir Putin ordered the invasion and occupation of the Crimea and its annexation from Ukraine for the Russian Federation. This was followed up on 6 April 2014 when Russian-backed separatists began a war against the Ukrainian government in the Donbas region of eastern Ukraine. The attempt aimed to wrest control of this eastern Ukrainian province, rich in minerals and industrial capacity, from Ukraine and unite it with Russia. Russia supplied these separatist rebels with an abundance of military equipment, and continues to do so today. It appears then that Ukraine might have done better had it kept its nuclear arsenal as a deterrent to any would-be invader, rather than depending on the empty promises of both the US and the Russian Federation to guarantee its borders.

As with all other acts of Russian aggression, the US and Europe's leading powers employed words of condemnation in 2014, but not much else. This is exactly what happened between 1934 and 1938. Was it a surprise to the US and the European nations that, after years of their turning a blind eye to what Putin was doing, he felt emboldened enough to invade another sovereign nation? In order to find an excuse to swallow up the rest of Ukraine, Putin has made the baseless accusation that the country is being run by Nazis. This is truly a classic case of psychological projection, given that Ukraine's president, Volodymyr Zelensky, happens to be Jewish, and the only person behaving like a Nazi happens to be named Putin. Just as the Western leaders had appeased Hitler for years, culminating in the signing of the infamous Munich Agreement, so has the West appeased Putin by allowing him to run roughshod over his neighbours for years.

With the formal invasion of Ukraine on 24 February 2022, the birds of appeasement and economic pragmatism have come home to roost, and only too late has the West realized that Putin needs to be confronted. Only when Adolf Hitler's forces marched into what was left of Czechoslovakia in March 1939, ending that nation's liberty, did the British Prime Minister Neville Chamberlain and the French Prime Minister Édouard Daladier finally realize that Hitler, like all schoolyard bullies, needed to be opposed. The months between September 1938 and March 1939 have gone down in history as a testament to what happens when democracies fail to confront tyranny. We must now add February 2014 to this shameful list. Confronting Hitler much earlier might have avoided war, or at least reduced the terrible cost in lives that the Second World War brought. By the same token, opposing Vladimir Putin earlier might have also prevented further Russian aggression. If he were alive today to witness the tragic events unfolding in Ukraine, Edmund Burke, the Irish-born British statesman, would have repeated his famous warning: 'All tyranny needs to gain a foothold is for people of good conscience to remain silent.' Again, the parallels between the Nazi period and now are uncanny.

The same old dream of empire-building

Today we are faced with a Hitler-wanna-be in the guise of the Russian President. Putin's goal is no less than the re-establishment of a Russian empire like the one that existed during the time of the USSR. Realizing that he can't live for ever, and contemplating how Russians will remember him, Putin is attempting to re-establish the territorial boundaries of what used to be the USSR as his legacy. Like all other tyrants before him, his goal will ultimately fail, but not before tens of thousands or even hundreds of thousands of innocent people lose their lives. The only thing that will defeat Vladimir Putin is the will and military support of the West, coupled with the resistance of the brave Ukrainian people. Unfortunately, western support for Ukraine is faltering. This is especially true with regard to the US, given that the election of 2024 will most likely decide if the US will continue to fight aggression by supporting Ukraine, or allow Ukrainian democracy to fall.

At home in Russia there are stirrings of dissent, but Putin's police state is firmly entrenched. In 2017 he created the *Natsional'naya gvardiya* (National Guard), known as the Special Police Force. This organization is a police formation of some 340,000 soldiers, whose members are only answerable and loyal to Putin himself. This paramilitary organization sounds very similar in make-up and allegiance to Hitler's *Sturmabteilung* (SA) Stormtroopers, or even the *Schutzstaffel* (SS). Now, the only way that Putin will fall from power is if military affairs take a further bad turn for Russia. Putin knows that his future as leader of the Russian Federation depends on victory in Ukraine, no matter what that victory might cost. If Putin is thwarted in taking Ukraine, he will lose power and most likely his life. Therefore, he will continue to act ruthlessly and show no mercy. His past track record suggests he will be willing to sacrifice everything, including the lives of the Russian people, to obtain that victory. Recently some politicians in the West have been pushing the Ukrainian government to make peace with Russia. What these 'armchair generals' don't realize is that allowing Vladimir Putin to keep what land he has stolen from Ukraine will only encourage him to continue his aggression at a later date. The temporary peace will also give him time to re-equip and retrain the Russian Army. The Ukrainians understand that they cannot compromise or try to reason with a man like Putin. To Putin, compromise is a sign of weakness. The only thing he understands is brute force. In this, he is accompanied by a legion of Russian tyrants who came before him, going all the way back to Ivan the Terrible. Putin is merely the latest Russian tyrant.

Behind the lines, the Ukrainian partisan movement has begun to take a toll on the Russian invader. The war, it seems, will last longer than Putin expected. Hopefully, Putin's attempt at empire-building will fail. In the meantime, those politicians, generals and rich oligarchs around Putin, who support his kleptocracy, are waiting to see if the Russian Führer suffers more military reversals, or if the West abandons Ukraine. If history is a harbinger, then this war of aggression will decide not only Ukraine's future but also Putin's ultimate place in history. Just as the Nazis failed at building an empire in the East, Putin too, it is hoped, will fail in his attempt to create an empire along the lines of his beloved USSR. Dr John Gray's observation that history is cyclical has to be considered, given the many parallels between the Nazi period and now. If Putin suffers more military reversals on the battlefield, then, as Hitler before him discovered, he may find himself inside a house of cards that is about to collapse on him. Benito Mussolini's famous quote, 'a regime, of whatever kind, collapses only under the weight of defeat', will then have been proven true.

Dr Antonio J. Muñoz

Introduction

A different kind of war

Why was it that Nazi Germany was unable to create an eastern empire that, many historians agree, could have supplied land and resources to keep the Third Reich alive for a thousand years? The answer lies in the nature of the Nazi system itself. During the Second World War Nazi policy regarding the combating of partisans, especially in eastern Europe, including the USSR, involved the tactic of *kollektive gewaltmassnahmen.*[1] This policy punished all for the acts of a few. For example, an attack by guerrilla forces against German units or interests made the local population near that attack as responsible for it as the guerrillas themselves. This and other German policies dealing with civilian and military matters would eventually work to undermine German rule in the East. The idea behind *kollektive gewaltmassnahmen* was the German belief that, fearing reprisals, the local population in an occupied region behind German lines would inform on the partisans before the guerrillas had a chance to launch any attacks against German interests. In addition, several orders created shortly before the start of the Russian campaign, collectively referred to by historians as the *Verbrecherbefehle*, were meant to give an air of 'legality' to such policies as *kollektive gewaltmassnahmen* that were criminal and illegal in wartime. These official announcements would quickly become standard policy in the East. They would also end up costing the lives of many civilians.

With the invasion of the Soviet Union on 22 June 1941, various Nazi ideologies would come together in a deadly cocktail that would shape the German struggle in the East. Anti-Polish and anti-Jewish sentiments were already causing the deaths of thousands in German-occupied Poland. The idea that the Jewish, Romany and eastern European people were inferior to Germans, and natural enemies of Germany, made it easier for the Nazis to prosecute the Russian campaign in a more barbaric manner. In effect, dehumanizing these people made it easier for Germans to kill them. It's an established fact that anti-Semitism was the principal factor in the Nazis' eventual decision to attempt to murder the entire Jewish population of Europe. Christopher Browning states that the society in which Germans lived at the time was imbued with a steady dose of anti-Semitic propaganda, which denigrated and marginalized the Jews to the point where they began to be seen as less than human and, by extension, life unworthy of life (*Lebensunwertes Leben*):

> As *Leutnant* Drucker said with extraordinary understatement, 'Under the influence of the times, my attitude to the Jews was marked by a certain aversion.' The denigration of Jews and the proclamation of Germanic racial superiority was so constant, so pervasive, so relentless, that it must have shaped the general attitudes of masses of people in Germany, including the average reserve policeman.[2]

Just as importantly, however, Christian Streit has described very persuasively how anti-communism was 'a factor of crucial importance' in the process of creating an extermination policy during the period prior to and during the Russian campaign.[3] A perfect example of this is the infamous commissar order, which gave all German troops, irrespective of branch of service or rank, the ability to execute any and all Red Army commissars either right after capture or immediately after interrogation. While the Nazis had behaved, and continued to behave, harshly towards the Polish nation, their cruelty there did not compare to that which they planned to inflict during their campaign in the Soviet Union.[4] That is not to say that Poland would be spared the full brunt of the Nazis' wrath. On the contrary, as soon as the German invasion of the Soviet Union began, Poland would feel the full weight of this war of extermination (*vernichtungskrieg*). Repression begets cruelty, and the Germans would increase their campaign of terror against the Polish nation as the war in the East progressed. In effect, these criminal orders allowed the *Ostheer* to operate under a completely different set of rules from those that had been followed when the Wehrmacht conquered western Europe.[5] In this new form of warfare, simply being a Jew became synonymous with being a partisan. As such, all Jews were subject to execution on sight.

In addition, the Russian military and civilian population would have no legal protection from killings of any kind. Since the USSR had never signed the Geneva Convention on the treatment of captured enemy prisoners, the Nazis considered they had *carte blanche* in treating all captured enemy combatants and civilians in whichever way they wished. This included the use of immediate executions if it was deemed necessary by the local German commander, meaning that the lowest-ranked German soldier (even a lowly corporal) had the right to execute captured prisoners if he deemed it necessary. Nazi ideology, coupled with what was virtually a mandate to kill, fused together in the Russian campaign to create the *Weltanschauungskrieg* (ideological war) against what the Nazis referred to as the 'Judeo-Bolshevist' threat. Given such wide latitude, the struggle in the East would be unprecedented in terms of its intensity, ferocity and brutality. With the Nazi belief that the *lebensunwertes leben* Jewish race was a polluting factor in German life, this idea was now further expanded upon to suit the circumstances of the war in the East. This was accomplished by (as stated earlier) making the killing of Jews synonymous with fighting the partisans. Adolf Hitler even said that the war in the East was an opportunity for the German troops to kill all those they felt opposed them.

The belief that *Jeder Jude ist ein Guerrillakampfer* (every Jew is a guerrilla fighter) was hammered home by officers not only within the SS and *Ordnungspolizei*, but throughout the entire Wehrmacht. As if to reaffirm this view, Wilhelm Keitel issued the following order, dated 16 December 1942, regarding the combating of partisans. The command seemed to reiterate the criminal orders completely, almost a year and a half after the German invasion. A portion of the order reads:

> The troops therefore have the right and the duty to use, in this fight, any means, even against women and children, provided they are conducive to success. Scruples, of any sort whatsoever, are a crime against the German people and against the front-line soldier who bears the consequences of attacks by bands of guerrillas and who cannot understand why any should be shown to them or their associates. These principles must serve as a basis for operations against bands in the East. No German participating in action against bands or their associates is to be held responsible for acts of violence either from a disciplinary or a judicial point of view. Commanders of troops engaged in action against the bands are obliged to see to it that all officers of units under their command be immediately and thoroughly notified of this order, that their legal advisers be immediately acquainted therewith and that no judgments be passed which are in contradiction thereto.[6]

This policy made it easy for regular German army troops to both work side by side with SS units fighting the partisans and assisting the *SS Einsatzgruppen* in eliminating the Jewish population, and commit crimes against the Jewish and non-Jewish population under the guise of combating the guerrillas. Romany were added to the category of *lebensunwertes leben*, so they too would be targeted wherever they were encountered. In many instances these murders were carried out independently of the SS mobile killing units, the *Einsatzgruppen*. Even rear area army garrison commanders have been shown to have cooperated with the SS and to have undertaken operations against Jews and Romany on their own initiative. The above order, issued by Keitel, stipulated that no soldier was to be punished for any acts which he committed while under the pretext of fighting the guerrillas and keeping order behind the lines. In addition, women and children were specifically mentioned as not being an exception to this rule.

What Keitel meant is clear enough: the killing of women and children in the East would be permitted. Notice also that all of this served, as he put it, as 'a basis for operations in the East', meaning that the war and the tactics which the *Ostheer* was employing in the Soviet Union were unique to this particular front. Was this the case because the Germans saw the eastern Europeans as subhuman and less worthy of life? Was it because Josef Stalin did not ascribe to the Geneva Convention? Was it anti-communist hatred? Was it the brutalization which occurred on the Eastern Front, as Omer Bartov and others have argued, which contributed to the barbarization of the German soldier? Was it anti-Semitism? Was it hatred of the *Zigeuner* (gypsies)? The answer (sadly) is all of the above. All of these representative biases and bigotries were inflamed by Nazi propaganda and indoctrination. The Germans brought these biases to the East, and when coupled together with criminal military orders, permitting brutality and mass murder, they engendered in the *Ostheer* a feeling that immoral conduct would be condoned. A major role in combating the partisans in the USSR was played not only by SS and police forces, but by the *Ostheer*. This included ancillary and volunteer auxiliary units of the German Army. In addition, Keitel's order also reinforced the German Armed Forces High Command directive against communist insurrection in occupied territories, issued on 16 September 1941, and also the infamous 'Reichenau Order' of 10 October 1941 on the conduct of troops in the eastern territories, which partly read as follows:

> The most important objective of this campaign against the Jewish-Bolshevik system is the complete destruction of its sources of power and the extermination of the Asiatic influence in European Civilization … Therefore, the soldier must have full understanding for the necessity of a severe but just revenge on subhuman Jewry. The Army has to aim at another purpose, i.e., the annihilation of revolts in the hinterland which, as experience proves, have always been caused by the Jews … This is the only way to fulfill our historic task to liberate the German people once and for ever from the Asiatic-Jewish danger.[7]

In 2004 Ben Shepperd published a work detailing the war guilt of (principally) two such German units: two security divisions as they operated in central Russia from 1941 to 1943.[8] Although his work covered only two security divisions, the author argued that their behaviour proved how National Socialist indoctrination, combined with the brutality of the war in the East, created the conditions that allowed for widespread murders under the guise of combating the Soviet partisans. Shepperd's approach was to build his case from the bottom up, by illustrating a consistent pattern of action within the battalions and regiments of these security divisions. His study is important because it reinforced existing research on the criminal excesses of the Wehrmacht in the East.

The book, however, would have been aided further if Shepperd had been able to cite other cases in similar German rear area and front-line commands, to support the theory that this type of behaviour in the *Ostheer* was widespread and commonplace throughout the entire width and scope of the Eastern Front. By citing examples of atrocities committed by these units, Shepperd showed how, in the region of central Russia and Belarus, the degenerative brutality that National Socialism caused, when combined with the constant and vicious combat of the war in the East, worked to harden the German soldier and accustomed him to murder, even illegal killings.[9] This work will argue that similar criminal behaviours were perpetrated by German rear-area security forces throughout the East, including Poland, and what comprised the USSR at the time.

My research has affirmed what Dr Shepperd and other academics refer to as the brutalization theory. But this is just one piece of the puzzle if we are to understand Nazi *Ost* policy. In this work, I have covered a wider area, citing numerous examples from the occupation of Poland, the Baltic States, Belarus, Ukraine and European Russia. The conclusions provide verifiable evidence of this widespread practice of criminal conduct which even seeped into the Nazi civilian administration in the East. Like Shepperd and other researchers, I have worked from the bottom up, by going through reels of captured German records detailing the history of these rear area forces that operated in the East from 1939 until 1944. Cases also abound of front-line troops behaving criminally during anti-guerrilla sweeps. All that happened in the East was in keeping with a strategy prepared before the invasion. *Generalplan Ost* was a Nazi plan developed as a blueprint for the genocide and democide that would take place in the East as a precursor to German colonization. This plan required the Germans to be brutal and ruthless in the East. Employing the typical German penchant for fulfilling obligations, the *Ostheer* carried out this order to devastating effect.

The debate over German Army criminality in the East

Gerald Reitlinger is one of the earliest, if not the first, historians to have brought up the subject of possible participation of the German military in the heinous murders of the Jewish population of the USSR. Prior to this early work, the only substantive reference to this German Army and Holocaust connection lay in the High Command trials that occurred within the context of the Nuremberg War Crimes Trials of 1946–1948. Reitlinger pointed to this in his ground-breaking 1956 study, *The SS: Alibi of a Nation.*[10] He began there, and others followed after him, with further proof that it wasn't just the

Jewish people who were targeted, but the civilian population as a whole – and the *Ostheer* was knee-deep in it all.

With this work, Reitlinger established a foundation upon which others would follow and contribute, in much the same way that the base of a house is built, and other workers later add the walls and roof. The crux of his argument was that by blaming all the evils committed by the Nazi regime on the SS, the German nation, and therefore the army as a whole, could be exculpated from any guilt. Reitlinger followed that classic work four years later in 1960 with *The House Built on Sand: The Conflicts of German Policy in Russia, 1939–1945*.[11] In it, he detailed how the Nazi leaders and their German Army counterparts had prepared for a different kind of war in the Soviet Union. The criminal orders made the campaign different, in that these orders were a virtual licence to kill. In this he was repeating points already made by Alexander Dallin in *German Rule in Russia, 1941–1945: A Study of Occupation Policies*, in which Dallin described the 'Commissar Decree' among other documents linking the German Army to the Holocaust and the illegal killings of the general population.[12]

Reitlinger pointed to documents written to senior German Army commanders by the Nazi leadership – collectively referred to by historians as the 'criminal orders' – which provided the *Ostheer* with its 'mandate' to allow for the killing of the local population, especially the Jewish population. These orders document how German military courts would not apply to Russian civilians, how the SS and police units were to work outside military commands, and also included the infamous Commissar Order and the Barbarossa Jurisdiction Order, to name a few. The Jurisdiction Order in effect gave a virtual *carte blanche* to any German soldier fighting in the East to shoot or kill anyone who was categorized as either 'agitators', 'partisans', 'partisan helpers', 'saboteurs', 'political commissars' or 'Jews' without fear of prosecution by any German court or tribunal. As stated earlier, the terms 'partisan' and 'Jew' were made synonymous, since treatment of both groups would be the same: execution. While many former German Army officers point to the fact that no order originated from the Wehrmacht which specified that the Jewish population was to be targeted for premeditated murder, historian Yitzhak Arad was correct when he stated that because Jews were included in the list of those persons who could be shot on sight, the effect was the same as if the Wehrmacht itself had written the order for the murder of the Jewish population.[13]

The criminal orders, therefore, directly link the Holocaust in the USSR to the German Army. Reitlinger related that shortly after the start of the Russian campaign, a meeting was held on 16 July 1941 in Angerburg. In attendance were Göring, Keitel, Rosenberg, Lammers, Bormann and Adolf Hitler. The Führer, Reitlinger explained, 'declared that Stalin had ordered partisan warfare behind the German front'. Hitler also commented that this partisan war gave them the ability to eliminate everyone who opposed them.[14] This, of course, included not only the Jews, but anyone considered by the Nazis as an enemy. As a result, on 22 July 1941 a new expanded order was put forth by Adolf Hitler and added to the Barbarossa Jurisdiction Order, which stated explicitly that where SS and other security forces were not available, the German Army itself was to take all measures necessary, even draconian steps, to control the rear areas and those who populated them. They were also to eliminate the partisan threat or 'other dangers' that placed the German armed forces or the war effort at risk. This, Reitlinger wrote, 'became the German soldier's charter for anti-partisan warfare'.[15]

In spite of these early and impressive starts, the study of the German Army connection to the Holocaust and other illegal murders in the East did not really begin to be considered fully until the mid-1980s. It was then that Professor Omer Bartov published his now-classic work, *The Eastern Front, 1941–45, German Troops and the Barbarization of Warfare*. In it, he proposed that the rigours of the Eastern Front – that is, the very nature of the warfare being fought between the Soviet Union and Nazi Germany, as well as pre-existing Nazi ideology – quickly accustomed the typical German soldier to brutalization, which made it easier for him to kill Jewish and non-Jewish civilians, captured soldiers and partisans with little thought to the legality or morality of his actions. Indeed, as stated decades before by Reitlinger and Dallin, the 'criminal orders' gave the members of the German Army, from high-ranking officer down to the lowliest *landser*,[16] the feeling that any action taken under the pretext of these orders would protect them from punishment by any German Army military tribunal.[17]

Bartov's incisive work was followed up three years later, in 1989, by a study titled *The German Army and Nazi Policies in Occupied Russia* by Professor Theo J. Schulte. Dr Schulte proposed that not only had the German Army been complicit in the Holocaust, but that it was part of a Nazi aim which sought 'the total destruction of another society as a fundamental prerequisite for the refashioning of German society'.[18] Here, Schulte was echoing the thoughts of historian Michael Geyer, who argued that the war of ideologies, the *Weltanschauungskrieg*, was not just fought with mere words, but was practised in the East with physical vigour.[19] Two years later, in 1991, Yitzhak Arad reappraised the various criminal orders and expounded and developed on their implications as part of the Yad Vashem Yearbook Series. This important article added 'cement' to the arguments that authors like Bartov and Schulte were developing. Even when discussing the non-military leadership that ruled the German eastern empire, we see the same ideology and action. Why did it take several decades from the publication of Reitlinger and Dallin's works for them to be followed by further research on the criminality of the Wehrmacht in the East? This is an important question.

It is beyond the scope of this work to go into the personal, social or political reasons why the topic remained relatively dormant for so many years, but in 2007 Professors Ronald Smelser and Edward Davies published a study which proposed several reasons for this apparent 20-year hiatus on the topic.[20] Although this study was fraught with numerous assumptions, the authors did conclude correctly that the Cold War may have played a role in sanitizing the German Army from its complicity in the horrors perpetrated in the East. This was done in order to use the full capacity of a revitalized West German state to help block Soviet aggression and intentions during the Cold War.[21] Throughout this period, Smelser and Davies argue, an entire myth about the valour and chivalry of the Wehrmacht was created by numerous American and European writers. In addition, at the end of the Second World War various powers were scrambling to grab as many Nazi scientists as they could get their hands on. The Americans and Russians were the biggest hoarders of German scientific knowledge. Professor Werner von Braun, the Nazi scientist who worked at Peenemunde perfecting the V-1 and V-2 rockets, and who later helped the Americans to reach the moon, immediately comes to mind. The Cold War was also a time when former Nazis, some involved in the Holocaust, were sought by Western intelligence agencies because of their supposed knowledge of the Soviet Union and its people.

An important study in understanding how it came to pass that 80 million Germans fell sway to Hitler and the Nazis and aided in the destruction of European Jewry came when Christopher R. Browning published his definitive study, *Ordinary Men: Reserve Police Battalion 101 and the Final Solution in Poland*. A few years later, in 1995, German author Paul Kohl published a little-circulated work called *Der Krieg der Deutschen Wehrmacht und der Polizei 1941–1944* ('The War of the German Armed Forces and Police 1941–1944'). In it, he argued that indeed the German Army had followed the *Führerprinzip* (Leader Principle) of the *Weltanschauungskrieg* to its inevitable conclusion.[22]

Following the work by Kohl, Walter Manoschek edited a book in 1996 titled *Die Wehrmacht im Rassenkrieg: Der Vernichtungskrieg Hinter der Front* ('The [German] Armed Forces in the Race War: The War of Annihilation Behind the Front'). The numerous contributors to this significant work, which included such notables as Raul Hilberg, Manfred Messerschmidt, Wolfram Wette, Christian Streit, Hans Safrian, Hannes Heer, Bertrand Perz, Ela Hornung, and Reinhold Gärtner, referenced incidences that occurred in the Soviet Union, but went a step further by describing the political and propaganda preparations and conditioning Germans were subjected to by the Nazi state before they even set foot on Soviet soil. Walter Manoschek, also managed to document a comparable occurrence of a German Army atrocity in Serbia, thus further cementing the truth of the unlawful activities prevalent in the Nazi-era German Army.[23] Willi Dreßen had also recorded Wehrmacht atrocities in Serbia and Russia in an article published in the 1993 edition of the Yad Vashem Yearbook Series.[24] The numerous eyewitness reports in his book cemented those accounts with apparently indelible ink. That same year Hannes Heer and Klaus Naumann edited and published an extremely important study, *Vernichtungskrieg: Verbrechen der Wehrmacht 1941 bis 1944*,[25] that propelled the topic of German Army complicity in atrocities to a whole new level by attacking the question from the top and bottom – that is, by not only presenting documentary evidence of guilt, but showing in a very lucid and straightforward manner how the very nature of the Nazi regime worked to create the conditions leading to complicity from all corners of the Wehrmacht and civilian apparatus.[26] The book turned out to be so popular and important that in 2000 it was translated into the English language in annotated format.[27] The book proved very successful in the US, but interest was especially high in Germany, where there was a growing awareness of what had been a taboo subject until 1990: German Army complicity in atrocities and sanctioned murder. An exhibit was eventually created. That exhibit toured Germany for many years in the 1990s and was considered extremely controversial.[28]

German military veteran groups protested that this exhibition was negatively painting too broad a picture of the Wehrmacht. A huge, oversized volume was produced in 2002: *Verbrechen der Wehrmacht: Dimensionen des Vernichtungskrieges 1941–1944*.[29] Its 764 pages are chock-full of documents, photographs, reports from diaries, interviews, eyewitness accounts and other documentary evidence about the crimes of the German Army during the Nazi period. The sheer size and scope of this volume attests to the extent of the German Army's participation in these crimes, for surely if today the institute that produced it, the *Hamburger Institut für Sozialforschung*,[30] could have amassed such a work, what other crimes were committed during the Second World War that for lack of evidence we shall never know about? That same year Wolfram Wette, who until then had been a contributing writer to this topic, published his first single and full study on the subject,[31] translated into the English language as *The Wehrmacht: History, Myth, Reality*. In it, Wette studied not only the top generals and middle-management officers but also included reports and testimonials from lowly privates as well. In his closing analysis, he stated:

> In recent years we have gained greater insight into the experience of the 'average Joe' in uniform meaning the many millions of enlisted men and noncommissioned officers who participated in the exterminationist campaign on the eastern front. Many of them followed the generals'

> ideological guidelines reluctantly, while others supported the campaign on the basis of their own convictions. Recent research has revealed a considerable amount of agreement with and support for the regime's goals at the bottom of the military hierarchy. Very few summoned the courage to resist this war – to the extent that it was possible at all. While the Wehrmacht was officially dissolved after the capitulation of May 8, 1945, that did not put an end to its history. Some believe that only after that date did the Wehrmacht achieve its ultimate victory, namely, in its struggle to preserve its image as an army with 'clean hands' in the eyes of the public both at home and abroad. The myth of the Wehrmacht lived on. The policy of apology evident in the memoirs of former generals – in concert with like-minded people in West Germany – worked successfully for decades.[32]

Wette reached the conclusion that perhaps by 2002 (the year when his work was published and several years after the *Hamburger Institut* exhibit) Germany was now ready to admit that the legend of the Wehrmacht's 'clean hands' could finally belong to the past.[33] However, old habits are hard to break. During the mid-1990s an American political scientist would reopen the old wounds caused by German war guilt that perhaps the travelling exhibit on Wehrmacht crimes had merely scratched. So heated and controversial were this author's assertions that the national media both in the US and in Europe picked up on it and carried the story for months. That author's name was Daniel J. Goldhagen, and the debate about the German Army's war guilt was about to expand to the whole German nation's war guilt. By the early 1990s the question over the extent of German Army complicity in *ha Shoah* (the Holocaust) almost certainly helped to partly inspire Goldhagen's work, *Hitler's Willing Executioners: Ordinary Germans and the Holocaust.*[34]

Goldhagen's book sold over 80,000 copies in its first print run, catching the attention not only of academics but of the general public. American and European media covered the story about the controversy that the book produced. It also stirred up a hornets' nest of arguments among academics for and against the theory which Goldhagen proposed. In the book he argued that the majority of Germans were willing participants in the Holocaust because of their predisposed negative conditioning towards Jewry. Accusations and counter-arguments appeared from every corner of academia. Julius H. Schoeps edited the first work which appeared in Germany to counter Goldhagen's argument: *Ein Volk von Mordern? Die Dokumentation zur Goldhagen-Kontroverse um die Rolle der Deutschen im Holocaust.*[35] Not all of the rebuttals to Goldhagen's book came from Germany. Domestic scholars like Fritz Stern, a German-Jewish refugee who, at the time Goldhagen's work was released, was teaching at Columbia University, had some tough criticism to dish out as well. Stern's counter-argument seemed persuasive, as did the strength of his words:

> Goldhagen singles out those murderers who were 'ordinary Germans' and who, he insists, were motivated solely by their 'cognitive model' of the Jew. He then moves from specific and harrowing examples to a grotesque extrapolation: having examined the acts of some hundreds or perhaps even thousands of people, he insists that almost all Germans were moved by the same hatred, approved the killing, and would have acted in like fashion if chance had so decreed. As he writes, '... the institutions treated here ... should permit the motivations of the perpetrators in those particular institutions to be uncovered, and also allow for generalizing both to the perpetrators as a group and to the second target group of this study, the German people.' The leap from individual cases to the German people at large is unpersuasive, but necessary for his indictment of his 'second target group'.[36]

That was but a taste of the argument that all Germans were willing participants in the Holocaust, based on several hundred or several thousand Germans who did take part. Dr Stern was pointing out the fact that you cannot assume that 80 million Germans were willing participants, based on thousands who did play a leading role in the Holocaust. This argument was reinforced when further research about the complicity of German Army units in the Holocaust began to be studied in greater detail (a process which began in the mid-1980s). It only affirms the continued importance of researching this topic even today. The implication of Goldhagen's work is clear: all Germans bear responsibility for the deaths of 6 million Jews. Thus, Goldhagen stirred many passions which have very real personal, social and political implications. Geoffrey P. Megargee's work *War of Annihilation: Combat and Genocide on the Eastern Front, 1941* is perhaps one of the better studies to be released, and referred to what Goldhagen was claiming. In it, Megargee merges some of the theories expounded by Goldhagen, arguing that Germans in general were predisposed to the kind of annihilation war waged in Russia. Most academics, however, have only proven the guilt of the Wehrmacht during the war. In his conclusions, Megargee states, according to his premise, the crux of German Army guilt:

> In order to ensure their victory, the generals also helped lay the plans for Hitler's vision of an exterminationist war. Later they would claim that the SS was solely responsible for the crimes in the east, but in fact the military's role was crucial. At the most basic level, the crimes could never have taken place if the Wehrmacht had not conquered the ground, but the generals' culpability extends well beyond that fact. They encouraged

their soldiers in an attitude that placed little or no value on the life of Soviet civilians, in fact, they ordered their men to use the harshest conceivable means to establish German dominance. They planned for the deliberate starvation of millions of people and for forced labor by millions more. They laid the groundwork for the fatal neglect of Soviet prisoners of war, whose care was their responsibility by international law. And they played a key role in planning for the elimination of the Communist leadership and intelligentsia, including those in uniform, as well as anyone who resisted German rule. That last goal provided the perfect cover for the SS *Einsatzgruppen* and other killing units to murder anyone whom they saw as a threat, including hundreds of thousands of Jewish men, women and children. Since most of the military's leaders believed that Jews were fundamentally hostile and dangerous, they were able to persuade themselves, with little apparent difficulty, that killing all the Jews was necessary to secure the conquered territories.[37]

The only drawback to Megargee's book is that he only used published works and as a result could only come to conclusions from the observations and assessments of other authors. However, he laid out exactly what the Wehrmacht generals did which stained their escutcheon of honour for ever. Another important work regarding German attitudes and decisions made in the East was published a year earlier, in 2005. It was titled *Abgehort: Deutsche Generale in britischer Kriegsgefangenschaft 1942–1945* ('Monitored: German Generals in British War Captivity 1942–1945'). This work, edited by Sönke Neitzel, is a massive compilation of secret conversations taped by British intelligence of German officers held in British prisoner-of-war (POW) camps from 1942 to 1945. The book was thought important enough to be translated into the English language in 2008. The importance of this study is that in many of these secret conversations, German officers talked openly of the annihilation war in the East. Not knowing that they were being recorded, they showed emotions ranging from arrogant joy to total indifference. One such example from the book describes a conversation secretly recorded in a POW camp by the British on 6 May 1945, between *Generalleutnant* Karlimilian Siry, the former commander of the German *347. Infanterie Division*, and *Generalstabsintendant* Pauer of the *Oberkommandos des Heeres*.[38] Pauer just listened while Siry expounded on how he would have handled the massive POW problem which the *Ostheer* had to deal with during the Russian campaign:

Siry: One mustn't admit it openly, but we were far too soft. All these horrors have landed us in the soup now. But if we'd carried them through to the hilt, made the people disappear completely – no one would say a thing. These half measures are always wrong. In the East I suggested

> once to the *Korps* [command] – thousands of POWs were coming back, without anyone guarding them, because there were no people there to do it. It went quite well in France, because the Frenchman is so degenerate that if you said to him: 'You will report to the POW collecting point in the rear' the stupid idiot really did go along there. But in Russia there was a space of 50–80km, that is to say, a 2 to 3 days' march, between the armoured spearheads and the following close formations. No Russians went to the rear, they lagged behind and then took to the woods left and right, where they could live all right. So, I said: 'That's no good, we must simply cut off one of their legs, or break a leg, or the right forearm, so that they won't be able to fight in the next four weeks and so that we can round them up.' There was an outcry when I said one must simply smash their legs with a club. At the time, of course, I didn't really condone it either, but now I think it's quite right. We've seen that we cannot conduct a war because we're not hard enough, not barbaric enough. The Russians are that all right.[39]

This outlook did not just arise out of the blue. The Nazis had nine years (1933–1941) to imbue the German nation with a hatred of Jewry and the Slavic people in the East. This hatred was nurtured, fed and finally legalized by a series of orders that, when combined with anti-Semitic and anti-communist ideology, worked to create conditions that caused criminality on a grand scale. However, we must admit that there existed in the German nation (and indeed in most European countries) a base level of antipathy by the gentile community towards the Jewish people. Religious anti-Semitism had existed in Europe for hundreds of years. What made the Nazi period different was that racial anti-Semitism was now added, in much the same way that one adds more kindling to a fire. The Nazis were able to exponentially increase that basic anti-Semitic sentiment to the point of madness. There is no doubt now that the German Army bears a good portion of the guilt for the horrors that occurred in the East. The outcome of the debate as to the degree of that war guilt on the part of the Wehrmacht is still incomplete. This work will hopefully add additional bricks and mortar to the studies mentioned in this introduction, but more precisely it provides additional documentation to Dr Timothy Snyder's magnum opus *Bloodlands: Europe Between Hitler and Stalin*[40] and Mark Mazower's equally important study *Hitler's Empire: How the Nazis Ruled Europe*.[41] The documentation herein affirms a cruel and extremely genocidal comportment on the part of the Germans that was particular to these regions of eastern Europe. This comportment was led by an ideology of exclusion and genocide. It was also the very reason why ultimately Germany was not able to establish an eastern empire as envisaged in *Mein Kampf*.

Chapter 1

German preparations for invading and occupying the USSR

We need only kick in the door, and the whole rotten structure will come tumbling down. [Adolf Hitler, June 1940[1]]

German attitudes towards the Soviet populace

When Hitler launched his armed forces against the Soviet Union on 22 June 1941, the world was stunned. Less than two years earlier, Hitler and Stalin had signed a non-aggression pact, which even included a trade deal. This treaty allowed Hitler to invade Poland without the fear of a war on two fronts. Moscow had then taken advantage of German aggression against Poland to seize large areas of that country and bring them under Soviet control. As soon as the Soviet Union was invaded, it became clear once more how revealing a manifesto Hitler's *Mein Kampf* had been. In what editors have declared a long-winded and badly written book, Hitler said what his intentions were:

> When we talk of new land in Europe, we are bound to think first of Russia and her border states. Fate itself seems to wish to give us our direction. For the organized Russian state was not due to any political capacity of the Slav race, but it was a wonderful example of the efficiency of the Germanic element in forming States among inferior races.[2]

Besides stating that he wished to conquer the East for Germany, he was also alluding to the fact that it was the German Army High Command that in the First World War had smuggled Vladimir Lenin into Russia, causing the Russians to leave the war and creating a new state – all because the Germans had so designed it by sending Lenin into the country. He went on to declare that no nation held any territory because of any right derived from Heaven. Frontiers were made by people and just because a nation had succeeded in acquiring an unfair share of territory, that was no reason for respecting its boundaries for ever. That a nation had acquired the land of another merely indicated which was the stronger, and this strength alone 'constitutes the right to possess'.[3] That these views continued to be held by Hitler was evidenced time and again in his pre-Second World War speeches. 'We have a very great interest in seeing to it that this Bolshevist plague shall not spread over Europe,' he declared in his Reichstag address on 20 February 1938, giving clear warning that he intended to fight communism.[4] He actually expected that people throughout the world would believe him when he said that the German war on Russia would be for the purpose of liberating Russia from communism, not annexing territory.

Hitler's decision to attack the Soviet Union had been made as early as November 1940 and his plans were definitely crystallized by the start of 1941, for on 17 March 1941 he told *Colonel-General* Franz Halder, Chief of the German Staff, that the ideological ties to the Russian people were not strong enough to survive a serious crisis: 'They would break up with the elimination of the Bolshevik functionaries.'[5] Exactly three months later he expressed his plans for the East to the various commanders of the German armed forces:

> The war against Russia will be such that it cannot be conducted in a knightly fashion ... communism is an enormous danger for our future. We must forget the concept of comradeship between soldiers. A communist is not a comrade before or after battle. This is a war of extermination. If we do not grasp this, we will again have to fight the communist foe. We do not wage the war to preserve the enemy ...[6]

In Halder's diary for the same date, 17 June 1941, there is this entry: 'war against Russia. Extermination of Bolshevik commissars and communist intelligentsia. The new state must be socialist but without an intellectual class of their own.'[7] If Hitler's understanding of the people of the Soviet Union was obscure, his plans for their destiny certainly were not. The war was to be called a clash of ideologies, and the extermination of communists and the intelligentsia was written into all orders given to German military planners. A captured German document talks about a conference held on 29 April 1941, during which Hitler offered twelve rules on how to act in Russia. Rule No. 9 stated:

> We do not wish to convert the Russians to National Socialism. We wish only to make them a tool in our hands. You must win the youth of Russia ... by taking them firmly in hand and administering ruthless punishment to those who practise sabotage or fail to accomplish the work expected of them.[8]

Under a dictatorship such as that imposed on the Germans by Hitler, policy swiftly took the form of a direct military order, often transmitted in the name of the Führer. An example is the directive issued by Field Marshal Wilhelm Keitel, Chief of the Armed Forces High Command, on 13 May 1941:

> Persons suspected of criminal action will be brought at once before an officer. This officer will decide whether they are to be shot. With regard

> to offences committed against enemy civilians by members of the Wehrmacht, prosecution is not obligatory even when the deed is at the same time a military crime or offence.[9]

Hitler was clearly preparing the way for the Wehrmacht to act quite differently in the East than they had previously done in conquering the western nations of Europe. That same day (13 May) Hitler issued an order concerning special military measures to be taken in the rear of the area where the invasion of the Soviet Union was to take place. This proves that the German High Command realized it would have to take action against the guerrillas. This directive ordered that:

> Guerrillas should be disposed of ruthlessly by the military, whether they are fighting or in flight. Likewise, all attacks by enemy civilians on the armed forces, its members and workers, are to be suppressed at once by the military, using the most extreme methods until the attackers are destroyed.[10]

As will become apparent later in this study, orders such as these placed military commanders in a rather precarious position given that the Soviet populace very often, at least early in the war, greeted the Germans as liberators. An invading army always fares better when it treats the occupied populace with respect, if not kindness. Here Hitler was telling his military to be cruel and ruthless. Indeed, the Führer warned that 'Anyone who talks about cherishing the local inhabitants and civilizing them will go straight to a concentration camp.'[11] Most members of the German military complied with this order, though a number of 'enlightened' officers thought it best to stay on friendly terms with the civilian population, the theory here being that you could get what you wanted more often if you used sugar instead of a stick. One of many orders issued in Russian by the German Army to the occupied populace in July 1941 read as follows:

> Toilers, workers, peasants. The German Army is entering the territory of the Soviet Union in order to liberate all the toilers from the Bolshevik yoke ... Therefore, carry out the following orders: 1. Do not run away to the countryside. Continue to work. Calmly stay where you are. Food for you is guaranteed. Beggars' wages will come to an end ... 2. Do not start the partition of the land on your own. Agricultural and industrial equipment should stay in place. Protect it from saboteurs. Do not let sabotage take place or any destruction. Protect your property ... Protect all the railroads and waterways, bridges, canals, ports and other means of communication ... When the ones responsible for your suffering and misery – leaders, commissars and their helpers – leave your village or city the German Army will appoint individuals of your choice for a temporary

> administration. Later on, a reconstruction of your country will be started under German leadership.[12]

To anyone who did not truly know the Nazis, this declaration sounded wonderful. But the reality was nowhere near what this propaganda flyer was alleging. The people living in the Soviet Union had already been the recipients of anti-German propaganda by Stalin's government. The peace treaty with Nazi Germany that was signed by Joachim von Ribbentrop and Vyacheslav Molotov was excused as merely a delaying tactic (which it really was). For the most part, everything that the Soviet government was telling the people about National Socialist Germany was true. The problem, however, was that by then most Soviet citizens had come to distrust the government in Moscow. In general terms, Ukrainians, Poles, Latvians, Lithuanians and Estonians favoured the Germans because it was Germany that allowed for their independence from Russia (if only temporarily in some states, like Ukraine). Those who were old enough to remember the First World War recalled that the majority of the Kaiser's troops had either been friendly to the locals, or at least had behaved fairly. That would not be the case under Hitler's rule.

The German invasion

The conquest of the Soviet Union was planned under the operation name Barbarossa.[13] The campaign, as envisioned by its planners and presented to the Führer by General Franz Halder, was expected to last between eight and ten weeks. When these plans were completed, Hitler said, 'When Barbarossa commences, the world will hold its breath and make no comment.'[14] The strategy for Operation Barbarossa called for 160 divisions, of which only 17 were armoured and 12 were motorized, to be divided into three army groups.[15] It was to be a broad frontal attack from Lapland (in northern Finland) to the Black Sea, aiming to engage and destroy the main Soviet armed forces, estimated at 150 infantry divisions, 36 motorized brigades and 32 cavalry brigades near the border. The attacks would involve pincer movements that would encircle the Russian formations in a matter of weeks, so as to prevent any withdrawal of forces into the vastness of the Russian hinterland. The German General Staff envisaged a successful invasion of the USSR as the destruction of the Red Army, while Adolf Hitler believed the objective of the invasion was the conquest of Soviet territory – basically, all of European Russia (that is, everything west of the Ural Mountains). Therefore, the German General Staff differed from the Führer as to what the final objective of the war against the Soviet Union should be.

In the first phase of the invasion, Army Group North was to seize Leningrad, Army Group Centre was to take Smolensk and Army Group South had

Kiev as its objective. The second phase was temporarily stalemated because of a sharp disagreement between Hitler and Field Marshal Walter von Brauchitsch, Commander in Chief of the German armed forces. Brauchitsch wanted the main drive directed against Moscow, since it was a major railway hub and thus an attack there would disrupt future Red Army troop movements. Moscow was also the political head of the Soviet Union and the seat of power for the communist state. Capturing it would not only disrupt command and control but would deal a huge psychological blow to the Soviet leadership. In contrast, Hitler, who was always guided by his intuition, and desirous of a rapid economic exploitation of the enemy's country, insisted on the major attack being made against industrialized Leningrad and the agriculturally rich Ukraine.[16]

Because of this disagreement, and later the inability of the *Ostheer* to effectively stop the Soviet winter offensive, Hitler would relieve Brauchitsch on 19 December 1941 and assume the supreme command himself.[17] Hitler is known to have boasted that he would not make the mistake Napoleon had made: 'when I march to Moscow, I will start early enough in order to reach it before winter'.[18] Operation Barbarossa was originally scheduled to be launched on 15 May 1941. However, its launch was unavoidably delayed by five weeks because in the autumn of 1940 Italy invaded Greece, albeit without success. Since Germany could hardly undertake a major campaign against the Soviet Union while her southern flank remained insecure, on 6 April 1941 German troops were diverted to the Balkans in order to help the floundering Italians. Hungarian and Bulgarian troops assisted the German and Italian military in occupying Yugoslavia. By 1 May the Yugoslav and Greek Armies had capitulated and the campaign in the Balkans was successfully ended. However, the Balkan delay would upset Hitler's timetable for the planned invasion of the USSR. As if to counterbalance this development, Finland entered the war on the side of Germany on 25 June, and two days later the Axis powers were joined by Hungary, who initially sent an expeditionary corps to Russia.[19] Nevertheless, the loss of five weeks of clear weather would prove decisive in defeating Hitler's plans for Operation Barbarossa.

The German summer offensive progressed relatively smoothly and it appeared to the rest of the world that another successful blitzkrieg was in the making. The advance appeared to be working perfectly until the battle for Smolensk, which delayed the Germans by two months. Although Red Army losses were staggering, a large number of Soviet forces managed to escape. In the meantime, Army Group North overran the Baltic States during the latter part of August but here again the Soviet forces were not annihilated. Soviet troops in this region numbered thirty-five divisions, including two armoured divisions and six armoured brigades. Only seven divisions were engaged with the enemy, the remainder being shifted toward Pskov by Marshal Kliment Yefremovich Voroshilov, the Commander of the Northern Front. Leningrad was surrounded but held firm. Army Group Centre was almost on schedule as it completed two successful pincer movements around Bialystok and Minsk. By 5 August the Smolensk pocket was cleared of Soviet troops.[20] The battle had been costly to both sides. Timoshenko had managed to delay the German advance by weeks. While this did not seem very consequential at the time, later it would factor as one reason why Moscow could not be taken in the autumn of 1941. As for Army Group South, it was opposed by Marshal Semyon Mikhailovich Budenny commanding the Red Army forces of the Southern Front. By the end of August the Germans had only progressed to the mouth of the Dnieper river. Kiev had not been taken.[21]

Although the Russians had already suffered staggering losses, their armies were still intact and were withdrawing eastward. In addition, the vast manpower reserves of a nation of 196 million people assured the Red Army a steady flow of replacements for existing units and even new combat formations that was the envy of German generals. The bulk of the German armies were still employing horses, with only a core being fully motorized or mechanized. It was this armoured spearhead that was rolling rapidly across Russia, in spite of the poor roads that lay therein.

The failure of the Barbarossa plan

The infamous Russian weather now came to the rescue of the Soviet army. Excessive autumn rains began to stall the German armoured vehicles, most of which possessed narrow tracks and were thus unsuitable in heavy mud. German artillery, which in some cases weighed more than a small tank, also suffered on account of *rasputitsa*.[22] Almost overnight, the entire German invading force ground to a halt, stopping any further German advance on Moscow. Then, on 29 November, Marshal Semyon Konstantinovich Timoshenko, who had replaced Marshal Budenny in the region of southern Russia, launched a counter-offensive and recaptured Rostov.

'General Winter' interfered with Army Group Centre as well.[23] The campaign to take Moscow began on 2 October 1941, and involved three panzer armies in a pincer movement, two to the north and one to the south of Moscow. The codename for the attack was Operation Typhoon. The climate became favourable for the Germans in November, when the cold weather froze the muddy ground. The Germans once again moved ahead on all fronts, but in the first week of December the temperature dropped to 40 degrees below zero. At that time, the Germans stood just 21 miles north and 40 miles south of the Soviet capital. At these harsh temperatures, the transmission fluid in German vehicles froze. The Soviets on the other hand were prepared.

By the start of December 1941 the divisions of Army Group Centre which had taken part in Operation Typhoon had been bled dry:

> German infantry divisions had lost 30–50 per cent of their combat strength after their ceaseless marching and heavy fighting, and the armoured divisions were mere shadows of their former selves, operating with barely one third of their normal strength, one begins to understand what happened at Moscow between 18 November and 5 December, and what it was that the Russian war historians call 'the miracle of Moscow'.[24]

Companies were down to a platoon in strength. Battalions were lucky if they had the strength of one company. Regiments were fortunate if they could muster an understrength battalion, and divisions had been whittled away to regiment size. The flower of *Heeresgruppe Mitte* lay dead and frozen on the road from Smolensk to Moscow.

On 5 December 1941, faced with the start of the Soviet winter counter-offensive in front of the Russian capital, General Heinz Guderian, commanding the German forces south of Moscow, advised Hitler that the operation to capture the Russian capital be postponed. In the north, General Georg-Hans Reinhardt doubted his ability to hold the front. On 13 December Field Marshal von Bock, commander of *Heeresgruppe Mitte*, communicated with Field Marshal von Brauchitsch to ask Hitler whether his army group was to hold where it was and risk being destroyed, or withdraw and run the same risk. If the decision was to be to withdraw, Bock doubted whether he could save enough equipment to hold a new and not previously prepared line.[25] The Red Army had employed large numbers of winter-trained and well equipped Siberian divisions. Facing these well trained and equipped troops were German soldiers who had no cold weather gear available because Hitler, when asked whether the Wehrmacht should prepare for a winter campaign, told the Quartermaster General that the Russian campaign would only last eight weeks.

Hitler's reply to Field Marshal von Brauchitsch was that the German armies were to hold all along the line, whatever the cost. This brought about many changes in the military high command. A number of generals were relieved and others asked for new assignments. Then, as already noted, on 19 December 1941 Brauchitsch was dismissed and Hitler took over as commander-in-chief. To an anxious world, it appeared that the Germans were but temporarily bogged down in the usual severe Russian winter.

A failed strategy

Many believed that with the coming of spring in 1942, Germany's successful blitzkrieg tactics would be resumed and another European nation would be ground under the Nazi jackboot. But it is now apparent that during the first months of the war in Russia, the Germans committed blunders when planning the Russian campaign. These blunders were not only military but also economic and political. The Germans overextended their lines of communication and supply in their area of operation, thus stretching their forces too thinly over a vast territory. The advancing panzer spearheads would capture tens of thousands of Russian soldiers, most of whom were simply told to walk unguarded towards the German rear for processing. Because the panzers were usually way ahead of the advancing German infantry, many Russian prisoners fled into the vast forests of European Russia, and eventually became partisans.

Climatic factors were not given the serious attention and consideration that they deserved. The military objective of annihilating the entire Red Army in a blitzkrieg sweep across European Russia never materialized. Sure, the Red Army took horrendous losses, but a nation of 196 million people could afford to take heavy casualties and still come out on top. There were only 80 million Germans and they were fighting the entire world. The problem of not being able to defeat the Red Army lay in the fact that the Soviet Union had a virtually limitless supply of men. So no matter how many divisions the German Army in Russia smashed, more kept popping up. It must have felt to the German commanders that they were playing an endless game of 'Whack-a-mole', where once a Soviet army was destroyed, another would pop up to take its place.

Heavy losses

The Germans on the other hand began to experience shortages in replacements and reinforcements as early as the spring of 1942. This is why early in 1942 the German Army requested that 20,000 German sailors and 200,000 German airmen be transferred over to the army, in order to make up for the heavy losses sustained by the *Ostheer* up until then.

This request set the stage for Reich Air Marshal Hermann Göring's refusal to allow those 200,000 men to be transferred into the army. Instead, he convinced Hitler that the German Air Force could raise infantry divisions and field them. Thus, the Luftwaffe field divisions were created. They proved to

Table 1.1. German losses on the Eastern Front and replacements.

1 November 1941–1 April 1942	Lost (all casualties)	Replaced
Officers, NCOs, men	900,000	450,000
Horses	180,000	20,000
Armoured fighting vehicles (all types)	2,300	1,800
Motor vehicles	74,000	7,400

be a recipe for disaster. Göring's selfishness in not wishing to give up his men would prove detrimental to the German war effort. The losses sustained on the Eastern Front from 1 November 1941 to 1 April 1942 simply could not be made up (see Table 1.1). The obvious conclusion is that the *Ostheer* was having to face the Red Army in 1942 with fewer men and less materiel than it had in 1941. The table also shows how the German Army in Russia was less mechanized in the spring of 1942 than it had been in 1941.

Keeping the communist economic system in place

In the economic sphere, the preservation of the collective farms was a mistake. Land was important to the Russian peasant, and yet the Germans cautioned 'Do not start the partition of the land on your own.'[26] By issuing orders forbidding partitioning, the Germans transmitted to the peasants some suspicion of the meaning of Nazi 'liberation'. During the Russian Revolution, when the peasants began dividing up the land from the nobles who owned most of it, the old Bolsheviks had endorsed the practice in order to win over the majority of the *muzjiks*.[27] An order dated 30 July 1941 proclaimed that the present form of the economy would remain in effect, the collectives', and then added:

> Those who work hard during the harvest will not only remain the owners of their garden plots but will be exempt from the tax and will also have a chance, after final authority is established, to increase their livestock. Those who will not help during the harvest, or who start sabotage, will be punished according to German military law.[28]

The introduction of forced labour was another serious policy mistake. As General Alfred Toppe, a veteran of the Russian campaign, wrote in retrospect:

> The economic exploitation of the occupied territories can be affected only by employing the local inhabitants to the greatest possible extent. Their employment as labour on a voluntary basis is the prerequisite for the successful accomplishment of the plan.[29]

The Germans never came to grips with the political ramifications of keeping the collective farms, not that they wanted to, because the plan all along was to have the USSR become a non-entity after the Nazi victory. Content with constantly repeating the goal of liberation from Bolshevism, the Germans prepared no concrete plan for the political future of Russia, because there was to be no future. This was done on purpose. German 'preparations' along these lines were designed to exclude the peoples of the USSR from having a future, political or otherwise. There were many Russians who wanted communism to end, and who were willing to help the Germans achieve that goal, but who were incensed when they realized that the Germans had no intention of allowing the establishment of any type of post-war Russian state. With their harsh policies, the Germans made it easier for the people of the Soviet Union to choose between a homespun despot (Stalin) and a foreign one (Hitler). This eventually gave those Russians who were fighting alongside the Germans, and those who were contemplating doing so, only two choices: support a domestic despot or a foreign one. Most chose the former.

Russia was to be a non-entity

No education of any kind, beyond the elementary stage, was planned for the people who comprised the Soviet Union. The *Ostvölk* were to perform only lowly and unimportant roles in the region's future, providing manual labour where necessary for the *Dritte Reich*. Moreover, the Nazi terror that accompanied the advance of the invasion frustrated the Soviet peoples' short-lived hopes of true liberation. The occupied began to be disenchanted with the occupier. The Soviet Government realized what was transpiring in the German-occupied areas. The timing of the German attack may have taken the Soviet Union by surprise, but on 3 July 1941 Stalin made a radio speech to the Soviet Union in which he briefly described the events of the German assault and appealed to the nation for support and sacrifice. Stalin emphasized that 'the enemy is cruel and is out to restore czarism and convert the peoples of the Soviet Union into slaves of German princes'.[30] He referred to issues involving national sentiment and feeling, but very wisely said nothing related to communism. He then called for unlimited guerrilla warfare with the words:

> In areas occupied by the enemy, guerrilla units, mounted and on foot, must be formed, diversionist groups must be organized to combat the enemy troops, to foment guerrilla warfare everywhere, to blow up bridges and roads, damage telephone and telegraph lines, set fire to forests, stores and transports. In the occupied regions conditions must be made unbearable for the enemy and all his accomplices. They must be hounded and annihilated at every step, and all their measures frustrated.[31]

A lost opportunity

Stalin's appeal didn't bring immediate results because in 1941 the Nazi beast had not yet completely showed itself. The Germans appeared to be interested only in hunting down and killing Jews. Given that there had always been anti-Semitism in Russia, the majority of the non-Jewish population in the USSR simply didn't care that Jews were being murdered, and continued to support the Germans. A limited degree of sabotage was reported but there is no evidence of a general uprising against the Germans in 1941. On the contrary, when the Wehrmacht first made contact with the Soviet populace, the general attitude they encountered was friendly, though it naturally varied from area to area. The Germans were initially greeted as liberators in Ukraine and the

Baltic States. Throngs of Ukrainian girls and women offered the German troops bread and salt, the traditional welcome gift for visitors. Ukrainians greeted the German invasion for several reasons. The bulk of the Ukrainian people resented collectivization, which had been forced on them by Stalin. Because they resisted collectivization and other communist measures, Stalin created an artificial famine that killed approximately 3.9 million Ukrainians. At that time this figure amounted to approximately 13 per cent of the population of Ukraine. To this day the Ukrainians refer to this famine as the 'Holodomor' ('Death by famine'). Finally, it was hoped that with the German invasion, the Ukrainian state could once again become a reality. Thus in the first year of the campaign the Germans literally threw away the support of the majority of the Soviet populace because of their actions.

Some regions, such as the Baltic States and the recently incorporated eastern part of Poland, even included elements hostile to the Soviet Union. According to German records, 'the population greeted the Germans with joy as liberators and placed themselves at our disposal willingly and freely with body and soul'.[32] These Baltic states had been forcibly absorbed and militarily occupied by the USSR since 1940. The very first thing the Soviets did was to imprison or murder the intelligentsia of these Baltic nations, while imposing forced collectivization, indoctrination of young people and the closing of churches and synagogues. These actions on the part of the Stalinist system presented the Germans with a great opportunity to win the hearts and minds of the millions of people who inhabited the Soviet Union. Nazi ideology, reflected by the policies which the Germans brought to the East, would eventually work to stifle that prospect.

The door creaks open

In the spring of 1942 the *Ostheer* had yet to recover from the grievous losses that it had sustained during the initial summer, autumn and winter seasons in the USSR. Even as the operation to capture Moscow was beginning in October 1941, General Keitel issued an order for Russian prisoners of war to be utilized by the German armed forces for railroad construction. This apparent 'about face' on this matter occurred mainly due to the realization that the Soviet Union would not be defeated in six months. However, it was the mounting German losses in the field that provided the *raison d'être* for Hitler's apparent reversal. However, by the time the *Führer* had consented to this policy, the numbers of possible volunteers had already been considerably reduced. The Germans had not counted on capturing well over 3 million Russian soldiers and they were totally unprepared for housing and feeding these prisoners. Most German soldiers were giddy and heady over the victorious summer of 1941, with its stunning victories and the vast number of Red Army prisoners, and the booty of weapons captured or destroyed. This feeling of invincibility was not a recipe for compassion towards the defeated and the conquered. Human nature being what it is, I am reminded of the quote from Virgil's *Aeneid*, '*Una salus victis nullam sperare salutem*'.[33]

It is no surprise, therefore, that most German commanders were in no mood to offer that kindness, especially to the Untermensch Slavic race, as the Nazis viewed them. Although the commanders in charge of the POW camps could have requested more assistance in accommodating and feeding these prisoners, no effort was made to do so, for the very reasons just outlined. Callousness and indifference to human suffering yielded a terrible death toll of captured Russian prisoners. Stalag 350, for example, which had been established in July 1941, housed 80,000 Russian POWs, even though the camp could only house and feed 6,000 prisoners. So, in this one camp alone, 74,000 Russians had to sleep out in the open, even in the winter. A supply of food sufficient for only 6,000 prisoners had to feed 80,000. Needless to say, by May 1942 only 50,000 of the original 80,000 prisoners remained alive. No fewer than 30,000 men had perished of malnutrition or the effects of the weather. Disease was also rampant, given the crowded conditions. This, too, worked to cull the prisoner population. According to the Germans themselves, around 2,500 Russian POWs were dying each day. A German officer named Herre, related to author Jürgen Thorwald, recalled what he witnessed during a visit to one such Soviet POW transit camp, located in Stalino, on 26 January 1942:

> In the gallery where students once sat, almost fleshless skulls were raised here and there. They stared at Herre like so many death masks. The camp commandant came up to him. 'Have you found what you were looking for, Major?' The look in his eyes was a blend of bafflement, self-righteousness and uneasiness. But Herre looked past him to a group of weeping Russian women who were standing outside the gate; they were vainly trying to throw a few cold potatoes and pieces of bread to the prisoners.[34]

This death toll, then, raises the question of why so many people in the Soviet Union decided to volunteer to serve the Germans. A good number of people were recruited from POW camps. It must be said that hatred of Stalin and Stalinism was one reason why Soviet citizens sided with the invaders. And faced with a slow death from disease or starvation, volunteering to serve in a pro-German combat battalion may have seemed to be the only way for a Russian POW to survive.

Recruitment begins

As mentioned before, the order of October 1941 allowed for the 'official' recruitment of Russian POWs and other volunteers for use by the Germans on the Russian railways. Indeed, by 1 January 1943 the total number of

German employees working on the Soviet rail system (in one capacity or another) was 111,899 but total natives working on the same rail system stood at an amazing 633,935 men and women.[35] Some German commanders, extremely short-handed of able-bodied men, did not restrict their employment of native volunteers by complying strictly with the order of October 1941, with its very limited clause on the use of Eastern volunteers.[36] Many took it upon themselves to use these men as cooks, drivers, work crews, interpreters, messengers, etc. Some particularly bold officers even went so far as to arm these native volunteers to have them act as village or town guards, and eventually even to act as security behind the German lines against partisan attacks. These volunteers were considered auxiliaries and became known as *Hilfswillige* (volunteers), or '*Hiwis*' for short, which literally translates to 'willing helpers'.[37] An example of just how thinly spread the German rear area forces were can be found by examining the German *Kommandant Rückwärtiges Armeegebiet 582* (582nd Army Rear Area Commander), abbreviated to Korück 582, which was the local army rear area military government organized into region, district, town and village, all under the direct control of the German Quartermaster General for the Eastern Front.[38]

The Korück commands were responsible for all matters of supply, administration and security in the rear area of the combat zone. This latter duty meant that they were ultimately responsible for defending against guerrilla attacks. Korück 582's area of responsibility encompassed 6,900 square miles of territory behind the German 9th Army lines in the region of Army Group Centre. It contained more than 1,500 villages, in addition to collective farms. Yet to cover this large area, Korück 582 could only count on 16 companies of about 85 men each, with a total of 1,400 men to act as guards for POW camps, protect the rail lines, the headquarters personnel, to act as town garrisons, etc. This work left only about 300 men for employment in anti-partisan operations.[39] Another issue was the advanced age of most troops serving in these rear area Korück commands. Older-age soldiers were not suited for the rigours of hunting down partisans in the woods or swamps. There was always a high rate of injuries and infirmities that men serving under the Korück would experience. The rate for heat stroke, for example, during the summer months was particularly high for the older-age German soldiers.

The rear area headquarters controlled a certain number of troops, and were also in charge of keeping order behind the lines. These army forces included army staffs, security troops, bicycle units, and supply and support troops. Every German Army had at least one Korück command. For the start of the Russian campaign, the following Korück commands were assigned to every German Army taking part in the invasion of the USSR: (22 June 1941): 2nd Army: Korück 580; 4th Army: Korück 559; 6th Army: Korück 585; 9th Army: Korück 582; 11th Army: Korück 553; 16th Army: Korück 584;

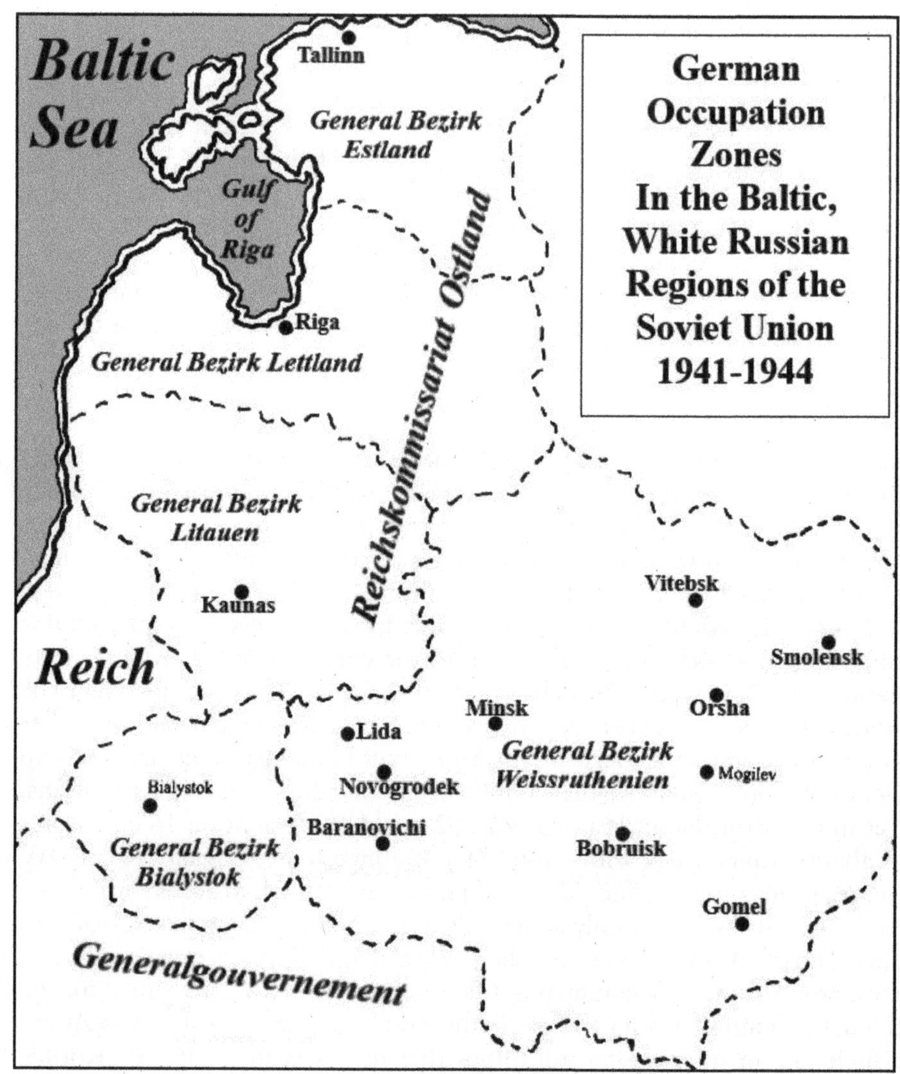

Map 1. The German occupation zones bordering the Baltic states, Belarus, East Prussia (Germany) and the so-called Generalgouvernement (occupied Poland).

17th Army: Korück 550; and 18th Army: Korück 583. The various *Panzergruppen* (later redesignated panzer armies) also had their own Korück command: *Panzergruppe* 1: Korück 531; *Panzergruppe* 2: Korück 532;[40] *Panzergruppe* 3: Korück 590; and *Panzergruppe* 4: Korück 593.[41]

The recruitment of native troops into the auxiliary battalions to serve either on the front lines or behind the lines fighting the partisans was not optional, but rather was a necessity. For example, the German 134th Infantry Division, which had apparently begun to recruit native volunteers on an equal footing as early as 1941, was made up of 50 per cent Russian and other Soviet volunteers by late 1942.[42] The 113th Infantry Division began to organize Hiwis in the summer of 1942.[43] An order dated 8 August 1942 called for the raising of Hiwis and eventually formed the following units:[44] *Ukrainische Hunterschaft Feldgendarmerie Trupp* 113 (Ukrainian Hunter Field Police Company 113) and *Kriegsgefangen Kompanie der Piohier Bataillon* 113.[45] When the 113th Infantry Division was surrounded and eventually destroyed in the Stalingrad pocket these auxiliary units also ceased to exist. As early as the summer of 1941 some German divisions began to illegally recruit native volunteers for what initially were non-combat duties behind the front lines.

Eventually, each German division would contain a determined number of *Hilfswilliger* within the framework of the divisional table of organization and equipment (TOE). This number varied but was usually around 3,000–4,000 men. A 1944 estimate suggested that there were between 600,000 and 1.4 million Hiwis serving in German units on the Eastern Front. This equates to about 20 per cent of the strength of the *Ostheer* in the USSR at the time. So by 1944 roughly one soldier in five wearing the field-grey uniform of the German Army on the Russian Front was a native volunteer. As mentioned earlier, mass recruitment of the native population began in earnest in the autumn of 1941, but most of these early recruitments were illegal, since many German commanders were actually arming these volunteers and allowing them to fight either on the front line or against the growing Soviet partisan menace. One German commander described it thusly:

> Everything I have been doing is illegal. There are no regulations for my men. No recognized ranks, no uniforms, no official pay, no clothing. No decorations. No German soldier will salute a Russian whom I have chosen to appoint an officer. Where opportunists are concerned, what motivates them is the belief that we are going to win. But the genuine volunteers are not with us for such reasons. How will both groups react when the war goes badly and they realize we are not meeting them half-way, not treating them as real allies?[46]

How would they react? This was the question that most German officers did not want to have answered, for deep inside they knew what the consequences would be. Those officers hoped that a change in policy from the top-down would soon come and repair the damage that had already been done and continued to occur. The bulk of these volunteers recruited by the Germans came from the Soviet Union, even from areas of the Soviet Union which were not located in what is termed 'European Russia'. Like so many wasted opportunities, the employment of Soviet citizens in German uniform proved to be, at best, an expediency to an end that failed, and not a concrete foreign policy, geared to undermine the support for Stalin and communism. The Nazis never offered the people of the Soviet Union true autonomy and freedom. It was only after much time had passed, with numerous heated debates, that Hitler reluctantly permitted the recruitment of battalion-sized units of *östlich Völker* ('eastern peoples'). By the time the Germans finally came around to supporting a 'Russian Liberation Army' in 1944, that opportunity had turned into an illusion. Like a house of cards, the Nazi attempt at empire building in the East fell by the weight of its own ruthless and cruel eastern policies.

Chapter 2

The *Ostland* (Baltic) and Belarus regions

The object of war is victory, the object of victory is conquest, and the object of conquest is occupation. [Napoleon Bonaparte]

A plethora of rear area forces and commands

When the Third Reich invaded the Soviet Union on 22 June 1941, her armies were followed by what at first seemed like a plethora of various rear area forces representing just about the entire Nazi political, civilian and military system. These copious German formations each had a unique and important role assigned to them in the German scheme to occupy and control the peoples and territories that in 1941 comprised the USSR. These organizations included principally the Nazi Party functionaries, with their staffs and headquarters, and the complete German law enforcement system (which could count on the various police arms such as the German *Ordnungspolizei* (Order Police), *Schutzpolizei* (the uniformed protection police), *Geheim Staatspolizei* (state secret police), *Landespolizei* (state police), *Gemeindepolizei* (municipal police) and *Gendarmerie* (rural police)), as well as services like the *Technische Nothilfe* (technical emergency services) and *Wasserschutzpolizei* (river police). These various organizations supplied the bulk of the manpower for the *Einsatzkommando* units, the mobile SS killing units which also engaged in combat behind the advancing German Army lines.

The majority of the personnel for the *Einsatzkommando* units came from various SS and police forces. The German Army also had its own rear area troops, namely its line of communications divisions, also known as *Sicherungsdivisionen* (security divisions). There were also other forces allocated to the rear area commands, including security battalions, bicycle units, regional defence battalions, etc. The number of troops that each Korück controlled varied greatly and sometimes even changed from month to month. For example, on 18 November 1943 Korück 593 of 2nd Panzer Army controlled the following forces: 783rd Turkestani Infantry Battalion, 802nd North Caucasian Infantry Battalion, I. Battalion, 454th Eastern Cavalry Battalion,[1] 583rd Cossack Infantry Battalion and the 1st Eastern Guard Company.

In addition to the army rear area commands, the *Ostheer* could also count on the *Feldgendarmerie* (military field police) and the *Geheimfeldpolizei* (secret field police, abbreviated in German as GFP). The *Feldgendarmerie* were responsible for traffic control and security immediately behind the army front lines. They also dealt with runaway soldiers and deserters. The GFP operated in company-sized units and, in conjunction with front-line and rear area forces, were charged with combating partisans and assisting the SS killing units. For the initial invasion of the Soviet Union, military field police battalions were assigned as follows:

- Army Group North: 561st, 689th and 691st Battalions;
- Army Group Centre: 531st, 591st, 690th, 695th, 696th, 697th Battalions; and
- Army Group South: 541st, 571st, 682nd, 683rd, 685th, 692nd, 693rd, and 694th Battalions.

The 571st Military Field Police Battalion initially operated in the region of Army Group North in 1941. In April 1942 it was transferred to Army Group Centre and in July 1942 it was once again shifted, this time to Army Group South. Additionally, in late July 1942 the 698th Military Field Police Battalion was established in southern Russia.

As a special branch of the German Army field police, the *Geheimfeldpolizei* (GFP) was more involved in the Holocaust than, say, the regular German Army military field police force. To begin with, GFP units were formed into small, highly mobile groups of no more than 80–100 men. Their mission was intelligence-gathering and the elimination of threats behind the German lines. As the war would prove, this mission included the killing of political commissars, Jews, partisans and any other elements deemed a danger to the prosecution of the war effort in the East. While the *Feldgendarmerie* committed murder on orders, the GFP would often give those orders. In 1941 only 43 GFP groups were operating in Europe. By 1942 the demands of the Russian campaign had forced the deployment of 83 GFP units, most of which were allocated for use on the Eastern Front.[2] The sheer vastness of the Soviet territories necessitated that the German planners divide the Soviet countryside into regions which could be controlled and managed properly.

The Baltic states of Estonia, Latvia and Lithuania, for example, were grouped into a civilian administrative area called the *Reichskommissariat Ostland*. This *Reichskommissariat* was split up into several *Generalkommissariate* that were further divided by country. As a result, three General Districts named 'Estonia', 'Latvia' and 'Lithuania' were organized under the staff and leadership of the *Reichskommissariat Ostland*. On 1 September 1941 the Bialystok District was attached to the *Reichskommissariat Ostland*. Immediately southeast of this region, neighbouring the Polish-Lithuanian-Belarus border

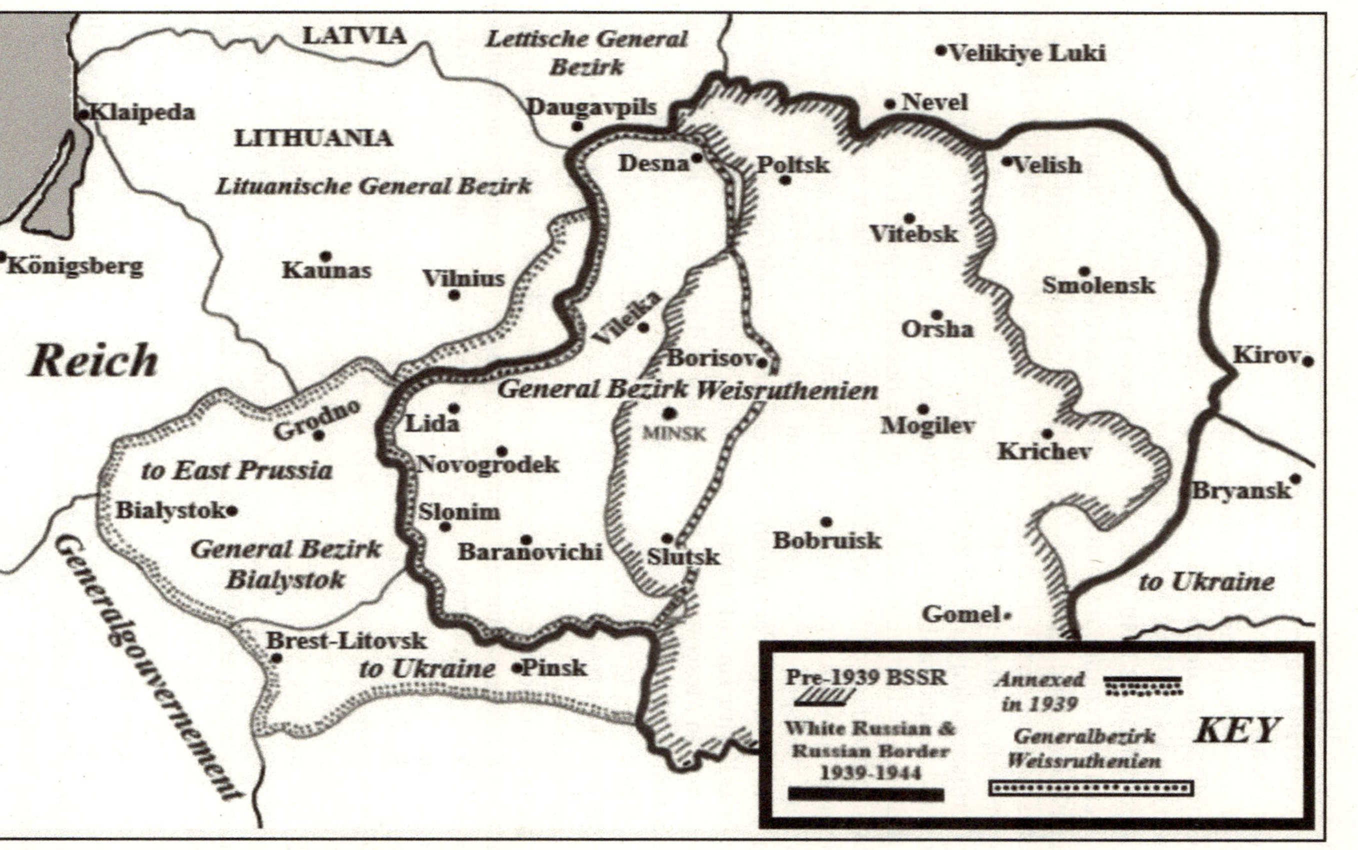

Map 2. The various borders of Belarus, 1939–1944.

area, was a district which the Germans called *Reichskommissariat Weißruthenien* (General District White Ruthenia).[3] This region had undergone many border changes throughout its existence. For example, in 1940 the western half of what was considered the Belarusian Soviet Socialist Republic had actually been the northeastern part of Poland until the USSR annexed that area in October 1939. A small part of southeastern Lithuania had also been ceded to Belarus in 1940. When the Germans invaded the Soviet Union, they too decided to change the borders of what was considered Belarus, most significantly by extending Belarus into parts of northeast Poland and by limiting Belarus on its eastern half to the regions of Desna, Borisov, Minsk and Slutsk.

In this way, most of pre-1939 central and eastern Belarus was ceded to what the Germans called Central Russia. Belarus lies in an area between the Baltic States and Poland in the west, Ukraine in the south and Russia proper in the north and east. Throughout its history the Belarusian people, also referred to as White Russians or White Ruthenians, have always been at the mercy of their more powerful neighbours. At the end of the First World War the Germans had sponsored the Belarusian National Republic. This move had been made to try to place another buffer state between Germany and Russia. The brief Belarusian independence lasted only until 1921, when the Bolshevik government in Moscow sliced Belarus in half in the Treaty of Riga. The Belarusian nation was cut between its western and eastern halves. The western part, which was predominantly Catholic, was ceded to Poland, while the eastern half, which was predominantly Eastern Orthodox, became a part of the Soviet Union.[4]

This split would eventually come back to haunt the White Ruthenians as it divided the Belarus community into two antagonistic (though nationalistic) political blocks. As described above, when the Germans invaded the Soviet Union, their forces were divided among three major army groups facing European Russia: Army Group North, which moved through the Baltic States towards Leningrad, Army Group South, which moved against Ukraine, and Army Group Centre, which sliced through Belarus and into the central region of Russia towards Moscow. Following in the wake of this huge force were the rear area security troops. Each army group had a headquarters command that controlled security forces immediately behind the various German army groups. In the region of Army Group Centre that command was titled *Befehlshaber des Rückwärtigen Heeresgebietes der Heeresgruppe Mitte.*[5] As stated earlier, in September 1941 the Bialystok District came under the control of *Generalkommissariat Ostland*. Shortly thereafter, all of Belarus – what the Germans called the *Generalbezirk Weissruthenien* – was attached to the *Ostland* civilian administration.

The *Ostland* government was led by *SA Gruppenführer* Heinrich Lohse, the *Reichskommissar für Ostland*.[6] Thus, initially Belarus was merged into the Nazi civilian apparatus controlling the Baltic States. A Higher SS and Police Leader North Russia headquarters was to control all SS, *Sicherheitsdienst* and police forces for the three Baltic *Generalbezirke*, as well as the Bialystok and Belarus *Generalbezirke*. National Leader of the SS Heinrich Himmler established three Higher SS and Police Leader commands which in 1941 were initially titled 'A', 'B' and 'C'. These headquarters were also to control the infamous *Einsatzgruppen* killing formations. The rear of Army Group North was assigned Higher SS and Police Leader A, while Army Group Centre and Army Group South received Higher SS and Police Leader B and Higher SS and Police Leader C respectively.[7] Higher SS and Police Leader A in the *Ostland* region eventually came to be called Higher SS and Police Leader Ostland and North Russia. This command controlled the following four subheadquarters:

- SS and Police Leader Lithuania (led by Lucian Wysocki);
- SS and Police Leader Latvia (led by Walter Schröder);
- SS and Police Leader Estonia (led by Heinrich Möller); and
- SS and Police Leader White Ruthenia (led by Carl Zenner).

The head of the Higher SS and Police Leader Ostland and North Russia command was SS Lieutenant General Hans-Adolf Prützmann.[8] Prützmann had access to the units under the control of the *Kommandostab Reichsführer SS* headquarters. The *Kommandostab Reichsführer SS* staff controlled various SS units which were initially held in reserve behind the front lines. These SS units were to be used at the total discretion of Prützmann and the other Higher SS and Police Leader commanders in the USSR. Requests for troops from the Waffen SS, *Sicherheitsdienst*, *Ordnungspolizei*[9] and SS killing units *Einsatzgruppe* A, B, C and D were to be directed to the *Kommandostab Reichsführer SS*, who would allocate the forces. Naturally, since Belarus had become part of the Higher SS and Police Leader Ostland and North Russia command in 1941,[10] the German Waffen SS, *Sicherheitsdienst*, *Ordnungspolizei* and *Einsatzgruppen* forces there were indirectly guided or assisted in one way or another by the Higher SS and Police Leader Ostland and North Russia headquarters. The *Reichssicherheitshauptamt* (Reich Security Main Office), which at the time was led by Reinhard Heydrich, had also established itself in the *Ostland* region with its infamous *Gestapo Amt-IV* (Department No. 4), commanded by Heinrich Müller. Müller created the *Befehlshaber der Sicherheitspolizei und Sicherheitsdienst Ostland* (Supreme Commander of the Security Police and Security Service Ostland) staff and assigned Heinz Jost to lead it. Jost in turn split up his command into similar regional groups in much the same fashion as the Higher SS and Police Leader commands. He named these subcommands *Kommandeur der Sicherheitspolizei und Sicherheitsdienst* (*KdS*)

(Commander of the Security Police and Security Service), and their commanders were as shown below:

- *KdS Litauen*: SS Colonel Karl Jäger (23 September 1941–23 May 1944)[11]
- *KdS Lettland*: SS Lieutenant Colonel Rudolf Lange (3 December 1941–January 1945)
- *KdS Estland*: SS Colonel Dr Martin Sandberger (July 1941–September 1943)
- *KdS Weissruthenien*: SS Lieutenant Colonel Dr Eduard Strauch (December 1941–May 1944)

Similarly, the head of the German *Ordnungspolizei*, SS Lieutenant General Kurt Daluege, sent in higher police headquarters staffs behind the three main German army groups in the USSR. In the region of the Baltic States (*Ostland*) and North Russia, he established the *Befehlshaber der Ordnungspolizei Ostland*. Kurt Daluege gave control of this post to Lieutenant General of the Police Georg Jedicke. Jedicke in turn established the following sub-commands, which were termed *Kommandeur der Ordnungspolizei* (*KdO*) (Commander of the Order Police), and their commanders were as shown below:

- *KdO Litauen*:
  Police Major A. Engel (14 September 1941–9 March 1942)
  Police Colonel Wolfgang Denicke (10 March–14 October 1942)[12]
  Gendarmerie Colonel Dr Hans Hachtel (15 October 1942–December 1943)
- *KdO Lettland*:
  Police Major Karl Knecht (28 August 1941–18 August 1943)[13]
  Police Lieutenant Colonel Johann Klepsch (19 August 1943–18 October 1944)[14]
- *KdO Estland*:
  Police Major Hermann Schallert (August 1941–10 March 1942)[15]
  Police Colonel Wilhelm von Thaden (28 July 1942–1944)[16]
- *Kommandeur der Schutzpolizei Minsk*
  Police Colonel Eberhard Herf (December 1941–15 February 1942)[17]
  SS Major General and Police Major General Erik von Heimburg (16 February–30 July 1942)[18]
  Police Lieutenant Colonel Johann Klepsch (8 August 1942–18 August 1943)[19]

While the *Befehlshaber der Sicherheitspolizei* (Commander of the Security Police) and *Befehlshaber der Ordnungspolizei* (Commander of the Order Police) were subservient to the *Reichssicherheitshauptamt* (Reich Main Security Office) under Reinhard Heydrich and the Order Police under Kurt Daluege, they could still answer directly to National Leader of the SS Heinrich Himmler through his Higher SS and Police Leader commands. This is the way Himmler wanted it, since he wished to circumvent his immediate subordinates if he ever wished to control a situation in the field or implement a decree immediately without having to go through the normal channels of command. This also gave Himmler greater flexibility of command. The downside was that some feathers would be ruffled whenever he circumvented some officers and their respective headquarters command. Table 2.1 lists the SS and police forces that were available in the USSR in the summer of 1941.

Thus, for the purpose of controlling the rear areas, performing anti-guerrilla operations and other security tasks, and even implementing the *Einsatzgruppen* killings, the offices of the Higher SS and Police Leader commands in the Baltic States, Belarus and Ukraine, as well as north, central and southern Russia, could count on numerous SS and police forces. These included the units under the Command Staff of the National Leader of the SS, as well as forces belonging to the Commander of the Security Police and Security Service and the Commander of the Order Police. In 1941 the forces allocated for guard duty, anti-partisan warfare and the killings of Jews, commissars and others the Nazis' deemed undesirables are listed in Table 2.1; to these formations of the SS and police we should also add the numerous *Geheimfeldpolizei* (Secret Field Police) units which, although a part of the Army, were nevertheless much more closely aligned with the activities of the *Einsatzgruppen*. The Secret Field Police also worked closely with the SS, the Security Police and regular Order Police forces in the USSR. Robert Barth, a former member of a *Teilkommando* from *Einsatzkommando* 10b (*Einsatzgruppe* D), stated after his defection and capture in Italy in 1943 that the behaviour of the Secret Field Police units in Russia was 'a close second to the *Einsatzkommandos* in the perpetration of horrors'.[20]

According to agreements made between the Security Service and Army prior to the start of the Russian campaign, the role of the Secret Field Police units was limited to counter-intelligence. Nevertheless, as we shall see, this role was soon expanded to include the elimination of anyone deemed a threat to the Nazi state. Because the Russian campaign would employ large numbers of Secret Field Police units, a post was established to control them: Head of the Secret Field Police East. Field Police Director Ernst Rassow held this position. His superior was Wilhelm Krichbaum, as Secret Field Police Chief. When the *Kommissarbefehl* (Commissar Order) was released, instructing all members of the German Army, police and SS forces to kill all Commissars, later expanded to include Communist functionaries, the role of the Secret Field Police was likewise widened. Now they were also expected to carry out this order and eliminate not only Jews, who were automatically considered

Table 2.1. SS and police units available for employment in the USSR in the summer of 1941.

Higher Command/Unit and Commander	Area of Operation	Notes
Command Staff of the National Leader of the SS. On 27 June 1941 Reichsführer SS Heinrich Himmler removed the *Kommandostab Reichsführer SS* from German Army control and placed it at the disposition of Higher SS and Police Leader SS Lieutenant General and Lieutenant General of the Police Erich von dem Bach-Zelewski, commander of Higher SS and Police Command C, soon designated *Weissruthenien* (White Russian). He could allocate those forces to any of the other Higher SS and Police Commands in Russia.		
1st SS Infantry Brigade (motorized): SS Brigadier General Karl Demelhuber	South, then Central Russia*	*Transferred to central Russia in Nov. 1941 as a rear area unit.
2nd SS Infantry Brigade (motorized): SS Brigadier General Karl von Treuenfeld	North Russia	
SS Cavalry Regiment 1*: SS Major Gustav Lombard	Central Russia	*SS Cavalry Regiments 1 and 2 were merged in Sept. 1941 to become the SS Cavalry Brigade.
SS Cavalry Regiment 2*: SS Major Franz Magill	Central Russia	*Committed to Army Group North in Nov. 1941.
SS Escort Battalion Reichsführer SS	Central Russia	
SS Flak Battalion East: SS Major Hallman	North Russia	
SS Volunteer Regiment Northwest*: SS Colonel Otto Reich (1941–1942)	North Russia**	* *Source*: Prechtl, *Unsere Ehre Heibt Treue*, p. 17. ** Served initially in an operation in the northern part of the Pripet marshes in Central Russia.
Battalion of the Waffen SS for Special Employment*: SS Major Eberhard von Kunsberg**	North, Central and Southern Russia***	*This battalion was not created until Aug. 1942 but its companies served in the 1941 campaign and were referred to as SS *Sonderkommando* AA. ** *Source*: NARA Microfilm T-175, Roll 191, Frame 2729914. *** The three companies were split up and distributed to each Higher SS and Police Leader Command.
Sonderkommando Dirlewanger*: SS Major Oskar Dirlewanger	Belarus	*This SS penal unit was stationed in Poland throughout 1941. It arrived in Belarus in Jan. 1942.
Commander of the Security Police and Security Service		
Einstazgruppen members totalled 3,000 in June 1941, 500 of whom were from the Order Police.*		* *Source*: Browning, *Ordinary Men*, p. 10.

Unit	Area	Notes
Einsatzgruppe* A: SS Major General and Major General of the Police Dr Franz Walter Stahlecker		* *Source*: Krausnick, *Hitlers Einsatzgruppen*, p. 128. ** *Sonderkommando* 1a and 1b were redesignated at the end of 1941 as Head of the Security Police and the Security Service in the Rear Army Area 101 (North) and *Sonderkommando* 1a and 1b.
Commander of the Security Police and Security Service Estonia* *Sonderkommando* 1a**: SS Major Dr Karl Martin Sandberger	Baltic States and North Russia	* Part of this unit became the basis for the security police and security service units and headquarters in Estonia on 3 Dec. 1941. ** In autumn 1941 *Einsatzgruppe* Reval (Tallinn) was formed from *Sonderkommando* 1a and became known as Task Force Reval of the Security Police and the Security Service. In Feb. 1943 it was redesignated Commander of the Security Police and Security Service Reval.
1–12 Estonian Auxiliary Police Companies: Major Ain Ervin Mere	Estonia*	* Twelve Estonian volunteer companies were raised by *Sonderkommando* 1a and the staff headquarters of *Einsatzgruppe* A in the summer of 1941 and stationed as follows: Order Auxiliary Police Company 1: Tallinn; 2: Harrien; 3: Jerwen; 4: Wierland; 5: Narva; 6: Tartu; 7: Voru; 8: Valga; 9: Petseri; 10: Poltsamaa; 11: Viljandi; 12: Oesel.
Commander of the Security Police and Security Service White Ruthenia* *Sonderkommando* 1b**: SS Lieutenant Colonel Dr Erich Ehrlinger***	North Russia, then Belarus	* This unit became the basis for the security police and security service units and headquarters in Belarus (White Russia) on 3 Dec. 1941. ** In summer 1942 this headquarters staff and its units were renamed *Sonderkommando* 1b of the Security Police and Security Service at 16th Army, Army Group North. It was disbanded in Oct. 1943. *** Source: Wilhelm, *Die Einsatzgruppe* A, p. 488.
Commander of the Security Police and Security Service Latvia* *Einsatzkommando* 2**: SS Major Dr Rudolf Batz	Baltic States and North Russia	* This unit became the basis for the security police and security service units and headquarters in Latvia on 3 Dec. 1941. ** In autumn 1941 *Einsatzkommando* 2 was redesignated Operations Command of the Security Police and the Security Service for the Rear Army Area 101 (North).
Commander of the Security Police and Security Service Lithuania* *Einsatzkommando* 3**: SS Colonel Karl Jäger	Baltic States and North Russia	* This unit became the basis for the security police and security service units and headquarters in Lithuania on 3 Dec. 1941. ** In the autumn of 1942 a *Teilkommando* from *Einsatzkommando* 3 was renamed Security Police and Security Service at 18th Army, Army Group North. In Feb. 1943 it was once again renamed Security Police and Security Service at the Commander in the Army Area North/*Teilkommando* 3.

Higher Command/Unit and Commander	Area of Operation	Notes
1st–5th Lithuanian Auxiliary Police Companies*	Kaunas, Lithuania	*These five initial companies were formed by *Sonderkommando* 1b. One company was stationed in Fort no. 7 in Kaunas, while another travelled with *Sonderkommando* 1b. The other three were taken up by the 11th Reserve Police Battalion when part of the battalion travelled to Minsk.
SS First Lieutenant Rosenow*		* *Source*: Prechtl, *Unsere Ehre Heibt Treue*, p. 244.
1st Company of Waffen SS Battalion for Special Employment*	North Russia	* *Source*: USHMMA, RG-48.004M Acc. 1993.A.0019. Selected Records from the Military Historical Institute Archives, Prague, 1941–1944. Records of *Bataillon der Waffen SS z.b.V.*, Rolls 3 and 4.
***Einsatzgruppe* B: Arthur Nebe**		
1st–5th Lithuanian Auxiliary Police Companies	Central Russia	
Representative of the heads of the security police and the security service at Commander of the Rear Army Area 102/Army Group Centre*		*In autumn 1941 became Chief of the Security Police and Security Service for Army Area 102 Centre.
Einsatzkommando 8: SS Lieutenant Colonel Dr Otto Bradfish and *Einsatzkommando* 9: SS Lieutenant Colonel Alfred Karl Filbert	Central Russia	
Einsatzkommando of the Security Police*		*In autumn 1941 became Security Police and Security Service at Army Area 102 Centre/*Einsatzkommando* 7b.
Einsatzkommando 7b: SS Major Günther Rausch**	Central Russia	** *Source*: Kampe et al., *Die Einsatzgruppen* in der besetzten Sowjetunion, p. 377.
Einsatzkommando der Sicherheitspolizei und SD beim Befehlshaber der rückwärtigen Heeresgebiet 102 Mitte		
Einsatzkommando 7a*: *SS Obersturmbannführer* Dr Walter Blume	North Central Russia	*In Nov. 1943 this unit was renamed and posted as Security Police and Security Service White Ruthenia/*Einsatzkommando* 7a.
Vorkommando Moscow* (later redesignated as *Sonderkommando* 7c)**: SS Brigadier General Dr Franz Six (until 20 Aug. 1941)*** then SS Major Woldemar Klingelhöfer****	Smolensk, Central Russia	*Unit disbanded Jan. 1942. The men and equipment were used to augment *Einsatzkommando* 7a. ** *Source*: Kampe et al., *Die Einsatzgruppen* in der besetzten Sowjetunion, p. 63. *** *Source*: Krausnick, *Hitlers Einsatzgruppen*, p. 362. **** *Source*: MacLean, *The Field Men*, p. 78.
Einsatzgruppe z.b.V.* (this unit operated briefly in 1941)**		*This *Einsatzgruppe* was a temporary affair. It was disbanded autumn 1941. **Its movements followed this path: Lemberg-Brest-Litovsk-Bialystok-Pinsk-Luck-Rovno-Kovel-Rava Ruska-Bialystok-Novogrodek-Baranovichi-Grodno.
SS Oberführer Dr Eberhard Schöngarth (the rank of *SS Oberführer* has no British or American equivalent)	Eastern Poland and Western Belarus	

Unit	Location	Notes
2nd Company, Battalion of the Waffen SS for Special Employment	Central Russia	
Einsatzgruppe* C: SS Brigadier General Dr Otto Rasch		* Until Oct. 1941 when SS Brigadier General Dr Max Thomas assumed command.
Einsatzkommando 4*		* A *Teilkommando* from *Einsatzkommando* 4 was used in autumn 1942 to form *Teilkommando* 4/Head of the Security Police and Security Service at 18th Army/Army Group North. This *Teilkommando* only lasted until the end of 1942.
Sonderkommando 4a*: SS Colonel Paul Blobel	Southern Russia	* Renamed Security Police and Security Service for the Rear Army Area 103 (South)/*Sonderkommando* 4a in autumn 1941. In Feb. 1943 it was renamed Security Police and Security Service with the Commander in the Army Area South/*Sonderkommando* 4a. One source states it was disbanded at the end of 1943, but the staff and rear area of the security police and security service posts it created existed into Nov. 1944 when it was finally redesignated Security Police and Security Service with the Commander in Army Group A.
Sonderkommando 4b*: SS Colonel Günther Herrmann	Southern Russia	* Disbanded in Jan. 1944.
Einsatzkommando 5*: SS Colonel Erwin Schulz**	Southern Russia	* Disbanded in Jan. 1942. Reformed in Oct. 1943 and its component parts used to form Security Police and Security Service White Ruthenia command in Jan. 1944. ** Until Oct. 1941 when August Meier assumed command.
Einsatzkommando 6*: SS Lieutenant Colonel Dr Erhard Kröger	Southern Russia	* Dissolved in Nov. 1943.
3rd Company, Battalion of the Waffen SS for Special Employment	Southern Russia	
Commander of the Order Police Eastland and North Russia: Lieutenant General of the Police Georg Jedicke* (22 June 1941–Mar. 1944) then Major General of the Police Otto Gieseke*		* *Source*: Mehner, *Die Waffen SS und Polizei*, p. 319** *Source*: Tessin et al., *Waffen SS und Ordnungspolizei*, p. 613.
SS and Police Leader Estonia: SS Brigadier General and Major General of the Police Heinrich Möller*		* *Source*: Jurs et al., *Estonian Freedom Fighters*, p. 86.
SS and Police Leader Estonia headquarters	Tallinn, Estonia	

Higher Command/Unit and Commander	Area of Operation	Notes
a) *SS and Police Station Post Pleskau**	Pleskau (Pskov), Russia	*The translation of this title was: SS and Police Site Leader. It was a post below that of the SS and Police Leader headquarters. This specific command was raised in autumn 1941 and disbanded summer 1943. The SS and Police Station Posts were responsible for overseeing security and police matters in a specific area. Their officers were typically appointed by the SS and held authority over both SS units and local police forces. Duties included maintaining order, enforcing Nazi policies, suppressing resistance, and coordinating with other branches of the Nazi regime, such as the Gestapo and the *Sicherheitsdienst*.
b) *SS and Police Station Post Dorpat*	Dorpat (Tartu), Estonia	
Commander of the Security Police Estonia: Dr Martin Sandberger*		* Sandberger served in this post until Dec. 1943 when he was transferred to Italy.
Commander of the Order Police Estonia		
Headquarters:	Reval (Tallinn), Estonia	
9th Police Battalion*: Police Major Paulus Meier		* This battalion was split and its 500 men used to augment SS *Einsatzgruppen*. In July 1942 the men were regathered and sent to Norway, the unit now redesignated III. Battalion, Police Regiment 27.
Police Regiment North*: Police Lieutenant Colonel Hermann Keuper**	North Russia	* Comprising the 61st, 112th and 132nd Police Battalions.** *Source*: Muñoz, *The German Police*, p. M27.
Police Technical Emergency Company of Police Regiment North	North Russia	
105th Police Battalion*: Police Major Helwes	North Russia	* This unit was created in northern Russia in July 1941 but was transferred to Holland in July 1942.
65th Police Battalion: Police Major Barkhold	North Russia	
69th Reserve Police Battalion Todt*	North Russia	* This unit made its appearance in Riga, Latvia, in Oct. 1941 and remained in Latvia until July 1942 when it was sent to France to become part of Police Regiment 28 Todt.
319th Police Battalion: Police Major Geissler	North Russia	
321st Police Battalion: Police Major Petersen	North Russia	
254th Police Battalion: Police Major Bendzko*	North Russia	* Initially held in reserve, along with the 304th, 315th and 320th Police Battalions.
Leader of the Order Police and Gendarmerie *Reval* (Tallinn)*	Tallinn, Estonia	* Created in the autumn of 1941 but struck from the rolls in Feb. 1943.

Estonian Self-Defence Battalion Dorpat*: Police Major Bergmann** (Aug.–Dec. 1941) then Police Major Franz Kurg (Dec. 1941–June 1944)	Dorpat (Tartu) Estonia	*Redesignated 37th Estonian Self-Defence Front Battalion in Nov. 1941.** *Source*: Jurs et al., *Estonian Freedom Fighters in World War 2*, p. 81.
Estonian Self-Defence Construction Battalion Dorpat (Tartu)*: Police Major Schiller**	Dorpat (Tartu) Estonia	*Created Sept. 1941; redesignated 42nd Estonian Engineer Self-Defence Battalion in Nov. 1941. ** *Source*: Jurs et al., *Estonian Freedom Fighters in World War 2*, p. 83.
Estonian Self-Defence Cadre Battalion*: Lieutenant Colonel Sarev. (Later, Lieutenant Colonel Vermet, another former Estonian Army officer, assumed command of the battalion)	Dorpat (Tartu), Estonia	*A cadre battalion created for forming Estonia *Schuma* battalions. Contained a staff and three recruit training companies. Renamed 41st Estonian Self-Defence Front Battalion in Nov. 1941. Expanded in summer 1942 to include a ski training company and engineer training company. Redesignated 41st Estonian Self-Defence Battalion (reinforced) in autumn 1942.
Estonian Self-Defence Battalion Poltsama*: Major Sobolev	Poltsama, Estonia	*Created autumn 1941 with a staff and three companies. Redesignated 39th Estonian Security Battalion in summer 1942 with a staff and five companies.
Estonian Self-Defence Front Battalion 36: Police Major Renter* and Captain Riipalu	Estonia**	*A German police officer held command initially but in autumn 1942 Captain Riipalu assumed command. At this time the unit was fighting the partisans in Ukraine. **Formed in Nov. 1941 from Estonian volunteers from Saaremaa, Haapsalu and Tartu.
181st Estonian Security Battalion	Estonia	
182nd Estonian Security Battalion	Estonia	
183rd Estonian Security Battalion*	Estonia	*The 181st–186th Estonian Security Battalions (later redesignated the 658th–665th Estonian Eastern Battalions) were created in Sept. 1941. In Oct. the 181st–183rd were sent to the German Army Rear Area Command (Korück 583) immediately behind the 18th Army front lines and placed on guard duty.
184th Estonian Security Battalion*	Estonia	*In Nov. 1941 it was sent to Korück 583 behind the lines of 18th Army in Army Group North and ordered to perform security duties.
185th Estonian Security Battalion	Estonia	
186th Estonian Security Battalion*	Narva, Estonia	*This unit would serve as the replacement battalion for the 181st–185th Estonian Security Battalions.
Estonian Self-Defence Battalion Pihkva*: Major K. Limpere	Pihkva, Estonia	*Renamed 40th Estonian Self-Defence Front Battalion in Nov. 1941.
Estonian Self-Defence Battalion Fellin (Viljandi)*: Lieutenant Colonel J. Raudmäe	Viljandi, Estonia	*Renamed 38th Estonian Self-Defence Front Battalion in Nov. 1941.

Higher Command/Unit and Commander	Area of Operation	Notes
1st Estonian Guard Battalion*: Police Major J. Kövenig** and Major J. Peiker	Tallinn, Estonia	*Formed on 1 Nov. 1941 from very old and young Estonian volunteers, and renamed *(Estnische) Front Bataillon 29* on 28 Nov. 1941. It was used as a guard unit in the Estonian capital.** Although Major J. Peiker was in command of the battalion, the Germans placed one of their own police officers, Police Major J. Kövenig, as the liaison officer.
SS and Police Leader Latvia: SS Brigadier General and Major General of the Police Walter Schröder		
SS and Police Leader Latvia Headquarters:	Riga, Latvia	
a) *SS and Police Station Post Libau*: SS Lieutenant Colonel Dr Fritz Dietrich	Libau [Liepaja], Latvia	
b) *SS and Police Station Post Dünaburg* [Daugavpils]: SS Major and Police Lieutenant Colonel Josef Vogts*	Daugavpils, Latvia	* Vogts was appointed in Sept. 1941 and held the post until 1943, when he became the Chief of Staff for the SS and Police Leader Lublin command. He became the Ia of this SS headquarters in Jan. 1944 and was promoted to SS lieutenant colonel in Sept. 1944.
Commander of the Security Police Latvia: SS Major Dr Martin Franz Erwin Rudolf Lange*		* Lange attended the infamous Wannsee Conference on 20 Jan. 1942, where the Nazis' 'final solution to the Jewish problem' was decided. Prior to this, Lange had been responsible for executing 35,000 people just outside Riga between 30 Nov. and 8 Dec. 1941. Overall, he would be responsible for the deaths of about 250,000 people in a six-month period. He was promoted to SS lieutenant-colonel in 1942 and SS Colonel in Jan. 1945. He was killed fighting in the defence of Posen (Poznan) in Feb. 1945.
Commander of the Security Police Latvia Headquarters	Riga, Latvia	
Commander of the Order Police and Protection Police Latvia		
Commander of the Order Police and Protection Police Latvia Headquarters	Riga, Latvia	
Reserve Police Battalion Eastland*: Police Captain August Hanner	Riga, Latvia	* Actually the 33rd Reserve Police Battalion, which appeared in Riga in July 1941. Soon redesignated Reserve Police Battalion Eastland. The unit recruited heavily from ethnic Germans in the Baltic states. The battalion was eventually sent to L'viv in Poland in Oct. 1941, and then to Zhitomir in Ukraine.
33rd Police Communications Company	Riga, Latvia	
16th Latvian Self Defence Battalion: Colonel Gustavs Mangulis*	North Russia**	* *Source*: Muñoz, *Hitler's Eastern Legions*, vol. II, p. 52. ** Formed in Oct. 1941 and immediately sent to the rear area of 16th Army, under the Rear Area Military Commander of 16th Army (Korück 584). It was assigned to security duties.

Unit	Location	Notes
Latvian Security Battalion Riga*: Captain Karlis Behms	Riga, Latvia	*Formed in Oct. 1941 in Riga and renamed the 18th Latvian Self-Defence Battalion in Dec. 1941.
19th Latvian Self Defence Battalion*	Riga, Latvia	*Created and initially stationed in Riga in the first half of Dec. 1941.
Latvian Engineer Security Battalion Abrene*	Abrene, Latvia	*Formed in Oct. 1941.
SS and Police Leader Lithuania: SS Brigadier General Lucian Wysocki (July 1941–July 1943)		
SS and Police Leader Lithuania	Vilnius, Lithuania	
SS and Police Station Post Vilna [Vilnius]	Vilnius	
Commander of the Security Police in Lithuania: SS Colonel Karl Jäger	Vilnius, Lithuania	
Commander of the Order Police in Lithuania: Police Colonel Wolfgang Denicke (Mar. 1942–13 Oct. 1942)*	Kaunas, Lithuania	*Denicke was succeeded by Gendarmerie Colonel Dr Hans Hachtel (5 Oct. 1942–Dec. 1943).
Lithuanian Guard Company Toropets*	Toropets, Lithuania	*Created in autumn 1941 but disbanded by autumn 1942.
Lithuanian Guard Company Dno*	Dno, Lithuania	*Disbanded in autumn 1943.
82nd Police Communications Company	Vilnius, Lithuania	
5th Lithuanian Self-Defence Battalion*	Kaunas, Lithuania	*Formed in Nov. 1941 from existing Lithuanian self-defence companies.
11th Reserve Police Battalion*: Police Major Lechthaler	Kaunas, Lithuania, then Minsk, Belarus**	*Arrived in Kaunas in July 1941 and set about raising three companies of Lithuanian auxiliary police. **Two of the four German police companies in this battalion left for Minsk in Sept. 1941. They took with them three companies of Lithuanian auxiliary police volunteers.
Higher SS and Police Leader Central Russia and White Ruthenia: SS Lieutenant General and Lieutenant General of the Police Erich von dem Bach-Zelewski (21 May 1941–21 June 1944)	Minsk	
SS and Police Leader White Ruthenia: SS Lieutenant General and Lieutenant General of the Police Jakob Sporrenberg* (21 July–14 Aug. 1941)	Minsk	*SS Brigadier General and Major General of the Police Carl Zenner held this post from 14 Aug. 1941 to 22 May 1942.
SS and Police Leader Bialystok*	Bialystok	*SS Oberführer and Police Colonel Werner Fromm (Jan. 1942–Jan. 1943); SS Lieutenant-General and Lieutenant General of the Police Otto Hellwig (May 1943–July 1944); SS Oberführer and Police Colonel Heinz Roch (July–Oct. 1944).

Higher Command/Unit and Commander	Area of Operation	Notes
SS and Police Station Post Baranovichi	Baranovichi	
SS and Police Leader Mogilev* with:	Mogilev	*Formed on 1 Aug. 1942. The first commander was SS Brigadier General and Major General of the Police Georg Graf von Bassewitz-Behr (1 Aug. 1942–20 Apr. 1943), followed by SS Brigadier General and Major General of the Police Franz Kutschera (20 Apr.–20 Sept. 1943) and SS Lieutenant General and Lieutenant General of the Police Hans Haltermann (20 Sept. 1943–12 July 1944).
a) SS and Police Station Post Mogilev*	Mogilev	*Established in autumn 1941 and disbanded in summer 1943.
b) SS and Police Station Post Smolensk	Smolensk	
c) SS and Police Station Post Vitebsk*	Vitebsk	*Disbanded in summer 1943 and its headquarters used to help form the Self-Defence Training Battalion Vitebsk in autumn 1943.
SS and Police Leader Pripet*	Pinsk	*Headquartered in Pinsk. The first commander was SS Oberführer and Police Colonel Ernst Hartmann (18 Dec. 1943–6 Sept. 1944). On 1 Aug. 1944 Hartmann was promoted to SS Brigadier General and Major General of the Police.
Commander of the Security Police White Russia (Belarus): SS Lieutenant Colonel Dr Eduard Strauch		
Commander of the Order Police White Russia*	Minsk	*Initially, no higher order police command was assigned to White Russia and Central Russia. In 1943 a KdO was established in Minsk, when the General Commissariat White Ruthenia came under the control of the Higher SS and Police Leader Centre Russia, which then became Higher SS and Police Leader Centre Russia and White Ruthenia in 1943. The following officers led this post: SS Colonel and Police Colonel Johann Klepsch (Nov.–Dec. 1941), SS Brigadier General and Major General of the Police Eberhard Herf (Dec. 1941 to 16 Feb. 1942), SS Brigadier General and Major General of the Police Erik von Heimburg (17 Feb. 1942 to 30 July 1942), SS Colonel and Police Colonel Johann Klepsch (1 Aug. 1942–10 Apr. 1943), SS Brigadier General and Major General of the Police Walter Abraham, temporary commander (11 Apr. 1943–1 Oct. 1943), and SS Colonel and Police Colonel Johann Klepsch (2 Oct. 1943–Nov. 1944).
SS and Police Station Post Mogilev*	Mogilev	*This staff and its sub-units were dissolved in summer 1943.
31st Police Communications Company*	Minsk	*Later served with the 31st Police Rifle Regiment in 1944.
32nd Police Battalion*: Police Major von Braunschweig	Minsk	*Arrived in Minsk in Dec. 1941.

Police Economic Warehouse Bialystok*	Bialystok	*Both the Police Economic Camp Bialystok and the Police Supply Camp Bialystok were established in autumn 1941. The units in Bialystok (northeast Poland) were listed because it bordered White Russia.
Police Supply Warehouse Bialystok	Bialystok	
71st Police Communications Company	Bialystok	
SS and Police Station Post Orel*	Orel, Central Russia	*Created in autumn 1941 and disbanded in autumn 1942.
131st Police Battalion*: Police Major Hans-Detlef Ohrt	North Central Russia**	*When the police regiments were reorganized and expanded in July 1942, this battalion's line companies were used to form the anti-tank companies of four police regiments (North, Centre, South and Special Employment). **On 4 Sept. 1941 the battalion headquarters was in Newel. The battalion staff and the 2nd Company were relocated to Velikiye-Luki until 18 Sept. 1941, under the command of *Feldkommandantur 181*. On 10 Oct. 1941 the battalion marched to the front in the Velikiye-Luki/Toropets region, and deployed east of Toropets 11–14 Oct. 1941. From mid-Nov. 1941 to 15 Dec. 1941 the battalion staff and the 1st Company were withdrawn to Vitebsk, while the 2nd and 3rd Companies secured the Orsha–Smolensk highway from Bogushevsk. On 16 Dec. 1941 the battalion was absorbed by Police Regiment Centre in Smolensk. In the Soviet winter offensive, it was deployed at the front in the Kaluga area, under the control of 290th Infantry Regiment. According to Max Montua, commander of Police Regiment Centre, the 311th Police Battalion collapsed under a heavy Red Army attack on 26–28 Dec. 1941. It suffered heavy losses due to frostbite as much as through enemy action. The unit remained in this area until 30 Dec. 1941, but was withdrawn to Luga in Jan. 1942 for refitting.
307th Police Battalion*	Belarus, Central Russia	*Transferred in early June from Police Regiment Lublin to Police Regiment Centre. On 3 July 1941 it was at Brest-Litovsk, where it aided in the killing of about 4,000 Jews. From 28 July to 12 Aug. it was just east of Slutsk. In mid-Aug. it took part in another *Aktion* against Jews in Bobruisk. It reached Mogilev by 31 Aug. From 22 Oct. to 3 Nov. it took part in anti-partisan operations around the Drut and Dnieper rivers. On 4 Nov. it went to Smolensk. In mid-Dec. 1941 it moved to Kaluga and fought there until 21 Jan. 1942, when it moved to the region of Army Group Centre to fight partisans. In spring 1942 the remaining men of the 308th Police Battalion were absorbed into the 307th Police Battalion.
309th Police Battalion: Police Lieutenant Colonel Ernst Weis	Belarus, Central Russia	

Higher Command/Unit and Commander	Area of Operation	Notes
317th Police Battalion: Police Lieutenant Colonel Erwin Gresser		
308th Police Battalion*	Belarus, then Yughnov (Central Russia)	*Did not appear until Jan. 1942, when it was committed to front-line fighting.
316th Police Battalion*: Police Major Karl Behr	Belarus, Central Russia	*Part of Police Regiment Centre in 1942. The battalion was withdrawn to Paris in July 1942.
322nd Police Battalion*: Police Major Nagel	Belarus, Central Russia	*Reached Belarus at the end of July 1941.
323rd Police Battalion*: SS Major and Police Lieutenant Colonel Bernhard Griese	Belarus, Central Russia	*The battalion was in Tilsit, East Prussia, in Dec. 1941, en route to central Russia. It was withdrawn to Paris in July 1942.
Police Regiment Centre*: Police Colonel Karl Montua	Belarus, Central Russia	*Formed using the 6th, 85th, and 301st Police Battalions.
Police Technical Emergency Company, Police Regiment Centre	Belarus, Central Russia	
Commander of the Gendarmerie Mazyr Gendarmerie Lieutenant Colonel von Bredow (25 Oct. 1941–Mar. 1943); Gendarmerie Major Max Hirsch (Mar.–Oct. 1943)	SE Belarus	
Commander of the Order Police Ukraine*: Police Lieutenant General Otto von Oelhafen (Sept. 1941–Oct. 1942)	Rovno, then Kiev, Ukraine	*Subsequently led by Police Lieutenant General von Bomhard (Nov. 1942–Oct. 1943), Gendarmerie Colonel Ernst Lorge (Oct. 1943–Dec. 1943), Police Lieutenant General Karl Brenner (15 Dec.–June 1944) and Gendarmerie Colonel Ernst Lorge (June 1944–Sept. 1944).
Police Leader and Commander of the Order Police and Gendarmerie in Chernigov*	Chernigov, Northern Ukraine	*Raised in autumn 1941; disbanded in summer 1943.
Police Leader and Commander of the Order Police and Gendarmerie Nikolayev*	Mykolaev**, Ukraine	*Raised in autumn 1941; disbanded in summer 1943. **The name of the city transliterates as Nikolaev or as *Nikolayev*.
Police Leader and Commander of the Order Police and Gendarmerie Kharkov*	Kharkov, Eastern Ukraine	*Raised in autumn 1941; disbanded in summer 1943.
Commander of the State Protection Police Kerch	Kerch, Crimea	
Police Station Post Kirovograd*	Ukraine	*Raised in autumn 1941; disbanded in summer 1943.

Police Station Post Sumy*	Eastern Ukraine	*Raised in autumn 1941; disbanded in summer 1943.
Police Station Post Kremenchug*	Central Ukraine	*Raised in autumn 1941; disbanded in summer 1943.
Police Station Post Krivoirog*	Southern Ukraine	*Raised in autumn 1941; disbanded in summer 1943.
304th Police Battalion*: Police Major Deckert	Ukraine	*Located in Starokostiantyniv (156km southwest of Zhitomir) from 21 Aug. to 4 Sept. 1941, where the battalion killed 500 people. On 5 Sept. 1941 it was in Vinnitsa, where it murdered about 2,000 Jews. By 13 Sept. 1941 it was in Ladyshyn, where another 486 people were shot.
Police Station Post Poltawa*	Ukraine	*Raised in autumn 1941; disbanded in summer 1943.
Police Station Post Cherson*	Ukraine	*Raised in autumn 1941; disbanded in summer 1943.
Police Station Post Nikopol*	Ukraine	*Raised in autumn 1941; disbanded in Aug. 1944.
Police Station Post Zaporhye*	Ukraine	*Raised in autumn 1941; disbanded in summer 1943.
Police Station Post Dnjepropetrovsk*	Ukraine	*Raised in autumn 1941; disbanded in summer 1943.
Police Station Post Melitopol*	Ukraine	*Raised in autumn 1941; disbanded in summer 1943.
1st Police Cavalry Battalion*: Police Major Adolf Hahn	Ukraine	*Comprised staff HQ and three squadrons, with an initial strength of 428 officers, NCOs and men.
Police Regiment for Special Employment*	Ukraine	*Its staff was formed in summer 1941 for the Higher SS and Police Leader for Special Employment, whose headquarters was intended for deployment in the Caucasus. The regiment controlled the 304th, 315th and 320th Police Battalions. Redesignated Police Regiment 11 on 24 Feb. 1943.
315th Police Battalion: Police Major Klaus*	Ukraine	*According to one source, Police Major Gewehr commanded 315th Police Battalion in Aug. 1943.
320th Police Battalion*: Police Captain Dall	Ukraine	*Combined with 304th Police Battalion and 315th Police Battalion to create Polizei Regiment 11. At its height, the regiment amounted to an astounding 2,132 men.
Police Regiment South*: Police Colonel Hermann Franz	Ukraine	*Comprised of three police battalions, the 45th (Police Major Besser), the 303rd (Police Lieutenant Colonel Heinrich Hannibal) and the 314th (Police Major Severt).
Police Technical Emergency Company of Police Regiment South	Ukraine	
Police Economic Camp Vinnitsa*	Ukraine	*Raised in autumn 1941; disbanded in summer 1942.

partisans or partisan sympathizers, but also political commissars and Communist Party officials. Later still, as the summer campaign in the Soviet Union was progressing, requests began to filter into Army Headquarters from different commanders, such as Lieutenant General Wolfgang Baron von Plotho, commander of the 285th Security Division, who wanted permission to treat all cut-off Red Army men still roaming behind the German front lines as partisans so they could be shot. The Commander of the Rear Army Group South, General of Infantry Karl von Roques, finally agreed to this, but with the exception of those Russian soldiers who had deserted from the Red Army.[21] From this point, the Secret Field Police units now also played a role in carrying out this order behind the German lines.

The KdS, BdS and *Einsatzgruppen* in the Baltic States

On 17 July 1941 Adolf Hitler officially created the Ministry for the Occupied Eastern Territories, appointing Alfred Rosenberg as its head. Since it was no longer used, the old Yugoslav Embassy building in the heart of Berlin was selected for the newly created ministry. The rapid advance of the German Army through the Baltic states of Lithuania and Latvia allowed for the Nazi civilian administration to assume power in those two states as of 1 September 1941. This was a region that before the war had been northeastern Poland, and Russian Belarus was also added to the responsibility of Heinrich Lohse, a former bank official turned *Gauleiter* (Nazi Party District Chief), who was now appointed to the task of running the Baltic States and White Russia. His title was Reich Commissioner for the Ostland, and he quickly set up offices in Kaunas, Lithuania. He has been described as mediocre and trivial in nature, but with a taste for the good life. He was in a hurry to get started – so much so that on the day that German Army turned over to Rosenberg the administration of Lithuania (25 July), Lohse rushed in.

On 5 December 1941 Estonia was also handed over to German civilian control. The Reich Commissariat Ostland was to be split up into four *bezirk* (districts), one for each of the major areas in the region. In Estonia, the German Civilian District headquarters was located in Reval (Tallinn), in Latvia it was situated in Riga, and in Lithuania it was in Kaunas, where Heinrich Lohse also kept the main headquarters of the Reich Commissariat Ostland. The Civil District headquarters in Belarus were located in Minsk. Every military and paramilitary organization that functioned and was sanctioned in the Third Reich was also represented in the Ostland region, including Organization Todt,[22] the civil and military engineering organization of the Third Reich, the National Socialist Motor Corps, the Reich Labour Service, the Reich Bank and others. Soon all of these organizations had offices in the East. The former Yugoslav Embassy building in Berlin, which now housed the new Ministry for the Occupied Eastern Territories, was a hubbub of activity and movement. Reich Marshal Hermann Göring, who had the dual responsibility of being both the head of the German Air Force and the head of the German economic Four-Year-Plan, was very much a constant visitor to Rosenberg's ministry.

The SS apparatus had also set up shop in the Ostland, beginning with the formation of the notorious *Einsatzgruppen*, whose purpose was the elimination of those whom the Nazis considered undesirables in the East. Three groups were created initially, with a fourth added later. After the initial killing sweep, *Einsatzgruppe* A was used to supply men for the basis of the Security Police and Security Service in the Ostland. SS Brigadier General Franz Stahlecker led *Einsatzgruppe* A from 22 June 1941 until 23 March 1942, when he was killed while leading combined police, security police and volunteer self-defence forces engaged in fighting Soviet partisans near Krasnovardeisk. SS Brigadier General and Major General of the Police Heinz Jost succeeded Stahlecker in the post but only briefly as he soon took up the liaison role between Alfred Rosenberg and Field Marshal von Kleist. Next to take over command of *Einsatzgruppe* A and the dual role as Commander of the Security Police and Security Service in the Ostland was SS *Oberführer* Dr Achamer-Pifrader. Before being posted to the East, Achamer-Pifrader had been Inspector of the Security Police and Security Service Wiesbaden.[23] Achamer-Pifrader led the Security Service units in the Ostland and north Russia region from 10 September 1942 until 4 September 1943.[24] By November 1942, however, he had established a forward command post for his battlegroup in Nataljevka, about 45km south-southwest of Leningrad. Two more SS officers were subsequently to have the title Commander of the Security Police and Security Service Ostland: SS Colonel Friedrich Panzinger (4 September 1943–May 1944) and SS Lieutenant Colonel Dr Wilhelm Fuchs (May–October 1944). The Commander of the Security Police and Security Service Ostland had several subordinate offices spread out all over the Ostland region. In 1942 the commanders of these lower posts were as follows:

- in Ponewesch (Panevezys), Lithuania: SS Colonel Karl Jäger;
- in Mitau, Latvia: SS Major Dr Fritz Lange;
- in Reval (Tallinn), Estonia: SS Major Dr Martin Sandberger; and
- in Minsk, White Russia (Belarus): SS Lieutenant Colonel Eduard Strauch.

Despite the formation of these Security Police and Security Service headquarters, the bulk of the killing commandos remained and their locations varied. In November 1941 the headquarters of *Einsatzgruppe* A and part of its component part *Einsatzkommando* 2 were stationed at Gatschina (Krasnovardeisk), about 72km southwest of Leningrad. *Sonderkommando* 1a, then located in Reval, had posts as far away as Narva, Dorpat (Tartu), Pernau, Arensburg-Oesel, Kingisepp and Volossovo (65km south-southwest of Leningrad). In November 1941 *Einsatzkommando* 3 was in Kaunas, Lithuania, while *Sonderkommando* 1b was at Staraya Russa, but by September 1942 *Sonderkommando* 1b (under SS Captain Dr Hermann Hubig) was located in Loknya, about 60km north of Velikiye Luki. *Sonderkommando* 1c, formed in the summer of 1942 and only operational from August to November of that year, was led by SS Major Kurt Graaf and was stationed in Krasnovardeisk.[25]

In February 1943 the *Einsatzkommandos* were reorganized and reinforced. Now they would be used primarily against the partisans. *Einsatzkommando* 1 (to which *Sonderkommandos* 1a and 1b belonged), under the command of SS Lieutenant Colonel Dr Erich Isselhorst, was to remain stationed at Krasnovardeisk. *Einsatzkommando* 2, under the control of SS Major Dr Manfred Pechau, was now located in Loknya, while *Einsatzkommando* 3, led by SS Lieutenant Colonel Karl Traut, was stationed in the Russian border town of Pskov (Pleskau), along the southeastern Estonian-Russian border. The structure and chain of command for the Security Police and Security Service stretched all the way from the desk of the National Leader of the SS (Heinrich Himmler) to the killing units in the field:

- National Leader of the SS and Head of the German Police (Heinrich Himmler)
- Reich Main Security Office, Department 4 (Secret State Police – *Gestapo*) (Heinrich Muller)
- Command of the Security Police and Security Service Ostland
- Command of the Security Police and Security Service Lithuania
- Command of the Security Police and Security Service Latvia
- Command of the Security Police and Security Service Estonia
- Command of the Security Police and Security Service White Ruthenia.[26]

Employment of Forces Behind the Lines

The *Kommandeurs der Rückwartigen Heeresgebiet* (Rear Area Army Commanders), abbreviated to Korück, were German Army rear area commands that were organized by region, district, town and city. They were all under the direct control of the Quartermaster General. The rear area was responsible not only for all matters of supply and administration of the field forces, but also for security in the combat zones. Discipline and the protection of lines of communication were the responsibilities of the regular military police, with each army usually having one motorized military field police battalion, though in some cases the army or army group in question was assigned two such battalions. Each Korück was assigned three security forces, whose main duties were to control the flow of supplies and to protect the supply depots, which were generally located about 80–120km apart. A block system of successive guard posts was set up to safeguard the flow of supplies to the front. A security force of division size would usually be responsible for approximately 5,000–10,000 square miles of Soviet territory. The troops assigned to guard this wide expanse of land were usually second-rate men with average-grade officers and inexperienced field-grade officers.

The equipment and numbers of troops for these security divisions were usually mixed and low in number. For example, the 281st Security Division, which was assigned to the rear of Army Group North, contained rifles and pistols from captured stocks from French, Belgian, Czechoslovakian and Dutch military origin. The weaponry was a hodge-podge of articles from different subjugated European nations, and a nightmare for any quartermaster general to handle. The divisional headquarters staff didn't even have a single motorized vehicle. It is no small wonder then that the German police battalions and regiments were often added to these security divisions in an attempt to increase their strength. An effort was also made to try to improve the firepower of these security divisions. For example, on 5 July 1941, following Hitler's orders, Keitel instructed the Chief of the Army's Armaments Programme to equip the security divisions, local defence formations and police units with captured French Army tanks. Korück 582 (Lieutenant General Oskar Schellbach), which was responsible for the rear of 9th Army in the area of Army Group Centre, is a perfect example of a typical German Korück in the USSR. It had to cover an area of 17,870 square km, which included more than 1,500 villages in addition to dozens of collective farms.

To secure this immense area Korück 582 had only fifteen weak rifle companies (of about eighty men apiece), for a total of 1,400 men. These men had to act as guards for local POW transit camps, headquarters, railways, train stations and supply installations. This left about 300 men, or roughly two companies, to perform patrols and anti-partisan operations. Similarly, the German 2nd Army lacked adequate forces for its rear area command and an attempt was also made to reinforce its rear area. Overall, all of the German rear area commands required additional troops. In order to help 2nd Army, the 307th and 309th Police Battalions were detached from 221st Security Division and employed in the rear area of 2nd Army to help deal with the growing partisan threat. On 1 August 1941 the 307th Police Battalion conducted a railway security sweep between Rogachev and Gomel, in conjunction with units of the 252nd Infantry Division, against a large force of Red Army stragglers who had been bypassed in July. The region in question was the northeastern part of the Pripet Marshes. Life in the forests, swamps and marshes of this region was hard on account of the heat in the summer and the cold in the winter. In addition, the forests, swamps and marshes were areas where mosquitoes, lice, leeches and snakes plagued man and beast. Nevertheless, these regions offered the Red Army stragglers refuge from the German war machine as it was harder for the Nazis to destroy the partisan bands in these locations. Because of this, establishing a partisan base in the forests, swamps and marshes was the ideal solution. The Germans always found it extremely difficult to enter these regions and to effectively destroy the guerrillas. The 307th Police Battalion, supported by elements of 252nd Infantry Division, eventually managed to defeat this enemy force, which later turned out to number some 1,800 men, including several artillery batteries and numerous heavy weapons.

Between 23 August and 1 September 1941 Police Regiment Centre was relegated to Korück 580, the rear area command for 2nd Army, and employed against guerrilla forces in the Mogilev region.[27] Thus, with the aid of one infantry division (252nd Infantry Division), one police regiment (Police Regiment Centre) and two independent police battalions (307th and 309th Police Battalions), 2nd Army recorded that between August and October 1941 its forces had arrested 1,836 persons suspected of being partisans and that of this number 1,179 had been shot.[28] On 9 October 1941 the 8th Company, Police Regiment Centre surprised a partisan company coming out of a marshy region near Mogilev. In the ensuing firefight, the German police company killed 24 guerrillas and apprehended 43 more. These partisan prisoners were later shot after being interrogated in the field.[29] Beginning on 9 September 1941, Police Regiment Centre was placed back under the control of the 221st Security Division and ordered to secure the road from Bobruisk to Mogilev and keep it free of partisans.[30] On 17 September a company from Police Regiment Centre, acting on a tip from the mayor of Prokenevitchi, who was a Nazi sympathizer, encountered a guerrilla group of ten men who were gathering supplies and trying to recruit new men in the town. The German police captured the guerrillas and shot them after interrogation, along with the two women who had sheltered them in the town.[31]

Similarly, the 307th, 309th, 317th and 131st Police Battalions were temporarily detached from their service with the 221st Security Division from 23 August until September 1941 and assigned to the various Korück commands belonging to the armies of Army Group Centre.[32] The 307th and 309th Police Battalions were assigned to Korück 580 (2nd Army), the 317th Police Battalion under Police Major Karl Stäglich was assigned to Korück 559 (4th Army) and the 131st Police Battalion was assigned to Korück 582 (9th Army).[33] In the meantime, the secret field police units had already been assisting the Korück commands behind the lines. In addition, several motorized field police battalions were attached to specific German Armies, and in the case of the rear area security divisions, to fixed units (see Table 2.2).

On 25 October 1941 the Jewish populations of Tatarsk and Starodub resisted the German attempts to kill them. The Germans had to bring in units from their army rear area security forces in order to quell both revolts. This included elements of the 221st Security Division, then operating in the Bobruisk area.[34] In this operation the 701st Guard Battalion, part of the 221st Security Division, was employed against the Jewish defenders of Tatarsk and Starodub. Artillery as well as aerial bombardment had to be used before the rebellions were crushed in both towns.[35] The 221st Security Division was responsible for a huge area of the German rear, in July 1941 covering an area approximately 60,430 square km in size.[36] Between 16 and 18 September 1941 the SS Cavalry Brigade was located in the towns of Mosyr (just southwest of Gomel) and Chiniki (southeast of Mosyr and southwest of Gomel). It was in Mosyr that the SS cavalrymen were fired upon by partisans located in the nearby hills.[37]

This attack was more of a nuisance than an actual threat, and by 18 September 1941 the SS Cavalry Brigade had destroyed the guerrilla band, capturing their equipment. On 26 September the SS Cavalry Brigade was still operating west and south of Gomel. It reported killing 280 partisans and capturing 87 persons whom they labelled as criminals in their daily situation reports. The reports state that although Belarus was the region of greatest partisan activity in 1941, groups of guerrillas there had only been established in two out of the ten Belarusian *Oblasts* and fifteen out of the 170 urban and rural Belarusian *Rayons.*[38] Hence, it is plausible that a significant portion of the partisan operations documented by the Germans in Belarus and central Russia in 1941 occurred as a result of bypassed remnants of Red Army soldiers who were refusing to surrender. This is the most likely scenario.

On 10 October 1941 the SS Cavalry Brigade was instructed to start operations in the Nevel region and was relocated to the town of Toropetz, 200km north of Smolensk. As a result, the SS Cavalry Brigade departed Belarus at the beginning of October 1941. In December 1941 the 707th Infantry Division was shifted from Smolensk to Minsk in Belarus because of the growing partisan threat to the area. Partisan activity in Minsk had begun as early as mid-July 1941. In Minsk itself the 707th Infantry Division – which had only two weak regiments (the 727th and 747th Infantry Regiments), plus an artillery unit (657th Artillery Battalion) – was ill-prepared to fight a prolonged guerrilla war.[39] The divisional commander, Major General Gustav Freiherr von Mauchenheim genannt von Bechtolsheim had only 24 infantry companies to garrison Minsk and the surrounding regions. That number was wholly inadequate for the mission assigned to the division.[40] For example, by 1 October 1941 the combined area of responsibility that the SS Cavalry Brigade, 309th and 707th Infantry Divisions needed to patrol and control was around 130,000 square km. This was an impossible amount of territory to control

Table 2.2. German security divisions in Belarus and central Russia, 1941.

Division	Date	Location	Notes
221st Security Division – Lieutenant General Johann Pflugbeil			
UNITS:	June 1941	Bialystok	
350th Infantry Regiment with I.–III.	July*		*307th and 317th Police Battalions arrive.
Battalions	Aug.	Bobruisk/Bryansk	
701st Guard Battalion	Sept.		
I. Battalion, Artillery Regiment 221 (1.–3. Batteries)	Oct.	Gomel, Mogilev	91st Police Battalion arrives
91st, 307th and 317th Police Battalions	Nov.		
Police Regiment Centre	Dec.		
339th Infantry Division – Lieutenant General Georg Hewelcke			
691st, 692nd, 693rd Infantry Regiments,	Sept. 1941	Vitebsk, Bobruisk	
I.–III. Battalions each	Oct.–Dec.	Bobruisk, Lutzk	
339th Artillery Battalion (1.–2. Batteries)			
339th Signals Company			
339th Engineer Company			
403rd Security Division – Lieutenant General Wolfgang von Ditfurth (15 Mar 1941–14 May 1942). Ditfurth was succeeded by Lieutenant General Wilhelm Rußwurm on 15 May 1942.			
406th Infantry Regiment with I.–III. Battalions	June 1941	Bialystok	**Source*: Haupt, *Army Group Center*, p. 234.
705th Guard Battalion	July		
Regional Defence Regimental Staff 177	Aug.	Vileika	
III. Battalion, Artillery Regiment 213	Sept.	Polotsk, Nevel	
(1.–3. Batteries)	Oct.	Vitebsk, Velikiye Luki*	
826th Signal Battalion	Nov.		
403rd Engineer Company	Dec.		

286th Security Division – Lieutenant General Kurt Müller (15 March 1941–14 June 1942). On 15 June 1942 Lieutenant General Johann-Georg Richert assumed control. He in turn was relieved by Lieutenant General Friedrich-Georg Eberhardt on 5 August 1944.

Units	Month	Location
354th Infantry Regiment with I.–III. Battalions*	June 1941	Bialystok
704th Guard Battalion	July	
II. Battalion, Artillery Regiment 213 (1.–3. Batteries)	Aug.	Orsha
	Sept.	
Regional Defence Regimental Staff 61	Oct.	
Nachrichten Kompanie 286	Nov.	
286th Signal Company		
286th Cavalry Squadron**		

*This regiment was transferred in Feb. 1942 to 403rd Security Division, which was sent to the region of Army Group South in July 1942. In its place, the 286th Security Division received Regional Defence Regimental Staff 122. In 1942 Regional Defence Regimental Staffs 61 and 122 were redesignated Security Regiments 61 and 122 respectively.

**This volunteer squadron was later expanded to a battalion.

707th Infantry Division – Major General Gustav Freiherr von Mauchenheim genannt von Bechtolsheim.

Units	Month	Location
727th Infantry Regiment with I.–III. Battalions	June 1941	Forming in *Wehrkreis VII*, Germany
747th Infantry Regiment with I.–III. Battalions	July	
657th Artillery Battalion (1.–3. Batteries)	Aug.	Smolensk
707th Engineer Company	Sept.	
707th Signals Company	Oct.	
	Nov.	
	Dec.	Minsk

Source: Muñoz, *The Druzhina SS Brigade*, p. 46.

with just one cavalry brigade and two static infantry divisions.[41] In addition to the countryside, the Germans also needed to control the towns and cities where, because of the invaders' exterminationist policies, the Jewish population was desperate and near rebellion. In fact, the spring of 1942 would witness several Jewish ghetto uprisings in the East. Author Gerald Reitlinger admits that the German accusation of guerrilla activity in Minsk by some of the Jewish population was not entirely untrue, although German anti-Jewish policies were the sole reason for any Jewish resistance. During one typical round-up in September 1941 the Germans had captured Nat Weinhaus, a member of the prewar Minsk Soviet, who had been working with the partisan leader, Stolyarevitch.[42]

That these German sweeps of the city netted thousands of innocent non-combatants was unimportant to the Germans. As Hitler had stated in July 1941: 'this partisan war has some advantages for us, it enables us to wipe out everyone who opposes us'.[43] On 4 October 1941 some Jewish partisans had set fire to a local tar factory and Major General Bechtolsheim requested additional reinforcements. The came in the form of the 11th Reserve Police Battalion, which proceeded to systematically conduct shooting raids in almost every village or town around the city of Minsk. This police battalion would go on to shoot many innocent civilians. For example, on 8 October 1941 the police battalion reported shooting a Red Army political commissar, nine partisans and '630 suspicious elements, Communists, and Jews'.[44] The

Map 3. Partisan concentrations in Belarus, 1941. Partisan areas listed with a number '**1**' indicates a guerrilla force of about 100–300 men; '**2**' indicates a guerrilla force of about 500–1,000 men; and '**3**' indicates a force of around 1,000–3,000 men.

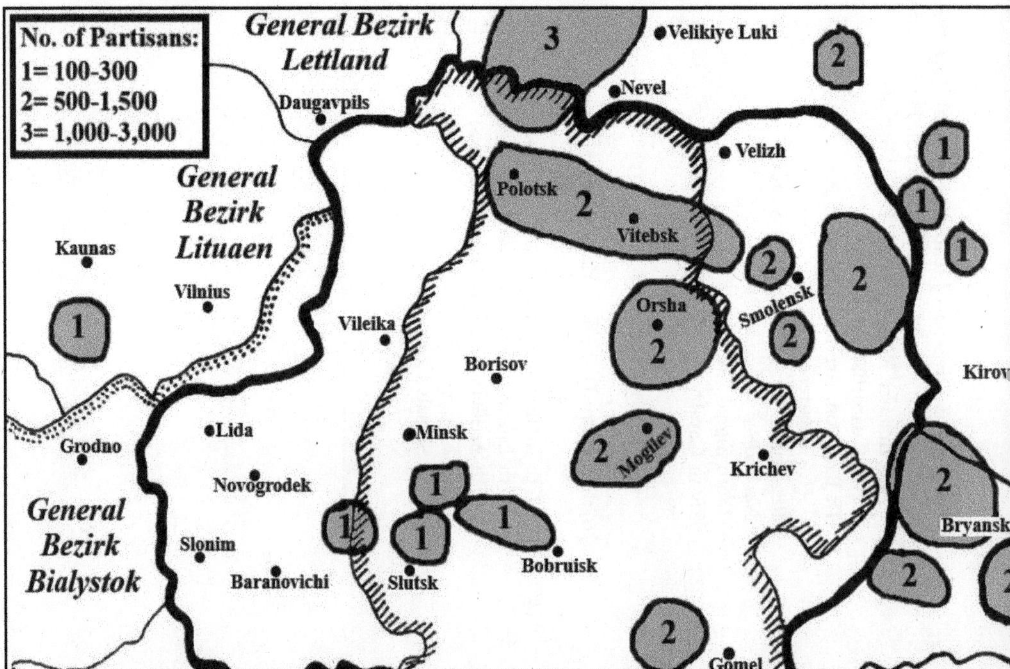

707th Infantry Division also took part in these killing operations. In fact, in the month in which it began operations in Minsk (December 1941), it reportedly shot 10,431 out of the 10,940 Russians it had apprehended.[45] By the end of 1941 the principal areas of partisan activity in Belarus included the forests around Usda, the regions east of Slutsk, south of Minsk, northwest of Bobruisk, west of Gomel, immediately surrounding and southwest of Mogilev, around Orsha, and in and around the regions connecting Polotsk and Vitebsk.

In addition, the areas of Army Group North around Velikiye Luki (north of Polotsk) and the regions of Army Group Centre around Smolensk and Bryansk were areas of vigorous partisan activity beginning in 1941.[46] In the areas of Map 3 showing the partisan concentrations in Belarus in 1941, the strengths of the guerrilla units varied depending on the region. The area that for the Germans was most difficult to control was the Nevel-Bezhanitsy-Idritsa triangle, which was infested with Soviet guerrillas from the summer and autumn of 1941; this area would never be completely neutralized throughout the German occupation, including the German withdrawal from there in February 1944.[47]

Chapter 3

The SS command in the Baltic States and North Russia and the employment of locally raised volunteers

Where a harsh law rules, people yearn for lawlessness. [Stanislaw Jerzy Lec]

Change in the structure of command

On 29 June 1941 Hans-Adolf Prützmann became the head of the Higher SS and Police Leader in Ostland and North Russia headquarters. This command was tasked with keeping order in the Baltic States and North Russia, as well as with fighting the partisan threat. In November 1941 Prützmann was assigned as Higher SS and Police Leader Ukraine and Russia South. Upon his departure to Ukraine, Himmler appointed SS Lieutenant General and General of the Waffen SS and Police Friedrich Jeckeln to Prützmann's previous post. On the afternoon of 10 November 1941 the newly appointed Jeckeln reported to National Leader of the SS Heinrich Himmler's Berlin headquarters at 8 Prinz Albrecht Strasse. There he received instructions on what Himmler wanted done in the Reich Commissariat Ostland and the region of northern Russia. Himmler told Jeckeln that the established lower SS and police commands that were subordinate to the Higher SS and Police Leader in Ostland and North Russia headquarters were to be employed principally in three major missions: (1) to combat the growing partisan threat, (2) to ensure the smooth functioning of the German administration in the Reich Commissariat, and (3) to make sure that supplies of men and war materiel reached the *Ostheer* fighting on the front lines. The Higher SS and Police Leader commands had authority over all civil and military matters behind the front lines. They controlled the lower SS and police leader commands, which in turn controlled the Commanders of the Order Police, the Security Police and the Gendarmerie, and even the various Army Korück commands. It also originated the employment of SS forces which the Himmler supplied to the three Higher SS and Police Leader headquarters in the East. The SS and police commands in this region are listed below.

Higher SS and Police Leader Ostland[1]
Headquarters: Riga, Latvia
Commanders:

- SS Lieutenant General Hans-Adolf Prützmann (29 June–9 November 1941)
  SS Lieutenant General Friedrich Jeckeln (11 December 1941–29 January 1945)
  SS Lieutenant General Dr Hermann Behrends (30 January–April 1945)

SS and Police Leader Lithuania (Commander of the Order Police; Commander of the Gendarmerie)
Headquarters: Kaunas, Lithuania
Commanders:

- SS Brigadier General Lucian Wysocki (4 August 1941–24 April 1942)
- SS Oberführer Karl Schäfer (25 April 1942–1 July 1943)
- SS Brigadier General Hermann Harm (2 July 1943–8 April 1944)

SS and Police Leader Latvia (Commander of the Order Police; Commander of the Gendarmerie)
Headquarters: Riga, Latvia
Commanders:

- SS Brigadier General Walter Schröder (4 August 1941–6 April 1942)
- SS Oberführer Karl Schäfer (7 April 1942)

SS and Police Leader Estonia (Commander of the Order Police; Commander of the Gendarmerie)
Headquarters: Reval (Tallinn), Estonia
Commanders:

- SS Oberführer and Police Colonel Hinrich Möller (4 August 1941–31 March 1944)
- SS Brigadier General and Major General of the Police Walter Schröder (1 April 1944–April 1945)

Higher SS and Police Leader in Central Russia and White Ruthenia
Commanders:

- SS Colonel and Police Colonel Johann Klepsch (November–December 1941)
- SS Brigadier General and Major General of the Police Eberhard Herf (December 1941–16 February 1942)
- SS Brigadier General and Major General of the Police Erik von Heimburg (17 February 1942–30 July 1942)
- SS Colonel and Police Colonel Johann Klepsch (1 August 1942–10 April 1943)

- SS Brigadier General and Major General of the Police Walter Abraham (11 April 1943–1 October 1943)
- SS Colonel and Police Colonel Johann Klepsch (2 October 1943–November 1944)

Higher SS and Police Leader in White Ruthenia (Commander of the Order Police; Commander of the Gendarmerie)
Headquarters: Minsk, Belarus
Commanders:

- SS Lieutenant General and Lieutenant General of the Police Jakob Sporrenberg (21 July–13 August 1941)
- SS Brigadier General and Major General of the Police Carl Zenner (14 August 1941–21 May 1942)
- SS Oberführer Karl Schäfer (22 May–20 July 1942)
- SS Lieutenant General and Lieutenant General of the Waffen SS and Police Curt von Gottberg (21 July 1942–21 September 1943)[2]
- SS Lieutenant Colonel and Police Lieutenant Colonel Ehrich Ehrlinger (22 September 1943–1944)[3]

The National Leader of the SS Heinrich Himmler also had at his disposal a command staff that would supply a number of SS and police forces to the Higher SS and Police Leader commands in the East. The pool of forces in this command would quickly diminish as the demands of the Eastern Front compelled the employment of more and more of these reserve SS and police forces. The command staff's headquarters was established between 7 April and 5 May 1941 and was initially referred to as the Operational Staff of the National Leader of the SS; on 6 May 1941 it changed to its final version: Command Staff of the National Leader of the SS.[4] At the time the forces available to the Command Staff were as shown in Table 3.1.[5]

Altogether, the units available to the Command Staff numbered around 29,000 men. SS Infantry Brigade 1 was initially committed to the rear of Army Group South until it was shifted to the rear of Army Group Centre in November 1941. In September 1941 both SS cavalry regiments were merged into the SS Cavalry Brigade and served behind the lines of Army Group Centre, slowly moving to the region of Army Group North in November until committed to front-line fighting in mid-December 1941.[6] Some units of the Command Staff were committed almost immediately, like both SS cavalry regiments, while some were committed later in the year, like SS Flak Battalion East. Other units did not make their appearance until 1942 or 1943. The location of these forces varied as well. For example, SS Flak Battalion I, which had been formed in Zhitomir in 1942, was in action under SS Kampfgruppe von Gottberg fighting the partisans in Belarus in May 1943. A month later it was stationed in Minsk, and in October 1943 it was located in

Table 3.1. Forces available to the Command Staff of the National Leader of the SS.

Unit	Commander	Notes
SS Infantry Brigade 1 (motorized)	SS Brigadier General Karl Demelhuber	
SS Infantry Brigade 2 (motorized)	SS Brigadier General Karl von Treuenfeld	
SS Cavalry Regiment 1	SS Major Gustav Lombard	
SS Cavalry Regiment 2	SS Major Franz Magill	
SS Volunteer Regiment Northwest		Employed in north Russia. *Source*: Prechtel, *Unsere Ehre Heisst Treue*, p.17.
SS Escort Battalion	SS Major Ernst Schützeck	*Sources*: Mehner, *Die Waffen-SS und Polizei*, p. 230; Westwood, *The Waffen SS*, p. 195.
SS Flak Battalion I	SS Major Hallman	Formed in 1942 in Zhitomir. *Source*: Stöber, *Die Flugabwehrverbände*, p. 381.
SS Flak Battalion II		Formed in 1943.
SS Flak Battalion East	SS Lieutenant Colonel Karl Burk	*Source*: Yerger, *Riding East*, p. 138.
Battalion of the Waffen SS for Special Employment	SS Major Eberhard von Kunsberg	
10th Police Signals Company		
SS *Sonderkommando* Dirlewanger	SS Major Oskar Dirlewanger	This *Waffen SS* penal unit was committed to White Russia in Jan. 1942.

Table 3.2. Command Staff unit strengths, June 1941.

June 1941	Officers	NCOs	Men	Total
HQ Staff	163	134	384	681
10th Police Signals Company	14	71	300	385
Escort Battalion	26	110	603	739
1st SS Infantry Brigade	258	1,309	6,074	7,641
2nd SS Infantry Brigade	246	1,308	5,747	7,301
SS Flak Battalion East	30	110	666	806
SS Cavalry Brigade	174	768	4,037	4,979
SS Volunteer Legion Netherlands	111	546	2,840	3,497
SS Volunteer Legion Flanders	31	160	865	1,056
Local Order Service Volunteers	4	98	22	124
SS Geological Battalion	8	40	324	372
SS Supply Battalion	28	70	380	476
Medical Service	21	36	191	248
Administrative Service	13	40	217	270
Veterinary Battalion	6	58	348	412
			Grand Total:	28,987

the Ukrainian city of Dnipropetrovsk. The 10th Police Signals Company operated in Russia until 1943, when it was disbanded. Table 3.2 shows the strengths of the Command Staff units in June 1941, shortly before the start of Operation *Barbarossa*.[7]

In total, Himmler would send about eleven police battalions – some 5,500 men – to aid in the extermination of the Jews and the control of the rear areas behind the lines in the USSR.[8] The numbers of units and men serving in the units of the Command Staff of the National Leader of the SS fluctuated from month to month, as would normally be the case when a combat formation gains or loses men and units due to transfers, or through battlefield deployment and losses. In April 1942, for example, the Command Staff no longer contained the Flemish and Dutch SS legions, nor the Escort Battalion.[9] The strength of the formations still under Command Staff control had also changed. Most had been substantially reduced in strength, indicating that combat losses had been taken (see Table 3.3).[10]

Individual call-ups were conducted during the late summer of 1941 to augment the German SS and police forces which were already committed to the campaign. On 27 July 1941 Himmler's office issued an order disbanding the *Gendarmerie* posts between annexed Polish territories and the General Government. The men released from this duty were sent to Russia. A further 128 *Gendarmerie* officers, NCOs and men were similarly dispatched on 8 August 1941. Eleven days later Himmler ordered a major mobilization of the *Gendarmerie* and Municipal Police. In this way, another 300 personnel

Table 3.3. Command Staff unit strengths, April 1942.

April 1942	Officers	NCOs	Men	Total
HQ Staff	55	75	267	397
10th Police Signals Company	17	34	316	367
1st SS Infantry Brigade	149	659	3,511	4,319
2nd SS Infantry Brigade	180	655	4,508	5,343
SS Flak Battalion East	10	29	406	445
SS Cavalry Brigade	131	363	3,734	4,228
Local Order Service Volunteers	5	46	173	224
SS Geological Battalion	12	66	576	654
SS Supply Battalion	15	50	296	361
Medical Service	29	41	146	216
Administrative Service	13	40	217	270
Veterinary Battalion	4	18	137	159
			Grand Total:	16,983

were gathered and formed into four detachments, which were sent to the cities of Dorpat (Tartu, in Estonia), Riga (Latvia), Kovno (Kaunas, Lithuania) and Minsk (Belarus). Each group contained 5 officers, 10 policemen and 60 police reservists.[11] The 69th Reserve Police Battalion was sent to Riga in October 1941 as reinforcements to help control the city. It remained in Latvia until July 1942, when it was sent to France to become part of Police Regiment 28 Todt.[12]

The Order Police command in the Ostland

In July 1941 the Higher SS and Police Leader Ostland and North Russia command had several lower SS and police headquarters to help control the region. In addition to the subordinate Commanders of the Order Police and Security Police, there were also four SS and Police Leader staffs, which in theory and practice controlled the lower-level commands of the SS, police and SS security police. In the nine largest cities and towns the SS command structure could also count on the SS and Police Station Post headquarters, which were immediately below the SS and Police Leader headquarters. Individual duty posts of the state police and the municipal police, as well as the *Gendarmerie*, constituted a major part of the initial police forces in the Baltic States. Regular Order Police forces numbered 1,695 men split up into three police battalions (the 61st, 112th and 132nd Police Battalions) under the control of Police Regiment North. In addition, there were two independent police companies with an additional 304 men.

The National Socialist Motor Transport Corps had made one transport company of 110 men available to the Higher SS and Police Leader Ostland command. There were also two SS signals companies: the 33rd Signals

Map 4. The Baltic States in 1941.

Table 3.4. Latvian police forces in Riga, August 1941.

Unit	Police Officers	Latvian *Schuma* (Police)	Grand Total
Headquarters of the Latvian Self-Defence Force	10	27	37
13 police stations	39	1,180	1,219
Harbour Police	11	149	160
Railroad Police	22	118	140
Ready Detachment	4	41	45
Six reserve and recruit companies	30	662	692
Prefecture Headquarters Command	39	241	280
Performing POW guard duty	19	381	400
Total number of men within the city limits of Riga	174	2,799	2,973

Company was stationed in Riga, Latvia, while the 82nd Signals Company was located in Vilnius, Lithuania. The number of individual duty members of the state police and *Gendarmerie* was initially only 1,330 men. This gave a total number of only 3,349 uniformed German police officers for the entire Baltic region.[13] In order to help augment this initial batch of forces, the Germans began to recruit locals into the auxiliary police and security service commands. Eventually, the number of Lithuanian, Latvian and Estonian volunteers who would serve in the German armed forces would number tens of thousands. As early as 10 August 1941, for example, the Germans had almost 3,000 Latvian auxiliary police forces in the city of Riga (see Table 3.4).[14] These men were armed with 983 pistols, 2,277 Russian and Latvian rifles, 3 heavy machine guns and 3 light machine guns. Approximately 129 of the 174 Latvian police officers were former members of the Latvian armed forces, which were disbanded when the Soviet Union annexed Latvia in 1940.

German and indigenous forces in the region of Army Group North

The forces available for SS and police duties included mobile killing units, since prior to the Russian campaign the German SS command had established that its SS and police forces were responsible not only for the control of the rear areas and the fight against guerrilla activity, but also for the elimination of the Jews in the USSR.[15] For this purpose, *Einsatzgruppe* A had been formed from security police, SS and police personnel for operations in the Baltic States and the northern part of the USSR. From the Waffen SS came members of the Waffen SS Special Employment Battalion,[16] from the Order Police came members of the 3rd and 9th Reserve Police Battalions, and from the Reich Main Security Office came members of the Security Police (the *Gestapo* and criminal police) and the SS security service.[17] The strength of

Einsatzgruppe A in October 1941 was 1,036 men, divided by service as follows: 89 *Gestapo* men, 41 criminal police members, 35 security service men, 340 Waffen SS members, 133 Order Police, 133 indigenous auxiliary police volunteers, 172 drivers, 51 interpreters, and 42 support personnel.[18] This represented the equivalent of a very strong battalion-sized unit. In percentage terms, 9 per cent of the unit was made up of *Gestapo* personnel, 4 per cent of security service men, 4 per cent of criminal police, 13 per cent of Order Police, 9 per cent of foreign personnel of the auxiliary police and 34 per cent of Waffen SS.[19] The remaining 27 per cent comprised support personnel such as drivers, secretaries, cooks, supply staff, etc. Command of this *Einsatzgruppe* was initially entrusted to SS Brigadier General and Major General of the Police Dr Franz Walter Stahlecker.[20] The *Einsatzgruppen* were split up into several lower echelon subcommands known as *Einsatzkommandos*, which were in turn sometimes split into *Sonderkommandos*. *Einsatzgruppe* A contained four lower-echelon formations:

- *Sonderkommando* 1a, commander: SS Major Dr Karl Martin Sandberger;
- *Sonderkommando* 1b, commander: SS Lieutenant Colonel Dr Erich Ehrlinger;
- *Einsatzkommando* 2, commander: SS Major Dr Rudolf Batz; and
- *Einsatzkommando* 3, commander: SS Colonel Karl Jäger.

In the autumn of 1941 *Einsatzgruppe* Reval (Tallinn) was formed from *Sonderkommando* 1a. It became known as *Einsatzgruppe* Reval of the Security Police and Security Service and in February 1943 it was redesignated as Commander of the Security Police and Security Service Reval. Thus *Sonderkommando* 1a became the basis for the security police and security service posts and personnel in Estonia. Likewise, *Sonderkommando* 1b became the basis for the security police and security service forces in Belarus on 3 December 1941. In the summer of 1942 *Sonderkommando* 1b was renamed *Sonderkommando* 1b of the Security Police and Security Service by 16th Army, Army Group North. It was then disbanded in October 1943. In the autumn of 1941 *Einsatzkommando* 2 was redesignated as the *Einsatzkommando* of the Security Police and Security Service for the Rear Army Area 101 (North). This was a precursor to the unit becoming the basis of all security police and security service forces in Latvia. Similarly, the other *Sonderkommando* and *Einsatzkommando* leaders and their respective forces established the Security Police and Security Service commands in their respective regions.

In the autumn of 1942 a *Teilkommando* from *Einsatzkommando* 3 was detached and became *Teilkommando* of the Security Police and Security Service for 18th Army, Army Group North. In February 1943 it was once

Table 3.5. Regular Order Police units employed in North Russia.

Unit	Commander	Notes
Police Regiment North	Police Lieutenant Colonel Hermann Keuper	At this time this regiment comprised the 61st, 112th and 132nd Police Battalions.
9th Police Battalion	Police Major Paulus Meier	Part of this 500-man battalion was split up and used to create the three SS *Einsatzgruppen*. In summer 1942 it was gathered together and sent to Norway as one unit, redesignated III. Battalion, Police Regiment 27.
Police Technical Emergency Assistance Company, Police Regiment North		
11th Reserve Police Battalion	Police Major Franz Lechthaler	On arrival in Kaunas, Lithuania, in July 1941, this battalion set about raising three companies of Lithuanian auxiliary volunteer policemen.
33rd Reserve Police Battalion	Police Captain August Hanner	Arrived in the Baltic States in late July 1941 and soon renamed Reserve Police Battalion Ostland. It recruited heavily for ethnic Germans from the Baltic States and was eventually sent to L'viv, Poland, in Oct. 1941.
Reserve Police Battalion Ostland	Police Lieutenant Colonel Herbert Braschnevitz	*Source*: Jurs et al., *Estonian Freedom Fighters in World War II*, p. 91. Herbert Braschnevitz (Herberts Brašševics) was an ethnic-German Estonian.
53rd Police Battalion	Police Captain Fechner	
65th Police Battalion	Police Major Walter Barkhold	In 1941 the battalion contained 591 men.
69th Police Battalion	Police Major Richard Sonnenburg	Arrived in October 1941.
105th Police Battalion	Police Major Helwes	
254th Police Battalion	Police Major Bendzko	Arrived in the late summer of 1941.
319th Police Battalion	Police Major Geissler	
321st Police Battalion	Police Major Petersen	

again redesignated, becoming Security Police and Security Service with the Commander in the Northern Army Area/*Teilkommando* 3. In addition to *Einsatzgruppe* A, the Higher SS and Police Leader in Ostland and North Russia command also had the 1st Company, Waffen SS Special Employment Battalion under the command of SS First Lieutenant Rosenow. It was also made available for use in the Baltic States and north Russia.[21] The mission of this special battalion, for which one company was assigned to each of the three rear area commands (North, Centre and South), was the accumulation of artworks and other valuables from the conquered territories. These captured valuables were to come from private Jewish collectors as well as from Soviet and other state museums, archives, etc.

The regular Order Police units employed in the north are listed in Table 3.5. Many of the police battalions were employed independently, either as part of a regiment (such as the 319th Police Battalion, which was initially part of Police Regiment North) or as part of a rear area security division or rear area army command. The 319th Police Battalion is a perfect example of this. In June 1941 this unit entered Latvia as part of Police Regiment North. Its 3rd Company was detached from July 1941 until January 1942 and fought in various operations throughout the Baltic States and North Russia under various security divisions. Between 23 August and 11 September 1941 it served with Kampfgruppe Fechner (composed primarily of the 3rd Security Regiment) of 285th Security Division. Previously, the 319th Police Battalion had fought under the 207th Security Division from 1 to 22 August 1941.[22] The 65th Police Battalion was just one of numerous police units sent to the front lines in the winter of 1941/1942. It would be caught up in the fighting for the surrounded town of Cholm, an epic battle that lasted from 21 January to 5 May 1942.[23] A few more German Order Police battalions made their appearance in the late summer and autumn of 1941, but the general lack of readily available forces forced the Germans to recruit auxiliary troops for their SS and police in considerable numbers, which one author has quoted at 31,562 men.[24] However, this figure probably includes not only the rear area auxiliary police forces but also the so-called self-defence front battalions which were raised to fight on the front lines. The Soviet winter offensive of

Table 3.6. German police losses, December 1941–March 1942.

Army Group	Police Officers	Enlisted Policemen	Casualties (%)
North	33	1,680	24
Centre	53	1,771	27
South	15	427	7
Grand Total:	101	3,878	20

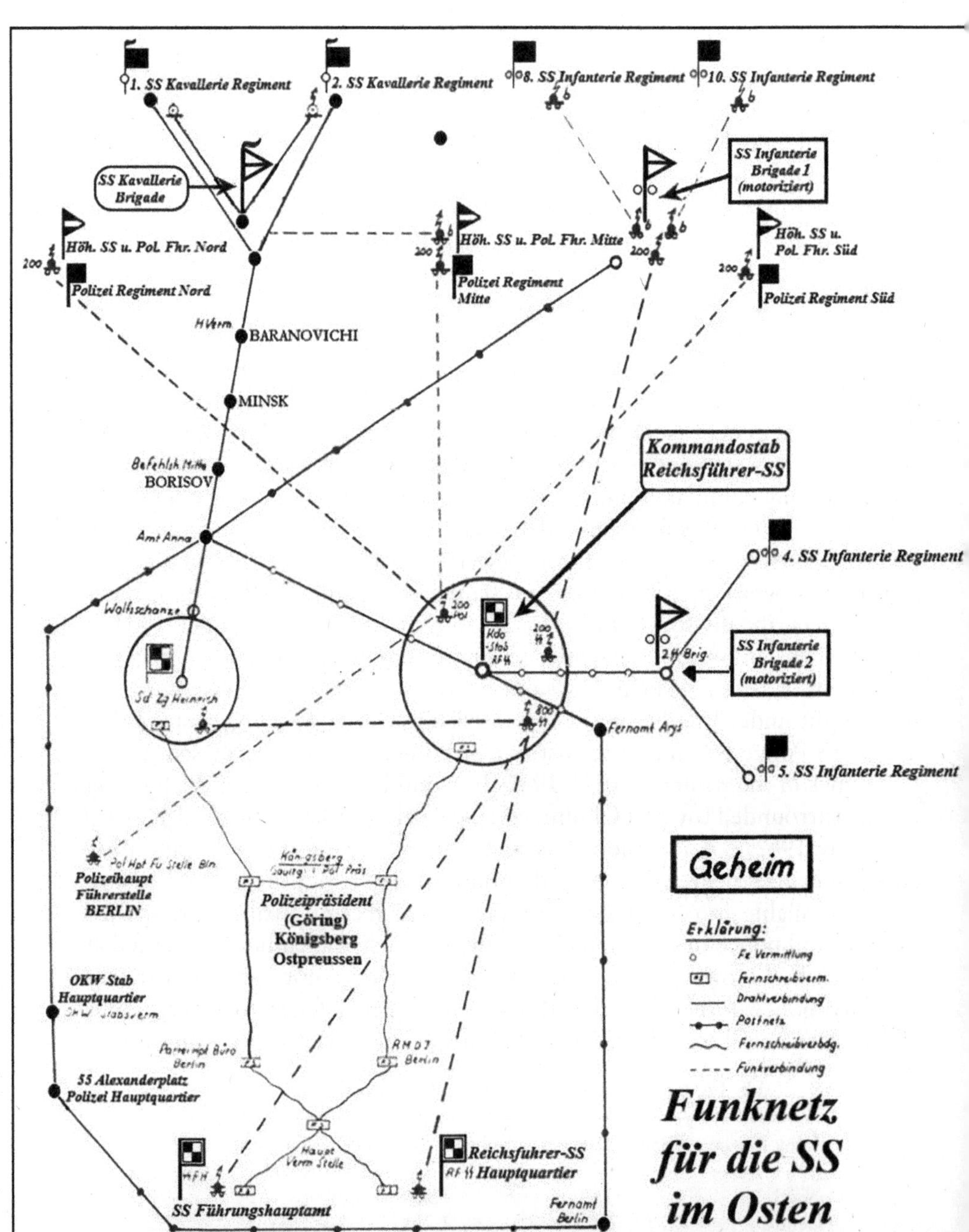

Map 5. Communications network for the SS in the East in the summer of 1941.

1941/1942 also placed a strain on the German police forces in Russia. Losses were heavy since the Germans had to commit many of these police battalions to front-line fighting. This is something they were totally unprepared for, as illustrated by the casualty figures given in Table 3.6.

The Main Office of the Order Police

The German Order Police, under the overall command of another SS department, the Main Office Order Police,[25] also made its presence felt in the Ostland region, especially behind the front lines of Army Group North. Headed by SS Colonel General and Colonel General of the Police Kurt Daluege, the Order Police was in charge of the uniformed police units. The structure and organization of the Order Police were similar to those of the Reich Main Security Office, which was headed initially by SS Lieutenant General and General of the Police Reinhard Heydrich until his death on 4 June 1942. On 30 January 1943 SS Lieutenant General and General of the Police Ernst Kaltenbrunner took over from Heydrich. The Commander of the Order Police Ostland was located in Riga, Latvia.

This command was led by SS Brigadier General and Major General of the Police Georg Jedicke, who was promoted to SS Lieutenant General and Lieutenant General of the Police on 12 December 1941. Jedicke was finally replaced in March 1944 by SS Brigadier General Gustav Giesecke. The Commander of the Order Police controlled several Command of the Order Police staffs, who in turn were in charge of various police posts and installations, like the security service and SS organization. From the very beginning, both the SS security police and the Order Police recruited volunteers from the local population to reinforce their limited forces. In fact, with only a few police battalions and one police regiment, in 1941 the Order Police in the Ostland did not have the number of troops necessary to police the huge territory for which they were responsible. For example, the Commander of the Order Police Ostland only had Police Regiment North, which comprised three Order Police battalions. SS *Einsatzgruppe* A, then operating in the Ostland region and behind Army Group North, also had some units from the 9th Police Battalion, whose 500 men had been split up in order to reinforce three of the four SS *Einsatzgruppen* shortly before the invasion of the USSR. Thus, of the approximately 3,000 men in the SS killing units, 500 (16 per cent) were men from the uniformed Order Police. In July 1941 the 11th Reserve Police Battalion made its appearance in Kaunas, Lithuania, and immediately recruited three companies of Lithuanian auxiliary policemen. The 11th Battalion did not remain in Lithuania for long. In September 1941 it sent two of its German police companies off to Minsk in Belarus, and they took with them the three attached Lithuanian companies. Therefore, this mixed battalion contained two German and three Lithuanian companies. A month later the rest of the 11th Reserve Police Battalion also moved to Minsk.

The 319th and 321st Police Battalions served under the Commander of the Order Police Ostland from the very beginning of the Russian campaign and at one time or another came under the control of Police Regiment North. These two battalions were withdrawn in July 1942 to Norway, where they helped to form Police Regiment 27. In August 1941 the 33rd Reserve Police Battalion was stationed in Riga and became the replacement unit for the other Order Police units in the Ostland region, its title changing to Reserve Police

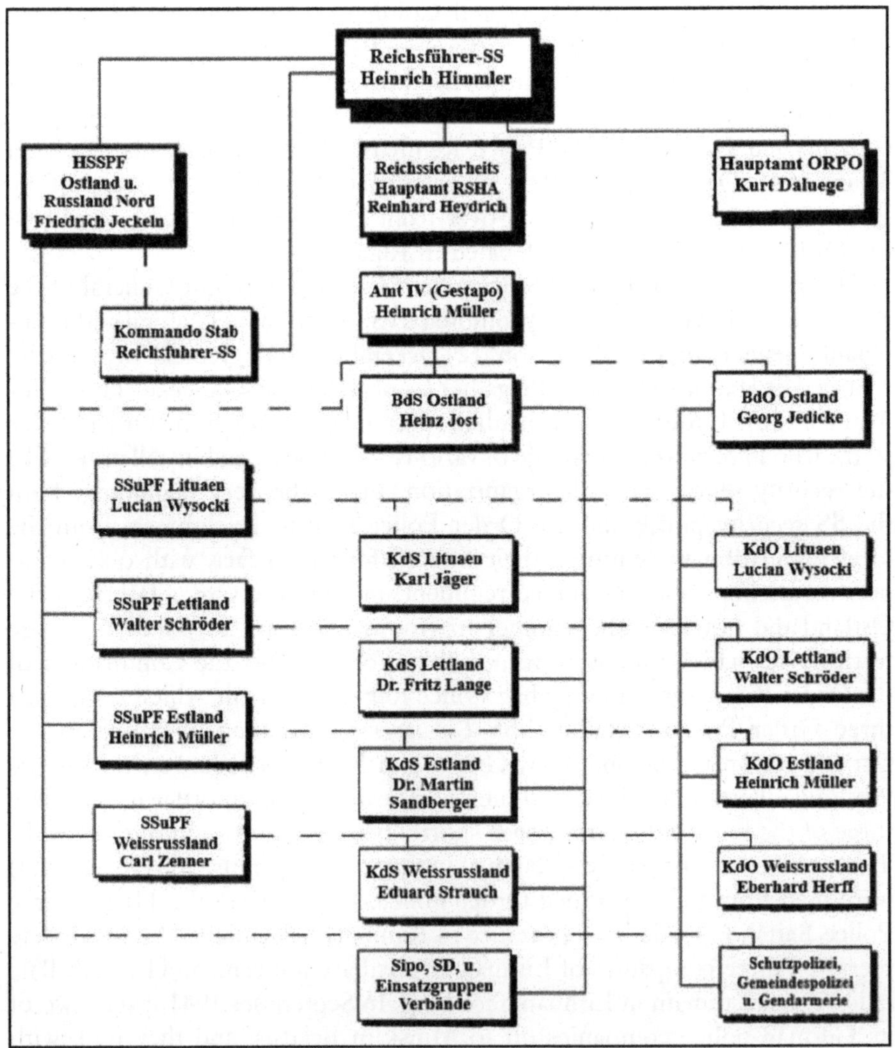

Figure 3.1. The SS and police command structure in the Baltic States.

Battalion Ostland. However, it reverted back to its numerical designation when it was transferred to Rovno and Kiev, Ukraine, in February 1942. The 105th Police Battalion was another unit that made an early appearance, in July 1941. Exactly a year later in July 1942 it was withdrawn and sent to Holland, where it became the nucleus of III. Battalion, Police Regiment 12. The 69th Reserve Police Battalion Todt was formed in August 1941 using three companies from the 66th Reserve Police Battalion and two companies from the 62nd Reserve Police Battalion in Cologne. In mid-September 1941 it was sent to the Baltic States, arriving on the Leningrad front in October 1941.[26] In July 1942 the companies of the 69th Reserve Police Battalion Todt became the III. Battalion, Police Regiment 17. July 1942 was a significant month for the Order Police in the Ostland and Army Group North rear area, since it was at this time that four police regiments were formed and made available for employment from nine recently arrived Order Police battalions. The battalions were divided into groups of three per regiment and their designation was changed, with each of them receiving a Roman numeral allocated depending on whether they were to form the I., II. or III. Battalion in each regiment. The following police regiments fought in the Ostland, mostly in rear of Army Group North:

- I. (ex-305th), II. (ex-306th), III. (ex-310th) Police Battalions of Police Regiment 15;
- I. (ex-56th), II. (ex-102nd), III. (ex-121st) Police Battalions of Police Regiment 16;
- I. (ex-42nd), II. (ex-74th), III. (ex-69th) Police Battalions of Police Regiment 17; and
- I. (ex-61st), II. (ex-112th), III. (ex-132nd) Police Battalions of Police Regiment 9.[27]

Other police regiments created in the summer of 1942 were employed either in central or southern Russia or were sent to other parts of occupied Europe. In addition, three of the newly created police regiments were dispersed behind the three main German army groups and assigned to various security divisions. One police battalion was given to each of the nine security divisions, as shown in Table 3.7.[28]

The Order Police command structure from Berlin to the Ostland region was as follows:

National Leader of the SS and Head of the German Police (Heinrich Himmler), then:
Main Office of the Order Police (Kurt Daluege), then:
Department VI – Colonial Police (Karl von Pfeffer-Wildenbruch), then:
Commander of the Order Police in the Ostland (Georg Jedicke) then:

Table 3.7. Police battalions assigned to security divisions, June 1942.

Rear Area Command	Security Division	Police Battalion	Renumbered Battalion
Korück 101 North Russia	207th	112th	II. Battalion, Police Regiment 9
	281st	132nd	III. Battalion, Police Regiment 9
	285th	61st	I. Battalion, Police Regiment 9
Korück 102 Central Russia	221st	91st	I. Battalion, Police Regiment 8
	286th	134th	III. Battalion, Police Regiment 8
	403rd	111th	II. Battalion, Police Regiment 8
Korück 103 South Russia	213th	318th	III. Battalion, Police Regiment 6
	444th	311th	II. Battalion, Police Regiment 6
	454th	82nd	I. Battalion, Police Regiment 6

- Command of the Order Police Lithuania (Lucian Wysocki)
- Command of the Order Police Latvia (Walter Schröder)
- Command of the Order Police Estonia (Hermann Schallert[29])
- Command of the Order Police White Ruthenia (Eberhard Herf)

The officer assigned to command the German police in Lithuania, Lucian Wysocki, was born in Gentomic, West Prussia, on 18 January 1899. He was an early member of the Nazi stormtroopers, attaining the rank of SA Major in 1933. A year later he led the 134th SA Regiment stationed in Duisburg, and three years later in 1937 he led the 171st SA Regiment in Wuppertal. That same year he became the commander of the 73rd SA Brigade in Essen, a post he held until 1940. In 1939 he was promoted to the rank of SA Oberführer and became an SA Brigadier General in 1941.[30] That same year he was also given the rank of General of the Police.[31]

The leader of the Command of the Order Police Latvia, Walter Schröder, was born in Lübeck on 26 November 1902. He joined the stormtroopers in 1925 and soon reached the rank of SA Lieutenant while serving in a stormtrooper battalion in Mecklenburg and in Lübeck. It quickly became evident to those who knew him that he had political aspirations. From 1930 to 1937 he was District Leader and Administrative Inspector of the National Socialist German Workers Party in Mecklenburg. In 1933 he was appointed as a representative of the German Parliament and in 1937 he was given the rank of police leader. A year earlier he had been promoted to colonel in the National Socialist Motor Transport Corps. In 1936 Walter Schröder was given a staff position in the National Socialist Motor Transport Corps Motor Group North, which was stationed in Hamburg. In 1938 he was promoted to the rank of NSKK *Oberführer*. That same year he transferred to the ranks of the SS and was given the rank of *SS Oberführer* on 20 April 1938. On 1 August

1941 he was assigned to lead the SS and Police Leader Latvia. He was also given the dual role of Commander of the Order Police Latvia. On 29 September 1941 he was promoted to SS Brigadier General and Major General of the Police.[32] Schröder is a fine example of the type of officers who were to man the SS and police commands: hardened SS men who had been wholly indoctrinated in National Socialist ideology. It was with such résumés that they assumed their posts, carrying out Nazi policy to the best of their ability. Unfortunately, this proved especially true with regard to the efficiency with which they set about exterminating the Jewish population.

As stated previously, there were not enough German policemen to properly occupy the vast areas of the Ostland region and the rear of Army Group North. This was also true in other parts of the occupied East and was a major factor in the recruitment of the local population by the *Ostheer*, SS, security service and Order Police. Table 3.8 clearly indicates the extent to which the Germans relied on indigenous volunteers to augment their SS and police forces. Strengths for the volunteer self-defence battalions are given separately from those volunteers who were serving behind the lines, wearing police uniforms and carrying out German police functions. The small numbers of German police in each city are given separately.

Dissension and power struggles in the East

We must now discuss the SS organization itself as it was set up in the Reich Commissariat Ostland. The establishment of what were termed the Higher SS and Police Leader commands inside and outside the borders of the Reich was done by Himmler to circumvent some of his own agencies and departments. It was a typical Nazi system, duplicating one service or channel by having more than one system in place. For Himmler, who had learned this tactic from the Führer, the creation of special SS staffs, responsible only to him directly, actually served two main purposes. First, it allowed Himmler to send in his own representative to areas of immediate attention or interest.

Table 3.8. German and foreign *Ordnungspolizei* (OD) and SD personnel, 1 October 1942.

Station Post	German Personnel	Order Service police	Self-defence battalions
Tallinn, Estonia	591	5,110 Estonian OD men	5,385 Estonian Schuma
Riga, Latvia (police)	1,000	9,000 Latvian OD men	9,000 Latvian self-defence
Riga, Latvia (security police)	987	563 Latvian security service men	
Kaunas, Lithuania	456	8,757 Lithuanian OD men	7,917 Lithuanians
Minsk, White Russia	1,394	8,374 Belarusian OD men	1,456 Belarusians
Grand Total	4,428	31,804	23,756

Theoretically this representative, almost always a high-ranking SS general, would report on the true status of the situation. In this way, Himmler could count on a regular report being filed by the local police, SS, security police or security service headquarters, but he was assured of a second opinion from his Higher SS and Police Leader headquarters. Secondly, and certainly almost as important, the structure and command of the Higher SS and Police Leader commands served as a balance and counterweight to the ambitions, aspirations and intrigues of those police, SS, security police and security service officers in Himmler's growing empire. If Himmler wished to keep one of his officers, departments or agencies out of a plan or project, he could always use one of his Higher SS and Police Leader commands to circumvent any particular office or official. For example, the *Einsatzgruppen* commanders, who held the post of Commander of the Security Police and Security Service, came under the direct authority of Reinhard Heydrich, through Heinrich Mueller's Department 4 (the *Gestapo*) of the Reich Main Security Office.[33]

The fact that Heydrich and later Ernst Kaltenbrunner (his replacement after Heydrich's assassination in June 1942) schemed to make themselves independent of Himmler not only affected the subordinate relationship of the Commander of the Security Police and Higher SS and Police Leader, but also confirmed Himmler's suspicions on the necessity of having an independent SS command and control group. It was essential, therefore, that he have a means to circumvent these departments and/or agencies (or individuals) whenever necessary. The Higher SS and Police Leader commands had the ability to take control of operations and the SS and police forces for those undertakings. Additionally, they had authority over the Command of the Security Police (KdS) and Command of the Order Police (KdO) headquarters, effectively circumscribing the Commander of the Order Police (BdO) and Commander of the Security Police (BdS) headquarters. With the creation of the Reich Commissariat Ukraine on 1 September 1941 a rift began to grow between the Commissariat's newly appointed leader, Erich Koch, and Alfred Rosenberg, head of the Reich Ministry for the Occupied Eastern Territories. The problem stemmed from a power struggle as to who would wield ultimate political power in the East. Rosenberg felt that an expanded civilian administration in the East that was hostile to his Reich Ministry for the Occupied Eastern Territories would eventually dilute whatever power he had garnered there.

Gottlob Berger, who was head of the SS Main Office, supported Erich Koch. When Koch was appointed Reich Commissar for Ukraine, he gained control over the Order Police and the *Gestapo* in the regions of Ukraine parcelled up for his Nazi civilian administration. This was a dilution of Himmler's power over these forces. Heinrich Himmler, like Rosenberg, also resented losing power and influence to a Nazi civilian administration, and initially supported Rosenberg against Koch, realizing that Koch's growing power was a threat to the influence that his Higher SS and Police Leader commands had wielded up until then. Prützmann's transfer to Ukraine and Jeckeln's transfer to the Ostland region were tied to this power struggle between Koch and Rosenberg.[34] On 14 December 1941 Alfred Rosenberg met with Adolf Hitler to discuss the growing rift between himself and Erich Koch, but failed to win Hitler's support. The Führer, who was interested in turning a section of southern Ukraine into a Reich enclave, eventually decreed on 1 April 1942 the creation of the East Working Area of the National Socialist German Workers' Party (*Arbeitsbereich Osten der NSDAP*) for the new occupied territories. This further weakened Rosenberg's hold over the eastern lands and increased Koch's growing power. Himmler was also upset at this turn of events, but wisely dropped his initial support for Rosenberg, now seeing that the winds of favour were blowing in Koch's direction. The culmination of this power struggle between Koch and Rosenberg occurred on 21 September 1944 when Koch replaced Hinrich Lohse as Reich Commissioner for the Ostland and his influence soared. Now Koch was overseeing the Nazi civilian administration in the Baltic States and Belarus as well.

Recruitment of Baltic volunteers

Initially, the raising of Baltic volunteers was done on a small scale. The larger Lithuanian, Latvian and Estonian anti-communist guerrilla units that were spontaneously created during the Soviet withdrawal from the Baltic region had actually been disbanded by the Nazis. Slowly but surely, however, the Germans began to partly reverse this policy of disbanding anti-communist Baltic guerrilla forces. The effect that these guerrillas had on the Soviet retreat was significant. One well known unit of some 600 Lithuanian partisans, under the command of Colonel Jonas Klimaitis, proved especially troublesome for the withdrawing Red Army. Before the German invasion, the head of the anti-communist Lithuanian resistance movement was Lieutenant Colonel Kazys Skirpa, who controlled the largest of the guerrilla cells. His units claimed to have 36,000 full- or part-time fighters. Beginning as early as 28 June 1941, and running until August 1941, the Germans disbanded dozens of units containing thousands of these patriot guerrillas. In the Vilnius district alone they encountered 3,600 Lithuanian deserters from the Soviet-raised 29th (Lithuanian) Territorial Corps.

Initially, *Sonderkommando* 1b organized five Lithuanian *Einzeldienst* (Individual Service) companies. The Latvian Individual Service worked under German supervision in the cities and in the countryside, relying on the already existing Lithuanian police organization. One of these companies was stationed in Fort No. 7 in Kaunas, while another company travelled with *Sonderkommando* 1b on its killing spree through the Baltic States, Belarus and North Russia.[35] The other three companies were attached to the 11th Reserve

Police Battalion when it was transferred to Minsk, Belarus. In addition, 1,150 Lithuanians under the command of Colonel Antanas Iskaukas volunteered for service in the SS. Initially the SS security police and security service command raised five companies of auxiliary policemen from these 1,500 volunteers. Some volunteers also served in the local SS *Einsatzkommando*. In Latvia on 3 July 1941 there were five provisional auxiliary police companies in existence. Thirteen days later *Sonderkommando* 1b reorganized 240 of these men into six police districts. These men were not only assigned to police duties, but also performed security police work. Initially these Latvian companies were referred to as *Ordnungs Hilfspolizei* (Auxiliary Order Police). It wasn't until the spring of 1942 that a Latvian security battalion appeared.

The Latvian volunteer battalions, commonly referred to as the *Arājs Kommando*, were named after their commander, Viktor Arājs. Originally a Latvian newspaperman, Viktor Arājs moved into politics and became the leader of the *Latvijas Pērkonkrusta partija*.[36] Units from the *Arājs Kommando* served under *Einsatzgruppe* A and were under the authority of the security service. As such, they served as auxiliary security service personnel. One published work states that the *Arājs Kommando* contained 1,200 men, initially formed into companies. Later, with the assistance of the German security police, these troops were organized into a Latvian security service battalion. It is estimated that throughout the war up to 45,000 Jews who lived in the Baltic States and Belarus were murdered by the *Arājs Kommando*. Other Latvian units were created and named *Ordnungs Hilfspolizei*.

These self-defence units were, in turn, divided into four sub-groups: *Wach* (Guard), *Ersatz* or *Stamm* (Replacement or Cadre), *Pionier* or *Bau* (Engineer or Construction), and *Front* (Front-line combat) battalions. Typically, a self-defence battalion was composed of between 400 and 700 men in 3 to 5 companies. Armaments were second- or third-rate hand-me-downs from various countries. For example, one could find at least half a dozen different types of rifles in a battalion, with just as many different numbers of machine guns. Uniforms were just as mixed, especially in the first two years of the war. In May 1943 these self-defence battalions became known as police battalions. During this same month the German police regiments received the honorary prefix 'SS' before their title, except the eastern police regiments, which were formed mainly from non-Germans and were instead titled police rifle regiments. These police rifle regiments served only in Poland, Belarus, Ukraine, and central and southern Russia. In Estonia, the northernmost Baltic country, a type of *Selbstschutz* (self-defence force) was established almost as soon as the front lines moved into the Soviet Union.

Initially, it was *Sonderkommando* 1a and even the headquarters' staff of *Einsatzgruppe* A which helped to organize and employ these small units. On 30 July 1941 the Germans ordered that all Estonian anti-communist units were to be disbanded. This was a mere formality, however, since the Germans did intend to use these men, but under German control. Two days later, on 1 August 1941, the Estonian *Ordnungs Hilfspolizei* (Auxiliary Police) was officially formed. Some authors assert that a day later (2 August) the name was changed to *Selbstschutz* (Self-defence). According to one source, Estonian Major Ain Ervin Mere did not become a staff leader of the Estonian regional *Selbstschutz* units until much later. It appears that initially these formations were under the overall command of Colonel Arnold Sinka. The Estonian word for *Selbstschutz* is *Omakaitse*, and service in this organization was compulsory for all male Estonians between the ages of 17 and 45 who were not serving in one capacity or another, such as in the *Schutzmannschaft* (Self-defence) battalions or the German Order Police or security police. Later on, the *Selbstschutz* was reorganized on a strictly territorial basis, with units subordinate to the local police post or station. These twelve companies were taken over and supplied and supported by *Sonderkommando* 1a and the staff headquarters of *Einsatzgruppe* A in the summer of 1941. They were stationed throughout Estonia (see Table 3.9).

In late 1942 or early 1943, this self-defence force was expanded and reorganized (see Table 3.10).[37] In addition to the self-defence battalions, a training school opened in Tartu and operated from 1942 until Estonia was abandoned in September 1944. The school was transferred to the town of Kehtna in early 1944 when the school and town of Tartu were threatened by the advance of

Table 3.9. Distribution of Estonian Auxiliary Police Companies, summer 1941.

Auxiliary Police Company	Location	Auxiliary Police Company	Location
1	Tallinn	7	Voru
2	Harrien	8	Valga
3	Jerwen	9	Petseri
4	Wierland	10	Poltsamaa
5	Narva	11	Viljandi
6	Tartu	12	Oesel

Table 3.10. Distribution of self-defence battalions, late 1942.

Self-defence Battalion	Location	Self-defence Battalion	Location
Harjumaa	Tallinn	Vôru	Viljandi
Järvamaa	Paide	Valga	Viljandi
Virumaa	Rakvere	Sakala	Viljandi
Narva	Viljandi	Pärnu	Haapsalu
Tartu	Viljandi	Läänemaa	Haapsalu
Petseri	Viljandi	Saaremaa	Kuressare

the Red Army. In addition to the German SS and police forces sent into the Soviet Union, auxiliary volunteer units made up of native volunteers were formed almost from the start of the campaign. As has been shown, these units were numerous and accounted for tens of thousands of indigenous personnel. They very quickly filled the ranks of the *Einsatzgruppen* – the murder commandos – as well as joining the Order Police, the security police and other security forces. The first instance of the use of these Estonian self-defence units against the Jewish population was on 12 October 1941, when it was reported that the Estonians attached to *Einsatzkommando* 1a assisted in the murder of 440 Jews in Reval and 474 Jews in Harku (both in the Tallinn District).[38] One unsubstantiated report, given to this author via an Estonian researcher,[39] listed the officers for the self-defence organization in the summer of 1941 (see Table 3.11).

According to the same Estonian source, the self-defence force had about 25,000 members in September 1941 and grew to 42,800 men by the end of the year. The Germans were thus able to recruit enough men to create 13 regiments, 52 territorial battalions and 270 companies. As stated earlier, the Estonian auxiliary police force was officially formed on 1 August 1941. It was a voluntary security organization which embraced the entire Estonian countryside. In addition to the formation of the initial Estonian self-defence companies, the Germans also began the full-scale recruitment of other auxiliary troops in the Reich Commissariat Ostland. As we shall see, this recruitment met with varying degrees of success, but proved in general principle to be worthwhile, mostly due to the local population's hatred of Stalin and

Table 3.11. The Estonian Self-Defence Organization, summer 1941.

Unit	Location	Commander
Home Defence Headquarters	Tallinn, Pagari Street	Colonel Arnold Sinka
Self-Defence Tallinn	Tallinn	Colonel Johann Paul
Self-Defence Harju County	Tallinn	Captain Evald Saidra
Self-Defence Järva County	Paide	Major Jaagund
Self-Defence Viru County	Rakvere	Captain Vaska
Self-Defence Narva	Narva	Major Joosep Lääne
Self-Defence Tartu	Tartu	Lieutenant Colonel Hugo Jaanson
Self-Defence Petseri	Petseri	Lieutenant Colonel Artur Viilip
Self-Defence Vôru	Vôru	Captain August Tiivel
Self-Defence Valga	Valga	Major August Sander
Self Defence of Sakala	Viljandi	Major Anton Pori
Self-Defence Pärnu	Pärnu	Major Paul Lilleleht
Self-Defence Lääne County	Haapsalu	Major August Kõrgmaa
Self-Defence Saaremaa	Kuressaare	Captain Peeter Kangro
Self-Defence School	Tallinn, Kehtna	Major Alfred Karik

Table 3.12. Estonian units created by the German Order Police in 1941.

Unit	Commander	Notes
Estonian Self-Defence Cadre Battalion*	Lieutenant Colonel Sarev**	* Created to supply trained Estonian recruits for the self-defence battalions. It contained a staff and three recruit training companies. Renamed the 41st Estonian Self-Defence Front Battalion in Nov. 1941. Expanded in summer 1942 to include ski training and engineer training companies. Redesignated the 41st Estonian Self-Defence Battalion (reinforced) in autumn 1942. ** Replaced by Lieutenant Colonel Vermet, also an ex-Estonian Army officer.
Estonian Self-Defence Battalion Dorpat*	Police Major Bergmann (Aug.–Dec. 1941) Major Franz Kurg (Dec. 1941–June 1944)	* Dorpat is the German name for the Estonian town of Tartu. This unit was redesignated the 37th Estonian Self-Defence Front Battalion in Nov. 1941.
Estonian Self-Defence Construction Battalion Dorpat*	Police Major Schiller**	* This battalion was created in Sept. 1941 and redesignated the 42nd Estonian Engineer Self-Defence Battalion in Nov. 1941. ** *Source*: Jurs et al., *Estonian Freedom Fighters in World War II*, p. 83.
Estonian Self-Defence Battalion Fellin*	Lieutenant Colonel J. Raudmäe**	* Fellin is the German name for the Estonian town of Viljandi, where this battalion was created in September 1941. ** *Source*: Jurs et al., *Estonian Freedom Fighters in World War II*, p. 81.
Estonian Self-Defence Battalion Poltsama*	Major Sobolev	* This battalion was created in the autumn of 1941 with a staff and three rifle companies. It was renamed the 39th Estonian Security Battalion in the summer of 1942 and expanded to a staff headquarters company and five rifle companies.
36th Estonian Self-Defence Front Battalion	Police Major Renter*	* Renter was a German Order Police officer; in the autumn of 1942 Estonian Captain Riipalu assumed command. At this time (autumn 1942) the battalion was in Ukraine fighting the partisans.
Estonian Security Battalion Pleskau (Pskov)*	Major K. Limpere	* The battalion was raised in Aug. 1941 from volunteers from the towns of Voru, Valga and Petseri. It was sent to Pskov in Oct. 1941. In the autumn of 1942 it was operating in the rear of Belarus but by the winter of 1943/1944 it was back at Pskov.

communism. Anti-Semitism was also an incentive for some volunteers. In addition to the volunteer companies formed by *Einsatzgruppe* A, numerous companies of Baltic volunteers were forthcoming in 1941, raised by both the German Army and the Order Police. The initial Estonian units created by the German Order Police in 1941 are shown in Table 3.12.[40] Other Estonian units were also raised by the German Army in 1941 (see Table 3.13).[41]

The 181st–186th Estonian Security Battalions were created in September 1941. A month later, in October, the 181st–183rd Estonian Security Battalions were sent to the German Korück 583, behind the lines of Army Group North. Placed immediately behind the front lines of 18th Army, they were used to combat the partisans as well as carrying out other security duties. A month later, in November, the 184th Estonian Security Battalion joined them. The 186th Estonian Security Battalion would serve as the replacement unit for the other security battalions.

Initial Latvian units raised by the German Order Police in 1941 included the following formations: the 16th Latvian Self-Defence Battalion commanded by Colonel Gustavs Mangulis;[42] the Latvian Security Battalion Riga, commanded by Captain Karlis Behms;[43] the 19th Latvian Self-Defence Battalion commanded by Captain Karlis Porietis; the Latvian Engineer Security Battalion Abrene[44] commanded by Captain P. Saulite;[45] and the 17th Latvian Self-Defence Battalion[46] commanded by Major Alfons Skrauja.

Table 3.13. Other Estonian units raised by the German Army in 1941.

Unit	Notes
Estonian Company, 184th Security Battalion	Detached and renamed the 657th Estonian Eastern Company in 1942. It was directly under the control of 18th Army.
181st Estonian Security Battalion	Redesignated the 658th Estonian Eastern Battalion in Oct. 1942.
182nd Estonian Security Battalion	Redesignated the 659th Estonian Eastern Battalion in Oct. 1942.
183rd Estonian Security Battalion	The cadre was used to help form the 661st Russian Eastern Battalion in Oct. 1942. The remaining Estonian personnel were sent to the 659th Estonian Eastern Battalion.
184th Estonian Security Battalion	Redesignated the 660th Estonian Eastern Battalion in Oct. 1942.
185th Estonian Security Battalion	The cadre was used to help form the 662nd Russian Eastern Battalion in Oct. 1942.
186th Estonian Security Battalion	The cadre was used to help form the 663rd Russian Eastern Battalion in Oct. 1942.

Table 3.14. Eastern troop strengths for Army Group North, February–July 1943.

HQ	February	March	April	May	June	July
18th Army	10,155	16,179	18,949	23,061	25,795	29,412
16th Army	10,590	12,644	14,728	21,957	23,666	27,158
Army Group North Rear Area	7,923	7,772	10,324	12,119	14,281	12,102
Total:	28,668	36,595	44,001	57,137	63,742	68,672

By 1943 the number of eastern troops employed by the Germans was much higher than it had been at the start of the Russian campaign. This was directly connected to the high daily casualty rates suffered by the Wehrmacht on the Eastern Front. Even on a quiet day, Hitler was losing around 3,000–4,000 men. In 1943 Adolf Hitler finally gave his (reluctant) consent for the official establishment of units of eastern volunteers larger than battalion-sized formations. Table 3.14 lists the numbers of eastern troops serving in the region of Army Group North in 1943.

Commander of the Gendarmerie Latvia

The Gendarmerie comprised the rural police in the countryside. In the Third Reich, including in the conquered areas, it operated in localities with a population of up to 5,000 inhabitants, but the general rule was a town or village of no more than 2,000 people. The smallest Gendarmerie unit contained about six men. With the exception of the motorized Gendarmerie platoons that were organized for operations in the East, the Gendarmerie usually lacked motorized equipment and depended almost exclusively on bicycles for transportation. The Gendarmerie had responsibility for all police tasks except: serious crimes that required a thorough criminal investigation; offences that were the responsibility of the State Police; and offences that required the employment of the State Secret Police. Traffic on the roads between villages and towns was the responsibility of the motorized Gendarmerie, not the local village and town Gendarmerie units. The war brought additional responsibilities for the Gendarmerie, especially in the occupied territories, where its units were now tasked with protecting a wide variety of localities, such as industrial sites, waterworks, bridges and even key roads. Gendarmerie units were also tasked with searching for escaped prisoners of war, forced labourers, etc., were responsible for ensuring that the local population followed all German decrees, especially with regards to ordinances and the Black Market, and supported the *Gestapo* in making arrests. In this latter capacity, the local Gendarmerie came under the nearest *Gestapo* or security police headquarters.

The Gendarmerie outside the Reich itself was organized into several Command of the Gendarmerie headquarters. These in turn controlled several

Gendarmerie districts, each containing several Gendarmerie posts. The Commander of the Gendarmerie Latvia headquarters was established on 13 August 1941. The initial German officer in charge was Gendarmerie Captain Richard Rehberg. On 1 October 1942 Rehberg was replaced by Gendarmerie Major Axt, who held the post until 30 April 1943. On 1 May 1943 Gendarmerie Major Oswald Espey assumed control and held it until most of Latvia was overrun by the Red Army in the autumn of 1944.[47] Sometime in the autumn of 1944 he led the Commander of the Gendarmerie Danzig, a post he held into 1945.

Among the initial Latvian units raised by the German Army in 1941 was the 652nd Latvian Eastern Guard Company, which was simply a redesignation of the 4th Company, 17th Latvian Self-Defence Battalion. This company was detached from the battalion and became an independent eastern company in the German Army, under the command of the Chief Quartermaster Army Group North.[48]

Other Lithuanian units raised by the German Order Police in 1941 included the Lithuanian Security Battalion Kaunas,[49] stationed in Kaunas; the Lithuanian Guard Company Toropets,[50] stationed in Toropets; the Lithuanian Guard Company Dno,[51] stationed in Dno; and the Lithuanian Self-Defence Guard Battalion Kaunas,[52] also stationed in Kaunas. In September 1942 the latter was renamed the 250th Lithuanian Self-Defence Battalion but it was then disbanded, and several of the existing Lithuanian guard companies were renamed and employed independently as German Army units. For example, the 650th Lithuanian Eastern Guard Company (ex-1st Company, 250th Lithuanian Self-Defence Battalion) and the 651st Lithuanian Eastern Guard Company (ex-2nd Company, 250th Lithuanian Self-Defence Battalion) both came under the control of the Chief Quartermaster Army Group North.

SS Kampfgruppe Jeckeln

The creation of this battlegroup was not a one-time event but a recurring necessity that would force its establishment on a temporary basis on numerous occasions throughout the war. The first time this combat group was organized was in mid-February 1942 when the Soviet winter counteroffensive of 1941/1942 was at its height, causing the *Ostheer* to withdraw in most places along the Eastern Front. The growing partisan threat behind the lines was also a reason for the creation of this emergency combat group. On 17 February 1942 SS Lieutenant General and Police General Friedrich Jeckeln was ordered to establish an emergency combat group from his Higher SS and Police Leader command and employ the formation under the 18th Army. One day later SS Kampfgruppe Jeckeln was directed to the front lines of 18th Army. The initial strength and composition of the battlegroup was as follows:[53]

SS Kampfgruppe Jeckeln

- V. Battalion, SS Adolf Hitler Bodyguard Regiment (1,000 men)
- SS Volunteer Legion Norway (1,100 Men)[54]
- 56th, 121st, 305th, 306th and 310th Police Battalions (3,000 men).

Grand Total: 5,100 men.

The initial reason for the creation of this combat group was also to allow for the withdrawal of the battered SS Police and 58th Infantry Divisions from the front lines. Between 19 and 24 February 1942 the combat group was brought to the front and went into front-line action in the first half of March 1942. The original kampfgruppe was soon expanded and by late March 1942 the strength and composition of the battlegroup was as follows:

- Headquarters of the 320th Infantry Regiment, 212th Infantry Division
- 37th Estonian Self-Defence Battalion
- 56th, 102nd, 121st, 305th, 306th and 310th Police Battalions (3,450 men)[55]
- Headquarters of the 409th Infantry Regiment, 212th Infantry Division
- V. Battalion, SS Adolf Hitler Bodyguard Regiment (1,000 men)
- SS Volunteer Legion Norway (1,000 men)
- 158th Reconnaissance Battalion
- Headquarters of Artillery Regiment 158, 158th Infantry Division.
- I., II. and III. Artillery Battalions, SS Police Division
- Eight infantry guns shared between the SS Police Division and the 58th Infantry Division.

Anti-partisan warfare in the Baltic states

The greatest concentration of guerrilla activity in the Baltic states during the Second World War was in the border region between Lithuania and Belarus. This region was the centre of guerrilla activity for many reasons. First, the area's geographic features, with its numerous forests, rivers, marshes and bogs, afforded any guerrilla unit the ability to hide. Secondly, larger numbers of possible partisan recruits were available in this region owing to the larger numbers of Jews living in Lithuania than in Latvia and Estonia before the war, and the fact that Belarusian recruits were also accessible to create or augment the partisan forces fighting in this border region.

Partisan activity in the Baltic states only began to cause concern for the German command from the autumn of 1942. The Soviet Central Partisan Command in Moscow understood the difficulty they faced in the Baltic states, given that 98 per cent of the population was hostile to the communists.

Stalin's occupation of Lithuania, Latvia and Estonia had only lasted about a year, from 1940 to 1941 but it was enough to cause lasting bitterness among the local population. The decision was quickly reached that partisan units operating in the Baltic states needed to have a core of trusted Russian men who could guarantee the effectiveness and reliability of the partisan forces. Eventually, more than 5,000 Russians were sent into the Baltic states to serve in these guerrilla groups or on special assignments. These were reliable individuals who could be trusted to perform any mission asked of them. They were deployed in two ways: first, as individual spies, scouts or assassins, if an important person needed to be eliminated or a region or installation needed to be scouted; and second, as the basis of new partisan formations, or to replace losses of men killed or wounded within an already established partisan unit.

The point from the Russian perspective was to remind the Lithuanians, Latvians and Estonians that the Russians had not completely gone, and would return. The strategy was more to give the Baltic peoples pause before they decided to assist or join the Nazis. The partisans there let it be known very early that they would be making lists of collaborators, and these people would be held to account when the Red Army returned. In spite of this threat, many Baltic peoples volunteered for service in the German military. In the region of Latvia, as elsewhere, given the animosity felt by the Baltic peoples towards the Soviet Union, support for a partisan movement was almost non-existent. The few hundred men organized into partisan groups in the summer and autumn of 1941 were soon wiped out. Some were even killed by the local people, many whom had taken up arms during the Russian withdrawal and after.

Up until the middle of 1942 the Soviets had not established one central partisan command that could coordinate the war effort behind the German lines. That changed when the Central Headquarters of the Partisan Movement was established on 30 May 1942. From the very creation of this headquarters, great attention was paid to trying to firmly establish a partisan presence in the Baltic states. Just east of Karsava in Latvia, near the Estonian-Latvian border, one partisan attack took place in December 1943. In the same month a major battle was fought there between the partisans and a combination of German and native troops operating in a battlegroup. This was Kampfgruppe Knecht, named after its commander, Police Colonel Karl Knecht. The composition of this combat group in December 1943 was as follows:

- 10th Gendarmerie Platoon (motorized)
- 276th Latvian Self-Defence Battalion
- 277th Latvian Self-Defence Battalion
- 278th Latvian Self-Defence Battalion
- 279th Latvian Self-Defence Battalion

- Signals Platoon Lewinski
- Flak Platoon Hatje.

According to most accounts, the partisan threat in Estonia was supposedly non-existent from 1941 to 1944. While this may have been true from 1941 to 1942, 1943 did see some partisan attacks on Estonian soil, close to the Latvian border. Throughout the Russian campaign around a thousand partisans operated in Estonia, mainly in the Estonian-Russian border region. These partisans were almost exclusively Russians. We know that throughout the war the Central Headquarters of the Partisan Movement sent approximately 5,000 Russian partisans to fight in the Baltic states. Around 80 per cent of them were sent to fight inside Latvia. Given that Lithuania experienced almost no partisan attacks during the war, we can assume that the remaining 1,000 Russians were sent to fight in Estonia.

We also now know from a series of *Bandenbekämpfungskarten* (anti-partisan warfare maps) held at the US Memorial Holocaust Museum that in December 1943 there were two acts of sabotage and four partisan attacks in and around the town of Naha, an Estonian village located on the lower western coast of Lake Peipus. In December 1943 the 321st Latvian Police Battalion was stationed there. In the immediate region surrounding the town of Voru, which happened to be the base for the 1st Company, 694th Security Battalion, several attacks also took place. Nine partisan attacks occurred in the same month, with two more south of the town. Similarly, southeast of the town, roughly halfway between Voru and Karsava, another five partisan attacks occurred along the Latvian-Estonian-Russian border.

Chapter 4

Controlling the rear areas of Army Group North

Don't these people know that they are conquered?
[Napoleonic officer complaining about the Spanish '*guerrilleros*']

Army rear area forces

Immediately behind the rear of 16th Army and 18th Army in Army Group North lay the Commander of the Army Rear Area headquarters (Korück). For the rear of 16th Army the Germans had Korück 584. This command was led by Lieutenant General Kurt Spemann until late June or early July 1943. Lieutenant General Curt von Krenzki assumed command on 1 September 1943 and remained in post until the end of the war. The 18th Army was assigned Korück 583. It was led by Lieutenant General Hans Knuth from 20 January 1941 until 20 June 1943. Then Lieutenant General Oskar van Ginckel assumed control from 26 June 1943 until 8 May 1945. According to one source, Spermann and Knuth held these posts until mid-June 1943.[1] The main duties of the Korück commands included military security of the rear army area, i.e. the security and defence of important facilities, especially railway lines and runways, as well as active combat against partisans and securing economic exploitation of local crops. They also included maintaining and expanding the civil administrative government and its services, managing march-through units to and from the front lines, accommodating troops and facilities of the Wehrmacht, keeping the roads passable, and the employment of security services for overall protection. Employed under the Korück commands, all of the SS, security police, security service, police and army units cooperated fully in the fight against the guerrillas. Two perfect examples of this type of cooperation were Operation *Ecklochjagd* ('Corner Hole Hunt') and Operation *Schonungslose Erledigung* ('Merciless Settlement'). These two operations were launched in the region of Army Group North on 18 August 1941. The units involved included a company from 561st Military Field Police Battalion under Korück 584, a company of Luftwaffe men acting as infantry, and a *Teilkommando* from *Sonderkommando* 1b led by SS Second Lieutenant Karolus.[2] This force swept the rail line between Ostrov and

Porchov and managed to kill five partisans and capture six others, while 425 local civilians were shot as suspected partisan helpers.

An early roster of the scheduled principal security and occupation forces slated for service behind the lines of Army Group North, dated 4 March 1941, listed the following initial divisions and sub-units:

207th Security Division:

- 817th, 818th and 819th Field Commands
- 852nd, 854th, 858th, 859th and 860th Local Commands
- 101st and 102nd Prisoner of War Transit Camps
- 75th Regional Defence Regimental Staff
- 266th, 853rd, 859th and 920th Regional Defence Battalions
- 706th Guard Battalion

281st Security Division:

- 820th, 821st and 822nd Field Commands
- 861st, 862nd, 863rd, 864th and 865th Local Commands
- 110th Prisoner of War Transit Camp
- 107th Regional Defence Regimental Staff
- 865th, 868th, 869th and 960th Regional Defence Battalions
- 707th Guard Battalion

285th Security Division:[3]

- 611th Field Command (28 June 1941)
- 134th Prisoner of War Transit Camp
- 3rd Security Regiment (July 1941)
- 619th and 620th Bicycle Guard Battalions
- 706th Guard Battalion
- 113th Regional Defence Regimental Staff (April 1941)[4]
- 853rd, 941st and 972nd Regional Defence Battalions[5]
- 207th Engineer Battalion
- 61st Reserve Police battalion
- 207th Bicycle Reconnaissance Squadron

Security forces commanders for Army Group North

In 1941 the commander of the Rear Area of Army Group North was General of Infantry Karl-Franz von Roques (15 March 1941–31 March 1943). He was replaced by General of Infantry Hans Kuno von Both, who assumed command of this post on 1 April 1943 and held it position until 26 March 1944. The Chief of Staff, Rear Area Army Group North, was Lieutenant Colonel Arno Graf von Kriegsheim.[6]

In 1941–43 the forces at the disposal of the Commander of the Rear Area Army Group North included the 207th, 281st and 285th Security Divisions,

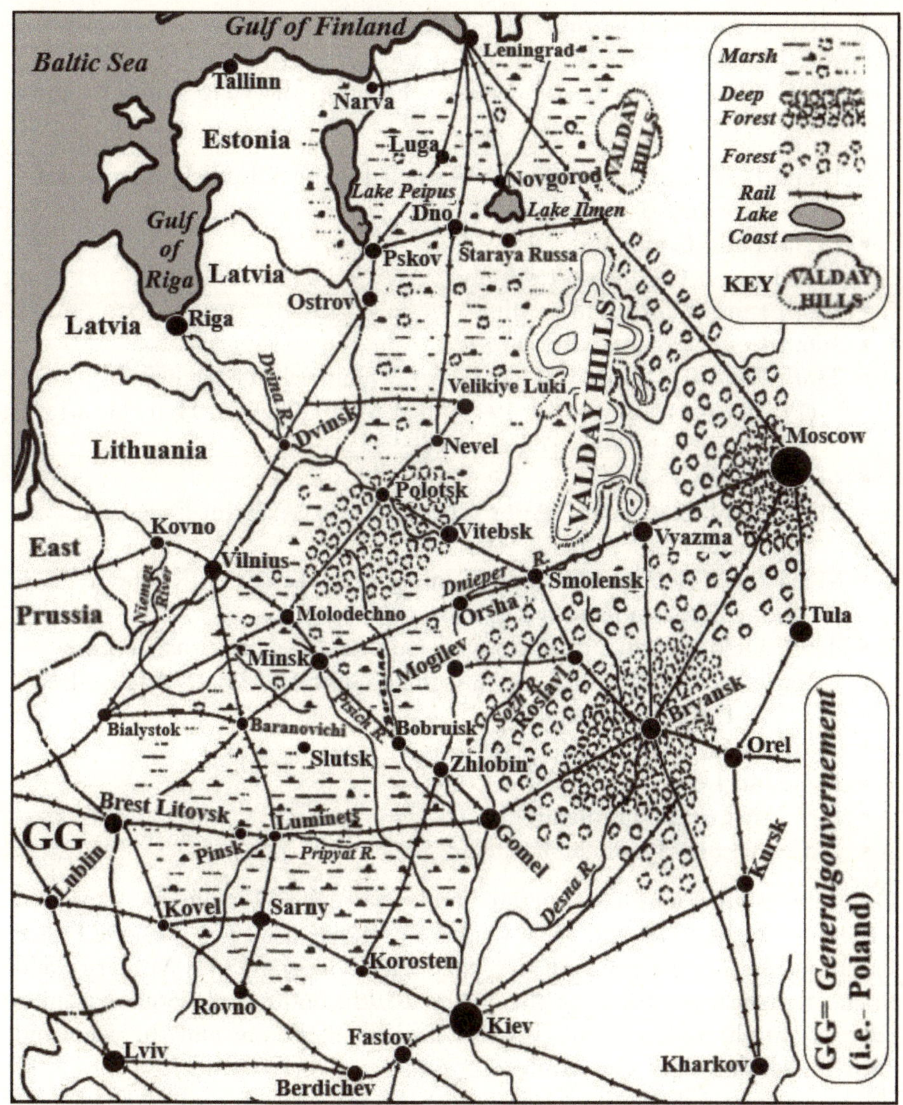

Map 6. Principal rail lines in northern and central Russia. The map also depicts the major topographical features of this region of Eastern Europe.

except in May 1942 when only the 207th Security Division and parts of the 281st Security Division were available. In November 1943 an additional unit, the 3rd Estonian SS Volunteer Brigade, was also attached, although it only remained with the Rear Area North command for that month. In November and December 1943 an additional unit, the Cavalry Regiment North, was also attached to the command.

The commanders of Korück 583 (18th Army) – Lieutenant General Hans Knuth (20 January 1941–20 June 1943) and Lieutenant General Oskar van Ginckel (21 June 1943–8 May 1944) – had the following forces at their disposal:

- 182nd Field Command: Major General Johannes Ludwig Sehmsdorf (15 February–1 March 1944)
- 192nd Field Command
- 332nd Local Command (Nõmmel)
- 360th Local Command (Tallinn)
- 366th Local Command (Paides)
- 238th Field Command: Major General Heinrich Aschenbrandt (15 August–9 November 1944) then Major General Hans Helwig (10 November 1944–21 February 1945)
- 611th Field Command
- 817th Field Command: Major General Erich Wilhelm Eisenbach (20 April–5 November 1944)
- 818th Field Command: Major General Hans Friedrich Küpper (assumed commmand on 2 January 1943)
- 819th Field Command (Haapsalu): Colonel Freiherr Ernst August Karlimilian Josef von Gise[7] (assumed command on 15 August 1943)
- I./322nd Local Command
- 283rd Local Command (Haapsalu)
- II./362nd Local Command
- II./371st Local Command
- I./574th Local Command

Other forces known to have operated under Korück 583 included: Armoured Train no. 30; the 531st and 571st Guard Battalions; the 105th Reserve Police Battalion; the 7th Technical Emergency Battalion; the 689th Military Field Police Battalion (motorized); the 658th, 659th, 660th and 666th Estonian Eastern battalions; the 664th Finnish Eastern Battalion; and the 36th and 38th Cossack Cavalry Companies.

The commanders of Korück 584 (16th Army) – Lieutenant General Kurt Spemann (1 September 1939–24 July 1943), Lieutenant General Curt Pfugradt (25 July–31 August 1943), Lieutenant General Curt von Krenzki (1 September 1943–31 October 1944) and Lieutenant General Kurt Fischer (1 November 1944–8 May 1945) – had the following forces at their disposal:

- 561st Field Command: Lieutenant Colonel Thümmel Kochem (Adjutant: First Lieutenant Möller)
- 579th Field Command: Major General Friedrich Haselmayr[8]
- I./629th Local Command: Major Sauer

- II./565th Local Command: First Lieutenant Baltin
- II./658th Local Command: Captain Maiss

Other forces known to have operated under Korück 584 included: the 667th and 668th Russian Eastern Battalions; the 493rd, 865th and 868th Security Battalions; the 267th Latvian Self-Defence Guard Battalion; the 5th, 10th and 13th Lithuanian Self-Defence Battalions; and the 561st Military Field Police Battalion (motorized).

To the above-mentioned units and headquarters must be added the higher rear area headquarters: 392nd Senior Field Command (Minsk), 394th Senior Field Command (Riga) and 396th Senior Field Command (Kaunas). These three commands were controlled by the Reich Commissariat Ostland leader until mid-1943, when their headquarters staffs were assigned to a new leadership staff: the German Armed Forces Military Commander for the Ostland. This new command, created in 1943, was also to control the employment behind the lines of German reserve divisions, as well as other formations such as the existing security divisions. The forces listed above were augmented even further by the addition of four German Army military field police battalions, which took up positions throughout the Ostland region and the rear area of Army Group North in 1941:[9]

- 691st Military Field Police Battalion (motorized) – Commander Army Rear Area North 101
- 689th Military Field Police Battalion (motorized) – 18th Army
- 561st Military Field Police Battalion (motorized) – 16th Army
- 521st Military Field Police Battalion (motorized) – 4th Armoured Group[10]

A closer look at the units under the three security divisions indicated that an attempt was also made to augment their strength:

207th Security Division (*Generalleutnant* Karl von Tiedemann)[11]

- 817th, 818th and 819th Field Commands
- 852nd, 854th, 858th, 859th and 860th Local Commands
- 101st and 102nd Prisoner of War Transit Camps
- 94th Regional Defence Regiment Staff (added 3 November 1941)
- 75th Regional Defence Regiment Staff (with 266th, 853rd, 859th and 860th Regional Defence Battalions)
- 706th Guard Battalion
- I. Battalion, 207th Artillery Regiment (1., 2. and 3. Batteries)
- 821st Signals Battalion (added 1 December 1941)
- 207th Cavalry Battalion (added 11 April 1942)
- 374th Engineer Company

281st Security Division (Lieutenant General Friedrich Bayer)[12]

- 820th, 821st and 822nd Field Commands
- 861st, 862nd, 863rd, 864th and 865th Local Commands
- 110th Prisoner of War Transit Camp
- 107th Regional Defence Regimental Staff (with 865th, 868th, 869th and 960th Regional Defence Battalions)
- 707th Guard Battalion
- II. Battalion, 207th Artillery Regiment (4., 5. and 6. Batteries)
- 281st Eastern Cavalry Battalion (added 1 December 1941)
- 822nd Signals Battalion (added 1 December 1941)
- 368th Engineer Company

285th Security Division (Lieutenant General Wolfgang Edler Herr und Freiherr von Plotho)

- 579th Senior Field Command[13]
- 190th and 569th Field Commands
- 320th Local Command
- 134th and 320th Prisoner of War Transit Camps
- 65th Reserve Police Battalion (attached on 22 June 1941)[14]
- III. Battalion, 207th Artillery Regiment (7., 8. and 9. Batteries)
- I., II. and III. Battalions, 322nd Infantry Regiment
- 113th Security Regiment (formerly 113th Regional Defence Regiment)[15] (with 853rd, 941st and 972nd Security Battalions)
- 823rd Signals Battalion (added 1 December 1941)

The security divisions

The condition of the security divisions assigned behind the front line was substantially below the normal standards of a front-line combat division. The 281st Security Division, for example, was pitifully outfitted with rifles, carbines and pistols captured from French, Belgian, Dutch and Czechoslovak armies. All of its vehicles were foreign, with no spare parts. Some had no tires. The divisional headquarters had no vehicles of any sort. Still, the unit was armed well enough for the purposes of security and guard duty, although as time wore on the fight against the Soviet partisans required stronger and better equipped units, given that over time those partisan forces would themselves become better armed and equipped. In 1941, however, the partisan threat was still not substantial enough for the Germans to concern themselves with strengthening their security or line-of-communication divisions. In fact, these security divisions were adequately equipped for the job to which they had been assigned: controlling the rear area of Army Group North. The following report from the Rear Area Commander Army Group North showed just how efficient these security units were in spite of the apparent deficiencies in their organization and equipment: 'Enemy activity behind the lines is infrequent and appears erratic. However, there are five major sectors (see attached map) where our rear area security forces have encountered concentrations of bandits. So far, our security forces have been able to contain them. Plans are being implemented to eradicate these bandit regions.'[16]

In the case of the 285th Security Division, the unit was augmented later in the month (on 15 March) with the following additional units: 322nd Infantry Regiment (reinforced) and III. Artillery Battalion, 207th Artillery Regiment (7., 8. and 9. Batteries). In December 1941 the 823rd Signals Battalion was added and on 29 March 1942 the 285th Cavalry Squadron was formed. On 27 May 1942 this cavalry formation was expanded to battalion size and was renamed the 285th Russian Cavalry Battalion. This was a Russian volunteer unit which had been fighting as a reinforced cavalry squadron since the autumn of 1941 and had slowly grown to battalion strength. In October the 285th Security Division underwent a dramatic change and increased in manpower. This was according to plans set out to reinforce and enlarge the rear area security forces, not only in the Rear Area Army Group North, but also in the Rear Areas Army Group Centre and Army Group South. The autumn of 1941 saw the rise of the partisan movement in most regions behind the

Table 4.1. Guerrillas and civilian suspects captured or shot by security divisions operating behind the lines of Army Group North, 30 September–29 October 1941.

German Security Division	Captured or apprehended	Shot	Handed over to security service for interrogation	Total killed or captured
281st Security Division				
Red sympathizers	418	26	323	444
Partisans	129	174	89	303
Male suspects and sympathizers	686	66	511	752
Female suspects and sympathizers	32	4	10	36
Total	1,265	270	933	1,535
285th Security Division				
Red Sympathizers	9,397[1]	237	1,698	9,397
Partisans	140	410	38	550
Male and female suspects or sympathizers	87	–	67	87
Total	9,624	410	3,803	10,034
207th Security Division				
Red sympathizers	17,542	1,085	2,581	18,627
Partisans	3,094	187	98	3,281
Total	20,636	1,272	2,679	20,823
Grand total (for one month)	31,525	1,952	5,415	32,392

German lines. Based on the General Plan East, as well as the orders and decrees regarding the treatment of the indigenous population and how the Germans were to conduct operations against the guerrillas, civilian losses began to mount. To be caught outside the region of your town, or simply in the woods, even if you possessed no weapons, was tantamount to being a *partisanhelfer* (partisan helper), which most likely ended with the person's execution immediately after interrogation. Table 4.1 illustrates the heavy civilian losses on the part of the Soviet population throughout the war.

The start of the partisan war in the North

As the Germans advanced through the Baltic States and entered northern Russia proper, the security divisions and other rear area forces followed in their wake. By 1 July 1941 the 207th, 281st and 285th Security Divisions were located behind the general front lines bordering Libau-Schaulen (Siauliai)-Jonava. By 7 July this line had shifted to Schlock-Bauske-Birsen and just southwest of Daugavpils.[17] A week later a third redeployment occurred and the three security divisions were moved again. This time the 207th Security Division was located in the Siauliai region, while the 281st was dispersed in and around Kovno (Kaunas) and the 285th was ordered to shift to the east of Kaunas. By August 1941 the 281st and 285th Security Divisions had left the Baltic States and advanced behind the rear of Army Group North in northern Russia. The 285th Security Division was assigned to operations behind the lines of 18th Army and south of the Gulf of Finland. The 281st Security Division was to provide security duty east and southeast of Lake Peipus, which also included the northern Soviet city of Pleskau (Pskov).[18] It appears that by the autumn of 1941 the security divisions had basically reached the region where they would operate for the next three years:

> The security troops made plans to spend the winter. The forward boundary of their area of commitment was again shifted at year's end. The line extended from Narva to the east to include Siverskaya and from there sharply to the south in an almost straight line through Dno on to the boundary with the army rear area of Army Group Centre. This line remained constant until the Soviet summer offensive of 1944.[19]

German security efforts in the rear areas were much needed, especially in light of the Soviet attitude of total war and all-out guerrilla war and the fact that tens of thousands of Red Army troops had been bypassed by the German Army during the summer of 1941. Many of these men were still wandering the woods in the autumn and were a potential source of manpower for the fledgling guerrilla movement. For example, as early as July 1941 the headquarters company of the 1st Infantry Division was ambushed by a Soviet partisan unit in the forest area around Lyadi. During the fight the divisional commanding officer, General of Cavalry Phillipp Kleffel, was seriously wounded, and many other members of the divisional staff were either killed or wounded.[20] Subsequently, command of the 1st Infantry Division passed to Lieutenant General Dr Friedrich Altrichter, who assumed control on 12 July 1941. Kleffel was sent to Germany to recuperate.[21] He eventually returned to active duty, becoming the commander of L Army Corps in January 1942.[22] At this time the 1st Infantry Division was part of the German advance with Army Group North. In July it was heading from Riga in Latvia towards Narva on the Estonian-Soviet border, with its eventual goal being the capture of Leningrad.[23] The division was disrupted for about half a day while it struggled to locate its command staff. This proved that the Soviet guerrillas

Map 7. Soviet partisan activity in the region of Army Group North, autumn 1941.

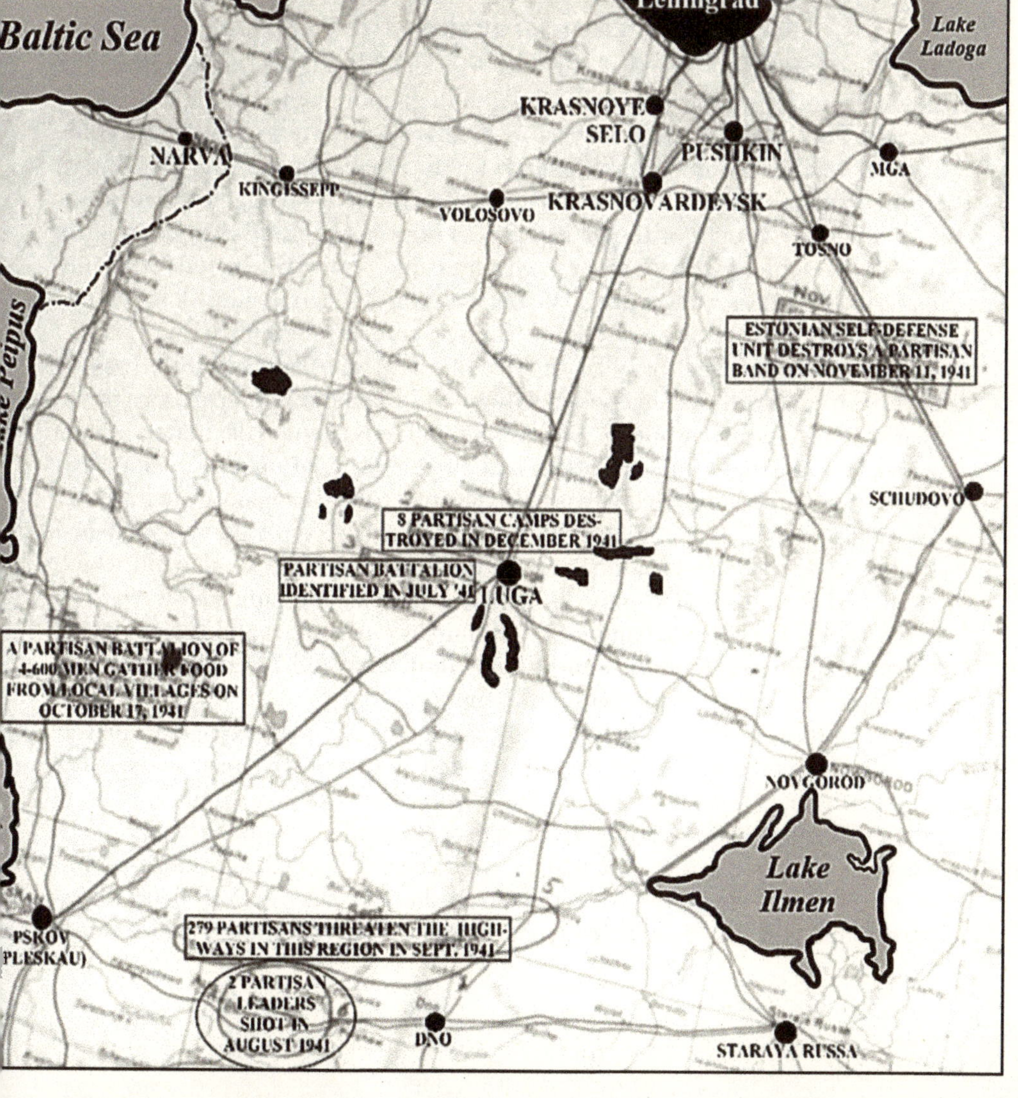

were capable of affecting the outcome of the campaign. Security of the rear areas was therefore of extreme importance.

The employment of non-German collaborationist battalions was an important and large component of the anti-partisan forces behind the lines of Army Group North in the autumn of 1942. As time passed, this dependence on foreign auxiliary troops would only grow, as the guerrilla situation became ever more serious. While Belarus proved to be the principal area of operations for the bulk of the Soviet guerrillas, the region of Army Group North also had its share of partisan problems. For example, in the Phorkov region, south of the Leningrad District, there existed a large 'partisan republic', which the Germans never quite got under their control.[24] This was a large region, bordered roughly by the Russian towns of Chudovo, Machinskaya, Siverskaya and Tosno.

Counter-measures against the partisans

On 20 August 1941 Marshal Kliment E. Voroshilov gathered together the members of his military council: Zhukov (then commander of the Leningrad sector), Popov, Subbotin, Kusnyetzov, Zhadanov and Merkulov (deputy commander of the People's Commissariat for Internal Affairs (NKVD)). Voroshilov addressed them in blunt terms: 'The enemy is strong and still fresh. You are to coordinate with partisan forces operating behind the enemy lines and support them in whichever way is possible. This will include not only materiel but personnel support. We must establish a strong guerrilla presence and not give the enemy any respite. This is comrade Stalin's wish.'[25]

At this time the Red Army facing the German 16th Army and 18th Army of Army Group North was in contact with only about a thousand partisans in the rear of both German armies.[26] But even though Soviet guerrilla units were yet to operate in large numbers, Stalin had already decided on a scorched earth policy that accorded perfectly with his view of a total war against the invading Germans. On 17 November 1941 Colonel General Volkogonov published Order no. 428 of the Headquarters of the Supreme High Command which stipulated that front-line units as well as partisans and subversives were to 'destroy and burn down completely all human settlements and houses in the German zone, to a depth of some 40–60 kilometers, and 20–30 kilometers to the right and left of roads, without exception'.[27]

The purpose here was obvious: deny the enemy any place to rest or quarter in order to make it difficult to control and dominate the rear areas. That Russian civilians – caught between the Nazis on one hand and Stalinism on the other – were to suffer terribly as a result of this order was inconsequential to Stalin. It was not the first time that a scorched earth policy had been employed as a delaying tactic by the Russians. From the very start of Napoleon Bonaparte's invasion on 22 June 1812, the Russian Czar Alexander I had ordered

Marshal Kutuzov to do several things: to deny the French Army battle by withdrawing into the Russian hinterland, to burn all towns and villages, and to destroy crops and animals so they could not be taken by the advancing French In this way, Napoleon's forces would not be able to live off the land. Before Napoleon captured Moscow, Alexander I ordered that the gaols be opened and instructed his gaolers to tell the criminals lingering in them that they could go free so long as they set fire to the city. These felonious, anti-social elements went about the task of setting fire to the city with glee. They thus denied Napoleon's forces any cover from the bitter Russian winter.

The initial partisan forces raised in the region of Army Group North were small and varied in size and strength. Partisan detachments of some 80 to 150 men were raised wherever they could be found. The city of Leningrad eventually contributed thirteen detachments by recruiting heavily from students

Map 8. Partisans in the area of Army Group North, December 1941.

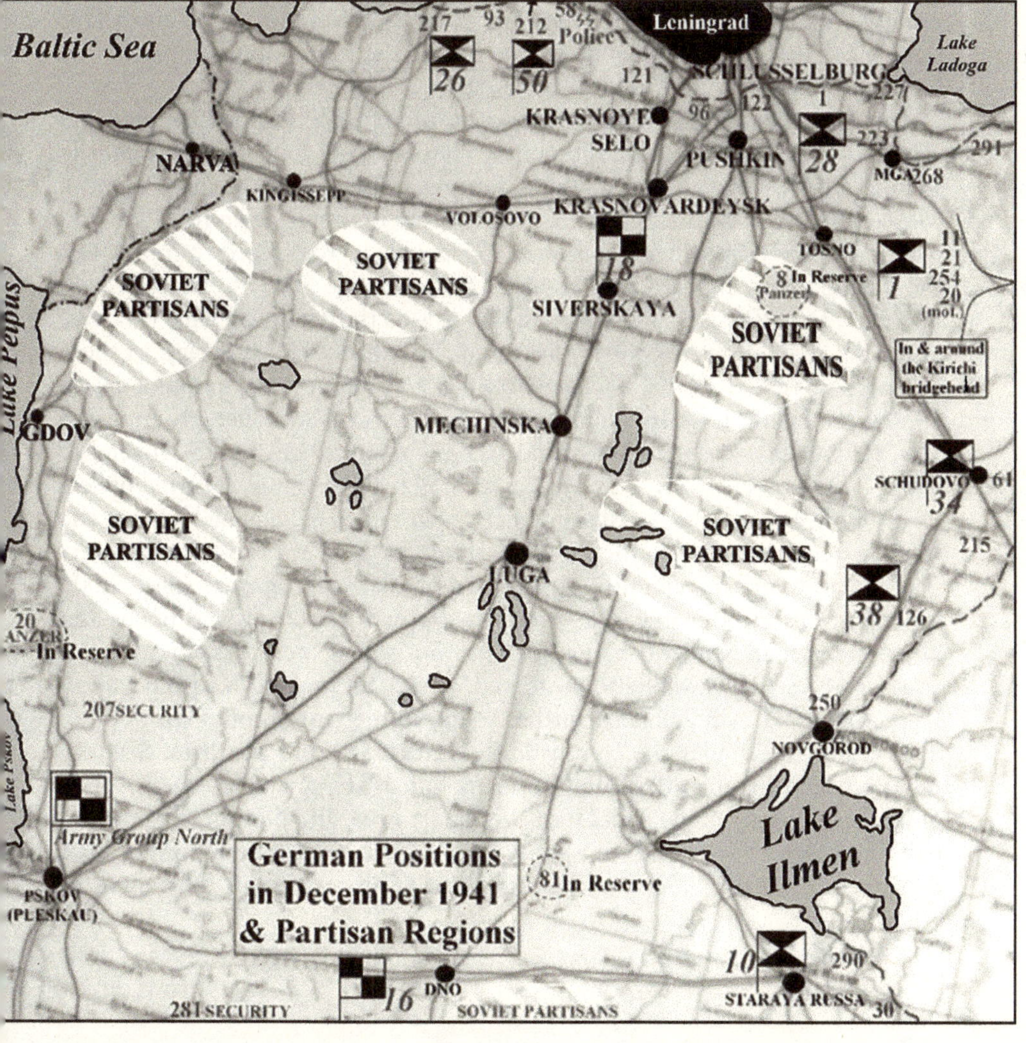

and faculty members of the Lesgaft Institute of Physical Culture. The first of these student/teacher detachments were formed as early as 24 June 1941.

The partisan menace grows

By September 1941 no fewer than 2,886 partisans were operating successfully behind the lines of Army Group North.[28] The end of that month saw the starting date (30 September 1941) for Operation Typhoon – the German drive to capture Moscow in the autumn of 1941. By this time the Soviets had another 10,000 partisans in the rear areas bordering Moscow, Tula and, most northerly of all, Kalinin.[29] The Germans tried to counter the guerrillas in much the same way, using their idiotic and insane tactic of collective punishment (*Gesamte strafe*). This tactic relied on a massive reprisal campaign that was indiscriminate and punished both active guerrillas and innocent civilian bystanders. Punishments included deportations and evacuations, as well as more severe measures that resulted in the death of many civilians. For example, when the Germans reached the area of Kalinin the Wehrmacht, hoping to deny the guerrillas any support from the local populace, proceeded to forcibly evacuate all the local inhabitants.

The Germans considered Kalinin to be of strategic importance since its capture by the 1st Panzer Division on 14 October 1941 had effectively cut the Leningrad-Moscow rail line, a vital feature in the overall plan to capture Moscow.[30] It was with this in mind that the deportations began from the first day of the city's capture. A total of 23,775 people were obliged to trek out of the region between 14 October and 16 December 1941.[31] These forced marches of the Russian civilian population caused the deaths of many civilians, especially the elderly, the very young and the infirm. The suffering of these evacuees increased after 1 December when the temperature plummeted to 30 degrees below zero. In addition, the local secret field police group in the area, GFP-580,[32] executed 340 of the local inhabitants between 15 November and 15 December 1941.[33] In December 1941 a combined security police, Order Police and Baltic auxiliary police force raid was launched against the partisan region closest to the city of Leningrad, between Tosno and Siverskaya. The 'partisan republic' in this area at that time housed some 2,000 guerrillas. During the attack the Germans burned 39 villages and towns and killed 486 people who were identified as Komsomol members. In addition, another 107 civilians were also murdered.[34] Another operation, also begun in December 1941, was launched further south, in the region southeast of Dno. This region was under the command of Korück 584 and the 281st Security Division. During this drive the Germans killed 317 guerrillas, and burned down 11 partisan camps and 23 villages and towns. In addition, 12 residential warehouses, 3 partisan hospitals and 7 ammunition storehouses were destroyed.[35] Further south, the partisans were also active in the region of

Cholm, especially after September 1941. A report from the local secret field police group there indicated the extent to which the guerrillas were willing to go: 'On 1 October 1941 Kozlov, a captured partisan, reported a suggestion of Kazalpov, a member of the Central Committee of the Party in Cholm, that German soldiers or wounded be tortured by mutilation before execution.'[36]

To any intelligence officer the implication of this suggestion was obvious. The Soviet Partisan Command wanted the Germans to be incensed so that their reprisals against the Russian civilian population would be brutal and extreme, thus causing the population to eventually turn against the Germans. This tactic was openly employed, but in many cases it was unnecessary given that many Germans were already behaving abysmally towards the civilian population. Alexander Shcherbakov, a member of the 18th Politburo and Chief of the Red Army Political Department, expressed that sentiment quite well during a meeting of the Central Committee of the Communist Party in early 1942: 'We should thank the Germans for their policies which have enabled us to fan the flames of the guerrilla movement.'[37] Before the end of the Soviet winter counter-offensive, the three Soviet fronts in the region – the Kalinin Front (Koniev), the West Front (Zhukov) and the Southwest Front (Sacharov) – would commit two entire cavalry corps and three airborne brigades to the support of the guerrillas in this region of the Soviet Union.[38] By the spring of 1942 total guerrilla numbers in the Tula and Kalinin regions stood at around 10,000 partisans. According to the Supreme Headquarters of the Partisan Command in Moscow, about 18,000 Germans had been killed by guerrillas throughout the Soviet Union during the winter of 1941/1942, while another 600 had been shot after being captured.[39]

By April 1942, 50 new partisan detachments totalling 4,000 men had been created and were operating around Leningrad. About 33 partisan detachments (2,000 men) were also working in the Karelia region of the Russo-Finnish border at this time.[40] Soviet sources, known for overestimation, state that during the winter of 1941/1942 the guerrilla movement was responsible for the destruction of 114 rail and road bridges, 26 warehouses, 69 tanks, 500 trucks and passenger cars of all sizes, and 13 planes, as well as the deaths of 15,000 Germans.[41] The figure of 15,000 Germans killed is 3,000 less than the number quoted by the Soviet partisan command, but still seems to be an overestimation. A more reasonable number for German losses at the hands of the guerrillas in the winter of 1941/1942 seems to be about 7,000–8,000 men. Of these, 3,610 Germans, 26 camps, 43 vehicles and 72 bridges were destroyed behind the lines of Army Group North by the end of 1941.[42]

The secret field police in Army Group North

The operational area of Army Group North would contain the shortest frontage for the German forces operating there than the length of the front lines in the regions of Army Group Centre and Army Group South. However, this part of the Russian Front would experience the largest concentration of Soviet partisan forces, second only to the region of Army Group Centre. It would also encompass the German civilian administrative region for the Baltic states (Lithuania, Latvia and Estonia) – the so-called Reich Commissariat Ostland.[43] The principal headquarters for the secret field police for the region of Army Group North was the Senior Field Police Director at the Commander of the Northern Army Area. This headquarters would act as liaison between the principal secret field police headquarters in Berlin and the various secret field police units in the field operating in the area of

Table 4.2. Location of the staff for the Chief of the Secret Field Police, Army Group North.

Dates	Town	Country
Feb. 1941–Feb. 1944	Voru (Verro)	Estonia
Feb.–Sept. 1944	Cesis (Venden)	Latvia
Sept.–Nov. 1944	Edola (Courland)	Latvia
Nov. 1944–Jan. 1945	Goldingen (Courland)	Latvia

Table 4.3. Location of the units under the Secret Field Police Chief, Army Group North.

Unit	Date	Town Posting	Country
GFP-705	1941–1943	Opochka	Russia
	1943–1944	Ventspils (Windau)	Latvia
	Oct. 1944	Courland	Latvia
GFP-713	Dec. 1941–17 Feb. 1944	Pskov	Russia
	Feb.–Sept. 1944	Cesis (Venden) in the Tuberculosis Institute	Latvia
	Sept.–Oct. 1944	Edole, in Courland	Latvia
	Oct. 1944–18 Jan. 1945	Danzig, Niedersiegen	Germany
	Jan.–May 1945	Neubrandenburg	Germany
GFP-714	1941–1942	Ostrov	Russia
	1944	Courland	Latvia
	1945	West Prussia	Germany
GFP-715	1941–1942	Strugie-Krasnye (Pskov District)	Russia
	1943–July 1944	Parnu (northern tip of the Gulf of Riga)	Estonia
	Aug. 1944–Jan. 1945	Warsaw	Poland
	Feb.–Apr. 1945	HQ OKH	Germany
GFP-722	July–Sept. 1944	Gdov (by Lake Peipus)	Russia
GFP-727[44]	1944	Novgorod (Lake Ilmen)	Russia
	Oct. 1944–May 1945	Courland	Latvia
GFP-728	1944	Luga	Russia

Army Group North. Throughout the war this headquarters staff would be located in the Baltic states of Estonia and Latvia. As the campaign in Russia dragged on, and the Germans began to withdraw, the location of this command changed at certain intervals (see Table 4.2).[45]

A number of territorial groups were directly subordinated to the Chief of the Secret Field Police, Army Group North, and later Army Group Courland (see Table 4.3). In the case of GFP-713, several *Aussenkommando* (external commands) were also created during the war (see Table 4.4).

In addition to these formations, two additional secret field police groups operated directly under army command: the 520th Secret Field Police Group (under 16th Army) and the 501st Secret Field Police Group (under 18th Army). In addition, the 744th Secret Field Police Group (L), a secret formation created from German Luftwaffe personnel, also operated at the disposal of the commander of Army Group North.[46] These were forces that were available to the army commander as additional security troops behind the lines.[47] The secret field police would be more involved in direct killings of the civilian population than was declared shortly after the end of the war. In fact, former secret field police officials made it a point to avoid relating the more criminal activities of the secret field police to the Allied interrogators who interviewed these men after the war. They avoided complicity with the SS killing units in the USSR, given the criminal nature of their duties. Table 4.5 illustrates the large numbers of people who were killed by secret field police units between 1941 and 1942.

Table 4.4. External commands created by the 713th Secret Field Police Group.

External Command	Date Formed and Date Dissolved	Country
Dorpat (Tartu)	1942–Dec. 1943	Estonia
Karamishevo	1942–Dec. 1943	Russia
Seredka	1942–Jan. 1944	Russia
Reval (Tallinn)	1942–Dec. 1943	Estonia
Kresti (Pskov suburb)	Aug. 1943–Feb. 1944	Russia
Slavkovichi (SE Pskov)	Nov. 1943–Feb. 1944	Russia
Volmar (Valmiera)	Mar.–Sept. 1944	Latvia
Lemsal (Limbazi)	Mar. 1944–Sept. 1944	Latvia
Army Group North		
Special Council R (*Sonderrat R*)	June 1943 (in the Pskov prison)	Russia
	Feb. 1944 (Valka, then Wenden)	Latvia
	Sept. 1944 (Edole, Courland)	Latvia
	Nov. 1944 (in the Petri School in Danzig)	Germany

Note: In September 1944 Foreign Command Special Council R absorbed almost all of the personnel of GFP-713. In essence, GFP-713 became a full-time interrogation company for returning German prisoners of war who had been in Russian custody.

Table 4.5. Partisans killed or captured by secret field police units, 1941–1942.

Formation/Date	Partisans captured and/or killed	Source
Secret field police, Army Group North		
12 Oct. 1941*	6,550	* BA-MA WF 03/15831, *Feldpolizeidirektor beim Befehlshaber Heeresgebiet 103.*
Secret field police, Army Group South		
May 1942*	2,729	*BA-MA RH 22/31, *Meldung Direktor GFP, Mai 1942.*
July 1942*	5,599	* BA-MA RH 22/173, *Meldung Direktor GFP, Juli 1942.*
July 1941–July 1942	5,000 in Zhitomir	
Aug. 1942–Dec. 1943	3,000 in Zhitomir	
Secret field police, Army Group B		
Aug. 1942*	291	* BA-MA RH 22/60, *Bericht GFP fur Heeresgebiet B, August 1942.*
Sept. 1942*	693	* BA-MA RH 22/86, s. 27.
Secret field police, Army Group Centre		
Oct. 1942*	1,001	* Christian Gerlach, 'Men of 20 July and the War in the Soviet Union', in Heer & Naumann (eds). *War of Extermination*, p. 134.
Total (1 July 1942–31 Mar. 1943)	21,683*	* BA-MA WF 01/2151, Bl. 816.

Note: The figure given for Army Group Centre is incorrect, for example, GFP-723 kept inaccurate records. The unit claimed in its reports that between July 1941 and the end of 1942 it had shot a total of 1,486 (including 133 Jews).

Chapter 5

The start of the war behind the lines

Guerrilla leaders win wars by being paranoid and ruthless. [Stephen Kinzer]

Rear area security forces and early massacres

As part of General Plan East, the Germans were instructed to act ruthlessly in order to obtain two major goals. The first was to cow the population into submission. The second was to cull the population in order to reduce the number of people in the USSR. This in turn would allow the Nazis to rule unchallenged and create territory for German colonizers. In effect, Russia would cease to exist as a nation. Those who were allowed to survive would do so only to serve their German masters in menial jobs. Education beyond primary school level would also cease to exist for the indigenous population. The New Order therefore offered nothing to the people of the East. How this culling would be accomplished was connected with how the Germans would fight the Soviet guerrillas. In many instances the killing of innocent civilians during anti-partisan sweeps was conducted under the guise of fighting this partisan war. An example of this can be shown in an operation that was launched in late July and early August 1941 in the Pripet marshes, a large swampy region of land that more or less divided Belarus from Ukraine.

This anti-partisan operation was the first major drive conducted in Belarus in 1941 and involved various units, including the newly created SS Cavalry Brigade,[1] as well as Army,[2] security police, security service and Order Police formations.[3] The area chosen was the northern Pripet marshes region, principally in and around the towns of Kobrin, Pinsk, Baranovici and Slutsk. The plan called for the encirclement of up to three Red Army divisions, plus an undisclosed number of partisans. These Red Army units included the 36th and 37th Cavalry Divisions, as well as the 121st Rifle Division. A German Order Police message, decrypted by British military intelligence (MI-14),[4] noted that the *SS Kavallerie Brigade* had executed 7,819 people to date in the region of Minsk, while SS and Police General Erich von dem Bach-Zelewski reported that in the region of Army Group Centre the police had shot around 30,000 people.[5] On 13 September 1941 SS Colonel General and Colonel General of the Police Kurt Daluege, the head of the German Order Police, warned all police commanders in Russia that there was a danger that matters of great secrecy, such as the exact number of executions, might be discovered by the Allies.[6] Based on these decrypted messages, it is obvious that as early as the autumn of 1941 the British knew what the Germans were doing in the Soviet Union. Soviet losses during the operation in the Pripet marshes region were announced on 16 August 1941 by Lieutenant General of the SS and General of the Police Erich von dem Bach-Zelewski, who was the head of the Higher SS and Police Leader Central Russia command. He listed a staggering 15,878 people killed and 830 captured for a German loss of only 17 dead and 36 wounded.[7]

The figure of 15,878 dead Red Army men is curious, especially when we compare this figure with the numbers of Jews killed by the SS Cavalry Brigade during the same period. Jewish researchers have listed the figure of 14,178 Jews killed and 1,001 Red Army soldiers killed during this German drive. These two numbers combined give a figure very close to the 15,878-figure given by author Mark Yerger as the number of Red Army soldiers killed. In addition, Jewish sources list 699 Soviet troops captured for this period. This figure too is not dissimilar to the number of 830 Red Army soldiers quoted by Yerger as captured by the SS Cavalry Brigade. Yerger used records of the actions of the SS Cavalry Brigade in this operation in his research. It is quite possible that the records of the SS Cavalry Brigade could have included the number of Jews killed in the area, in order to increase the body count of enemy dead and thus make the operation seem a greater success when presented in a report. This possibility is not so far fetched, especially when we recall the obsession of the high command of the US Army during the Vietnam war about increasing the kill ratio of US forces, a ratio that was often inflated with civilian deaths.

Early beginnings of the partisan movement

One of the earliest partisan groups organized was created from a core of 30 communist party functionaries from the Chernigov region on 8 August 1941.[8] This *Otriad* (partisan group) was organized into two teams: a demolition group and a combat group. In the spring of 1942 it formed the basis for a partisan brigade. As stated earlier, the campaign against the partisans in 1941 was initially considered negligible by the Germans, given that the guerrilla movement was disorganized and still in its infancy. Partisan 'companies' were in reality made up of 28 to 40 men apiece. One example was a 28-man unit formed with the aid of the Chovet Polessia Kolhoz, in the vicinity of the Rok District, and led by a Jewish commander named Bredyekovich. In September 1941 the 'Victory or Death' Partisan Battalion was established in the Podolsk Rayon, while another, as yet unidentified, partisan battalion was formed near Kharkov around the same time.[9] In Krichev local Komsomol members

ıbers of the *Reichsarbeitsdienst* (National Labour Service) stand guard with their dogs. ıbers of this organization were not only tasked with numerous construction jobs, but were employed as guards, and when necessary could also serve in the field as auxiliary troops. ır versatility was vital in occupied territories of the Soviet Union. (*Author's collection*)

German soldiers using German Shepherd dogs for tracking. These animals were invaluable in the fight against the guerrillas. In the early 1930s the German Army rebuilt its military hound training school in Brandenburg near Berlin where it could accommodate and train u to 2,000 dogs at any one time. By the start of the Second World War around 200,000 dogs h been trained. (*Bundesarchiv*)

German soldiers stand at ease as the armoured train commander addresses the reinforced platoon. Armoured trains, like dogs, proved to be vital in protecting not only the transport of supplies to the front but also the railway itself and the surrounding installations from the threat of partisan attacks. (*Bundesarchiv*)

Members of a German 37mm Flak gun stand at rest as their armoured train rumbles throug the Ukrainian countryside. By 1943 the Luftwaffe no longer controlled the skies in the USSR and it became necessary to outfit the German trains with both armoured wagons that carrie cannons and anti-aircraft weapons to protect the train from enemy air attacks. (*Bundesarchiv*)

improvised armoured train rumbling through the Russian countryside, autumn 1942. Here see men on a flat car that has been outfitted with firing slits. Behind is a captured French k that is either being transported or being employed as an armoured platform for the oured train. *(Bundesarchiv)*

Reserve Police Battalion 101 marching in front of its commander, 1940. The German Order Police proved critical to the occupation of territories captured by the Germans during the war. The German police comprised one leg in the framework of security forces and became heavily engaged in the fight against the partisans. (*United States Holocaust Memorial Museum*)

olice commander and his staff giving out final instructions before an operation. The police e not only instrumental in leading the attack against the partisans: the entire organization complicit in the murder of Jews, gypsies and others whom the Nazi state considered mies of the Reich. (*Author's collection*)

Members of a police unit after an *Aktion*. The employment of police battalions and regiments in the USSR proved to be substantial. However, as the war turned against the Reich, the Germans found themselves employing these police units on an emergency basis on

lembers of a police armoured car unit study a map during an anti-partisan operation in the ummer of 1942. The Order Police created several armoured car and tank companies for ervice principally against the partisans. Usually, these companies utilized captured enemy quipment. Here a pre-war Austrian Steyr armoured car is shown. (*Bundesarchiv*)

As the partisan war continued and the guerrillas grew in number, the Germans found it necessary to recruit local volunteers to help fight the partisan menace. Here is General Bronislav Kaminski (*second from right*), conferring with German Order Police personnel. Kaminski led a full brigade of Russian volunteers in the Bryansk region of central Russia. In 1944 he and his unit were withdrawn to Lepel in northern Belarus, where they continued to assist the Germans. One regiment from the Kaminski Brigade also took part in crushing the Warsaw Uprising in 1944. (*Bundesarchiv*)

SS Lieutenant-General and Lieutenant-General of the Police Erich von dem Bach Zelewski. In 1942 Heinrich Himmler appointed him to lead the entire anti-partisan war effort in the Soviet Union. In August 1944 he was also made responsible for crushing the Warsaw Uprising. (*Bundesarchiv*)

Multiple hangings of suspected partisans. The harsh manner in which the Germans ruled in the USSR, and the equally brutal way they fought the anti-partisan war, only fuelled more anti-German resistance. Wholesale executions were meant to cow the population, but these heinous acts simply added more fuel to the fire of resistance. (*Minsk State Archive*)

A *Schutzmannschaft* member beckonging to fellow soldiers. In the background is a house recently gutted by fire. The guerrilla and anti-partisan struggle in the USSR was waged with particular brutality. (*Museum of Modern History*)

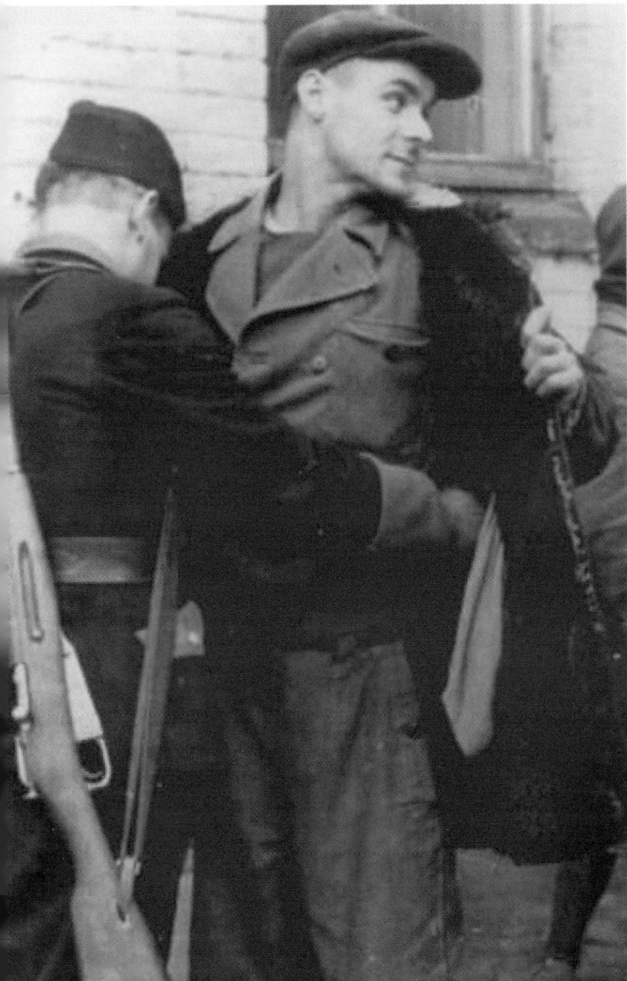

Schutzmannschaft members passing another burning home during the same action. In Belarussia alone, the war, as well as the campaign behind the front lines, destroyed 80% of all housing between 1941 and 1944, in villages, towns and cities alike.
(*Museum of Modern History*)

A *Schutzmannschaft* volunteer checks the pockets of a partisan suspect. For a person caught with a weapon, the penalty was death. (*Minsk State Archive*)

A German Gendarmerie NCO recruits a Russian volunteer for service in the *Schutzmannschaf* spring 1942. *(Minsk State Archive)*

While SS officers stand and observe, *Schutzmannschaft* recruits are taught the basics of marksmanship, some time in 1943. *(Minsk State Archive)*

nmer 1941 and the first partisan units are being formed. In this propaganda photo from the iod, an old veteran from the Russian Civil War teaches students and workers the basics of ıting with a bayonet. *(United States Library of Congress)*

1941 turned into 1942, the Central Headquarters for the Partisan Movement began to send n behind the German lines. These specialists were knowledgeable in demolitions, nmunications and weapons, and typically parachuted in behind the lines. In some instances ere the local partisans had a small airstrip, they were flown in using a Polikarpov Po-2 lane. *(United States Library of Congress)*

By the autumn of 1941, the Soviet partisan presence was causing trouble behind the German lines. When the Red Army launched their winter counteroffensive on 5 December 1941, the guerrillas who had been hiding in the deep forests and swamps of the USSR sprang into action. Nowhere now was it safe for a German to travel alone. (*Bundesarchiv*)

had established the 'Krasny October' Partisan Battalion, while the 'Komarov Partisan Battalion' was organized near Pinsk.[10]

The platoon-sized partisan formation was organized in late September 1941. A month later, in October, this 'company' was grouped with two other guerrilla companies, forming a 180-strong partisan unit. Led by a Jewish partisan commander named Davidovich, the formation's first engagement included the destruction of a German truck and ten Germans riding inside.[11] Other engagements included battles near the town of Limovichi, blowing up a bridge over the Orissa river, and destroying the Palichi railway station. This small group was part of the cadre that in 1942 numbered nearly 5,000 partisans in and around Gomel. Thus a small nucleus of guerrillas that formed in 1941 had blossomed into a 5,000-strong partisan force by 1942. Numerous other groups of guerrillas such as these were formed in Belarus during the summer and autumn of 1941, but the Germans never regarded them as important during that initial year of the invasion, as attested by this post-war estimate:[12]

> In general, from the German point of view, control of the occupied territory had been adequately organized in 1941. Its main purposes were to subjugate and exploit a conquered population and to keep the front commands' lines of communication open, and those were being accomplished. Consequently, the army group rear area commanders, Korück, and SS police commanders did not stage extensive anti-partisan campaigns.[13]

Thus, by ignoring small units of guerrillas as being too small to waste effort on, the Germans allowed a partisan cancer to slowly grow behind the German lines. This German reluctance to spend much effort and time going after small units of guerrillas was repeated again and again during 1941. In all fairness, it was also true that security forces were stretched to the limit by the autumn of that year. By then these small platoon-sized units had grown into company-sized formations and were therefore becoming more dangerous. For example, by early August 1941 the situation behind the lines of the German 2nd Army was such that it had become difficult for supplies to get through due to attacks by bypassed Red Army forces operating from the numerous forests in the area. In spite of this threat, and in variance of Hitler's order that the local populace would be punished for any guerrilla activity, General Field Marshal Maximilian Freiherr von Weichs, the commander of 2nd Army, passed on instructions to his various corps commands that the indigenous inhabitants were not to be shot unless irrefutable proof existed as to their guilt in partisan activity.[14] At the same time 2nd Army had requested additional *Sicherheitsdienst* forces in its rear, with the excuse that only the trained SS security service units could ferret out the Soviet communist

'Bolshevik' elements that were directing the guerrilla attacks behind its lines. The unit requested was *Sonderkommando* 7b, led by SS Major Günther Rausch, but *Sonderkommando* 7b was said to be too preoccupied and had too few resources to aid 2nd Army.[15] Eventually, the German XIII. Army Corps detached one of its units, the 252nd Infantry Division, for employment against the guerrillas operating behind its lines in August and September 1941.[16] By their actions in the rear of 2nd Army, the Soviet partisans had forcibly diverted a German division from the front lines.

The partisans and the German rail system in Russia in 1941

In 1980 the Commandant of the Marine Corps, General Robert H. Barrows, remarked that 'Amateurs talk tactics, but professionals study logistics', and there can be no truer statement on the importance of supplies in war. The German Army Quartermaster General in 1941 was General of the Infantry Georg Thomas, who served as the Chief of the General Office of the Army Economy (General Army Office), overseeing logistics, supply and procurement for the German Army. General Thomas played a significant role in managing the immense logistical challenges faced by the German military during the war, including coordinating the allocation of resources, equipment and supplies for the Army's operations on multiple fronts. But it was his immense efforts on the Eastern Front that earned him a reputation as an excellent organizer and miracle worker. The problem he faced in Russia was not merely that his supply trains would have to travel through hostile territories in order to reach the front-line troops – indeed, there were myriad issues that needed to be overcome.

The first of these was the difference in the gauge of the European railway tracks versus the Russian gauge. During the Second World War the standard gauge for most European railway tracks was 1,435mm (4ft 8.5in), while the standard gauge for Russian railway tracks, known as the Russian gauge, was wider, at 1,520mm (4ft 11.8in). This difference created logistical challenges for military operations, particularly during the German invasion of the Soviet Union, since trains and equipment designed for one gauge could not easily operate on the other gauge without modification or the use of special adapter cars. As a result, efforts were made to adapt railway infrastructure and rolling stock to facilitate transportation between European and Russian territories. These efforts included the construction of dual-gauge tracks in some areas, the use of specialized equipment to transfer cargo between different gauge tracks, and the standardization of equipment to minimize logistical constraints. However, despite these efforts, the difference in gauges remained a significant logistical hurdle throughout the war, impacting the efficiency and flexibility of transportation networks on the Eastern Front.

In addition, the Russian winters were so severe that the German locomotive engines of the Reichsbahn (German National Railway) would often not work in severe cold conditions. Even the coal that was dug up from the Donetz basin in eastern Ukraine needed to be mixed with European coal supplies because the German locomotives would not run on pure Soviet coal. In addition, European locomotive engines could not endure cold conditions. During the winter of 1941/1942, for example, 80 per cent of German locomotives were put out of action owing to the cold weather.[17] During 1941 partisan attacks on the German rail system inside the USSR proved to be minimal. Even in January and February 1942, at the height of the Red Army winter counter-offensive, no more than twenty or thirty attacks on the railways were made by partisans in the region of Army Group Centre. As for supplies getting through by road, it was true that more and more attacks were taking place as the summer of 1941 drifted into autumn and then winter. But these partisan attacks were still relatively small in size so that General Thomas could rightly claim that the Soviet guerrillas were not impeding the flow of supplies in any significant way.

Nevertheless, there were sensational attacks against the German rail system in 1941 that eventually prompted Adolf Hitler to remove control of the rails in the East from the German National Railway and assign it instead to the military in the spring of 1942. The most notable and infamous episode involved the derailment of a German hospital train as it was taking wounded German soldiers from central Russia back to the Reich. The train was derailed by partisans at night while it was travelling in western Belarus. The guerrillas killed the surviving German guards and the medical staff accompanying the injured, before the wounded passengers who had survived the crash were drenched in paraffin and set ablaze. They died in agonizing pain.[18] The following day the Germans took their revenge and destroyed three nearby villages, killing everyone. Of course, this only produced the kind of hatred that created more guerrillas. This incident epitomized what author Alan Clark meant when he wrote: 'A new dimension of cruelty began to throw its shadow over the war in the East.'[19]

The rise of an organized partisan army and early strategy

The beginning of the partisan movement in the Pripet marshes region originated from the men of numerous shattered and splintered formations belonging to the Soviet Fifth Army. In the summer of 1941 the Fifth Army was located in the eastern Pripet marshes, strung out along a 150-mile line straddling the right flank of Army Group Centre: 'Under Popov they were busy restoring cohesion to their shattered brigades, laying the foundation of the partisan movement, and operating vigorously with their cavalry – the only mobile arm left to them in any strength.'[20]

In the autumn of 1941 the partisan movement began to be organized in the rear of the German front lines in the USSR. By then, numerous partisan units were in radio contact with the head of the partisan movement in Moscow. The employment of more partisan bands equipped with radios also aided the Red Army's intelligence-gathering effort. The priority which Moscow gave to its guerrilla bands was clear: target local collaborators and intimidate the population into cooperating with us. Those who refused to comply were killed, often in a most brutal fashion. A strategy developed where the Soviet partisans were to mutilate any German soldiers that they had killed or captured, and leave their bodies along roadsides, at road intersections or at the edge of a town or village, so that the German command could easily find them. Once the local German command discovered the crime, the Germans themselves would do the work of alienating the local population by turning their vengeance on innocent civilians living in the area. This, of course, was the whole point of this partisan strategy.

The Germans, who entered the USSR with the intention of behaving harshly towards the local population, never thought twice about these punitive, collective-guilt measures, which in turn helped to create animosity and more partisan volunteers from the populace. By the spring of 1942 the Soviet partisan movement was ready to flower and expand.

Chapter 6

Collaboration in Belarus and central Russia, 1941–1942

It's not treason if you win. [Lisa Shearin]

Willing collaborators

As they had done elsewhere in Europe, the Germans wanted to wage a war of annihilation against the local Jewish population, in addition to fighting any organized resistance. The rear area forces, therefore, needed to be sufficient for both tasks. When it appeared that their forces were insufficient, even after a considerable reinforcement in the spring of 1942, the Germans resorted to recruitment of locally raised collaborationist forces. In fact, the number of these indigenous volunteers would increase by almost a factor of ten from 1941 to 1942. In 1941 only an estimated 33,000 Estonian, Latvian, Lithuanian, Ukrainian, Belarusian and Russian volunteers were serving in the German SS and police forces. That number would increase to around 300,000 a year later.[1] Guerrilla activity in 1941 was limited; the Soviet partisan movement was not yet organized. As the German armies surged forwards in the summer and autumn of 1941 many Red Army units were bypassed. Other Soviet units had surrendered and were told to march back (even without guards) to the slowly advancing German infantry. Many of these men ran away and ended up hiding in the forests behind the German rear areas. These men would emerge in the spring of 1942 as the backbone of the Soviet guerrilla movement. From the very start, the *Vernichtungskrieg* against the Jews in the USSR was followed with great vigour and enthusiasm. Alan Clark has suggested that this enthusiasm was not limited to the Jewish population, but was also meted out to the general Soviet population, and further, that this enthusiasm to punish also came with what the Germans refer to as *schadenfreude*, a sadistic pleasure gleaned from the misfortune of others.[2] The Nazis had indoctrinated the German soldier to consider a Jewish person not only less than human, but synonymous with being a partisan fighter. Therefore, by this definition simply being Jewish made you an enemy of the Third Reich and subject to immediate execution if captured. The phrase *Jeder Jude ist ein Partisanenkämpfer* ('Every Jew is a partisan fighter') became the catchphrase that permitted not just the SS and police but the German Army as a whole to commit legalized mass murder.

The other primary function of rear area forces was the establishment of a safe rear area for the advancing German armies by rounding up bypassed Soviet military forces, protecting vital road, rail and communication centres, airfields,[3] bridges and other structures and buildings of importance to the war effort. The rear area commands were also responsible for suppressing any resistance activity which threatened the lines of communication. The German command had issued a series of orders prior to the start of the Russian campaign which had been geared to legally clear any German soldier or unit from accusations of murder (aside from fighting on the front lines and killing the enemy). Thus, when the Russian campaign began, the German military was operating under a different set of rules from those that had pertained during their conquest of western Europe. The Nazis intentionally set the scene for the German military to act more brutally towards the indigenous population. It wasn't just the illegal orders permitting executions to take place without due process, but years of indoctrination embedding in the average German soldier the belief that the eastern Slav was subhuman and therefore unworthy of life (*Lebensunwertes Leben*).

This led the Germans to wage a war in the East the likes of which had never been fought before. The very harshness of the Russian campaign also numbed those who waged it until they valued life very cheaply. German wholesale massacres of the Jews and *Zigeunerinnen* (Romany), coupled with the brutalization of the non-Jewish population, would work to eventually turn most of the people in the occupied East against the Germans. It also led directly to the growth of the partisan movement, with many Jews opting to join the partisans, even though the probability of survival was not great. One such example comes from Belarus in early 1942:

> Confronted by such sadism, Jews everywhere sought some means of survival. But even in White Russia, where units of Red Army partisan groups had begun fighting behind German lines, the path to resistance was perilous. After the Purim massacre in Minsk, many Jews had tried to escape from the [Minsk] ghetto to join the partisans. One group, led by Nahum Feldman, reached the forests just as a battle was being fought between Germans and partisans, and, unable to approach the battle zone, was forced to return to the ghetto. Others who escaped were caught by the Germans while on their way to the forests and shot. One well known Jewish Communist in Minsk, Hirsh Skovia, reached the partisans, but died when his feet froze during a German attack on the partisan base.[4]

However, in the summer and autumn of 1941 the Germans had yet to fully alienate the local non-Jewish population. This was particularly true in the

Baltic States and in Ukraine, where the older generation still remembered the independence they had gained from Russia shortly after the end of the First World War because of German assistance. It was only after the German Army withdrew that the Russian Bolsheviks once again squashed Ukrainian and Baltic aspirations for independence. In fact, so hated was the communist system that recruitment of the Belarusian male population into the pro-German auxiliary police forces had begun almost from the start of the German occupation – so much so that by the end of December 1941, 3,682 Belarusians were serving in the Auxiliary Police Order service in more than 55 Gendarmerie posts throughout the region.[5] Soviet guerrillas were also vying for Belarusian recruits to fill the ranks of the partisan forces. In September 1941 a Belarusian villager explained to a Soviet partisan, dropped by parachute to help organize a guerrilla unit, why his village was reluctant to take part in any anti-German guerrilla actions:

> Horses pulled a cart into Lukoml, and inside the cart was an interpreter who had been shot dead and a German officer who was breathing his last. He was laying there, his face downwards with a knife sticking out of the nape of his neck. People say he just about managed to whisper: 'A Jude, a Jew, that is, killed me,' before kicking the bucket. So, by the order of the Kommandant they collected the Jews of Lukoml, about one hundred and fifty families, just imagine. The children they buried alive. And you are telling us to attack them in our village.[6]

The first to recruit these willing Belarusian volunteers were the secret field police units, which wished to take advantage of the locals' intimate knowledge of the countryside and its people.[7] This was done at a time when recruitment of eastern troops was still against Hitler's wishes. German reports from *Einsatzkommando* 8 also mention the recruitment of volunteers in the Belarusian region of Baranovichi as early as the beginning of July 1941. In fact, before the German occupation of Belarus was over, the SS security service would raise a special battalion, manned by volunteers dressed in security service field uniforms. Units would be well armed, with both German and Russian weapons. The first known action against the Belarusian Jews by fellow non-Jewish Belarusians occurred in October 1941 in the town of Borisov. The incident was described to Admiral Wilhelm Canaris of the *Abwehr* (German Armed Forces Intelligence) by way of a letter from one of his émigré Russian special officers named Sönnicken, who acted as interpreter and liaison between the Germans and the indigenous population. The report stated that it concerned the massacre of 7,620 Jews in Borisov in October 1941, which was carried out entirely by the local administration appointed by the Germans, with the aid of the local Belarusian security police.

In Sönnicken's opinion, the members of the new Belarusian volunteers of the German security police were mostly former communists, while the assistant to the Belarusian mayor of Borisov was a former regular policeman who recalled the Pogroms of the pre-revolutionary period with satisfaction and glee. The German Order Police in Belarus would raise half a dozen battalions, beginning in 1942. Initially, these self-defence units were known as the Belarusian Self-Defence Force (abbreviated in the local language as BNS). In addition, a Belarusian *Heimwehr* (Home Guard) was created, akin to the German *Volkssturm* ('People's Assault', i.e., Home Guard). It comprised men too young or too old to serve in the BNS.[8] It was at this time that a Russian émigré named Dimitri Kozmovich appeared in Belarus. He had come to the attention of the Germans on account of his successful operations against Soviet guerrilla forces in the Smolensk and Bryansk regions of central Russia. Kozmovich was thought to be just another Czarist-era intellectual; his family apparently came from the Belarusian *Krestyanin* (peasantry).[9] But he had done something that was rare during the Czar's time: he had actually gone through the ranks of the Russian Imperial Army, eventually becoming an officer. After the Bolsheviks won the Russian Civil War, he, alongside other Czarist officers, went into exile and settled in Belgrade, Yugoslavia.

As soon as the Germans entered the Soviet Union, the sheer vastness of the country quickly made them realize that the number of police and army forces allocated for the rear areas was wholly insufficient. A pro-German Belarusian civilian administration was organized in the autumn of 1941. This indigenous civilian body was to work with the local German military and civilian heads. Each Rayon established the security forces for that region. Among other duties, they were responsible for creating a list of volunteers and ordering the call-up of men for the self-defence companies and battalions that were being established. The order to create these units originated from the German Order Police, which was establishing outposts for the local police and Gendarmerie precincts all over the occupied regions. In the major towns and cities the Germans also had the *Gemeindepolizei* (municipal police), tasked with operating in the major civilian population centres. These posts also demanded volunteers. Eventually six major police commands – known as Police State Administration Posts – were established in White Russia. The number of men in each command depended on the size of the locality, but on average they contained between 30 and 100 men. The posts were as follows:[10]

- I – Glebokie
- II – Vileika
- III – Minsk and Slutsk
- IV – Lida and Novogrudok
- V – Slonim
- VI – Baranovichi and Hansevitchi.

In July 1941 the German Gendarmerie strength in the region of Belarus was only 75 men. On 19 August that figure had been increased to 315 men and by

14 October another 250 men had arrived. In July and August 1941 more police reinforcements were called into the USSR as the Order Police Main Office in Berlin received more and more reports about how large an area needed to be patrolled. In addition, as the German armies advanced, more and more enemy territory was captured which required more security forces. When organized partisan attacks began, the need for further troops was soon realized. The necessity for more policemen became so great that Himmler dissolved the police outposts between the annexed Polish territories and the so-called *Generalgouvernement* on 27 July 1941 in order to send these men to the USSR. On 7 August an additional 8 Gendarmerie officers and 40 enlisted men, plus 80 police reservists, received orders to report to the commander-in-chief of the uniformed police in Cracow. From there they were to be sent to Russia. On 19 August 1941 a major mobilization of the German rural and municipal police was ordered, followed in October 1941 by another call up:

> By order of the RFSS, Gendarmerie mission detachments (*Gendarmerie Einsatzkommandos*) consisting of 5 officers, 10 police troops and 60 police reservists were to be established in the cities of Dorpat, Riga, Kovno and Minsk ... On 14 October Himmler authorized the mobilization of 200 Gendarmerie personnel, community police personnel and police reservists for assignments to the Ukrainian General Commissariat of Volhynia alone. On the same day, a separate order directed the assignment of 250 uniformed police personnel and police reservists for individual duty in the General Commissariat of Belarus. The *Ordnungspolizei* accomplished these mobilizations by siphoning forces from numerous Reich regions.[11]

In spite of the assistance given by the local civilian administration in calling up volunteers, from 1 July until 31 December 1941 there were only 28 auxiliary policemen in Baranovichi, which was part of the Police State Administration Post VI district. The overall numbers increased dramatically in 1942. Even so, depending on the size and importance of the locality, the number of men ranged from 20 to 120. By the spring of 1943 partisan attacks were increasing in number and becoming bolder. While attacks on police posts were rare in 1941 and 1942, they increased in 1943. These attacks usually caused losses within the ranks of the collaborationist police and civilian administration. Table 6.1 shows the numbers of auxiliary police recruited for the Baranovichi region, 1941–1944.[12]

Experimental volunteer units in Belarusia, 1941–1942

During the first year of the invasion of the Soviet Union, many citizens of the USSR who came under the authority of the Germans either by being taken prisoner or by simply living in regions that were now controlled by the Third Reich, saw an opportunity for change. Many people living in the USSR had

Table 6.1. Belarusian Auxiliary Police recruits in Baranovichi, 1941–1944.

Date	Enlisted Auxiliaries	NCO Auxiliaries	Total Recruited
1 July–31 Dec. 1941	22	6	28
1 Jan.–30 June 1942	8	1	9
7 July–31 Dec. 1942	94	5	99
1 Jan.–30 June 1943	35	–	35
1 July–31 Dec. 1943	18	–	18
1 Jan. 1944	20	–	20
Recruit date unknown	131	1	132
Total	328	13	341

chafed at the totalitarianism of Stalin's regime, and hoped that one day they could free themselves of it. It was in this initial year of the Russian campaign, when the local population had yet to ascertain exactly who the Nazis were, that many came forward to try to assist the German invader. In this way several pro-German units were created.

Graukopf Verbände

In the autumn of 1941, in a large industrial plant called Osintorf (not far from Smolensk), a new experimental Russian unit was formed from former Russian prisoners of war by German Army intelligence.[13] The Germans unofficially referred to it as the *Graukopf Verbände* ('Greyhead Brigade'), after its first commander who had greying hair.[14] The Russian commander was Colonel Konstantine Kromiadi.[15] The unit initially had a strength of perhaps 350–400 men and was intended to be used for special operations behind the Red Army lines.[16] It was formed officially in March 1942.[17] The unit included former Red Army as well as Czarist officers. The known Czarist officers included ex-Colonel Konstantin Kromiadi, Second Lieutenant Igor Zakharov and Lieutenant Grigory von Lamsdorff, an émigré Russian count. These last two officers had fought in the Spanish Civil War before signing up as interpreters in the German Army intelligence service. Although the formation only had about six battalions and was therefore the strength of a brigade, it was grandiosely titled the Russian National People's Army. The originators of the unit were Russian émigrés, but the majority of the men were ex-Red Army soldiers who had been recruited from the large number of German prisoner-of-war camps that had sprung up all across the rear areas of the advancing German armies.

Living conditions in these prisoner-of-war camps was abysmal. The vast majority of Red Army soldiers captured in 1941 had to march hundreds of miles to makeshift German camps. The Germans were completely caught by surprise at the sheer number of Russians that fell into their hands. The captured Russian prisoners taken between June 1941 and February 1942 totalled an astounding 3,300,000. But by February 1942 only about 1,300,000 were still alive. Some 2 million men had died of malnutrition or had been executed for being a Communist Party functionary or for being Jewish. The cruelty of the war in the East, exacerbated by Nazi racial theories, created the conditions that allowed the Germans to starve millions of Soviet prisoners to death. Between 800,000 and 1,000,000 men eventually volunteered to serve in the German armed forces. Many simply did so to escape a slow death in the camps. Some may have been motivated by a hatred of communism, but the desire to survive was likely the paramount reason for wishing to volunteer.

The uniforms used in the Graukopf Brigade were Russian-style gymnast blouses and trousers, with Czarist Army epaulettes for the officers. Some of the Russian émigré officers who volunteered to join the brigade had been *Sonderführer* (special officers) in German commands, basically acting as interpreters. They therefore wore initially German uniforms and insignia. This soon changed when they removed the German Army emblems and replaced them with Czarist-era badges and insignia. The German blouses and trousers were retained, however. The last Russian commander of the Graukopf Brigade was Colonel Vladimir Boyarsky, who had been a General Staff officer in the 41st Guards Rifle Division until he was wounded and captured during the summer of 1941. Sven Steenberg has described Colonel Boyarsky as a bright yet impulsive Russian nationalist, who hated Stalinism and was prepared to cooperate with the Germans so long as their goal was liberation and not conquest.

Colonel Boyarsky had been recruited at a special Russian prisoner-of-war camp near Lötzen in Germany which housed high-ranking Red Army officers. Other officers in the unit included the émigré Igor Sakharov, who was the 31-year-old son of a Czarist-era general, and Konstantine Grigorievich Kromiadi, who was a Russian of Greek origin. A camp for the unit was established at Osintorf near Smolensk. By the autumn of 1941 the unit was well into being formed. At its height it would contain six infantry battalions but in the autumn of 1941 it was little more than an over-strength battalion and was initially titled *Bataillon z.b.V.* (Battalion for Special Employment) under *Unternehmen Graukopf* (Operation Greyhead). The 203rd Defence Group, a German Army intelligence unit stationed in Smolensk, was responsible for the organization.

The Belarusian police

The first formations of the Belarusian auxiliary police appeared in the eastern part of Belarusian territory even before the General District of White Ruthenia was established by the Germans. The creation of these formations was done on the initiative of those Germans who were concerned about increasing the numbers of security troops in the rear of Army Group Centre. The result was that by 1942 dozens of White Russian Auxiliary Service (*Ordnungsdienst*) police units were operating in eastern Belarus. The units were created principally by the Belarusian émigrés Dimitry Kosmovich and Mikhail Vitushka. They were made up of infantry and cavalry formations, most of which were led by former Red Army officers. These units were created by recruiting men from German prisoner-of-war camps. The troops were a mixture of volunteer civilians and recently released Red Army men, organized into companies of between 100 and 150 men each. A series of procedures was introduced in order to persuade the locals to join or assist these collaborationist formations. The mission of these auxiliary police units entailed food requisitioning, protecting the harvest, tax collecting and general police duties. It is important to note that in some cases these units cleared some regions of Belarus from communist control without the presence of German troops.

In August 1941 Belarusian nationalist forces in the area of Polesie and Mozyr conducted sweeps that bagged numerous Red Army stragglers, some partisan forces and even a few People's Commissariat for Internal Affairs units. The Belarusians were aided by the 10,000-strong Ukrainian nationalist guerrilla force led by M. Borovets. This force was part of the *Ukrayins'ka povstans'ka armiia* (*UPA*, Ukrainian Insurgent Army). The Germans did not participate in this drive, but merely observed. In the regions that were no longer under the control of Soviet forces but not yet under full German control, Belarusian and Ukrainian nationalists established a civilian administration, even publishing newspapers, and temporarily ended collectivization by redistributing the land to the peasants. In Polesie armed Belarusian units were spontaneously organized and began operating as a local constabulary. These indigenous police forces operated irrespective of the Germans, who only began to organize control of the region around October 1941.

The amount of autonomy offered to Belarusian collaborators varied from region to region and town to town. In one area the Germans allowed schools to reopen, while in others they closed them. The same thing occurred with regard to farm collectives, where some were ordered to be kept, while in some regions the more enlightened German administration allowed them to be broken up and divided amongst the farmers (despite the fact that this ran contrary to standing German orders to maintain the Soviet collectives). Chaos reigned, especially in the first year of the war, as the Germans struggled to decide just exactly what they wanted to do with the newly conquered territories. Unfortunately for the pro-German collaborationist movement, there were more unenlightened German administrators than good ones who understood that the only way to defeat Stalin and Stalinism was to offer the Soviet people a better alternative to communism.

The most common German civilian administrators were the knuckle-dragging, low-brow types who had little or no experience in dealing with any foreign peoples. Most had little or no administrative experience whatsoever. If lucky, they were the recipients of a 90-day crash course in 'schools' which taught foreign administrative rule. In reality they learned nothing that would help them to understand the very people they were to rule. These men were quickly nicknamed *Goldfasanen* (Golden Pheasants), after the golden epaulettes worn on the shoulders of their brown Nazi Party uniforms. Most were middle-aged men who had gone through the defeat of the First World War and the humiliation of the Treaty of Versailles. To them, hatred and bitterness had become a way of life. They brought with them to the East that hatred, and a desire to even the score. The recipients of their wrath turned out to be those they were meant to rule and administer.

After the creation of the Belarusian General District by the Germans, responsibility for maintaining order was assigned to the SS and Police Leader White Ruthenia headquarters, which at this time was led by SS Brigadier General and Major General of the Police Carl Zenner, who held the post from 14 August 1941 to 22 May 1942. In due course, all Belarusian police forces created from the population were reformed under his tutelage; they were initially referred to as *Hilfspolizei* (auxiliary police), but later the term *Schutzmannschaft* (Self-defence) was employed. The term was used to denote the indigenous auxiliary police volunteers. City and rural (Gendarmerie) police were also formed from Belarusian volunteers after the Germans had occupied all Belarusian cities and the larger towns. This was also done in conjunction with the local civilian collaborationist government.

In July 1941 the émigré Dimitry Kosmovich became the chief of all the Belarusian auxiliary police, with his headquarters in Minsk. The local police chief of a region would supervise the auxiliary police volunteers, but regionally they were still subject to the local SS and Police Leader command. The two principal duties of the auxiliary police were the maintenance of the order in the occupied areas and the surveillance of the local population, with the emphasis on checking the papers of suspicious persons. As the partisan threat grew, the Germans attempted to enlarge the Belarusian auxiliary police. They also tried to make them more mobile and thus more flexible in order to better deal with the growing partisan menace. A meeting was held at the beginning of October 1941 at the headquarters of Army Group Centre regarding this growing partisan danger.[18] The meeting netted two major results. First, the decision was made to employ, whenever possible, regular German Army units in the suppression of partisan activity. Secondly, the Nazi belief that *Jeder Jude ist ein guerrillakämpfer* was brought to its hateful fruition when the decision was made that in the fight against the partisan threat the army was to take part in targeting *any* Jews within their area of operation. The first employment of this new policy saw the massacre of 150 Jewish men, women and children in the central Belarusian town of Krucha on 10 October 1941. The murders were perpetrated by members of the 3rd Company, 691st Infantry Regiment, part of the 339th Static Infantry Division which at the time was serving as part of the German rear area security forces for Army Group Centre. In connection with this effort to improve the effectiveness of the auxiliary police, the German Armed Forces High Command eventually published instructions on how to deal with the partisan menace. The notes taken at the meeting held in early October 1941 at Army Group Centre headquarters were added to other directives on how to deal with the guerrilla threat and published in early December 1941. The new pamphlet was titled 'Special Instructions for Fighting Partisan Bands'. In particular, it stressed that 'the use of local auxiliary groups in the struggle against the guerrillas is justifiable and necessary. The knowledge of the local region, climate and language makes it possible for these indigenous troops to apply guerrilla tactics against the partisans and combat them more effectively.'[19]

Thus, according to this new German directive, the employment of indigenous collaborationist forces alongside German troops was of great importance in successfully dealing with the partisan threat. The directive also allowed for further recruitment of the local population, even at the static level, where villagers were recruited to serve as static self-defence forces known as *Heimatschutz* (Home Defence) by the Germans. The static defence units were easily armed with leftover Red Army rifles and pistols. The rapid withdrawal and destruction of Red Army forces in Belarus during the summer and autumn of 1941 had enabled many weapons to be gathered. The principal role of the Home Defence units was the guarding of crops and livestock against theft by either Polish or Red Army partisans. Apparently, the rapid German advance in the summer months of 1941 had prevented the Red Army from fully mobilizing a large number of able-bodied men of military age before the Soviet Army withdrew from Belarus. These men were now selected for service by both the Germans and the Belarusian collaborationist authorities. The local partisans also saw these men as potential recruits.

Chapter 7

The war against the Jews and the partisans resurgent

One death is a tragedy, but a million is just a statistic. [Joseph Stalin[1]]

Organization for murder

Before the start of Operation Barbarossa, the Nazis organized four Special Action Groups – mobile killing units in order to destroy the Jewish population in the East. They were named *Einsatzgruppe* A, B, C and D. *Einsatzgruppe* A – was assigned the job of eliminating the Jewish population in the Baltic States. However, it would be a small, ad-hoc, independent killing unit that would actually begin the war against the Jews in this area. This formation set out from the city of Tilsit as early as 23 June 1941, just a day after the start of the German invasion of the Soviet Union. In Tilsit SS Major Hans-Joachim Böhme moved his men in the direction of Kaunas (Kovno) with an improvised SD-Einsatzkommando. This ad-hoc group included SS Major Werner Hersmann and members of the Memel[2] city state protection police force, who drove into Lithuania with the *Einsatzkommando* under the leadership of their police director, *SA Oberführer* Bernhard Fischer-Schweder. By 25 June 1941 SD Commando Tilsit had arrived in Kaunas.[3] The unit began a series of killings that very day, shooting 214 people in Krottingen (German spelling), then moved on and killed another 111 people in Polangen on 27 June 1941.[4] On 2 July the Tilsit force killed 133 people in Tauroggen and a day later they shot another 317 men and 5 women in Georgenburg (German spelling), then proceeded that same day to shoot 316 people in Augustovo and 68 in Mariampole.[5]

On 16 July 1941 the headquarters of *Einsatzgruppe* A was located in Riga, Latvia, while one of its component parts, *Einsatzkommando* 1b, was situated in Dünaburg (Daugavpils). On 22 July the records for *Einsatzgruppe* A diligently recorded the killing of one Jew in Pagirai. A day later it was the turn of the Jews in Kedainiai, where the Germans liquidated 125 people. Of this number, 95 were listed as communist Jews, while the rest were written down as non-Jewish, Lithuanian communist functionaries. On 24 July 1941 the security service unit from Tilsit was once again in action, killing 201 people in the town of Garsden.

Genocide in the East

The killings went on. On 25 July 1941 the Tilsit force killed 103 Jews in Mariampole. Of that number, 90 were adult males and 13 were Jewish children. Three days later one of the mobile-killing units entered Panevezys and proceeded to kill 288 people. The tally sheet for the day separated categorized them as 234 Jewish adults, 15 Jewish children, and 19 Russian and 20 Lithuanian communists. A day later 257 people lost their lives in Raseiniai. Of this number, 254 were Jews and just three men were listed as communist functionaries. On 30 July the towns of Agriogola and Wendziegola were searched. Members of *Einsatzgruppe* A killed 27 Jews and 11 communist functionaries in Agriogola, while two Jews and 13 communist suspects were liquidated in Wendziegola. On 31 July 1941 the tally sheet was increased when an *Einsatzkommando* entered Utena and killed 296 Jews and two communist functionaries. A day later, in Ukmerge, they killed another 296 Jews and two other people accused of being communists. Kovno (Kaunas) saw its own killings on 2 August, when two people were shot for being communists and 245 Jews were murdered – of whom, 74 were children. On 10 August the headquarters of *Einsatzgruppe* A moved to Novoselye. In late October 1941 Franz Stahlecker, the commander of *Einsatzgruppe* A, boasted that a total of 71,105 Latvian Jews had been killed.[6] A month later, at the end of November, the tally sheet listed a total of 113,750 Lithuanian Jews killed by *Einsatzgruppe* A. Of that number 44,498 were women and 24,005 were children.[7] The killing units advanced into Estonia, but the murder of Lithuanian and Latvian Jews continued through the autumn of 1941. *Einsatzkommando* 2 of *Einsatzgruppe* A was responsible for the deaths of 34,193 Lithuanian and Latvian Jews. *Einsatzkommando* 1a had a tally sheet of 26,131 Jews, of whom 964 were Estonian Jews. *Einsatzkommando* 1b had the lowest tally sheet: 16,780 Jews, mostly from Latvia. *Einsatzkommando* 3 killed a total of 137,346 Jews during 1941. Of that number 95,518 Jews were from Latvia and Lithuania, while 41,828 were Jews who were killed in Belarus.[8]

The movements of the various *Einsatzgruppen* were as follows. *Einsatzgruppe* A moved through the Baltic States and into North Russia, in the region of Leningrad. *Einsatzgruppe* B moved through the area designated for operations of the German Army Group Centre. As such, it traversed Belarus before entering central Russia. *Einsatzgruppe* C travelled from the Galicia District to western Ukraine and then into central and eastern Ukraine. *Einsatzgruppe* D first travelled through Bukovina and Bessarabia, those territories that had been seized by Stalin from Romania. It then moved through southern Ukraine and eventually entered the Crimea. On 2 January 1942 Otto Ohlendorf reported that *Einsatzgruppe* D had murdered 17,645 Jews in western Crimea between 16 November and 15 December 1941. According to his report, an additional 2,504 Krimchak Jews, 824 Roma and 212 communists and partisans had been executed. *Einsatzgruppe* C's final movement eastward brought it to the Caucasus Mountains in the summer of 1942, following in the wake of the German summer offensive. These four *Einsatzgruppen* never amounted to more than 3,000 men, yet these four killing units were responsible for the murders of between 1,500,000 and 1,750,000 people, mostly Jews. The bloody tally sheet for *Einsatzgruppe* A for the period 22 June–31 December 1941 was said to be 229,052 lives, as testified in a detailed report compiled by Franz Stahlecker in January 1942. A more precise estimate would be 210,785 Jews killed in the Baltic States. This number does not take into account the additional 41,828 Jews killed in Belarus by *Einsatzkommando* 3, which was also a part of *Einsatzgruppe* A (see Table 7.1).

SS Brigadier General Dr Franz Walter Stahlecker's report to Security Service Chief Reinhard Heydrich, made on 31 January 1942, boasted of killing 229,052 Jews in the Baltic States. This seems a slight exaggeration. It is also possible that Stahlecker might have included the killings of Romany in the Baltic States in this figure. A total of 4,500 Romany people were murdered there during the war, which would have increased the tally sheet for 1941 from 223,010 to 227,510 Jews killed in the Baltic States from June to December 1941. Finally, there were about 2,000 non-Jews who were shot by the *Einsatzgruppe* for being communists. If we add this figure, we come to the total Stahlecker boasted about. At the end of November or beginning of December 1941 SS Colonel Karl Jäger reported that there were still about 34,500 Jews left in Lithuania, being used as slave labour in the following localities:[9] 4,500 in Schaulen (Siauliai);[10] another 15,000 in Kaunas (Kovno) and 15,000 in Vilnius. A further 29,500 Jews were still alive in Latvia as of January 1942.[11] Estonia was listed as *Judenfrei* (free of Jews) by this same time. According to scholar Gerald Reitlinger, about 248,200 Jews lived in pre-war Latvia and Lithuania. Of this number, Reitlinger states that an estimated 60,000 fled eastwards as the Germans advanced, or were deported during the Soviet occupation of the Baltic States in 1940–1941. This number of 60,000 is too high if we count the total deaths in all three Baltic countries between June and December 1941 (223,010). To add to the confusion, the Germans began deporting Reich Jews to the Baltic States in the autumn of 1941.

With this in mind, we must therefore presume that it was physically impossible for the 990 men of *Einsatzgruppe* A to have murdered so many people in such a short span of time, especially since half of the unit was sent to Krasnovardeisk, just south of Leningrad in northern Russia, towards the latter half of 1941. Of the total number of 990 men belonging to this *Einsatzgruppe*, 340 were from the Waffen SS, 35 from the security service, 41 from the criminal police, 89 from the state protection police and 133 from the Order Police; 87 were locally raised volunteers of the newly created *Hilfspolizei*. The

Table 7.1. Numbers of Jews killed in the Baltic States, 1941–1944.

City/Town	Country	Date	Killed	Notes
Rietavas	Lithuania	22 June–15 July 1941	500	
Vanziogala	Lithuania	22 June–16 July	34	
Vilna (Vilnius)	Lithuania	4–20 July	5,000	
Kaunas (Kovno)	Lithuania	17 July–31 Aug.	2,581*	*Including 245 murdered on 2 Aug.
Liepaja (Libau)	Latvia	July–Aug.	3,000	
Kaunas (Kovno)	Lithuania	2–4 Sept.	4,636	
Kaunas (Kovno)	Lithuania	Sept.–Oct.	10,500	
Kaunas (Kovno)	Lithuania	Nov.	5,000	
Daugavpils	Lithuania	16 July	1,150	
Mariampole	Lithuania	3 July	68	
Pagirai	Lithuania	22 July	1	
Virbalis	Lithuania	22 July	500	
Agriogala	Lithuania	30 July	27	
Wendziegola	Lithuania	30 July	2	
Wilkia	Lithuania	30 July	402	
Kedainai	Lithuania	30 July	2,201*	*Including 95 killed on 23 July.
Vilna (Vilnius)	Lithuania	17 July–31 Aug.	1,444	
Joniskis	Lithuania	17 July–31 Aug.	355	
Pasvalys	Lithuania	17 July–31 Aug.	1,349	
Rokishkis	Lithuania	17 July–31 Aug.	4,188	
Seduva	Lithuania	17 July–31 Aug.	664	
Panevezys	Lithuania	17 July–31 Aug.	8,837*	*Including 249 shot on 28 July.
Alytus	Lithuania	17 July–31 Aug.	952	
Prienai	Lithuania	17 July–31 Aug.	1,078	
Mariampole	Lithuania	17 July–31 Aug.	156*	*Including 103 murdered on 25 July.
Raseiniai (Raseinen)	Lithuania	17 July–31 Aug.	3,043*	*Including 254 shot on 28 July.
Kaisiadorys	Lithuania	17 July–31 Aug.	1,911	
Jonava	Lithuania	17 July–31 Aug.	552	
Ukmerge (Vilkomir)	Lithuania	17 July–31 Aug.	1,647*	*Including 296 murdered on 1 Aug.

Volkavyskis	Lithuania	17 July–31 Aug.	900	
Utena	Lithuania	31 July	251	
Dvinsk	Latvia	July–Aug.	565	
Dagda	Latvia	July–Aug.	216	
Rokishkis	Lithuania	15–16 Aug.	3,207	
Panevezys	Lithuania	18 Aug.*	8,837**	**Source*: Kampe et al., *Einsatzgruppen*, p. 37. ** 6,211 Jews (1,609 adults and 4,602 children) were shot on 23 Aug.
Raseiniai (Raseinen)	Lithuania	18 Aug.	1,926*	* Including 1,020 children.
Panevezys	Lithuania	23 Aug.	7,523*	* Including 1,609 children.
Obeliai	Lithuania	25 Aug.	1,060	
Zarasai	Lithuania	26 Aug.	2,569*	* 767 men, 689 women and 1,113 children.
Moletai	Lithuania	29 Aug.	2,744*	* Those killed in Moletai and Utena on 29 Aug. included 1,731 children and 767 men.
Utena	Lithuania	29 Aug.	1,038	
Mariampole	Lithuania	1 Sept.	4,898*	* Including 1,731 children and 1,763 men.
Ukmerge (Vilkomir)	Lithuania	5 Sept.	4,709*	* Including 1,737 children.
Alytus	Lithuania	9–12 Sept.	1,279	
Tartu (Dorpat)	Estonia	18 Sept.	50	
Liepaja (Libau)	Latvia	22 Sept.*	61**	* *Source*: Benz, Kwiet and Matthäus, *Einsatz im 'Reichskommissariat Ostland'*, p. 90.** All killed by an officer and 14 enlisted men of the Gendarmerie from *Sammelstandort Dresden*.
Liepaja (Libau)	Latvia	24 Sept.	37*	* Shot by members of the recently created SS and Police Site Leader Libau (Liepaja).
Liepaja (Libau)	Latvia	25 Sept.	123*	* Shot by members of the recently created SS and Police Site Leader Libau (Liepaja), who apprehended 88 other persons accused of being communist functionaries or partisans.
Ventspils (Windau)	Latvia	26 Sept.	183*	* Shot by members of the recently created SS and Police Site Leader Libau (Liepaja), who also rounded up 80 suspected communists and 7 other communist functionaries.
Eysisky (Eisishkes)	Lithuania	27 Sept.	3,446	
Liepaja (Libau)	Latvia	30 Sept.	21*	* Shot by members of the recently created SS and Police Site Leader Libau (Liepaja), who also liquidated 83 political prisoners.

City/Town	Country	Date	Killed	Notes
Vilna (Vilnius)	Lithuania	30 Sept.	1,446	
Zagare	Latvia	Sept.	2,386	
Mariampole	Lithuania	Sept.–Oct.	7,000	
Vilna (Vilnius)	Lithuania	Sept.–Oct.	19,311	
Sakiai	Lithuania	Sept.–Oct.	890	
Naumiestis	Lithuania	Sept.–Oct.	650	
Butrimonis	Lithuania	Sept.–Oct.	976	
Trakai	Lithuania	Sept.–Oct.	1,446	
Jahiunai	Lithuania	Sept.–Oct.	575	
Niemenczyn	Lithuania	Sept.–Oct.	403	
Novo Vileika	Lithuania	Sept.–Oct.	1,159	
Polygon	Lithuania	Sept.–Oct.	3,726	
Swieciany	Lithuania	Sept.–Oct.	8,000	
Zagare	Lithuania	2 Oct.	2,236	
Liepaja (Libau)	Latvia	3 Oct.	37	
Liepaja (Libau)	Latvia	4 Oct.	18	
Semiliskes	Lithuania	6 Oct.	962	
Liepaja (Libau)	Latvia	8 Oct.	36	
Svenciany	Lithuania	9 Oct.	3,726	
Liepaja (Libau)	Latvia	11 Oct.	67	
Reval (Tallin District)	Estonia	12 Oct.	440	
Harku (Tallin District)	Estonia	14 Oct.	474*	* According to author H-H Wilhelm, of this number 500–600 were women and children.
Lazdiya	Lithuania	3 Nov.	1,535	
Riga	Latvia	Nov.	10,000	
Vilna (Vilnius)	Lithuania	Nov.	1,341	
Liepaja (Libau)	Latvia	13 Dec.	53	
Liepaja (Libau)	Latvia	17 Dec.	2,746*	* *Source*: Benz, Kwiet and Matthäus, *Einsatz im 'Reichskommissariat Ostland'*, p. 98.
Liepaja (Libau)	Latvia	1–31 Dec.	3,500	
Jody	Latvia	Dec.	700	

Riga	Latvia	Dec.	15,000	
Vilna (Vilnius)	Lithuania	Dec.	385	
Grand Total	Baltic States	22 June–31 Dec.	223,010	
Liepaja (Libau)	Latvia	18 March 1942	9*	* *Source*: Benz, Kwiet and Matthäus, *Einsatz im 'Reichskommissariat Ostland'*, p. 98.
Jody	Latvia	2 May	40*	* Murdered by the *Sicherheitsdienst*.
Kaunas (Kovno)	Lithuania	Oct. 1943	3,000*	* These people were not immediately killed. They were sent to Estonia and murdered there.
Narva	Estonia	Jan.–Feb. 1944	86	
Grand Total	Baltic States	22 June 1941–Feb. 1944	226,145	

rest were radiomen, motorcycle dispatch riders, telegraph operators and other administration personnel. This means that of the 990 men in the killing unit, only about 725 men were actually doing the killing. It is therefore almost a foregone conclusion that they had to be assisted by other agencies of the German military. Assistance came from various units and formations of the Order Police, as well as parts of the regular German Army. As has already been discussed, local volunteers also took part in the destruction of the Jews in their native lands and elsewhere. Active cooperation with all sections of Himmler's SS and police empire was necessary in order to carry out the Final Solution in the East. In his interrogation on 14 December 1945,[12] Friedrich Jeckeln of the Higher SS and Police Leader command detailed the operations that fell within the framework of the Final Solution in the East:

> The shootings were carried out under the direction of Colonel Dr Lange, Commander of the SD and *Gestapo* in Latvia. Knecht was in charge of security at the liquidation sites. I, Jeckeln, took part in the shootings on three occasions; the same holds for Lange, Knecht,[13] Lohse and Lieutenant Colonel Osis, commander of the traffic police [*Verkehrspolizei*] in Riga.

Further to the notes found in Friedrich Jeckeln's appointment book, the interrogators asked numerous questions regarding the killings in the Baltic States:

> Q: Who did the shooting?
> A: Ten or twelve German SD soldiers.
> Q: What was the procedure?
> A: All of the Jews went by foot from the ghetto in Riga to the liquidation site. Near the pits, they had to deposit their outer clothes, which were washed, sorted and shipped back to Germany. Jews – men, women and children – passed through police cordons on their way to the pits, where they were shot by German soldiers.
> Q: Did you report the execution of the order to Himmler?
> A: Yes, indeed. I notified Himmler by phone that the ghetto in Riga had been liquidated. And then when I was in Lötzen, East Prussia, in December 1941, I reported in person, too.[14] Himmler was satisfied with the results. He said that more Jewish convoys were due to arrive in Latvia, and these were to be liquidated by me also.
> Q: Go into more detail.
> A: At the end of January 1942,[15] I was at Himmler's headquarters in Lötzen, East Prussia, to discuss organizational matters regarding the Latvian SS legions. There Himmler informed me that additional Jewish convoys were due to arrive from the Reich and from other countries. The

destination point would be the Salaspils concentration camp, which lay 1¼ miles from Riga in the direction of Dünaburg. Himmler said that he had not yet determined how he would have them exterminated: whether to have them shot on board their convoys or in Salaspils, or whether to chase them into the swamp somewhere.

Q: How was the matter resolved?

A: It was my opinion that shooting would be the simpler and quicker death. Himmler said he would think it over and then give orders later through Heydrich.

Q: What countries were the Jews in Salaspils brought from?

A: Jews were brought from Germany, France, Belgium, Holland, Czechoslovakia and from other occupied countries to the Salaspils camp. To give a precise count of the Jews in the Salaspils camp would be difficult. In any case, all the Jews from the camp were exterminated. But I would like to make an additional statement while we are on this topic.

Q: What statement would you like to make?

A: I would like to say for the record that Göring shares in the guilt for the liquidations of Jewish convoys that arrived from other countries. In the first half of February 1942, I received a letter from Heydrich. In this letter he wrote that Reich Marshal Göring had got himself involved in the Jewish question, and that Jews were now being shipped to the East for annihilation only with Göring's approval.

Q: This does not diminish your guilt. Describe your role in the Jewish liquidations in Salaspils.

A: I have already said that I discussed the extermination of Jews in Salaspils with Himmler in Lötzen. That alone makes me an accessory to this crime. Beyond that, Jews were shot in Salaspils camp by forces recruited from my SD and Security Police units. The commander of the SD and *Gestapo* in Latvia, Lieutenant Colonel Dr Lange, was directly in charge of the shootings. Other officers who reported to me on the shooting of Jews in the camp were the commander of the SD and *Gestapo* in the Baltic States, Major General Jost; Colonel of Police Pifrader; and Colonel of Police Fuchs.

Q: Specifically, what did they report to you?

A: They reported that two to three convoys of Jews were to arrive per week, all subject to liquidation.

Q: Then the number of Jews shot in Salaspils ought to be known too, isn't that correct?

A: Yes, of course. I can give you the approximate figures. The first Jewish convoys arrived in Salaspils in November 1941. Then, in the first half of 1942, convoys arrived at regular intervals. I believe that in November

1941 no more than three convoys arrived in all, but during the next seven months, from December 1941 to June 1942, eight to twelve convoys arrived each month. Overall, in eight months, no fewer than fifty-five and no more than eighty-seven Jewish convoys arrived in camp. Given that each convoy carried a thousand men, that makes a total of 55,000 to 87,000 Jews exterminated in the Salaspils camp.

Q: This figure sounds low. Are you telling the truth?
A: I have no other, more exact figures. It should be added, however, that before my arrival in Riga, a significant number of Jews in the Ostland and in White Ruthenia were exterminated. I was informed of this fact.[16]

Q: By whom, specifically?
A: Stahlecker; Prützmann; Lange; Major General Schröder, the SS and Police Leader in Latvia; Major General Möller, the SS and Police Leader in Estonia; and Major General Wysocki, the SS and Police Leader in Lithuania.

Q: Be specific. What did they report?
A: Schröder reported to me that over and above those Jews who had been exterminated in the ghetto in Riga an additional 70,000 to 100,000 Jews were exterminated in Latvia. Dr Lange directly oversaw these shootings. Möller reported that in Estonia everything was in order as far as the Jewish question was concerned. The Estonian Jewish population was insignificant, all in all about 3,000 to 5,000 and this was reduced to nil. The greater part was exterminated in Reval. Wysocki reported that 100,000 to 200,000 Jews were exterminated, shot in Lithuania, on Stahlecker's orders. In Lithuania the Jewish exterminations were overseen by the commander of the SD and *Gestapo*, Lieutenant Colonel of Police Jäger. Later Jäger told me that he had become neurotic as a result of these shootings. Jäger was pensioned off and left his post for treatment. All told, the number of Jews exterminated in the actions in the Baltic East reached somewhere in the vicinity of 190,500 to 253,000.[17]

By January 1942 the headquarters of *Einsatzgruppe* A was located in Krasnovardeisk, where it remained during the winter months. On 12 January 1942 men from the *Einsatzgruppe* murdered 14 Jews found hiding in Novgorod. More killings would follow but the bulk of the murders had by then been perpetrated. Table 7.2 shows the numbers of people murdered at the hands of the Nazis in the East, 1939–1945.

All told, between 1939 and 1945 the Nazis killed or caused the deaths of approximately 26,988,000 people in Eastern Europe. This number is higher than the 20 million dead that Stalin was responsible for. (Note that this figure does not include other regions of Europe, nor Africa and the Middle East.)

Table 7.2. Estimated numbers of victims killed by the Nazis in the East, 1939–1945.

Ethnic/National Group	Millions
Soviet soldiers killed in action	6.75
Soviet Jewish citizens	2.7
Soviet non-Jewish citizens	5.7
Soviet prisoners of war	3
Polish soldiers killed in action	0.4
Polish Jewish citizens	3.4
Polish non-Jewish citizens	5
Romany	0.038
Total	26.9

The Red Army partisan forces resurgent

The Red Army counter-offensive in front of Moscow, which began on 5 December 1941 and did not end until the spring of 1942, had a direct effect on the growth of the partisan movement in central Russia and Belarus. This was not only because the offensive had given hope to those partisan forces fighting behind the lines, but also because the attack had allowed for those guerrilla units close to the front to make contact with advancing Red Army forces. Additionally, German units, which had up until then been fighting the partisans, now had to be redeployed on the front lines: 'Army and Waffen-SS units as well as police battalions had to be withdrawn from Rear Army Area Centre and employed at the front. In consequence, Soviet partisans controlled large parts of the region; Infantry General von Schenckendorff judged that he was 'no longer master of the situation' in spring 1942.'[18]

The first hint that the war in Russia was going to last longer than six months occurred in late autumn 1941 when German police units began to be called into front-line service. Two police units, the 131st and 307th Police Battalions, were detached from the 403rd Security Division and sent to the city of Kaluga. The XLIII Army Corps had been forced to withdraw from Kaluga in mid-December 1941, in spite of the fact that the Germans had thrown into the fight the 19th Panzer Division, the 15th Infantry Division and the 2nd SS Brigade (motorized). The latter had been partially brought up from Cracow by transport planes. The two police battalions helped to stem the Red Army drive by assisting the German Army to recapture the city.[19] Similarly, the 65th Reserve Police Battalion was sent to the northern sector of the Russian front where it was employed as a principal component of Battlegroup Scherer, which, although surrounded, held onto the city of Cholm from January until the siege was broken in early May 1942.[20] Also taking part in the defence of Cholm was the 16th Latvian Self-Defence Battalion.

During the winter of 1941/1942, and up until the end of March, Police Regiment North was committed to front-line fighting under the 81st Infantry Division (X. Army Corps).[21] The Soviet offensive regained a sizeable amount of territory. These initial German military reversals had a detrimental effect on the morale of the auxiliary volunteer units and it was in the winter of 1941/1942 that we see the first desertions of men from the order service to the partisan forces. One example was recorded in the war diary of the Grishin Partisan Regiment, which documented the addition of '41 deserter-policemen, 17 railway workers, 6 medical workers from Cherikov, and 19 escaped prisoners'[22] into their guerrilla unit in just two days in January 1942. The regimental commander noted sadly that most of these new partisan recruits had arrived at the guerrilla camp totally unarmed.

The procurement of weapons in 1941 and 1942 was a constant problem for the guerrilla forces throughout the occupied areas. The Red Army tried to supply its partisan units with weapons, but as Table 7.3 shows, more often than not half of the arms in the partisan ranks were captured enemy stocks.

The withdrawal of the German police battalions and regiments for front-line service therefore had a direct effect on the increase in guerrilla units

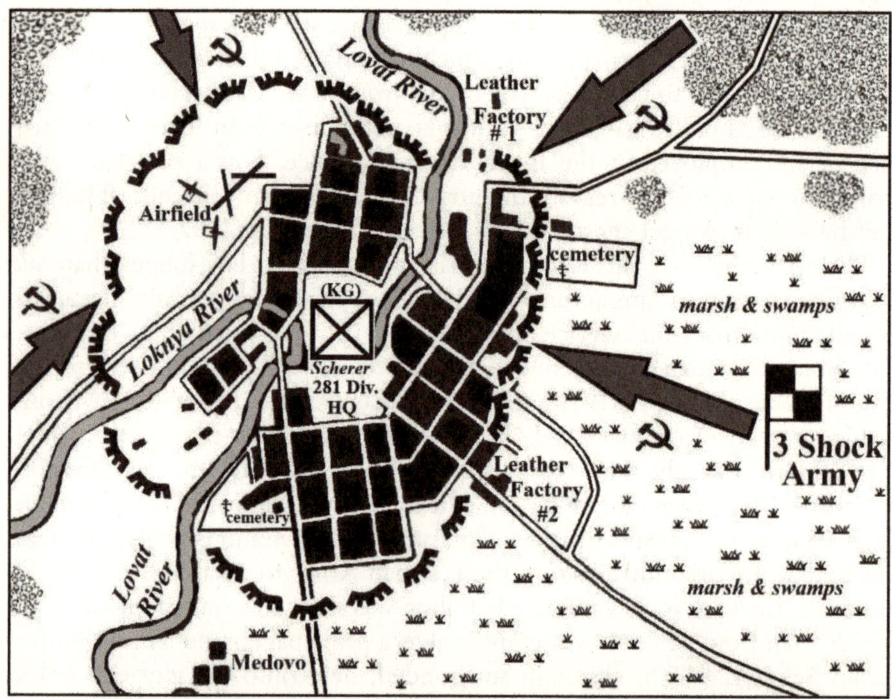

Map 9. Cholm and the surrounding area, 18 January 1942. At one point the Red Army had captured half the town. The siege of Cholm would last from 18 January until 5 May 1942.

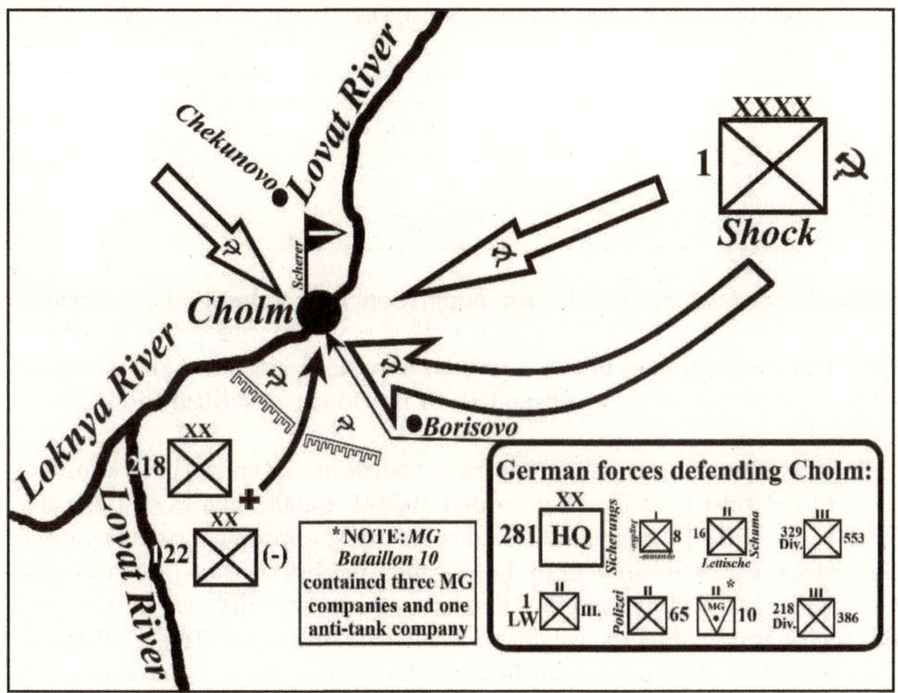

Map 10. The military situation in Cholm on 21 January 1942. The headquarters of the 281st Security Division would take charge of the defence. Also taking part in the battle was the 16th Latvian Self-Defence Battalion.

Table 7.3. Arms supplied to the White Russian Partisans in 1942.

	Rifles	Rifle Rounds	Mines	Machine Guns	Pistols	Sub-Machine Guns
Captured	4,000–7,000	67,500+	?	256	?	735
Soviet supplied	4,000	3,660,000	10,860	402	?	630
Grand Total:	8,000–15,000	3,727,500	10,860+	658	?	1,365

and activity behind the German lines. However, this effect did not actually manifest itself into substantially larger numbers of guerrilla attacks until the spring of 1942, partially through a lack of targets. For example, 80 per cent of German supply trains were not running in December 1941, primarily due to the severe weather and mechanical breakdowns. In addition, partisan attacks on the Belarusian rail lines in January and February 1942 only amounted to about twenty attacks per month, indicating a low level of guerrilla activity.[23] German police losses in front-line service during the winter of 1941/1942 reflected the large deployment of police units, which had been temporarily

Table 7.4. Police losses in front-line combat, December 1941–March 1942.[24]

Army Group	Officers	NCOs and Men	Casualties (%)
North	33	1,680	24
Centre	53	1,771	27
South	15	427	7
Grand Total:	101	3,878	20

diverted from killing the Jewish population and fighting the guerrillas. Between December 1941 and March 1942 some thirty-one police battalions served on the front lines but as their men were not trained to fight as regular infantry, their losses were substantial, as previously described in chapter 3 (see Table 7.4).

By all accounts, it seems that the Soviet partisan movement in Belarus and parts of central Russia stood at around 30,000–40,000 men as of 1 January 1942.[25] At the end of the winter battles, the most important partisan gain in Belarus was the establishment of the so-called Vitebsk corridor, an area of the German front that jutted out into Red Army territory to the east. In July 1942 this region was held by the newly established 1st Belarusian Partisan Brigade. This brigade had its origins in the Shmyrev *Otriad*, whose commander was Mihay Filipovich Shmyrev.[26] By the beginning of 1942 many of the partisan *Otriads* were being expanded to regiment or brigade level, but these titles were at times deceiving. For example, at its peak strength in 1942 the Grishin Partisan Regiment (led by Sergey Grishin) had only 737 men. In fact, even the largest partisan groups in the USSR in 1942 would contain no more than 12,000–20,000 men, although this was a significant increase from 1941.

In February 1942 a large partisan brigade, named Batia ('Father' in Belarusian), was organized in the northwest portion of the Smolensk District using ten *Otriads* of various strengths. This amalgamation of forces eventually became the 1st Smolensk Partisan Division in April/May 1942. When organized, the unit contained 6,000 men.[27] Its commander was V.I. Vorontschenko and the divisional commissar was F.N. Demenkov. This partisan division would assist the 2nd Guard Cavalry Corps (Lieutenant General Belov), which was surrounded in the Smolensk-Vyazma-Yelnya triangle, the so-called Vyazma pocket. General Belov was trying to organize a defence using his cavalrymen, Soviet paratroopers and the local guerrilla forces.[28]

Additional guerrilla units in the Vyazma pocket included the 24th Year and Laso Partisan Regiments. The commander of the 24th Year Partisan Regiment was F.D. Gnesdilov, while the unit's political commissar was G.S. Amirov. The commander of the Laso Partisan Regiment was V.V. Kasubski, while his political commissar was A.F. Yudenkov. These two regiments had

Table 7.5. Partisan brigades in Belarus, February 1942.[29]

Unit	Brigade Commander	Brigade Commissar
1st Belarusian Partisan Brigade	M.F. Schmyrev	R.V. Schkredo
Alexey Partisan Brigade	A.F. Danukalov	P.I. Mironenko
2nd Belarusian Partisan Brigade	M.I. Dyatschkov	J.M. Barsukov
Death to Fascism Partisan Brigade	V.V. Melnikov	I.F. Koronevski
Dsershinski Partisan Brigade	S.M. Korotkin	V.M. Frolov
Voroshilov Partisan Brigade	F.F. Kapusta	I.K. Shishik
Czechist Partisan Brigade	G.A. Kirpitsch	F.M. Sedlezki
Stschors Partisan Brigade	F.I. Pavlovski	S.V. Machanko

2,363 and 2,143 men respectively. Overall, partisan strength in the Smolensk region in February 1942 stood at around 19,500 men. The establishment of a guerrilla region in the Usachi Rayon, south of the town of Polotsk, occurred in early 1942. Surprisingly, this area remained free of any anti-partisan operations until 1944, when its strength in numbers of guerrillas had risen to around 12,000 men.[30] In February 1942 Russian partisan strength in the region of White Russia stood at 23,000 men, split up into 19 guerrilla brigades containing about 227 partisan battalions (see Table 7.5). Many of these partisan battalions were, in reality, little more than company size at 100–200 men, while the brigades had perhaps 1,500–3,000 men. Overall, the Belarusian partisan movement was in a much better condition when the spring of 1942 rolled around than it had been in the second half of 1941 when it was established. It appears that partisan regions closest to the front line contained the largest numbers of guerrilla forces.

An open wound: siphoning German forces to fight the partisans

Records of the Supreme Commander of the Order Police for February 1942 state that 19,389 policemen were fighting in Russia. This included 3,880 men fighting in the region of Ukraine, 3,439 in the Baltic States and 12,070 in central Russia and Belarus. Before the war was over, the total number of police troops killed would reach 63,000, indicating just how closely involved the German police forces were in the war.

Early in 1942 a special police mountain regiment was ordered to be formed, which was also to contain a company of armoured cars.[31] The police units were split up as follows: 9 police battalions were serving in the security divisions, 1 with the security service and 1 with the Organization Todt, while 3 police battalions and 2 companies were operating in the Ostland region, and 3 police battalions and 1 police cavalry battalion in Ukraine.

Massacres in Belarus

When the German security forces spread out into Belarus in June and July 1941 the population of Jews in that region stood at approximately 375,000 men, women and children. By the time the German forces were expelled in the late summer of 1944 approximately 245,000 Jews – about 65 per cent of the pre-war Belarusian Jewish population – would be dead.[32] The German Order Police took part not only in the war against the guerrillas, but also in the war against the Jews. The beginning of the campaign against the Jews of Belarus came on 27 June 1941, when the 309th Police Battalion killed about 2,000 Polish Jews in Bialystok (northeast Poland).[33] On 12–13 July the 316th Police Battalion executed another 3,000 Jews in Bialystok after a visit from the National Leader of the SS Heinrich Himmler and the Supreme Commander of the Order Police, Kurt Daluege on 8 July 1941.[34]

On 2 August 1941 the 3rd Company, 322nd Police Battalion, shot 77 Jews between the ages of 16 and 45 near the Bialowicza prison camp.[35] On 15 August 1941 a further 232 Jews were killed at Kobrin by the same police battalion. In late October 1941 the 11th Reserve Police Battalion arrived in Minsk alongside several Lithuanian auxiliary police companies and immediately proceeded to Slutsk, south of the Belarusian capital. They had been ordered to go from Kaunas to Belarus as a component of the 11th Reserve Police Battalion. Their mission was to kill Jews. The battalion proceeded to go on a shooting spree, killing about a thousand Jews living and working in Slutsk. Many of them were tradesmen. They were taken out in trucks and shot in a nearby forest. The Lithuanian order service auxiliary police companies assisted throughout the operation. During these shootings a young Lithuanian auxiliary policeman declared that he could not shoot men, women and children, whereupon the company commander, Juozas Kristaponis, invited any of his men with similar objections to move to the side. Some did, but most did not. Later this unit was involved in more killings, and in Slutsk there were instances that prompted a German police officer to call the Lithuanians 'pigs'.[36] A captured report from the German Commissioner of Slutsk, dated in the month of October 1941, listed in detail what transpired in the town:

> The 1st Lieutenant explained that the Police Battalion had received the assignment to effect the liquidation of all Jews here in the town of Slutsk, within two days ... Then I requested him to postpone the action one day. However, he rejected this with the remark that he had to carry out this action everywhere and in all towns, and that only two days were allotted for Slutsk. Within these two days the town of Slutsk had to be cleared of Jews by all means ... All Jews without exceptions were taken out from the factories and shops and deported in spite of our agreement. It is true that part of the Jews was moved by way of the ghetto, where many of them

> were processed and still segregated by me, but a large part was loaded directly on trucks and liquidated without further delay outside of the town ... For the rest, as regards the execution of the action, I must point out my deepest regret that the latter bordered already on sadism. The town itself offered a picture of horror during the action. With indescribable brutality on the part of the German police officers and particularly the Lithuanian partisans,[37] the Jewish people, but also among them White Ruthenians, were taken out of their dwellings and herded together. Everywhere in the town shots were to be heard and in different streets the corpses of shot Jews accumulated. The White Ruthenians were in greatest distress to free themselves from the encirclement. Regardless of the fact that the Jewish people, among whom were also tradesmen, were mistreated in a terribly barbarous way in the face of the White Ruthenian people, the White Ruthenians themselves were also worked over with rubber clubs and rifle butts. There was no question of an action against the Jews and any more. It rather looked like a revolution (1104-PS.)[38]

From 10 to 12 September the III. Battalion, Police Regiment Centre, performed an anti-guerrilla sweep in six towns surrounding the city of Mogilev. The initial results yielded the execution of eight women, one of whom was labelled a Jewish partisan sympathizer. Eight guerrillas were killed by the battalion in these three days, one of whom was found to be a Jew fighting with the partisans. Later still, on 29 September 1941 the same III. Battalion launched another drive in the vicinity of Daschkovka, which netted 63 dead guerrillas after a fierce but brief firefight. In addition to the 63 dead partisans, the battalion also listed the killings of 13 Jews (six men and seven women) who had been accused of inciting anti-German activities.[39] Another 3,700 Jews were killed in Mogilev in November 1941 when the 316th Police Battalion went on another shooting spree. Meanwhile, the SS *Einsatzgruppen* had not been kept idle. It is a fact that of the estimated 253,000 Jews living in the Baltic States immediately prior to the war, somewhere between 224,000 and 228,000 were said to have been killed by war's end.[40] Likewise, of the 375,000 Jews living in White Russia, about 245,000 were said to have perished by the end of the war.

Since *Einsatzgruppe* A was said to have operated in White Russia, the Baltic States and northern Russia, it stands to reason that it was responsible for most of those 473,000 Jewish deaths. In fact, a chart produced by *Einsatzgruppe* A during the war states that by the end of 1941 the number of Jews killed in the Baltic States and Belarusia was 214,450 men, women and children. Of this number, 963 had been killed in Estonia, 35,238 in Latvia, 136,421 in Lithuania and 41,828 in White Russia.[41] Most of Estonia's Jews had evaded capture by withdrawing deep into the USSR. Of the estimated 7,661 Estonian

Jews living in the Baltic States before the war, 963 were killed by *Einsatzgruppe* A.[42] In addition, released Lithuanian convicts and political prisoners beat hundreds of Jews to death while Germans watched. Altogether, the USSR would lose a million Jews killed during the war. Table 7.6 lists the main confirmed killings in 1941.

Table 7.7 lists the Order Police and *Einsatzgruppen* formations linked to the specific killings in the Baltic States and Belarus in 1941.

The figure of 413,153 Jewish men, women and children killed in the Baltic States and Belarus in 1941[43] is very close to the official number of Jews killed (473,000) in these two regions between 1941 and 1944.[44] Of the former figure (413,153), 214,450 or about 50 per cent can be attributed directly to murders committed by *Einsatzgruppe* A in 1941 alone. The records of *Einsatzgruppe* A itself attest to this.[45] If the German SS records for *Einsatzgruppe* A are correct, it means that approximately 198,662 Jews had to have been killed by *Einsatzgruppe* B in 1941. This figure is higher than the number of deaths attributed to *Einsatzgruppe* B (134,000 in one record).[46] In fact, it is higher by 64,662 deaths but is, in my estimation, a more precise number if one compares the statistics as presented by the German *Einsatzgruppen* documents as well as post-war studies on *ha-Shoah* (the Holocaust). The figures of Jewish deaths quoted from previous works have turned out to be quite modest. In fact, as the figures of those killed in the years 1942–1944 will show, the total number of Jewish lives lost in these regions for the entire war period in which Belarus was occupied by the Germans (June 1941–August 1944) will prove to be much higher than previously thought possible.

The partisan war in Belarus in 1941

The establishment by the Soviets of a guerrilla organization in Belarus – the *Belaruskaya Narodnaya Partizanka* (Belarus National Partisans)[47] – in September 1941 was the most notable factor that occurred in the region during 1941. It was done in conjunction with the help and full support of the Communist Party and forces from the People's Commissariat for Internal Affairs (NKVD). The NKVD actually began to parachute guerrilla cells behind the lines of Army Group Centre as early as August 1941. These cells were to help organize Red Army forces trapped behind German lines, as well as raise destruction battalions and guerrilla units from the local population. In this, they were to be aided by local Communist Party functionaries.[48] There were numerous examples of partisan units created from bypassed Red Army soldiers. One such was the detachment formed by M. Prudnikov, a border guard officer whose unit was active in Belarus in the autumn and winter of 1941/1942. It operated behind the German lines in the Klichev region. Another was a guerrilla detachment raised by Colonel V. Chlebtsov from members of the 110th Rifle Division, which fought the Germans in the Mogilev District of Belarus.[49]

Table 7.6. Extermination of the Jewish population in the Baltic States and Belarus, June–December 1941.

City or Town	Region	Date	Deaths	Notes
Kovno	Lithuania	28–29 June	300*	*Murdered by released Lithuanian convicts and political prisoners while the Germans watched.
Latvia	Baltic States	22 June–16 July	12,204*	*Including Jews from Riga, Jelgava, Siauliai, Jekabpils, Virbalis, Vandziogala, Mariampole and Vilnius.
Lithuania	Baltic States			
Kovno	Lithuania	2 July	3,000*	*Killed by Lithuanians prior to the arrival of *Einsatzgruppe* A.
Pripet marshes	Belarus	Late July	6,500*	*The 1st and 2nd SS Cavalry Regiments participated in an anti-partisan sweep in the Pripet marshes, killing 259 Red Army soldiers and 6,500 civilians. It is not known how many of the civilians were Jews.
Kovno	Lithuania	Late July	10,000	
Minsk	Belarus	July	2,000*	*Mostly Jewish intelligentsia.
Lyakhovichi	Belarus	1 July	100	
Novogrudok	White Russia	3 July	100*	**Source*: Hogan, *Holocaust Chronicle*, p. 244.
Fort No. 7 outside Vilnius	Lithuania	4 July	463*	*Including 416 men and 47 women. These were Lithuanian Jews killed by Lithuanian auxiliary volunteers. (They were part of the 12,204 Jews killed in Latvia and Lithuania, 22 June–16 July 1941.)
Vilnius	Lithuania	5 July	93*	**Sonderkommando* 1a directly took part in the murder of these Jews. (They were part of the 12,204 Jews killed in Latvia and Lithuania, 22 June–16 July 1941.)
Fort No. 7 outside Vilnius	Lithuania	6 July	2,000*	*Killed by Lithuanian order service auxiliary police members. (They were part of the 12,204 Jews killed in Latvia and Lithuania, 22 June–16 July 1941.)
Slonim	Belarus	17 July	1,159	
Minsk	Belarus	21 July	45*	*When non-Jewish Belarusians were ordered to bury their Jewish neighbours alive, they refused. Men from *Sonderkommando* 1b then shot the neighbours and buried the 45 Jews alive.
Kovno	Lithuania	25–26 July	3,800*	*German SS and Lithuanian auxiliary police officers took part in this pogrom.

City or Town	Region	Date	Deaths	Notes
Vilnius	Lithuania	20 July–8 Aug.	1,444	
Eastern towns and cities	Lithuania	17 July–31 Aug.	33,561*	*Including deaths in Josniskis, Pasvalys, Rokishkis, Panevezhys, Zarasai, Utena, Ukmerge, Kedainai, Seduva, Raseiniai, Agriogala, Wilkia, Jonava, Kaisiadorys, Prienai, Kovno, Alytus and Mariampole.
Dvinsk, Dagda, Aglona	Latvia	17 July–31 Aug.	781	
Vileika, east of Vilnius	Belarus	Aug.	250	
Libau	Latvia	Aug.	3,000*	*Shot by members of *Sonderkommando* 2.
Ponary	Lithuania	2 Aug.	4,000*	*Killed by 80 inebriated Germans.
Kovno	Lithuania	2 Aug.	200*	*Including an American Jewish woman.
Mitau	Latvia	3 Aug.	1,500	
Minsk area	Belarus	7 Aug.	7,819*	*Killed by the SS Cavalry Brigade.
Dvinsk	Latvia	8–9 Aug.	3,000*	*Transported to the Pogulanka Forest, forced to dig their own graves and then shot.
Pripet marshes	Belarus	1–12 Aug.	14,178*	*Killed by the SS Cavalry Brigade, specifically battalions under SS Major Franz Magill. In addition, Magill's combat group killed 1,001 partisans and 699 Red Army soldiers. The German order police and security service also assisted in this drive.
Mogilev	Belarus	19 Aug.	3,000*	*Killed by *Sonderkommando* 8.
Starobin, in the Pripet marshes	Belarus	23 Aug.	500*	*1st SS Cavalry Regiment helped to shoot the entire male Jewish population of Starobin after accusations that the Jews had killed two German-appointed mayors for the town and the established auxiliary police force.
Kedainiai	Lithuania	28 Aug.	2,000*	*Awaiting execution, a Jewish butcher fatally bit the throat of an *Einsatzgruppen* member, at which point all Jews were immediately shot.
Vilnius	Lithuania	31 Aug.	3,600*	*Taken to Ponary and murdered in reprisal for a partisan attack on a German rear area patrol.
Bobruisk	Belarus	Aug.–Sept.	380*	*Killed by Police Regiment Centre, most likely in the last week of Aug. 1941.
Krupki	Belarus	Sept.	1,500	
Eisishkes, south of Vilnius	Lithuania	Sept.	3,446	
Mariampole	Lithuania	Sept.	7,000	

Ukmerge (Vilkomir)	Lithuania	Sept.	4,000	
Parichi	White Russia	Sept.	1,700	
Vilnius	Lithuania	12 Sept.	3,434*	*Taken to Ponary and shot.
Hancewicze	Belarus	13–15 Sept.	3,000	
Kovno	Lithuania	20 Sept.	3,000*	*Mainly women and children.
Olkieniki, north-northwest of Lida	Belarus	25 Sept.	1,000	
Swieciany	Lithuania	26 Sept.	8,000*	*Massacred in Polygon Woods. Several hundred Jewish males escaped.
Ejszyszki	Belarus	Sept.	3,200*	*Executed at pits outside the city.
Slutsk	Belarus	Oct.	1,000*	*Killed by the 11th Reserve Police Battalion.
Yanovichi	Belarus	Oct.	1,180	
Antopol, southwest of Hancewicze	Belarus	Oct.	50	
Kostopol	Belarus	Oct.	1,400*	*All women and children.
Ostrog	Belarus	Oct.	2,500	
Miedzyrec, southeast of Kostopol	Belarus	Oct.	1,500	
Krasnopole	Belarus	Oct.	1,940	
Lelchitsy	Belarus	Oct.	1,400	
Mogilev	Belarus	Oct.	2,760	
Vilnius	Lithuania	1 Oct.–22 Dec.	33,500	
Kovno	Lithuania	4 Oct.	1,500*	*Murdered inside Fort No. 9.
Dvinsk	Latvia	6–7 Oct.	2,000*	*Reports that the majority of Jews in Dvinsk are killed.
Vitebsk	Belarus	8 Oct.	16,000	
Uzlany-Rudensk	Belarus	8 Oct.	640	
Rudensk	Belarus	9–12 Oct.	800*	*Referred to as 'partisans, communists, Jews and other suspicious riff-raff'.
Borisov	Belarus	18–21 Oct.	8,000*	*Killed by *Sonderkommando* 7b, aided by the 709th Secret Field Police Group.
Mogilev	Belarus	19 Oct.	3,700*	*Killed by the 316th Police Battalion.
Kodianov	Belarus	21 Oct.	1,500*	*All the Jews living in the town are killed
Starodub	Belarus	25 Oct.	270	
Slutsk	Belarus	28 Oct.	300*	*Half of the killers were Lithuanian and half German. Most likely, they belonged to the 11th Reserve Police Battalion, which in Sept. had killed another 1,000 Jews in Slutsk.

City or Town	Region	Date	Deaths	Notes
Lida	Belarus	28 Oct.	2,000	
Fort No. 9, Kovno	Lithuania	28 Oct.	9,200*	*Including 4,300 children.
Nesvizh (Nieswiez), southeast of Lida	Belarus	30 Oct.	5,000*	**Source*: Gilbert, *Atlas of the Holocaust*, p. 77.
Kleck, south of Nesvizh	Belarus	31 Oct.	4,000	
Kovno	Lithuania	Nov.	5,000	
Novogrudok	Belarus	Nov.	400	
Slonim	Belarus	14 Nov.	9,000*	*Killed by 6th Company, 727th Infantry Regiment.
Mir	Belarus	Nov.	1,500	
Woloczyn (Voloshin)	Belarus	Nov.	300	
Swierzen	Belarus	Nov.	500	
Lyubavichi	Belarus	Nov.	700	
Rogachev	Belarus	Nov.	3,500	
Berezina	Belarus	Nov.	1,000	
Borisov	Belarus	Nov.	7,000	
Mogilev	Belarus	Nov.	3,700*	*Killings attributed to the 316th Police Battalion.
Vitebsk	Belarus	5 Nov.	4,090	
Minsk	Belarus	7 Nov.	12,000*	*May have included a sizeable population of German Jews recently transferred from the Reich. The 322nd Police Battalion took part in these murders.
Bobruisk	Belarus	7 Nov.	20,000	
Pogulanka, near Dvinsk	Latvia	7–9 Nov.	5,000	
Czepielow	Belarus	14 Nov.	9,000*	*Brought to Czepielow from Slonim and murdered.
Minsk	Belarus	20 Nov.	7,000*	*Killed at Tuchinka. The 322nd Police Battalion took part in these murders.
Riga	Latvia	27 Nov.	10,600*	*Taken to Rumbula Forest and systematically shot.
Mogilev	Belarus	Dec.	315	
Mekhov	Belarus	Dec.	200	
Parichi	Belarus	Dec.	1,500	
Polotsk	Belarus	Dec.	7,000	

Vilnius	Lithuania	Dec.	385	
Jody	Lithuania	Dec.	700	
Liepaja (Libau)	Latvia	Dec.	3,500	
Novogrudok	Belarus	6 Dec.	5,000*	*200 Jews resisted, killing some 50 of their German tormentors before being gunned down alongside the other Jews who did not fight.
Riga	Latvia	7–9 Dec.	25,000*	*Taken to Rumbula Forest and shot. These killings were attributed to the 22nd Reserve Police Battalion. The 1st Company also took part in the shooting of around 100 gypsies near Frauenburg (Frombork) in 1941.
Novogrudok	Belarus	Dec.	4,000	
Total Baltic States and Belarus*		June–Dec.	476,354	*In some instances, 'Belarus' also includes villages, towns and cities that bordered Belarus in Lithuania, Poland or central Russia.

Table 7.7. Murders linked specifically to certain SS, police and secret field police units, June 1941–January 1942.

Unit	Killed	Date	Region	Notes
Sonderkommando 1a	26,131	22 June 1941–31 Jan. 1942	Baltic States and Leningrad region	The figures for *Sonderkommando* 1a and 1b are estimates based on Jewish sources for Jews killed in the Baltic States and captured *Einsatzgruppe* A documents. Most of these murders occurred in Latvia.
Sonderkommando 1b	16,780	22 June 1941–31 Jan. 1942	Baltic States	The Jews this SS unit killed were evenly divided between Latvian and Lithuanian Jews.
Polizeiregiment Mitte	20,000	7 Nov.	Bobruisk, Belarus	Polizeiregiment Mitte were not the sole culprits in these deaths.
Einsatzkommando 8				
Einsatzkommando 2	34,193	22 June 1941–31 Jan. 1942	Baltic States	
Einsatzkommando 3	137,346	22 June 1941–31 Jan. 1942	Baltic States and Belarus	Including 41,828 Jews killed in Belarusia. *Source*: MacLean, *The Field Men*, p. 228.
Sonderkommando 7a, aided by Lithuanian auxiliaries	517	4 July	Vilnius, Lithuania	
Sonderkommando 7b	100	1 July	Lyakhovichi, Belarus	
Sonderkommando 7b and GFP-709	8,000	8 Oct.	Borisov, Belarus	
Teilkommando of *Einsatzkommando* 8 and 316th Police Battalion	1,159	17 July	Slonim, Belarus	*Source*: Kampe et al., *Die Einsatzgruppen*, p. 56.
Einsatzkommando 8	3,000	19 Aug.	Mogilev, Belarus	
Einsatzkommando 8	4,090	5 Nov.	Vitebsk, Belarus	
Einsatzkommando 9	16,000	8 Oct.	Vitebsk, Belarus	According to Krausnick (*Hitlers Einsatzgruppen*, p. 159), this was the only *Einsatzgruppe* unit in Vitebsk on 8 October 1941.
Two companies, 11th Reserve Police Battalion	1,000+	Sept. 1941	Slutsk, Belarus	
Einsatzgruppe A	214,450	22 June 1941–31 Jan. 1942	Baltic States, Belarus and the Leningrad region	
Einsatzgruppe B	198,662	22 June 1941–31 Jan. 1942	Belarus and central Russia	

Two companies, 11th Reserve Police Battalion; 640th Secret Field Police Group; Lithuanian auxiliaries	640	8 Oct.	Uzlany-Rudensk, Belarus	Those killed were described as 'Jews and communists'.
Two companies, 11th Reserve Police Battalion; 640th Secret Field Police Group; Lithuanian auxiliaries	800	9–12 Oct.	Rudensk, Belarus	Those killed were described as 'partisans, communists, Jews and other suspicious riff-raff'.
Two companies, 11th Reserve Police Battalion; 640th Secret Field Police Group; Lithuanian auxiliaries	1,300	14 Oct.	Smilavichy (Smilovichi), Belarus	
Two companies, 11th Reserve Police Battalion; 640th Secret Field Police Group; Lithuanian auxiliaries	1,000	21 Oct.	Koidanov, Belarus	
22nd Reserve Police Battalion, Police Regiment North	100	5 Dec.	Fronino (Frauenberg), Russia	The headquarters of Police Regiment North moved to Opochka in October 1941. Fronino lies 10km south-west of Opochka. The victims here were Romany.
22nd Reserve Police Battalion, Police Regiment North	25,000	Nov.–Dec.	Riga, Latvia	
316th Police Battalion	3,799	Nov.	Mogilev, Belarus	
316th Police Battalion	5,281	19 Dec.	Bobruisk, Belarus	
322nd Police Battalion	914	31 Aug.–1 Sept.	Minsk, Belarus	
322nd Police Battalion	3,700	19 Oct.	Mogilev, Belarus	
322nd Police Battalion	19,000	Nov.	Minsk, Belarus	
III. Battalion, Police Regiment Centre	2,208	7–29 Sept.	6 to 8 villages around Mogilev, Belarus	
Police Regiment Centre	380	Last week of Aug.	Bobruisk, Belarus	
Total	745,550+			

The success of this guerrilla effort in 1941 has to be viewed as not very effective. First, the partisan organization was in its infancy and therefore the rank-and-file guerrilla units were neither well led nor well coordinated. Nor were they as numerous as they would become by 1943. It had been decided that the leadership for the Russian partisan movement was to be created, if possible, using the existing Communist Party and Red Army officer and commissar cadre. However, many functionaries from these Soviet branches of the military and government ignored Stalin's order to form cadres behind the German lines. Second, communications were still rudimentary and the main partisan headquarters in Moscow had yet to establish regular radio contact with more than a small number of guerrilla units behind the German lines. Third, arms for the guerrillas were insufficient and irregular. For example, the total number of supplied and captured weapons given to guerrillas in Belarus in 1941 could barely outfit about one and a half rifle divisions (see Table 7.8).[50]

Reports state that another factor behind the limited guerrilla activity in 1941 was the belief held by the overwhelming majority of the Soviet population under German occupation that the Soviet system had proved weak and would not be re-established. Belarus peasants in 1941 continued to help feed cut-off Red Army troops and give information to the occasional partisan unit, but they did so more out of fear than conviction. However, the Germans were also able to secure volunteer informants on a large scale, both from sincere opponents of the Soviet system and from opportunists.[51] Many citizens of the USSR also informed on their Jewish neighbours and, as has been shown, even took part in the destruction of Soviet Jewry. The Germans themselves made every effort to associate communism with Judaism.

A perfect example of the type of partisan unit in 1941 was the Shmyrev Otriad, which was operating west of Smolensk in July 1941. At that time the unit had lost 14 men to desertions, while in August it was able to raise its numbers to 88 men. However, by then 38 other partisans had deserted from the unit or been thrown out for cowardice, while one had actually been shot.[52] However, though it had problems with retention, the Shmyrev unit was also successful. On 25 July 1941 it launched its first attack, surprising a group of

Table 7.8. Belarusian partisan weapons, autumn 1941.

	Grenades	Rifles	Rifle ammunition	Artillery pieces	Machine guns	Pistols	Sub-machine guns (and cartridges)
Captured	750	1,125	30,000	3	133	1,400	124 (27,000)
Soviet	30,000	9,560	1,710,000	–	–	3,800	265 (125,000)
Total	30,750	10,685	1,740,000	3	133	5,200	389

German cavalrymen bathing in a river. Between 20 and 25 Germans were killed before the guerrillas departed. By its own records, the Otriad would claim around 200 Germans killed by the end of September.[53] Still, the partisan units operating in Belarus and central Russia in 1941 were sufficient to cause concern and some actual losses to the German command. General Heinz Guderian himself was said to have complained that of the seventy railroad cars which Army Group Centre needed to maintain its advance in September 1941, only twenty-three actually arrived at the front on time as a result of guerrilla activity against the rail lines. But Soviet post-war estimates of guerrilla forces behind the German lines in 1941 number about 40,000 fighters. Western sources state that perhaps 30,000 partisans were actually active in 1941. A good estimate would be that the actual figure for 1941 was somewhere around 22,000 partisans, and the total amount of land held by the partisans behind the German lines at the end of 1941 was only estimated to be 5–6 per cent of the land controlled by the partisans at that time.[54] The partisan movement in 1941 was not yet a serious threat to the Germans, but it should have been a bellwether of things to come. The rise in guerrilla activity in 1942 proved that, as did the rise in partisan strength and in partisan activity. The period between June and December 1941, therefore, was the quietest phase behind the Nazi lines that the Germans would experience throughout their entire invasion of the Soviet Union.

Chapter 8

Rear area security in Ukraine and southern Russia

He will win who knows when to fight and when not to fight. [Sun Tzu]

The wrong policies

As elsewhere along the Russian Front, the German rear areas in Ukraine and southern Russia suffered from partisan activity, although not to the extent experienced by the Germans in central and northern Russia and especially in Belarus. Numerous operations involving rear area garrison commands of the army and the army economic office, as well as rear area security units and front-line forces, were launched from as early as the late summer of 1941. What ties these disparate anti-partisan operations together is a consistent pattern of criminality regarding the treatment of the Soviet civilian population and, in particular, the Jewish population. As author Wendy Lower attested, cooperation and coordination between the indigenous collaborationist units, the SS, the police and Wehrmacht forces appear to have been routine. German forces were indifferent to the suffering of the civilian population and captured Russian soldiers. Retribution massacres occurred on a regular basis. Even people suspected of being partisan helpers were subject to elimination. Anyone who has seriously studied low-, medium- or even high-intensity resistance movements will know that the key to defeating them is the winning of the hearts and minds of the local civilian population. That is the most crucial factor in conducting a successful campaign against guerrilla forces. This is why the Nazi tactic of collective guilt and collective punishment proved to be so counterproductive for the German war effort.

When dealing with partisans or partisan suspects, or those labelled 'suspicious persons', the standard German procedure during the campaign in the East was to *auf Nummer sicher gehen* ('play it safe') and *das Problem beseitigen* ('eliminate the problem') by shooting them. In effect, what all of these anti-guerrilla operations demonstrated is a consistent pattern of criminal behaviour that authors including Ben Shepperd, Omer Bartov, Theo Schulte and others have already documented in other regions of the Eastern Front. Given that this comportment was apparently rampant throughout the scope and breath of the Russian Front, we can make the strong argument that this was a policy of murder that was accepted on the Eastern Front: a policy in which the Wehrmacht was made a willing accomplice.

The partisan movement in Ukraine, 1941–1942

The summer, autumn and winter of 1941 were relatively free of partisan activity in the region of Army Group South. We can attribute this partly to the initial, friendly attitude which the Germans encountered when they entered Ukraine. Anti-Stalinist feelings were running very high in this region of the USSR. Local independence had been crushed after a brief taste of freedom in 1918–1920. During the early 1930s most Ukrainians were resisting the collectivization being imposed on them by the Communist Party. In anger, Joseph Stalin punished the Ukrainian people by forcibly withholding foodstuffs and creating an artificial famine that eventually killed millions of Ukrainians. It was a horrific crime. When a member of the Politburo dared to question how the western powers would portray the suffering and the deaths in Ukraine, Stalin simply shrugged off the concern as unimportant.

Stories of cannibalism during the famine proved to be true, and most Ukrainians rightly blamed Stalin and communism for these deprivations. Furthermore, latent anti-Semitism in the Ukrainian population, when mixed with the rabidly anti-Semitic and anti-communist ideology of the Nazis, worked to create the conditions where some Ukrainians volunteered to serve not only as auxiliary soldiers for the invaders, but even as willing executioners of their own Ukrainian Jewish neighbours. In 1973 one Ukrainian-Jewish survivor, Michael Hanusiak, privately published a work about this Ukrainian involvement. The importance of the work lay not merely in his testimonials, but in the voluminous documents and wartime newspaper reports which he had accumulated and used in writing his book. One of those Ukrainian newspaper articles seemed to signal to the local population that it was now time, like in the days of the Czar, for another pogrom against the Jews:

> On July 16 1941, Ivan Hladilovych wrote an article entitled 'Jews – a Bacillus of Decomposition' in which he enthusiastically commented on the Nazis' order for Jews to wear bandages (arm bands) with six-pointed stars: 'The general public of L'viv has greeted with relief this wise initiative which has made it impossible for the 'Sons of Israel' to conceal their 'racial background', as well as their instincts within the mass of Ukrainians, Poles and Muscovites.'[1]

It was therefore no surprise that the Ukrainians, remembering the brief and relatively lenient German occupation during the First World War, believed the Germans to be their liberators. After all, it had been the Germans who had allowed the Ukrainian nation to come into being in 1918. The over-

Map 11. Ukraine, southern Russia and the northern Caucasus Mountains, showing the areas of partisan activity by the autumn of 1941. The guerrilla movement in Ukraine at this time was still nascent. It would not be until the late summer and early autumn of 1942 that the partisan presence in Ukraine would become a larger threat to the Germans.

whelming majority of Ukrainians had no idea who the Nazis were and what they represented, and thus supported the Nazi invasion as a way of freeing themselves from communist tyranny. All over Ukraine, as German troops entered a town or village, the *Landsers* would be pleasantly surprised to see women and girls running up to them and handing them bread and salt – the traditional Ukrainian welcome gift.[2] This act of kindness was even extended at Jewish villages, as many Jews in the USSR could not believe the horror stories that the Communist Party was feeding them about Nazi Germany. Most believed these stories to be exaggerated and mere propaganda, intended to keep the civilian population hostile to Germany.

Of course, this all changed if the German troops exhibited hostility towards them, or when the SS killing units appeared immediately behind the main line of German front-line troops. The fond remembrances of the Kaiser's troops from the First World War were replaced by the terrible and immediate realization that these Germans, wearing a double thunderbolt or skull and crossed bones insignia on the collars of their tunic, were now herding them together, ready to take away their most precious possession: their lives.

The lack of any initial significant partisan activity in Ukraine also appears to have been partly a result of the region's topographical landscape, with its vast steppes. There was little natural cover, such as woods, marshes, hills or mountain ranges. The only exceptions were the Pripet marshes region, which separated Belarus from western Ukraine, and the wooded area referred to as the 'Black Forest' near Cherkassy, both of which lay west of the Dnieper river region.[3] Nevertheless, some partisan formations were created in Ukraine in 1941. For example, a partisan destruction battalion was established in the area around Stalino in August 1941.[4] That same month the 'Victory or Death' Partisan Battalion was created in the Podolsk Rayon. The 'Krasny October' Partisan Battalion was formed near Krichev in early August 1941, while the 'Komarov' Partisan Battalion was established near Pinsk. Another partisan formation was established in the Krivoi Rog region in September but the 213th Security Division encountered the guerrilla unit on 18 October 1941 and killed 1,025 people. The report said that the 1,025 included partisans and 'partisan helpers'. No doubt a good proportion of those killed were civilians who happened to live in the area.[5]

The 'Black Forest' near Cherkassy was evidently a gathering point for partisans from a considerable area of central Ukraine; apparently the band here was liquidated by early 1942, but nothing is known of its organization. Smaller bands east of the Dnieper in the scattered forests of Kiev and Poltava Oblast were evidently under the control of the underground party and NKVD structures. They also vanished by early 1942, with the members possibly seeking refuge in the deeper woods to the north. Small groups in the forests of Kharkov Oblast were liquidated by Ukrainian auxiliaries of the

Germans in late 1942. A succession of small bands appeared in the Donbas, but they were apparently sent in by the Red Army. A post-war US Army interrogation report of three German Abwehr officers,[6] Major Johannes Gänzer, Captain Helmut Damerau and Captain Kurt Kohler, stated that in 1941 partisan action in Ukraine was at a minimum. The testimonials were basically true, although partisan activity actually began to grow in the autumn of 1942 and not in 1943 as these Abwehr officers claimed:

> Conditions differed in the area of *Heeresgruppe Süd* [Army Group South]. Having enlisted the anti-Bolshevik sympathies of the Ukrainians to a considerable extent, the Germans had no partisan trouble there until they began to lose the war. Ukrainian partisan bands began to form in the summer of 1943 and ultimately dominated all of Ukraine. Polish nationalists and communist bands had their beginnings at approximately the same time in Poland and Lithuania. Toward summer 1944, only Estonia and parts of Lithuania were free of partisans.[7]

Another report compiled by the head of *Wirtschaftsinspektion Süd* (Economic Inspectorate South) for the month of April 1942 (dated 1 May 1942) listed several other regions in Ukraine where partisan activity was detected. It reported that a 1,000-strong guerrilla group, led by Red Army and NKVD officers, was operating in the forest region near Selino (Selin) in the Chernigov region, northeast of Kiev, close to the border region with Belarus.[8] The general area from roughly west of Pinsk and following through to the east of Chernigov would be a continuous area of Soviet partisan activity throughout the German occupation.[9] A 50-man partisan band was also discovered operating in the region of Ombish, which lies about two-thirds of the way from Kiev to Konotop, between the Nezhin and Chernigov Oblasts. A 500-man guerrilla force was also reported operating in the region of Michałówka, approximately halfway between Rezeszow and L'viv (present-day sub-Carpathia, Poland). The same report listed guerrilla losses for just one month in the region of the German 2nd Army as 2,000 partisans killed, with 2 artillery pieces, 4 anti-tank guns and 15 machine guns captured.[10] This unit was part of the main Chernigov partisan band, led by a Communist Party official named Oleksii Federov.[11]

Federov's formation became active in the autumn of 1941 and operated in the Gomel-Kletnya-Konotop-Chernigov areas well into 1942.[12] Federov's group would become one of the larger Red Army partisan formations operating in Ukraine but initially it consisted only of about 242 men and women guerrilla fighters.[13] The report by the Economic Inspectorate South also listed a 700-strong guerrilla force operating in the area of Gluchov in the Sumy Oblast. Gluchov is located between Konotop in Ukraine and Bryansk in central Russia, close to the Ukraine-central Russia border region. The distance from Gluchov to the cities of Bryansk, Orel and Kursk is approximately the same. This town and the region surrounding it, therefore, was an important staging area for partisan forces. Another partisan band, composed of about 500 fighters, was operating in the Michailovka-Dimitrovsk region in the Donetsk Oblast.[14] This region lay halfway between Izyum and Mariupol in southeastern Ukraine. The report also lists an estimate of some 20,000 Soviet partisans, divided into 25–30 guerrilla groups, thought to be operating in the Crimea. Altogether, the figures amounted to some 23,000–24,000 guerrillas operating in the region of Ukraine and southern Russia by spring 1942, most of whom were in the Crimea. This, then, was the size and strength of the Soviet partisan movement in Ukraine in 1941 and 1942. The importance of this is that by knowing where guerrillas were likely to be operating during this period, we can better gauge whether a so-called anti-partisan operation was being launched against actual guerrilla forces or if, for lack of actual partisan units, those German 'anti-partisan actions' were in actuality targeting the local civilian population. For example, in 1941 a joint German Army and police anti-partisan operation was launched near Kornin, about 27km west of Fastov, although the available data suggest that no sizeable guerrilla force was listed as operating in this area at that time. Thus, we can better argue that the 'partisans' targeted there were most likely local civilians.

Ukrainian auxiliaries and German Army rear area commands

By June 1942 the Germans had recruited some 30,000 Ukrainians for service in the self-defence battalions.[15] In fact, by November 1942 the total number of Ukrainians serving the German war effort in the Reich Commissariat Ukraine was around 238,000. In June 1943 the number of Ukrainians serving in the self-defence battalions alone was around 80,000 men.[16] Between June 1942 and January 1943 a total of fifty-eight self-defence battalions were created from volunteers. These battalions, which would be principally employed in fighting the partisans, were formed in ten different Ukrainian towns and cities. During anti-partisan operations it wasn't just the local German rear area garrison forces that participated or took part in illegal shootings. The German commanders employed Ukrainian auxiliaries to work alongside the German Army, SS, police, field police and secret field police forces. However, it was the Wehrmacht village and town commanders who actually enlisted them, outfitted them and assigned them to their routine tasks of guarding buildings and roadways and transporting prisoners.[17]

According to Edward Westermann, Ukrainian auxiliaries were employed by the Germans as early as August 1941.[18] In the region under the control of I./882 Local Command, the Ukrainian auxiliary police force stood at

423 men as of 9 April 1942. These were distributed as follows: 95 men in Michailovka Rayon, 74 in Beloserka Rayon, 89 in Lepeticha Rayon and 165 in Kamenka Rayon.[19] It was in the Beloserka Rayon that German troops from the I./882 Local Command discovered about forty Romany men, women and children hiding out in an abandoned factory. A company of Germans supported by a platoon of auxiliary policemen forced the Romany from the factory and drove them to a nearby wooded area just outside the facility, where they shot them.[20] The garrison command covered up the murders by using the excuse that the Romany were fomenting dissension among the Ukrainians, but even if this were true, it did not justify their execution. The local German command did not try to hide the incident and in fact reported the event. The German Army rear area command's tacit approval meant it was therefore taking responsibility for the massacre. Raul Hilberg believes that the local auxiliary forces took part in the killing of the Jewish population on a regular basis:[21]

> In the military areas, the army's native stationary police were another backup force, particularly for the arrest of Jews in hiding. These personnel served under the local indigenous mayors and rural indigenous rayon chiefs under the supervision of the army. In the area of Army Group North, the stationary police were first called *Selbstschutz* and then *Hilfspolizei* (Hipo), in the center *Hilfspolizei* and then *Ordnungsdienst* (OD), in the south *Selbstschutz*, then *Miliz*, and then *Hilfspolizei*. On occasion, some of these auxiliaries were lent to the SS and Police as needed, and later on some became part of the Schutzmannschaft stationed in the *Reichs-kommissariat* and in Ukrainian regions remaining under military control.[22]

Cleansing actions and decrees regarding the war in the East

Between 1 January and 31 March 1942 the 444th Security Division continued to serve in the Dnepropetrovsk, Zaporozhe, Pavlograd, Vasil'kovka, Ssinelnikovo, Orechovo and Melitopol regions, mainly employing the 679th and 774th Field Commands and the 726th and 774th Secret Field Police Groups, the 311th Police Battalion and the 708th Guard Battalion. The 444th Security Division performed operations against Red Army parachutists and partisans, secured bridges, railways and highways, and constructed strong points, as well as engaging in other security duties. Reports from this time were typed in typical efficient fashion and almost always described the partisans as 'bandits'. Terms like *Säuberungsunternehmen* ('cleansing operation') or *Aufräumarbeiten* ('clean-up work') were common.[23] One such report described in a matter-of-fact manner the 'cleansing' of the localities of Yevekaya, Andreyevka and Michaylovka by the 725th Secret Field Police Group.[24]

During the month of March 1942 the 444th Security Division was partly pressed into front-line service in the Pavlograd area after the Soviet break-through at Izium. The Russian winter counter-offensive forced the Germans to commit forces to their front lines that would otherwise been employed in the rear areas, and it was to their detriment that these anti-partisan units were not equipped nor trained for actual front-line combat. During this time the 311th Police Battalion was committed in the Pavlograd region and suffered accordingly. From 11 to 28 February 1942 this battalion lost 29 men killed and 122 wounded.[25] This was quite a reduction in strength from a tally taken of the battalion on 15 January 1942, when its roster listed a total of 582 officers, NCOs and enlisted men.[26] The entire 444th Security Division on this date had exactly 6,369 men, a relatively small number but typical of the security divisions. The same document listed the strength reports for the 711th, 720th and 726th Secret Field Police Groups which were attached to the 444th Security Division.[27] At the start of the Russo-German war, each secret field police group contained, on average, anywhere from 80 to 120 men (about a company in size). At this time, however, all three groups combined could barely muster enough men for one company.[28] A report was released to all troops serving within the 444th Security Division, but directed at all soldiers serving in the region of Army Group South, in which the Army Group commander, Field Marshal von Bock[29] issued the following statement:

> Treatment of German Prisoners – The Supreme Commander of Army Group [South] acknowledges the following: In the Crimea, it has been absolutely witnessed that German soldiers who surrendered after discarding their weapons were shot by the Red Army. Their corpses were subsequently plundered. I state this not to approve the same measures, but rather to bring to the attention of all soldiers under my command that the bestial Bolshevik opponent observes no norms of military behaviour. Each soldier must be aware of what this means and to be clear to avoid retreat or surrender.[30]

While this minor note might be ignored at first as inconsequential, it is important in the overall behaviour of the German Army vis-à-vis how the German soldier perceived the enemy. Any soldier reading or hearing this declaration by such a noted German officer as Field Marshal von Bock would naturally believe the report, and as a result might afterwards be inclined to treat Russian soldiers or partisans more harshly because of it. This would be a totally normal reaction and quite within the realm of possibility. While we cannot say for sure if stirring up hatred and anger was the intention of the report, it nevertheless most likely had that effect. At the very least a German soldier listening to this report would be disinclined to surrender to the Red Army. The issue as to whether the Red Army did indeed kill Germans who were trying to surrender is a mixed bag. It appears that in the case of SS men who gave themselves up to a partisan unit, surrendering was not a good idea:

> The mass of people darted toward the prisoner, shoving each other, stepping over one another. The first to reach the SS man was Pupko, the oldest man in the Otriad, described by some as 75 years old, by others as 80. With knife in hand, Pupko screamed, 'God. My grandfather was not a murderer, my father was not a murderer, but I will be a murderer.' Something in the old man's voice stopped the crowd's advance. It halted with their eyes glued to Pupko's knife. As if in a trance, this main actor began the job of cutting up the SS man. A murmur of approval escaped from the mass of people. This wordless conversation urged Pupko to continue, to finish the job. In a few intense, highly charged moments, the SS man was unrecognizable and dead. The two other prisoners were shot.[31]

If SS soldiers were to surrender to regular Red Army units, they could expect similar treatment, given the ideology which their SS uniform stood for and represented to most Russians: a philosophy of extermination. Just as Russian prisoner-of-war deaths were high because of German abuse and neglect, so German prisoner-of-war deaths were equally elevated because of Russian abuse.[32] The level of cruelty in the East truly made this a war of annihilation. During the war about 260,000 German soldiers who had been captured by the Red Army died in Russian captivity.[33] This figure, however, pales in comparison to the estimated 3 million Soviet POWs who died in German custody. It was the Germans' *Weltanschauungskrieg* policy that caused so many deaths. They captured vast numbers of Red Army soldiers, especially during the first six months of the campaign, when the Russian soldiers were unaware of the treatment they would receive at the hands of the Germans. Millions of these Red Army prisoners of war would die of neglect while in German captivity. Between 25 and 70 per cent died while in transit to the camps, basically through exposure, hunger and thirst.[34]

For the German soldier who surrendered, the question boiled down to which Red Army units accepted prisoners and which did not. If a German soldier was lucky, he could surrender, but the act was always a lottery. Most likely the typical German *Landser* would almost certainly now begin to believe (if he didn't before) that the orders issued to the army regarding the shooting of all Russian prisoners immediately after interrogation were justified because of the uncompromising manner in which the Russians seemed to be conducting the war. This order had cost about 45,700 lives between July and November 1941.[35] In fact, by March 1942 German statistics regarding the anti-guerrilla struggle listed 63,257 partisans killed vs. 638 Germans killed and 1,355 wounded. Hannes Heer states that the low number of German

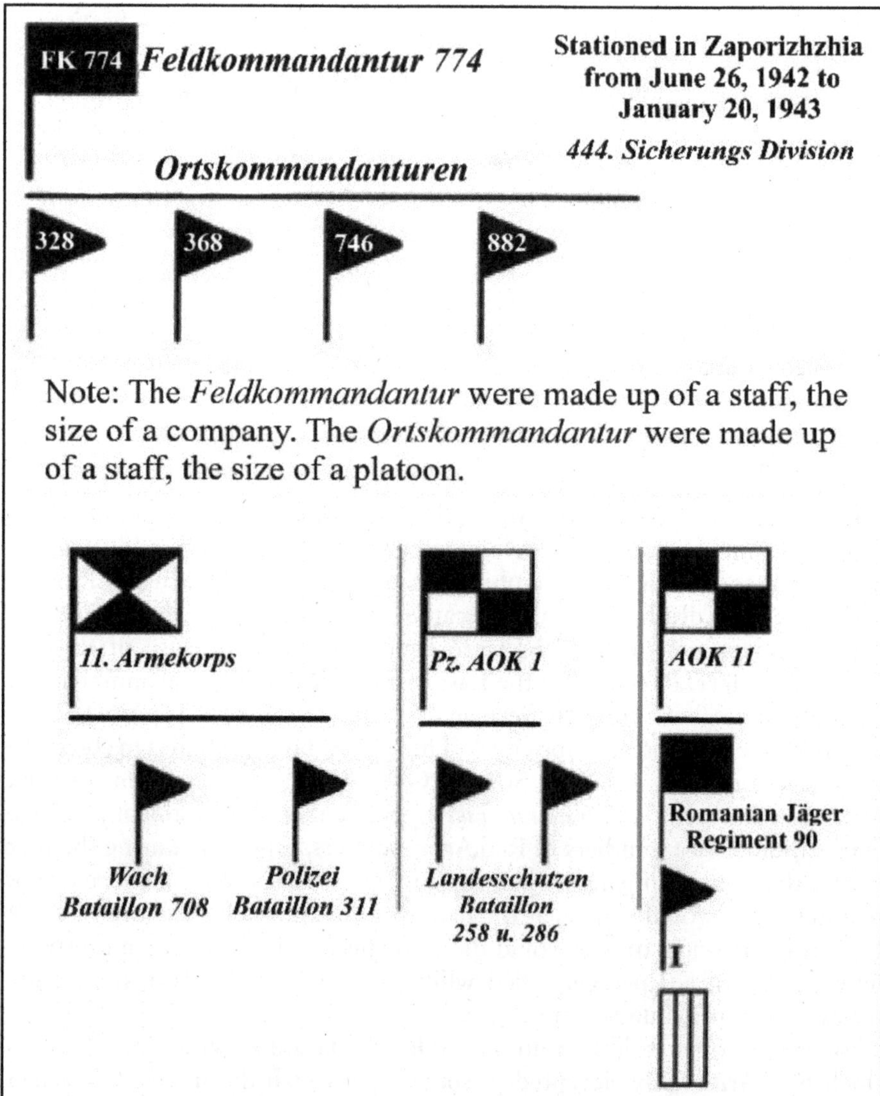

Figure 8.1. Field commands and local commands under 444. Sicherungs Division, March 1942.

losses compared to the high 'partisan' figures indicates that most of the 'partisans' were actually civilians, and that they had not been killed in combat.[36] By 4 March 1942 the 444th Security Division had been dramatically expanded on account of the need for more security forces.[37]

This expansion was important because the division would soon be directed to follow the German summer offensive and as a result more territory would come under German control. Additional units would be attached to the division for this reason.[38] As for the criminal orders, which in effect gave the Wehrmacht a licence to kill, they were reinforced by further decrees during the campaign. The first major directive which affirmed and expanded these orders was the Armed Forces High Command directive on communist insurrection in the occupied territories, dated 16 September 1941. The order read in part that 'no matter what the individual circumstances that it is of communist origin'.[39] So any act considered damaging to the German war effort was now to be considered communist-inspired. Even though this statement seems to expand the decrees to include any act which the Germans deemed detrimental to the German war effort by simply labelling someone or some act as 'communist', it was the second clause which showed just how little regard Wilhelm Keitel, the head of the Armed Forces High Command, had for non-Germans:

> In order to nip these machinations in the bud, the most drastic measures should be taken immediately on the first indication, so that the authority of the occupying forces may be maintained, and further spreading prevented. In this connection it should be remembered that a human life in unsettled countries frequently counts for nothing and a deterrent effect can be attained only by unusual severity. The death penalty for 50–100 communists should generally be regarded in these cases as suitable atonement for one German soldier's life. The way in which sentence is carried out should still further increase the deterrent effect.[40]

Thus, to General Keitel non-German life counted for nothing, and 50–100 civilian deaths were to be exacted for every German killed behind the lines. In addition, he demanded that the manner in which the civilians were to be killed was to have a further deterrent effect. One can only surmise that he was probably speaking about, say, hanging civilians, which is a much more gruesome death than just shooting them. The final clause of this decree stated that only the death penalty was a sufficient deterrent, leaving the Wehrmacht officers in charge of carrying out punishment for acts deemed counter to the German war effort with only one option: murder.

The next order of significant importance was the infamous Reichenau Order of 10 October 1941 on the conduct of troops in the eastern territories. Field Marshal Walter von Reichenau was the commander of 6th Army, then operating in the region of Army Group South. In this order he stated:

> Therefore, the soldier must have full understanding for the necessity of a severe but just revenge on subhuman Jewry. The Army has to aim at another purpose; i.e., the annihilation of revolts in the hinterland which, as experience proves, have always been caused by Jews ... The feeding of the natives and of prisoners-of-war who are not working for the armed

> forces from army kitchens is an equally misunderstood humanitarian act as is the giving of cigarettes and bread. Things which the people at home can spare under great sacrifices and things which are being brought by the Command to the front under great difficulties should not be given to the enemy by the soldier, not even if they originate from booty. It is an important part of our supply.[41]

To Reichenau, feeding the local Soviet civilian population or captured Red Army prisoners of war, even if they were starving, was tantamount to betraying not only the Wehrmacht, which he described as making great efforts to bring forward these supplies, but the *Heimat* (homeland) as well. The obvious attempt here was to try to give the German soldier reasons why he should behave more severely and eliminate from the German war machine any traces of humanity by interpreting any acts of pity for the Soviet civilian or prisoner of war population as a betrayal of his community (the Wehrmacht) or his *volk* (people).

Although this order was Reichenau's most infamous, it was by no means his first or last criminal decree. An earlier 6th Army command order, dated 21 August 1941, went into detail about how Wehrmacht troops on patrol were to treat suspicious persons and persons who were identified as not being from the region they were apprehended in. The title of the order was 'Arrest by patrols of suspects and persons not living locally'.[42] It stated clearly that 'All suspicious persons (men and women)[43] are to be arrested and checked. Those that are thought to be spies, saboteurs or partisans are to be shot after interrogation by the Secret Field Police.'[44] The most important words here are 'thought to be', since this phrase implies that no verifiable proof was needed in order to shoot these civilians, only the arbitrary suspicions of the soldiers who had detained them while on patrol. That belief was sufficient to allow the German soldiers to shoot them. However, the one stipulation that Reichenau listed was that such persons would first be interrogated by the secret field police, ostensibly to try to obtain information from them about the local partisan movement, before they were executed.

The next important decree was issued by another army commander, Erich von Manstein, head of 11th Army in the region of the Crimea, in Army Group South. The order dealt with the organization and execution of the combating of partisans, and was signed on 29 November 1941. The first thing that one notices when looking at this decree is that Manstein makes it explicit that replacement and supply troops would be employed in helping to combat the guerrilla menace. Thus, being in a reserve or non-combat formation behind the lines no longer exempted a German soldier from being employed against the partisans. This basically showed that all the German formations behind the front lines were now potential anti-partisan troops – and thus also potential murderers. Part 6 of this order indicated clearly that Wehrmacht and *SS* cooperation was to be very much a common occurrence:

> All headquarters are to be instructed to give far-reaching assistance to the 'Staff for the Combating of Partisans' and to the *Sonderkommandos* and Army units employed by it, by allotting to them reinforcements and supplies. Section DQMG, GHQ 11th Army has received special orders in this respect.[45]

Therefore, von Manstein's army troops were to give full aid and cooperation to the *Sonderkommandos*. The significance of this is that in the end the Wehrmacht was both directly and indirectly helping in the murder of innocent civilians, this time on the pretext of fighting the guerrillas, by aiding these SS killing units. Such Wehrmacht and SS cooperation, and its consequences, can be seen in an incident that occurred in the Crimea in January 1942. It appears that a Soviet partisan battalion of about 650 well armed guerrillas had entered the city of Evpatoria.[46] The 105th Infantry Regiment and the 70th Engineer Battalion under the command of Colonel Müller were trying to expel the guerrillas from the city. A call for support by the army garrison command went out. *Sonderkommando* 11b was brought in to help support the army effort, but the first thing it did was to murder 1,200 civilians in a local warehouse:

> Part of the civilian population was pro-German. It was proposed therefore that Riesen, the Abwehr officer should accompany Werner Braune and 'advise' the leader of *Sonderkommando* 11b on which of these civilians were sympathetic German supporters. A total of four GFP officials accompanied Reisen and *Sonderkommando* 11b into Evpatoria. Of the four GFP officials, two had arrived separately on 7 January 1942. Fighting was still occurring inside the city, but Colonel Müller stated that the last 'resistance nests' were being demolished. *Sonderkommando* 11b's answer to the fighting in the city was to shoot 1,200 civilians in a warehouse.[47]

An attempt was made to rein in Braune and his SS killers by 'assisting' them to differentiate between friendly locals and the partisans fighting within the city. That is why Major Riesen, a German Army intelligence officer, and four secret field police officials accompanied SS First Lieutenant Dr Werner Braune and *Sonderkommando* 11b into Evpatoria – so that abuses could be prevented. However, as can be seen, the murderous cruelty which some in the army feared occurred nonetheless. While Braune and his SS men were directly responsible for the executions, the Wehrmacht is partly accountable because they employed this SS killing unit knowing full well what it was accustomed to doing. The Wehrmacht effort to advise Braune clearly indicates that they knew what was likely to happen if they allowed *Sonderkommando* 11b into the city. And yet they permitted it within the context of fighting the guerrillas. According to Martin Gilbert, 1,300 Jews were murdered in Evpatoria between 1 and 15 January 1942, with an additional 22 Jews murdered on 17 January 1942.[48]

If the civilians murdered in the warehouse are the same Jewish people Gilbert mentions, then here again is another example where Jews were murdered on the pretext of fighting the guerrillas, and the mentality that 'every Jew is a guerrilla fighter' reaches its horrific conclusion. Did the secret field policemen and the army intelligence officer escorting Braune and his SS men help them to decide who was a Jew and who was not? After all, the Germans themselves stated that there were civilians in the city friendly to the German cause. Did Major Riesen and the secret field police help to identify and apprehend the Jews in the city? We cannot answer this with any certainty. But the fact that they were present with this SS killing unit is, at the very least, subject to the accusation of guilt by association – or even that they were just as responsible for the massacre as if they had taken part in it themselves.

This, then, is the crime of the Wehrmacht at Evpatoria in January 1942: it was aware of the reputation of this SS killing unit, but decided to employ the force anyway, just for the sake of retaking the city. To make a better case against the unit's employment, Colonel Müller himself had stated that the 'last resistance nests were being demolished',[49] so the employment of *Sonderkommando* 11b most likely was not necessary in defeating the partisan battalion. In fact, even though the unit was deployed there, it fought no guerrillas but was instead used against unarmed civilians – something at which it seemed to excel. While the Wehrmacht command had no direct control over this SS unit, it did have control over fighting the partisan war, so the local Wehrmacht division, corps or army headquarters stationed in the area certainly had the power to prevent the employment of *Sonderkommando* 11b if it had wanted to. What all this means is that the immoral behaviour of the Wehrmacht in the East was condoned because of the criminal orders and a regime that further affirmed and legalized these criminal mandates.

The various criminal orders combined with the ideological war to create a poisonous cocktail that affected many Germans who served in the *Ostheer*. Here anti-Semitism was heightened by anti-communist sentiment, and morphed into what the Nazis referred to as 'Judeo-Bolshevism'. By turning morality upside down, the Nazis were able to achieve their annihilatory aims in the Soviet Union, not merely by employing the SS *Einsatzgruppen*, but by making the Wehrmacht complicit in what was basically a racial and ideological struggle. To a great degree, it appears that the Nazis were able to accomplish this with little difficulty. That mindset, as typified by the following excerpt, was in many cases the norm for German behaviour in the East.

During a conference on 18 June 1941, dealing with the criminal orders, Chief Court Martial Councillor Dr Weber declared at an officers' meeting of 11th Army that:

> Every soldier must know that he has to defend himself against all attacks in battle, and that in cases of doubt he has to bring detained persons to the nearest officer. Every officer must know that he can have detained persons shot or released, that political commissars are to be taken aside and finished off. Every battalion commander must know that he can order collective forced measures.[50]

Thus, the ideological war was to be ingrained into the mindset of every soldier, and every officer was to know to what extremes he would be allowed to operate in the East. The following accounts describe some of the documented consequences of this policy and these attitudes throughout the rear areas,[51] and the Wehrmacht forces which were involved. In some instances, army participation was direct; in others, it was indirect. However, in all instances some degree of criminality, whether great or small, must be attributable to the *Ostheer*. Individually most of these cases may seem trivial, perhaps insignificant, but when added together they illustrate a pattern of abuse that points to a systemic, intentional policy regarding the way in which the indigenous population was treated. The brutalization of warfare in the East is another factor that contributed to the harsh manner in which German forces operated, both in the front lines and in the rear areas.

Murder in the Ukrainian town of Fastov, mid-August 1941

An early case of a criminal act by army security units operating in the USSR occurred in mid-August 1941 in the Ukrainian town of Fastov, which at the time was an important rail junction southwest of Kiev. It appears that secret field police personnel and members of a regional defence battalion belonging to the 213th Security Division[52] shot about 30 so-called snipers and around 50 Jews shortly before the arrival of an SS mobile killing unit, *Sonderkommando* 4a. According to one report which survived, the actions caused such an uproar among the population of the town that order there could only be restored 'after *Sonderkommando* 4a shot all the Jewish inhabitants between 12 and 60'.[53] This report was part of a series of captured documents now held by the United States and German governments. Apparently, SS Lieutenant Colonel Dr Theodor Paeffgen[54] had been charged with destroying these documents (among many others) at the end of the war, but had forgotten to do so.[55] Paeffgen had previously served in the Baltic States in 1941–1942.[56] In 1942 he was promoted and placed at the head of Department VI-D (Foreign Intelligence) of the SS Security Service in Berlin.[57]

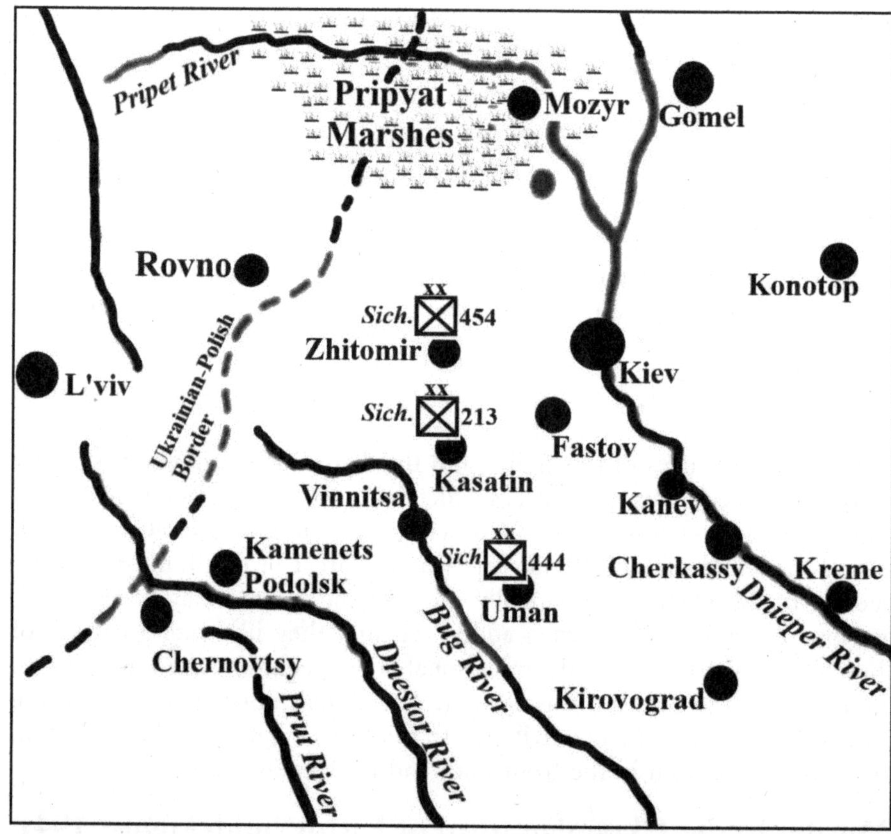

Map 12. Location of German security divisions in western Ukraine, 10 September 1941.

There is no way to prove if indeed the thirty Russians accused of being snipers were really guilty. We only know that the Germans shot them. Even if the accusation were true, it still does not explain why fifty Jews were liquidated alongside the snipers. Again, we are drawn to the criminal orders and the ideological war, which clearly gave these men what they saw as a mandate for murder. Jews here, as shown in a previous example, are seen being selected for murder and the local Soviet civilian population is treated to harsh and arbitrary judgement. The pattern of abuse and outrageous behaviour on the part of the Germans had begun to show itself in this region of the USSR.

Cleansing action by the field police in Tokmak[58], October 1941

At the end of October 1941 *Einsatzkommando* 12 of *Einsatzgruppe* D, nominally under the jurisdictional control of 11th Army, headed for Stalino, accompanied by the 3rd Company, 683rd Military Field Police Battalion (motorized).[59] On the way both units entered the forest region between the towns of Tokmak and Yefimovka. There, the military field policemen and members of *Einsatzkommando* 12 apprehended many 'suspected partisans' and Jews and hanged them before heading out to Stalino.[60] The exact numbers killed between Tokmak and Yefimovka are unknown, but we do know that in April 1942 some 1,600 Jews still lived in Stalino itself and that between April and June, when *Einsatzkommando* 6 of *Einsatzgruppe* C finally entered the city, the entire region around Stalino had suffered 75,000 deaths due to these 'cleansing' operations and anti-guerrilla sweeps.[61]

Hunting for food near Belaya-Tserkov, Zhitomir region, 4 November 1941

The deposition of one German Army soldier, Albert Bartel, gives us an insight into the kind of occurrences which took place and the almost matter-of-fact brutality with which some Germans operated in the East. His short testimony relates how on one day, 14 November 1941, he had seen one of his immediate superiors, *Leutnant* Haas, returning to the bivouac area with meat for dinner:

> We spent a month resting in Belaya-Tserkov. Our officers made small raids on the neighbouring settlements in order to 'improve' the food supply. On 14 November 1941 Lieutenant Haas returned with some meat. When questioned by the [other] officers, who were interested in knowing how he managed to meet with such success, he calmly answered in his Breslau dialect: 'The damned people did not want to give it up; I had to kill them first.'[62]

What this shows is the total disregard for the Russian civilian population and a general callousness shown by many German soldiers. Haas's solution to the problem of obtaining the meat was brutal. He simply killed the civilians because they would not give up their food. He could have threatened them, or even wounded one or two to dissuade the others from resisting. Yet he chose to kill them all. In his mind, we can assume they were *Lebensunwertes Leben* (life not worthy of life). It is a perfect paradigm of the ideological war put into practice. If Field Marshal von Reichenau had heard of this incident, he would have most likely been pleased. He had recently released an order, dated 10 October 1941, specifically encouraging harshness on the part of the German soldier in denying the Russian civilians or prisoners of war any food supplies. We cannot ascertain how much influence the Reichenau Order had on the behaviour of Germans in the USSR, but it must have added more fuel to the fire.

Retribution massacre, Myrgorod region of southern Russia, 9 November 1941

German Army complicity in illegal killings during the war was not limited to the rear areas where the security divisions operated. In many instances, front-line units were pulled out of the lines and used in so-called 'cleansing' operations, especially in cases where the German command felt that retribution had to be exacted. One such incident occurred in November 1941 in southern Russia, in the village of Baranivka, in 6th Army's operational area. On 4 November a partisan band had attacked and killed a German Army colonel and several staff members at Baranivka. This colonel happened to be known personally to *Generalfeldmarschall* Walter von Reichenau, the current commander of 6th Army. A battalion of the 62nd Infantry Division, which at the time was assigned to the anti-partisan staff of Army Group South in the Myrgorod region, was chosen to search for the partisan perpetrators and destroy them. On 9 November 1941 the 11th Company, III. Battalion, 190th Infantry Regiment, arrived at Baranivka, recovered the German bodies and then sought out the guerrillas, who had long since departed. Unable to find the perpetrators, the Germans shot ten local inhabitants and burned the village to the ground. The report claims that explosions from hidden grenades or munitions occurred as a result of the fires.[63] Thus under the pretext of fighting the guerrillas, a German Army company had committed an atrocity. Again, we see the criminal orders creating the conditions which legalized this kind of barbarity on the part of the Wehrmacht against the Soviet civilian population within the context of fighting the guerrillas.

Massacre of Jewish refugees in the village of Yuryevka, 23 November 1941

Following in the wake of the massacre at Baranivka, the 7th Company of II. Battalion, 164th Infantry Regiment, 62nd Infantry Division, entered the village of Yuryevka, which was located about 7km northeast of Liutenka.[64] They then marched off to the nearby collective farm, where they asked a local if there were any Jews about. One farmer told the Germans about a group of Jews who had arrived fleeing the German advance and had been allowed to stay on the farm. Truman Anderson described the events that followed:

> The German report on this incident says only that twenty-three Jews were shot and offers no pretext for the killing. A resident of Yuryevka who claimed to have witnessed this execution as an 11-year-old girl said in an interview with the author that these Jews were refugees from somewhere to the west. They had fled before the German advance and gone to the local collective farm seeking help. The council agreed to help them and had given them jobs on the farm and a house in Yuryevka.

> When the patrol from the 7th company arrived on the 23rd, they asked a man who lived in Yuryevka whether there were any Jews in the village, and he told them about the refugees. The Germans ordered them from their home and shot them all – men, women and children. By all appearances this was, like the massacre of Jews in Myrgorod, a clear-cut instance of racial murder. As with the Myrgorod killing, this execution was reported up the chain of command in a very routine fashion, and there is no evidence of disapproval in either the Heeresgebiet or 62nd Division records.[65]

According to Anderson, the 202nd Replacement Brigade assumed the security duties which the regiments of 62nd Infantry Division had been performing on 21 December 1941.[66] This replacement brigade continued to search for guerrillas operating in the region of Poltava. With this example we see yet again how the jurisdictional decree empowered an army soldier to kill Russians suspected of partisan activity and all Jews, without trial or any shred of evidence.[67]

Forest area by Novo-Moskov-Pavlograd, 9 December 1941–1 January 1942

This operation involved various regional defence battalions located in and around Novo Moskovsk and Pavlograd and was aimed at clearing the railway line that ran from Dnepropetrovsk to Pavlograd. The Red Army winter counter-offensive was driving a bulge west of the Donetz river by Izyum, north of Pavlograd. This area of the Soviet advance eventually came to be known as the 'Izyum bulge'. The partisans hoped to help the Red Army offensive in that region by disrupting the railway line. The following forces were employed in the anti-partisan drive:

- Elements of 213th Security Division
- 711th, 720th and 725th Secret Field Police Groups
- 213th and 444th Cossack Cavalry Squadrons
- 414th Regional Defence Battalion
- Company from the 901st Regional Defence Battalion
- 311th Police Battalion
- I. and III. Battalions, 190th Light Regiment (listed in a later frame)
- 679th Local Command (Zaporozhye)
- 270th Field Command (Choplino)
- 286th Field Command (Zaporozhye)
- 829th Field Command (Pavlograd)
- 835th Field Command (Dnepropetrovsk)
- 837th Field Command (Novo Moskva)

The first official anti-partisan operation launched in Ukraine by the 213th Security Division occurred on 18 October 1941 just north of Krivoi Rog. In the second week of December 1941 another major drive took place in the forest region of Novo Moskov-Pavlograd.[68] The partisans in this area were supposed to have numbered about 500 men and were split up into 'West' and 'East' groups. The 'East' group was said to number 200 guerrillas, while the 'West' group could count on 300. The headquarters in charge of the operation was the 837th Local Command,[69] which was previously stationed in France, but had been sent to the East and attached to the 213th Security Division on 1 April 1941.[70]

Troops assigned to the operation included the 711th, 720th and 725th Secret Field Police Groups, the 213th and 444th Cossack Cavalry Squadrons, the 414th Regional Defence Battalion, 4th Company, 901st Regional Defence Battalion and the 311th Police Battalion. A later frame also lists the I. and III.

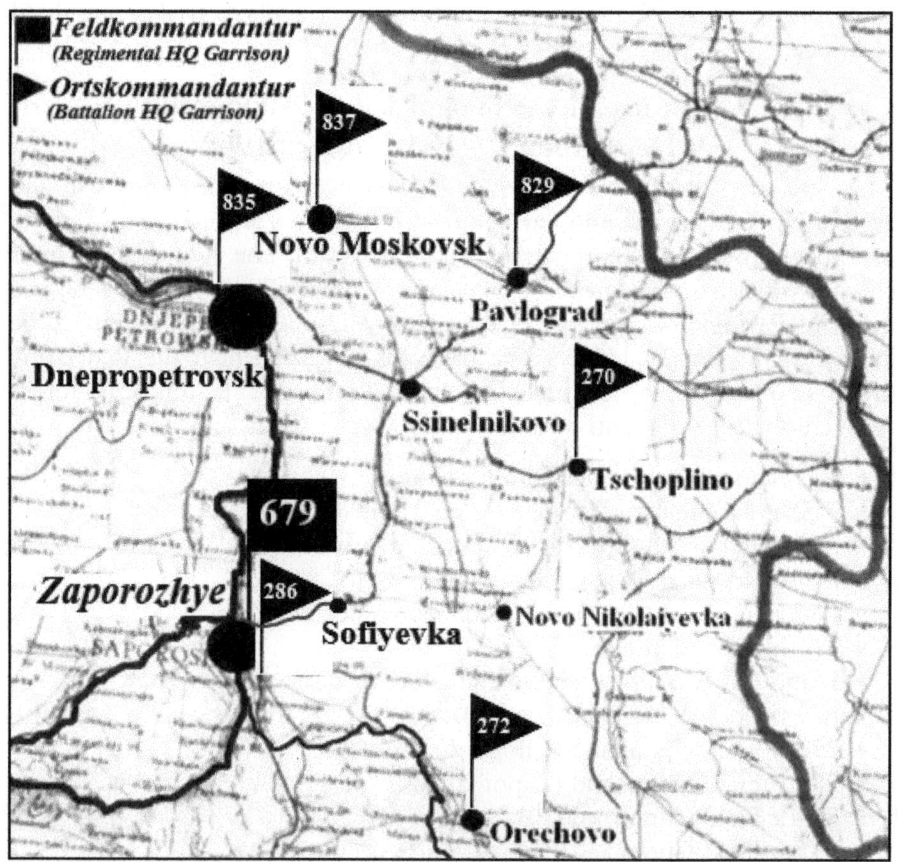

Map 13. Anti-partisan drive in Novo Moskov-Pavlograd, December 1941 to January 1942.

Battalions, 190th Light Regiment, as taking part in the operation.[71] According to one source, the 318th Police Battalion was assigned to the 213th Security Division in the summer of 1941,[72] while the 311th Police Battalion was attached to the 444th Security Division, but it may just be that these two battalions were transferred between the two security divisions on a need-for-need basis, given that a pre-invasion document stated that the 318th Police Battalion belonged to the 213th Security Division and the 311th Police Battalion was assigned to the 444th Security Division.[73]

Therefore, the employment of the 311th Police Battalion alongside the 213th Security Division must have been on a temporary basis. Under the control of the 213th Security Division, the 318th Police Battalion would be implicated in the massacre of the Jewish communities in Volhynia, Luck (Luzk) and Rovno, to name a few.[74] The operation in a forest area near Novo Moskov-Pavlograd was carried out by a combined army and police force. While we cannot say for certain how many Jews were killed by the police or how many were killed by the army, the fact that army forces were needed to augment the small police force which took part in this operation makes them just as guilty of this crime because without their help, the operation could not have achieved the same results. The one German police battalion in the operation, the 311th, had served in Poland before being sent to Russia. According to one source, the 311th Police Battalion was responsible for the deaths of 5,186 non-Jewish civilians.

However, the larger and more significant killing tally for the 311th Police Battalion occurred on 11 October 1941, when its companies shot at least 11,000 Jews in Dnepropetrovsk.[75] Not all of the units originally involved in the anti-partisan drive that began on 9 December 1941 followed the operation through into late December. Those which did included the following formations[76], which at the time were operating under the 213th Security Division:

- 414th Regional Defence Battalion
- 444th Cossack Cavalry Squadron
- 720th Secret Field Police Group
- one battalion from the 162nd Artillery Regiment
- 1st Company, 246th Construction Battalion
- 3rd Company, 531st Construction Battalion
- 311th Police Battalion

German losses proved insignificant, indicating that perhaps the number of actual guerrillas may have been inflated by adding innocent civilians to the tally, thus making the operation seem all the more successful.[77] The partisan battalion which had been the principal target for this anti-partisan operation had been raised in the region of Dnepropetrovsk in August 1941.[78] It had immediately headed for the Novo Moskov woods in order to prepare to fight the Germans in that region.[79] In 1939 the Jewish population of Dnepropetrovsk stood at a sizable 129,439 men, women and children.[80]

The operation netted the following 'bandit losses' (*Verluste der Banditen*):

- 260 *Banditen erschossen* ('bandits shot')
- 2 *Flintenweiber erschossen* ('female gunmen shot')
- 76 *Banditen Gefangen* ('bandits taken prisoner')
- 4 *Flintenweiber Gefangen* ('female gunmen taken prisoner')
- 39 *Kriegsgefangene erschossen* ('POWs shot')
- 56 *Wieder gefangen* ('recaptured')
- 372 *Sonstige verdachtige Personen verhaftet* ('suspicious persons apprehended')
- 136 *Juden erschossen* ('Jews shot').[81]

It is clear from this operation that some differentiation was made by the German Army's 213th Security Division staff between 'bandits' and 'Jews' by listing them separately, although in practice Nazi propaganda made Jews synonymous with partisans, and all were eventually shot. In the case of the bandits, it appears that initially at least they were kept alive, as the list indicates. However, with the Jews the record simply lists them as 'shot'. If the Jews had been combatants, then perhaps they might have been listed as 'bandit Jews shot', but because there is no indication that the Jews listed here were involved in the 'banditry' (as the Germans referred to the guerrilla movement at this time) then we can surmise that the 136 Jews shot may have simply been Russian Jewish civilians taken during the operation and then shot for being Jews. It might also be possible that the Germans grouped combatant and non-combatant Jews that they encountered during the operation into one group so that their command would know how many Jews were killed during the drive. In any event, it clearly shows a German obsession with targeting Jewry for destruction. What is also significant about this operation is that it shows army and police cooperation in hunting down and killing Jews. Without army cooperation, it is unlikely that the police force available would have been sufficient to conduct the operation and kill as many partisans and Jews as it eventually did. Therefore, another important point to derive from this operation is that army assistance was critical to the success of the operation and therefore, to the murder of the Jews taken during the drive. The Wehrmacht forces taking part in this operation are as guilty of the crime as if they themselves had carried out the shootings.

Chapter 9

German security divisions in Ukraine and southern Russia

A good guerrilla leader strikes at the appropriate time.
[Emmerson Mnangagwa]

The 213th, 444th and 454th Security Divisions in Ukraine and Russia, 1941

The 444th Security Division was established on 15 March 1941 in the town of Ohlau (Military District VIII). By May it was stationed in the East in anticipation of its employment in the rear of Army Group South. Its order of battle just before Operation Barbarossa is shown in Fig. 9.1. From April 1941 until February 1942 Lieutenant General Wilhelm Rußwurm was its commander.[1]

The 454th Security Division was to form part of the rear area security force for Army Group South in the coming invasion of the Soviet Union. Like its sister division, the 444th, it moved immediately behind the advancing German forces on 22 June 1941. Both divisions had a limited number of motorized vehicles and were considered limited mobility units. Like the

Figure 9.1. The 444th Security Division on 15 May 1941.

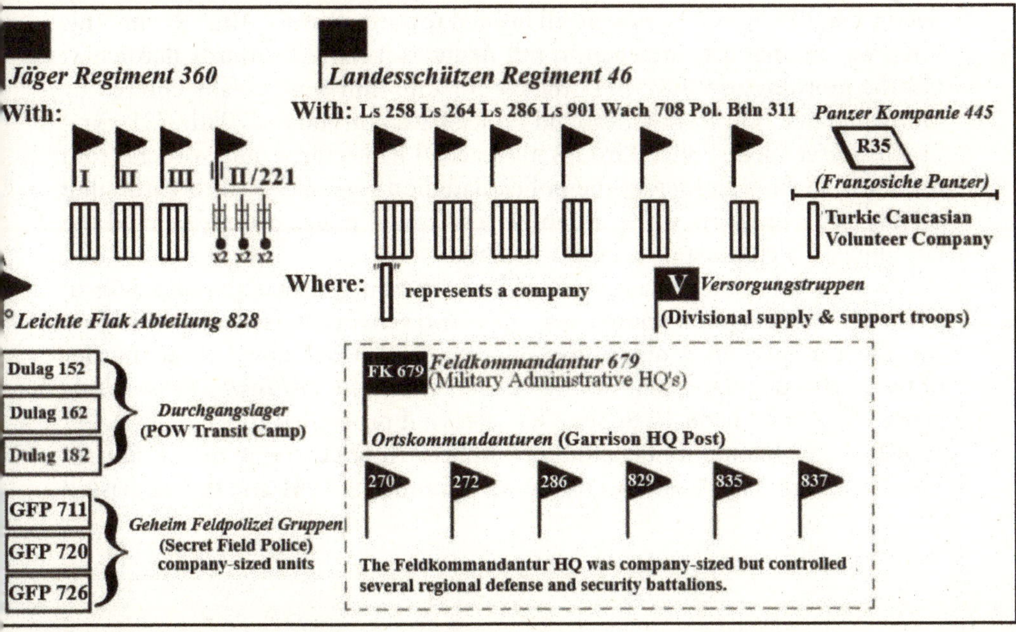

311th Police Battalion, the 444th Security Division, the 82nd Police Battalion was the only fully motorized unit in the 454th Security Division. On 23 June 1941 the 82nd Police Battalion was moving towards the Trepcza-Temeszow region, but on the night of 23/24 June it became the 454th Security Division's reserve unit and was stationed in the area of Pielnia, about 56km south of Rzeszow.[2] On 26 June 1941 the 4th Technical Emergency Company, Police Regiment South was attached to the 454th Security Division in the region of Temeszow, about 40km west-southwest of Przemysl, and 35km south-southeast of Rzeszow.[3] The following day, 28 June, a war diary report for the division stated that the 82nd Police Battalion had 'cleaned out the enemy' in a forest area by Olchovski.[4] For this action, the commander of the 82nd Police Battalion, Police Captain Ebert,[5] received the Iron Cross, 2nd Class on 28 June. On 1 July 1941 the same police battalion was operating in the Rybotycze-Przemysl-Bircza area in what was termed a 'cleansing' operation.

The war diary report also noted that the local Ukrainian population wished to create a Ukrainian *Selbstschutz* ('self-defence') force, to be attached to the 454th Security Division. Rybotycze had a pre-war Jewish population of 314 people, while Przemysl had 17,326 and Bircza had 1,038.[6] Four days later, on 5 July, the 82nd Police Battalion, acting on orders from the 454th Security Division, and supported by a secret field police force (also from the division), marched through the localities of Chyrov, Sambor, Rudki and Wlk Lubien, and then turned north towards L'viv.[7] It was in L'viv that the headquarters of the 454th Security Division was ordered to create a prisoner-of-war transit camp in a large warehouse in the city, which would eventually hold 3,000 prisoners. At this time the 721st Secret Field Police Group happened to be stationed in L'viv and assisted in the housing of these prisoners.[8]

By 18 July 1941 the 82nd Police Battalion and the 708th, 721st and 730th Secret Field Police Groups were all headed towards Rovno. After Rovno, this force was temporarily attached to 6th Army as it moved towards Berdichev. On the morning of 9 July 1941 the city of Zhitomir was initially entered by German units.[9] On 19 July the 82nd Police Battalion and the 708th, 721st and 730th Secret Field Police Groups all reached Zhitomir. Under orders from the local SS *Einsatzgruppen*, the police battalion was relegated to cordoning off the city's outskirts while the three secret field police groups entered the city under SS command looking for Jews.[10]

It was at this time, according to Gerald Reitlinger, that the massacre of Zhitomir's Jewish population occurred.[11] Also arriving at Zhitomir on 19 July was the headquarters group of *Einsatzgruppe* C,[12] which now led the murder of the Jewish population in the city. A source claims that *Einsatzkommando* 4a arrived at Zhitomir on 19 September 1941 and proceeded to wipe out 3,145 Jewish men, women and children.[13] Andrej Angrick states that Reinhard Heydrich visited the Eastern Front in the summer of 1941 and that he passed

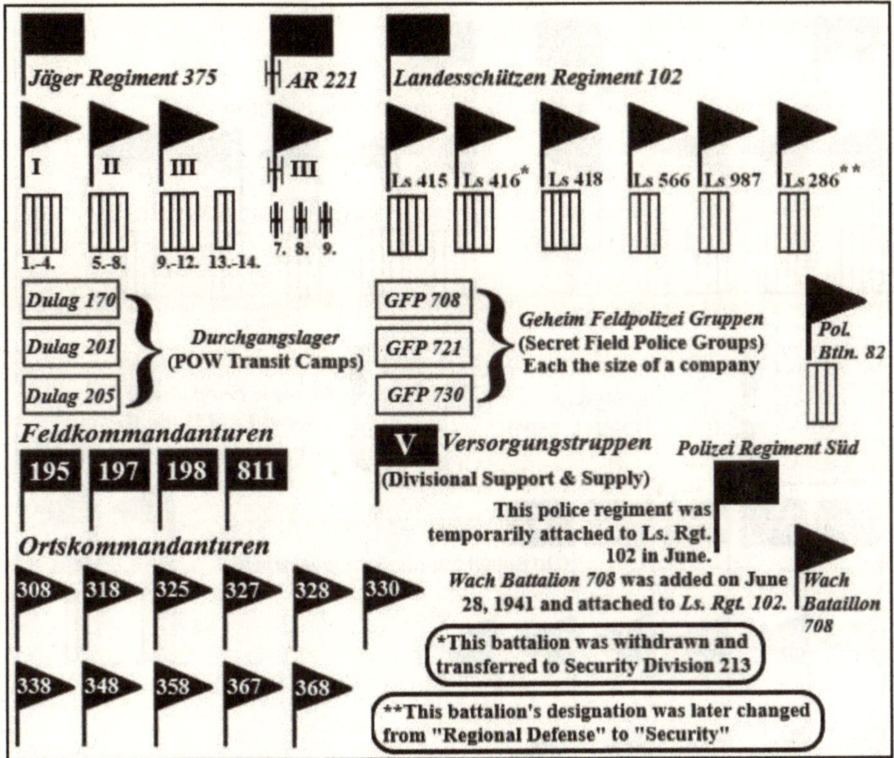

Figure 9.2. The 454th Security Division on 15 May 1941.

by Zhitomir in August 1941.[14] This means that Zhitomir was fairly safe for him to visit by then, affirming that the city was firmly in German hands by then. This possible conflict of dates was explained by Martin Gilbert, who stated that Zhitomir experienced not just a single massacre, but several.

The first massacre occurred in the third week of July and cost 2,530 lives, while the second occurred on 19 September when another 3,135 Jews were killed.[15] Another 4,355 people were executed between 20 September and 31 October 1941.[16] In the initial killing spree, however, the secret field police units of the 454th Security Division (the 708th, 721st and 730th Secret Field Police Groups) assisted *Einsatzgruppe* C inside the city.[17] However, not all the 2,530 Jews were shot in July: about 400 were killed on 7 August. This means that in July 1941 about 2,130 were massacred. Another large number of Jews (1,500) were shot on 4 September.[18]

In total, 2,530 Jews were killed in Zhitomir between 17 July and 3 August 1941, while another 7,500 Jews were killed between September and October 1941.[19] This *Aktion* indicates some very significant things. First it shows army, police and SS cooperation. The secret field police units belonged to the

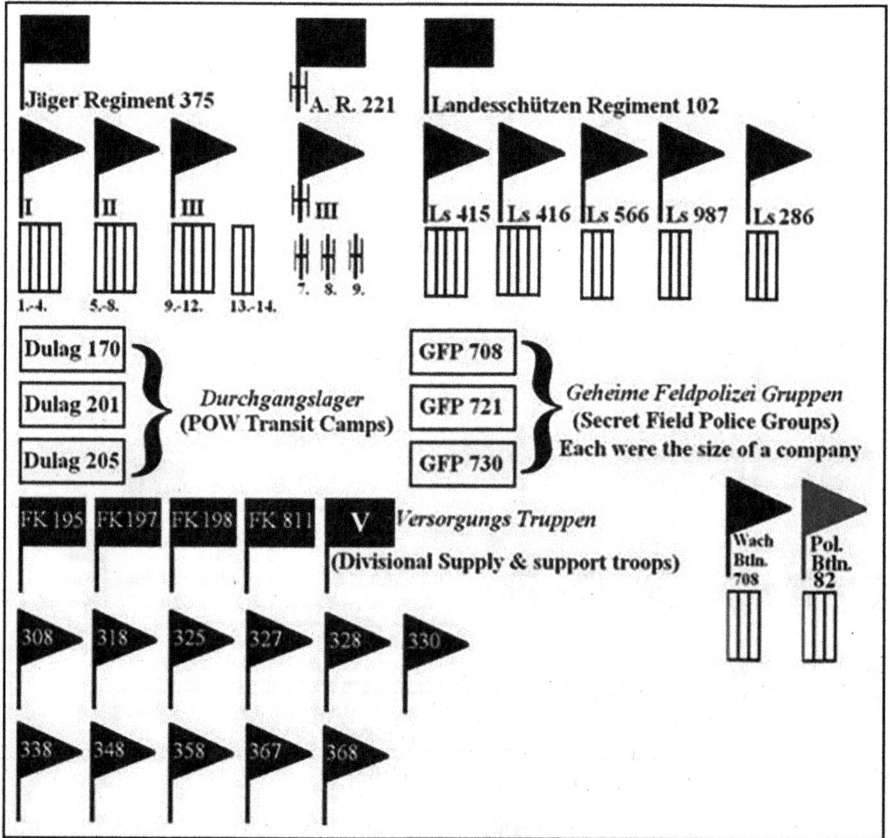

Figure 9.3. The 454th Security Division in August 1941.

Wehrmacht and were under the command of the 454th Security Division. While the 82nd Police Battalion belonged to the Order Police, it too was under the control of the 454th Security Division. Second, we see Wehrmacht complicity in war crimes. Those people killed in August 1941 were actually photographed by the German Army's 637th Propaganda Company.[20] The event was the execution by hanging of 400 Jews in the town's marketplace. Wehrmacht soldiers from the 637th Propaganda Company added fuel to the fire by asking local Ukrainians to now take revenge for any slight which may have been perpetrated on them by any of the condemned Jews. A witness to the incident reported:

> The guards asked the people standing there if someone had business to settle with anyone. Then Ukrainians spoke up who accused this or that Jew of some offence or other. While still in a seated position, these Jews were then beaten and kicked and otherwise mistreated, mostly by

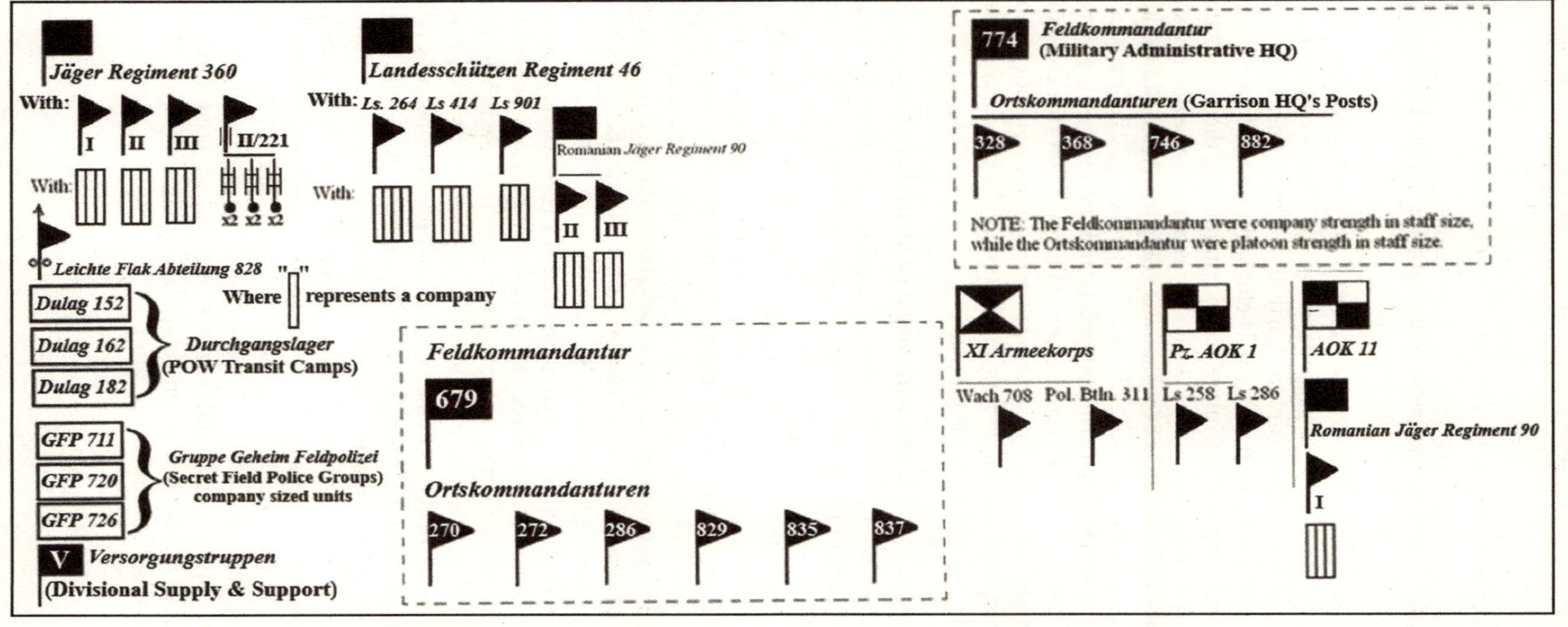

Figure 9.4. The 444th Security Division in March 1942.

Ukrainians. The Landsers who were watching shouted 'slowly, slowly', so they could take better photographs.[21]

A close look at the photographs shows Wehrmacht men from the 637th Propaganda Company observing the hangings. Their expressions vary from straight-faced morbid curiosity to clearly discernible grins. The implication is that at the very least members of the Wehrmacht watched the executions with curiosity, and seemed more interested in entertaining themselves than caring about the fate of these civilians. From the report, they evidently showed no concern, nor did they object to what was going on. Again, we see an attitude of indifference to the suffering of other human beings which was encouraged and nurtured by the Nazi criminal orders and the regime in general. In this particular case, we cannot even use Omer Bartov's view that constant combat on the Russian front 'brutalized' these men since they were not combat troops and the campaign was barely four months old. The conclusion must be that these soldiers enjoyed the spectacle.

A terminology of murder

On 26 July the 82nd Police Battalion, alongside a unit from the Organization Todt, took part in disarming several thousand Russians who were encountered 17km southwest of Zhitomir.[22] On 2 August 1941 the 82nd Police Battalion was in the area of Bila Tserkva. Together with one platoon from the 14th Company, 375th Infantry Regiment, the police battalion combed the surrounding region for Soviet paratroopers who were apparently heading southwest. The Germans caught up with them near Kornin, about 27km west of Fastov. The partisan group was about 200 to 300 men in strength, so one additional company from the 416th Regional Defence Battalion was brought up for the 'cleansing' operation, as it was termed.[23] The 82nd Police Battalion, which was presently located in the area of Fastov, came into contact with an enemy reconnaissance force in Tarascha in the early hours of 3 August 1941. For reference, Fastov is located just west of Kiev and north of Berdichev. This reconnaissance platoon was composed of an officer and twenty men. The leader of the platoon was shot and one prisoner was taken, while the remaining enemy soldiers were able to escape. A motorized reconnaissance troop in the area of Goroschki, which was headed towards Alexandrovka, was ambushed by an enemy group of about thirty men and had to withdraw after a violent firefight. German losses included two dead and three wounded, and one vehicle destroyed.[24] The war diary of the 454th Security Division during the summer months of 1941 is filled with many such recorded engagements. In addition, the terminology used during the entire campaign, but which most often comes up during the period 1941–1943 is *Säuberungsaktion* ('cleansing operation').[25]

As stated previously, the recruitment of Ukrainian auxiliaries was quickly made an integral part of both the Nazi extermination plan for the Jewish race in the Soviet Union, and the anti-partisan war. One such *Hilfspolizei* (auxiliary police) unit was stationed in Osikovo. It was there on 5 August 1941 that this local Ukrainian militia, supported by I. and II. Battalions, 375th Infantry Regiment, engaged a guerrilla band of about 100 men and eliminated them.[26] On 8 August the entire 375th Infantry Regiment, alongside the 82nd Police Battalion, as well as III. Battalion, 10th SS Infantry Regiment, together with what were termed *ukrainische Vertrauensmänner* ('reliable Ukrainian men'), launched another so-called cleansing action which would cover the following regions:[27]

- 82nd Police Battalion (motorized): Fasova and surrounding region;
- III. Battalion, 10th SS Infantry Regiment: withdrawn and transferred back to Zhitomir;
- III. Battalion, 375th Infantry Regiment: north of Goroschki, checking for isolated and armed civilians in the woods; and
- I. and II. Battalions, 375th Infantry Regiment: cleansing operation in the forested region north of the Zhitomir railway line.

This list once again shows the police, SS and army cooperation and the participation of army forces in these cleansing actions. On 7 August another report noted that 200 Soviet paratroopers had landed near Troyanov, about 15km southwest of Zhitomir. The army command sent the 82nd Police Battalion against them. The 1st Company left Zhitomir and headed towards Troyanov, while the 2nd Company left Berdichev and headed towards Sosnovka. Meanwhile, with the assistance of Ukrainian guides, the III. Battalion, 375th Infantry Regiment, discovered a band of about forty or fifty men and succeeded in dispersing this group in the area of Osikovo, killing eight in the process while the rest escaped through the shrubs and woodlands. On 12 August the 3rd Company, 82nd Police Battalion, discovered what were described as 'thirteen Soviet paratroopers, together with five women' near the town of Barychevka. Later an additional five paratroopers were located. The war diary stated that these and other groups were plundering and obstructing the work of the 560th Bridge Construction Battalion. The commander of the 82nd Police Battalion wrote in his war diary regarding this guerrilla force: *Diesen Bänden zu säubern.*[28]

Cleansing action near Starikovskaya and Romanovka, August 1941

On 17 August a man from the town of Starikovskaya, about 60km north of Zhitomir, reported that many inhabitants of the town had fled on 16 August because a partisan group entered the village and wanted to force the male population to join its ranks. The men seemed to have a mark on their wrist which identified them as communists. He himself had seen eighty bandits. About noon a strong combat reconnaissance troop of the motorized 82nd Police Battalion was dispatched to Starikovskaya on the orders of the 454th Security Division and was soon able to annihilate the partisan group after surprising them.[29] On 20 August the 82nd Police Battalion was performing another 'cleansing' operation north of Fasova. A day later men of III. Battalion, 375th Infantry Regiment, arrested five Jews in the area of Romanovka and immediately shot them.[30] Here again, we see that Jews are treated as partisans and no quarter is given, even if they are initially taken alive. On 26 August III. Battalion's 5th Company raided a reported weapons storehouse in Verchovnya, finding fifty rifles and eight Jews. The weapons were confiscated and the Jews immediately executed.[31] The secret field police groups attached to the 454th Security Division were not idle during this time – in fact, they operated hand-in-hand with other police and rear area security forces. Where secret field police units were not available, action against partisan suspects was taken by the local army battalion commander. In most cases, this meant shooting suspects. After moving through Berdichev, Bialacerkiev and Fastov, the 708th Secret Field Police Group reached the city of Zhitomir on 3 September 1941.

Cleansing action at Czervone, August 1941

On 31 August 1941, after leaving Korosten, the 721st Secret Field Police Group headed for the region of Richovka, Vila and Beserovka.[32] Another cleansing operation was now planned in the region of Czervone for this police group, alongside the 82nd Police Battalion. Jews were found living in a sugar factory. The Germans believed these Jews had helped to make a modified airfield next to the sugar processing plant, and also assumed – correctly – that the airfield was used by the partisans in order to receive supplies. According to the divisional war diary, further searches by the 721st Secret Field Police Group and the 82nd Police Battalion discovered weapons and ammunition in the village of Czervone. Based on this information, there is no doubt that Police Major Ebert was guilty of the murder of the Jews found in the sugar plant. In addition, 63 villagers were executed by the 721st Secret Field Police Group on Ebert's orders.[33] Author Klaus Geßner states that this Wehrmacht secret field police unit was particularly murderous, having been 'credited' with numerous massacres, including the murder of eighteen Russian mayors during one operation and the mass murder of 327 men in another particular incident.[34] Overall, the unit was linked to well over forty separate massacres involving about 15,000 people. The commander of this active secret field police unit was Criminal Police Inspector Arnold Kostrowski.[35] Certainly the ideological war was having a terrible effect, but the Germans were by no means finished. On 1 October 1941 the 2nd Company, 82nd Police Battalion, was performing another *Säuberung der Rollbahn* ('cleansing of the railway line') north of Zhitomir.[36]

Support between army and SS forces, Pripet marshes, October 1941

The 213th Security Division was ordered to employ the 375th Infantry Regiment[37] and the 566th Regional Defence Battalion under the Commander of the Rear Army Area South headquarters for another cleansing operation. This time the target area was located in the Pripet marshes region. The zone selected was along the Dnieper river, northeast of Kiev and near the Belarusian-Ukrainian border.[38] In October 1941 II. Battalion, 375th Infantry Regiment (reinforced), was in the process of completing an operation in the area of Gornostaipol, due west of Kiev. It was expected to join the operation in the Pripet marshes very soon.[39] This was in keeping with the employment of the 454th Security Division.[40] This German rear area command, also referred to as Commander of the Rear Army Area South 103, contained a mixture of SS and army units (listed below) and is a perfect example of how various services were brought together to fight the guerrilla war.[41]

- 213th Security Division
- 444th Security Division
- 454th Security Division
- Slovak Fast Division (mobile)
- 1st SS Infantry Brigade (partly).[42]

These units knew that the key to a successful operation was teamwork and that the numbers of partisans killed and Jews murdered always increased when such cooperation was good because there was less chance for the guerrillas and Jews to evade the German encirclement. For this reason, army cooperation during operations which yielded Jewish and civilian death tolls, even if only at the hands of SS troops, should be viewed as indirect assistance in these murders and therefore, indirect guilt. The Germans paid the Pripet marshes region a lot of attention. This region roughly divides the southern part of Belarus from the northern part of western Ukraine. Since the region consisted mainly of bogs and marshes, it was ideal for hiding in and Soviet partisan bands were invariably attracted to it like bees to a honey pot. Jews trying to escape the massacres also gravitated towards the Pripet marshes in order to evade capture and death.

In October 1941 the 1st SS Infantry Brigade (motorized) consisted of the 8th and 10th SS Infantry Regiments, the 1st Battery of the 51st SS Heavy

Artillery Battalion, the 8th and 9th Flak Batteries from the 51st SS Flak Company, and several supporting units. Part of this brigade was committed to operations in the Pripet marshes region from 1 to 9 October 1941.[43] On 10 October the brigade halted operations on account of the inclement weather, as persistent rain and snowfall had rendered roads unusable. A large number of the vehicles and all the motorcycles in the brigade had broken down, and in any case it was virtually impossible to remove the mud from the tracks of the vehicles. Finally, any vehicles that were still in good working order were halted for lack of petrol.

As stated earlier, the 213th Security Division also took part in the Pripet marshes operation. In fact, cooperation between the 10th SS Infantry Regiment and the 375th Infantry Regiment in hunting down Jews had already occurred as early as August 1941.[44] The operation employing these same two units in the southeastern part of the marshes caused the deaths of 570 Jewish men, women and children between 1 and 10 October.[45] During the operation, parts of the 375th Infantry Regiment swept as far north as Yelsk and Mozyr in southern Belarusia.[46] It wasn't until 7 October that the 82nd Police Battalion was ordered to move towards Osztyer-Kosolez. Continuing east, it arrived at Gluchov on 10 October 1941. Meanwhile, the rest of the 454th Security Division was ordered to move east of Kiev towards the Sumy Oblast. On 10 October the 13th Company, 375th Infantry Regiment, came across a partisan band of fifty men in the region north of the Teterev railway station, and killed most of them.[47] Again we see that army cooperation with the SS yielded more deaths for the Soviet population, especially the Jews.

Anti-partisan Operation Cherkasy, 5–11 November 1941

This operation was undertaken in the area of Cherkasy, approximately 65km southeast of Kanev. The drive netted 36 partisans killed and 17 captured. Taking part in this operation were units from the 454th Security Division, including the 375th Infantry Regiment (reinforced) and the 987th Regional Defence Battalion, as well as the 8th Battery of III. Battalion, 221st Artillery Regiment. In addition, 251 people picked up during the sweep without identity papers were handed over to the local secret field police for 'special handling' – a euphemism for execution.[48] There were three secret field police unit operating in this region at this time: the 708th, the 721st and the 730th, which were all operating under the 454th Security Division during the summer and autumn of 1941.[49] The 730th Secret Field Police Group was currently assigned to the rear area of 6th Army, and the 708th Secret Field Police Group was covering the rear area of 1st Panzer Army, further south of the area in question, which belonged to 6th Army's operational area. The 721st Secret Field Police Group was also currently operating in the rear area of 6th Army, but at this time was in the region of Romny. Although we cannot say for sure, by a process of elimination we can conclude that the 730th Secret Field Police Group was the most likely police unit which 'handled' these 251 luckless Soviet citizens.

Conclusions

Victory has a hundred fathers, but defeat is an orphan.
[Count Galeazzo Ciano]

What were the goals of Operation Barbarossa?

At the start of Operation Barbarossa, the Third Reich had allocated what they believed to be sufficient rear area security forces for a six-month campaign. Military planning had gone no further than the proposed goals, and no contingency plans had been put in place in case the operational goals of the invasion were not met. The operation as envisaged by Hitler and the Armed Forces High Command had several goals:

- Destroying the Soviet Union. Adolf Hitler's primary objective in Operation Barbarossa was the total destruction of the Soviet Union as a political entity. He aimed to defeat the Soviet military, occupy key territories and dismantle the Soviet state.
- Eliminating Communism. Hitler saw the Soviet Union as the stronghold of communism and sought to eradicate it. He believed that by defeating the Soviet Union, he could eliminate communism and create *lebensraum* (living space) for the German people in the East.
- Acquiring Resources. The Nazi regime sought to exploit the vast resources of the Soviet Union, including agricultural land, raw materials and oil fields. Control over these resources would strengthen Germany's war effort and support its long-term economic goals.
- Weakening the Allies. By attacking the Soviet Union, Hitler hoped to eliminate a possible supporter of the western Allies, particularly Britain. He believed that defeating the Soviet Union would weaken the Allied war effort and pave the way for German victory in Europe, perhaps through a negotiated peace with the United Kingdom.
- Ideological and Racial Goals. Operation Barbarossa was driven by Nazi ideology, including beliefs in racial superiority and the need for *lebensraum* in the East. Hitler viewed the Slavic peoples as racially inferior and sought to subjugate or exterminate them, along with Jews and other 'undesirable' groups.

Overall, Operation Barbarossa was a massive military campaign aimed at achieving strategic, ideological and economic objectives for Nazi Germany. Despite the German Army's initial successes, including the rapid advance into Soviet territory, the operation ultimately failed to achieve its goals, leading to the eventual defeat of Nazi Germany three years later.

Why did Operation Barbarossa fail?

The reason why the operation failed has been the subject of much debate and scores of history books. The most common thinking boils down to two points: first, the fact that the campaign had to be delayed until 22 June 1941 on account of the need by the Wehrmacht to invade Greece and Yugoslavia, and secondly, Hitler's decision to strike south after capturing Smolensk, instead of heading straight for Moscow. Some believe that Hitler was right to halt the German advance on Moscow in August because the Red Army's counter-attack at Smolensk had severely depleted the divisions of Army Group Centre, especially the panzer divisions. In addition, it can also be argued that the German flanks were too exposed and the supply lines too long for a proper advance to be made on Moscow in August. If Army Group Centre had advanced on Moscow with insufficient supplies and without properly covering its flanks, the Red Army could have outflanked the German army group and destroyed a good portion of its striking power. Such are the arguments against heading for Moscow in August 1941. However, I have never bought into this argument for the following reasons.

First, although the Third Reich was able to capture over 600,000 soldiers and a huge amount of enemy equipment, taking western Ukraine cost Army Group Centre dearly, because in helping Army Group South to capture Kiev and trap more Red Army units, Army Group Centre lost men and armoured vehicles that could have proved crucial to capturing Moscow. By the time the Germans were ready to launch Operation Typhoon against Moscow on 30 September 1941, the Russians had enough time to prepare defences and to bring forward a significantly large force of fresh troops from Siberia and elsewhere. The delay was thus advantageous for the Soviets, but not so for the Germans because when Army Group Centre began its assault, its divisions had been reduced to brigades in strength, and that was only because reinforcements had arrived between August and September. In August 1941, for example, the 6th Panzer Regiment, 3rd Panzer Division, was down to 10 tanks from the 150 tanks that it had at the start of Operation Barbarossa. The division's motorized infantry companies, which had begun the campaign with 200 men apiece, were down to about 50 men each.[1] Two months later, by early December, the divisions of Army Group Centre were lucky if they could muster the strength of a regiment. By launching the attack on Moscow in August, Army Group Centre could have possibly taken Moscow by October or early November, which would have disrupted the entire political and military planning of Stalin's regime. Moscow had the largest railway hub in the USSR, and its loss would have thrown the Red Army's rail transportation system into turmoil.

Of course, attacking Moscow in August 1941, as Guderian wanted, did have risks. It is totally plausible that Army Group Centre might have been cut off, or at least partially defeated by a flanking manoeuvre. That aside, Guderian was correct in wanting to head for Moscow in August in lieu of aiding Army Group South at Kiev. Given the vastness of the Soviet Union and the seemingly inexhaustible numbers of men and materiel that the Red Army could muster, a strike against Moscow in August would have been a gamble, but it was a gamble that offered the only chance of a German victory in 1941. The attack on Moscow in October was doomed from the start. It took place because Hitler's pride and vanity prevented him from accepting the reality that his forces were in no condition to continue the attack. In contrast, by October the Red Army in front of Moscow had been heavily reinforced and the Russians had enough time to build up strong defences. That Army Group Centre was able to overcome many of these defences and, at great human effort and cost, to get as close as they did to the Russian capital is testament to the bravery and skill of the German soldier. That bravery, however, was not sufficient to overcome the personnel and materiel losses that between June and December 1941 bled the *Ostheer* white.

Kiev, the capital of Ukraine, was a major industrial centre and transportation hub and thus a key strategic objective for the Germans. Capturing Kiev would provide significant economic and logistical benefits to the German war effort, including access to resources and the disruption of Soviet supply lines. Smolensk, located to the northwest of Kiev, was a major Soviet defensive position. By striking at Kiev after Smolensk was captured, the Germans aimed to encircle and trap the large Soviet forces defending Kiev and its surrounding areas. This encirclement strategy was a key element of German military doctrine and had been successful in previous campaigns, such as the Battle of France in 1940. Nevertheless, the decision to strike south just as Army Group Centre was a mere 395km from Moscow proved to be a fateful one.

The battle for Kiev resulted in a significant delay for the German Army. The battle began on 23 August and lasted until 26 September. The marshy terrain and inclement weather conditions, including heavy rains, further hindered the German advance towards Kiev. As the battle dragged on, the Soviets were able to reinforce their defences around the city, making it increasingly difficult for the Germans to achieve a quick victory. Overall, the battle of Kiev resulted in a significant delay for the German Army's advance on Moscow. The decision to swing Army Group Centre's panzer forces away from Moscow to assist in capturing Kiev was objected to by General Heinz

Guderian, who believed that Moscow was within the grasp of the *Ostheer* if only Hitler would allow it. Field Marshal Walther von Brauchitsch, who served as the Commander in Chief of the German Army (*Oberbefehlshaber des Heeres*) during Operation Barbarossa, would later be opposed to an advance on Moscow in October.[2] Nevertheless, Hitler insisted on it. The Germans would have done better to hunker down in the territory they had taken, rather than throw away what striking power remained to them on a fruitless effort to capture Moscow in the autumn of 1941.

What was wrong with the plan?

This all leads us to an implication. If taking Moscow in August 1941 was a big gamble, but also the only hope for a German victory, what was wrong with the Barbarossa plan to begin with? The answer is that Operation Barbarossa was flawed from the start, because it assumed too many things. It *assumed* that the campaign would not last longer than six months – that is, that the entire Soviet Union and its 196 million inhabitants could be conquered in half a year. It *assumed* that the Red Army would be defeated near the border. It *assumed* that the Red Army would not fight as hard as it did. It *assumed* that Russia's military industrial might was not as large as it turned out to be. It *assumed* that Stalin's purge of the Russian officer corps in the late 1930s had left the Red Army emasculated. It *assumed* that Hitler could alter the Barbarossa plan on the fly, just as he did with the decision regarding Kiev, without suffering any consequences. Thus, Operation Barbarossa relied on too many assumptions. Moreover, Hitler also kept prevaricating about whether the attack was aimed at the political heart of the communist regime (Moscow) or its economic belly (Kiev and Ukraine).

The implications of taking Moscow in 1941

Kiev and Moscow were both military and economic targets. However, in addition Moscow was of great political importance and its fall would have been a great psychological blow signalling the beginning of the end for Stalin's regime. Its capture would certainly have demoralized the Red Army and would inevitably have had political repercussions around the world. Turkey, for example, which had remained neutral up until then, might have opted to join the Tripartite Pact, which would have opened a back door to the Middle East through Turkey. Other neutral but friendly countries, such as fascist Spain, might have also contemplated joining the Axis cause. Had that happened, British-controlled Gibraltar would have been doomed. Rommel's Afrika Korps might have reached Alexandria in Egypt if the British 8th Army had also had to contend with a second front in the Caucasus Mountains or from Turkish territory. Capturing Moscow in 1941 meant that there would not be a Stalingrad in 1942 or a Kursk in 1943.

Guarding the conquered Soviet territories in 1941

Once the campaign started and the fighting increased in intensity, it became quite clear that the security forces allocated to Operation Barbarossa were insufficient. This was made clear by the fact that almost from the very beginning the Germans began to recruit indigenous volunteers to aid them in occupying the vast Soviet territories and to fight the growing partisan menace. Local battalions were also raised to fight with the Germans on the front lines.[3] By the autumn of 1941 some 85 million Soviet citizens lived under Nazi rule. On average, a regiment of German rear area security troops was expected to cover somewhere in the neighbourhood of 80–100 square miles. This was clearly an impossible task and explains why very quickly the Germans settled on holding major stationary positions that were militarily or economically important, such as key towns or cities that were transportation hubs, as well as important railway lines, airfields, munitions depots and large collective farms.

At the same time they developed forces that were allocated into temporary *kampfgruppen* (battlegroups) to be employed in specific areas behind the lines where the guerrilla threat was greatest. In the summer and autumn of 1941 such anti-guerrilla drives were few, but in the spring of 1942 that all began to change. Additional security forces were brought into the Soviet Union, including Axis allied forces that were organized by region and employed in larger and more numerous anti-partisan operations. A future study to follow this one will cover the history of the partisan and anti-partisan war in the USSR from the spring of 1942 to the spring of 1943. The height of partisan and anti-partisan drives occurred in 1943. In that year dozens upon dozens of operations were launched by the Germans all across the vast expanse of the occupied USSR. The defeat of Operation Barbarossa not only signalled that the war in the East was going to last longer than Hitler had anticipated, it also indicated that the partisan war behind the lines would not disappear but would only grow. Indeed, the partisan war in the East would last from the summer of 1941 until its conclusion in the summer of 1944.

Appendix

Russian volunteer formations in the East, 1941–1942

August 1941

Intervention Group Tietjen. Formed on 24 August 1941 from the 9th Company, 18th Infantry Regiment, 6th Infantry Division, VI Army Corps, 9th Army, Army Group Centre. The company was led by Captain Georg Tietjen. This anti-partisan force began recruiting Russian volunteers.

October 1941

Defence Operation Tiger B. Formed on 18 October 1941 from German personnel from the 800th Special Purpose Brandenburg Regiment.[1] The group also included Russian prisoners of war who had volunteered for service. This unit was raised by the *Abwehr*.

November 1941

Staff Officer of the 582nd Eastern Troops Command. Formed under Korück 582 behind the lines of 9th Army, Army Group Centre. This staff was organized to control the large influx of Russian volunteers who were beginning to enter German service.

At this time, *Defence Operation Tiger B* comprised 300 Russian volunteers divided into six companies of 50 Russians each.[2] Each of these companies had perhaps 25 or 30 Germans attached. These German soldiers were from the 9th Company, 18th Infantry Regiment, which had been split up in order to provide cadre personnel for the Russian companies.

3rd Prisoner-of-War Labour Engineer Battalion. Formed on 12 January 1942 from Russian prisoners of war who volunteered for construction work in the German Army. The prisoners came from camps in *Wehrkreis XII* (Military District No. 12) in Germany. The battalion was sent to Oslo in Norway but by the spring of 1942 it had been shifted to southwestern Norway.

March 1942

Intervention Group Tietjen. Continued to serve under Korück 582 of 9th Army, Army Group Centre. The 582nd Eastern Artillery Battery, with four Soviet-made 76mm guns, was added to the unit on 1 March 1942.

April 1942

207th Cavalry Battalion. Formed on 11 April 1942 with two cavalry squadrons. It was attached to the 207th Security Division behind the lines of Army Group North.

246th Eastern Construction Battalion. Formed from Russian prisoners of war for work in the German Army. Its German cadre staff came from the 246th National Labour Service Battalion, which had been employed as an infantry unit and been virtually destroyed while fighting during the cold Russian winter of 1941/1942. The new battalion was formed in the region of 4th Panzer Army, Army Group B, in southern Russia.

Eastern Combat Battalion Dnieper. Formed on 29 April 1942 from Special Staff Hohlfeld.

617th Eastern Battalion. Formed on 28 April 1942 under Korück 532 of 2nd Panzer Army, Army Group Centre.

1st Prisoner-of-War Labour Battalion. Formed in Arnsberg from Russian prisoners housed in Stalag XX near Thorn (Torun), Poland. The unit was organized by the 6th Reserve Construction Battalion and also contained a good number of Polish prisoners. It was created officially on 8 April 1942.

Special Staff Hohlfeld. This headquarters unit was raised on 29 April 1942 in the region of Army Group Centre from a German cadre staff to control Russian volunteers. It helped to organize *Eastern Combat Battalion Dnieper*, a former unit of the Graukopf Brigade, and other eastern battalions for employment in Belarus and the region of central Russia where Army Group Centre was operating.

Special Staff Knoth. As *Special Staff Hohlfeld*, but stationed in Belarus.

Glossary of German military and political terms

Abschnitt – Sector, district.
Abteilung – Battalion. It could also mean Section or Department.
Abwehr – The Intelligence and Clandestine Warfare Service of the German Armed Forces High Command.
Abzeichen – Insignia, badge of rank, appointment or distinction.
Adlerhorst – Eagle's nest. The name given by British intelligence to Hitler's mountain-top retreat located in Berchtesgaden in the Bavarian Alps.
Afrika Korps – The German military force led by Erwin Rommel that fought in North Africa, 1941–43.
Amt – Office, Bureau or Department.
Angriff – Attack.
Angriffspunkt – Attack point.
Anwärter – Cadet or candidate.
AOK – see *Armee-Oberkommando*.
Arbeit – Work.
Arbeitsdienst – The literal translation is 'work service' but it meant a labour service.
Arbeitskommando – Work commando or work group.
Arbeitslager – Work camp.
Armee – Army.
Armeegebiet – Army region or district.
Armeekorps – Army corps.
Armee-Oberkommando (*AOK*) – Army headquarters.
Artillerie – Artillery.
Aufklärung – Reconnaissance.
Ausbildung – Training.
Bahnlinie – Rail line.
Bahnschutzpolizei – Railway security police.
Bandengebiet – Bandit region (partisan-controlled region).
Banditen – Bandits. The Germans referred to the partisans behind the front lines as bandits.
Barbarossa – Codename for the German invasion of the USSR.

Bataillon – Battalion.
Bataillonsführer – Battalion commander.
Bataillonskommandeur – Battalion commander.
Batterie – Battery.
Bau – Construction.
Baudienst – The national labour service of the Reich.
Baupionier – Construction engineer.
BdO – see *Befehlshaber der Ordnungspolizei.*
BdS – see *Befehlshaber der Sicherheitspolizei.*
Befehl – Command. The plural form of the word is *Befehle.*
Befehlshaber – Commander.
Befehlshaber der Ordnungspolizei (*BdO*) – Supreme Commander of the Order Police.
Befehlshaber der Sicherheitspolizei (*BdS*) – Supreme Commander of the Security Police.
Begleit – Escort, usually denoting an elite unit.
Belarus – White Russia.
Beobachter – Artillery or air observer.
Beutepanzer – Captured tank or armoured vehicle.
Bewachungsmannschaft – The literal translation is security crew, but in Third Reich era terminology it referred to an SS guard detachment in a concentration camp.
Bezirk – A district or administrative unit of the German civilian government.
Brigade – A brigade of troops.
Brigadeführer – Generalmajor in either the SS or Police.
Brücke – Bridge.
Brücken – Bridging.
Bürgermeister – The mayor of a town or community.
Chef – Commander of a unit or sub-unit.
Chef des Generalstabes – Chief of the General Staff.
der SS – Belonging to the SS. Usually a Germanic SS unit was prefixed with the title '*SS*' while non-Germanic formations were referred to as '*der SS*' (of the SS).
Dienst – Service.
Dienstgrad – Rank.
Dienststelle – An administrative department or administrative office.
Division – A division-sized military unit.
Dnjepr – German spelling for Dnieper.
Dorpat – German spelling for the town of Tartu in Estonia.
Drang nach Osten – Spread to the East, or Push to the East. It was the nineteenth-century German nationalist *zeitgeist* for a desire to expand German territory into eastern European lands.

Eingeschlossen – Surrounded, trapped, encircled.
Eingreifgruppe – The literal translation is 'response group', but in military terms it meant 'assault group'.
Einheit – A detachment or a unit.
Einsatz – Mission, action.
Einsatzgruppen – An operational group made up of the *Sipo* (Security Police), *SD* (Security Service) and Order Police units used for special missions, initially for liquidation of the Jewish population, communist commissars, etc., but later used to fight the partisans. One *Einsatzgruppe* could have as many as six *Einsatzkommandos*.
Einsatzkommando – A sub-group detachment of the *Einsatzgruppen*.
Ersatz – Replacement.
Ersatzheer – Replacement army.
Estland Estonia.
Estnische (*Est.*) – Estonian.
Fallschirmjäger – Paratrooper.
Feind – Enemy.
Feldausbildungs – Field training.
Feldheer – Field army.
Feldkommandantur – Field command: a German Army military administration headquarters.
Feldwebel – Sergeant.
Feldzug – Military campaign.
Fellin – German spelling for the Estonian town of Viljandi.
Festung – Fortress.
Feuerpolizei – Fire Police.
Finnische – Finnish.
Flak – Anti-aircraft.
Fluss – River.
Frankreich – France.
Freiwilliger – Volunteer (pl. *Freiwillige*).
Front – Referring to the front line or a front-line unit. Example: (*estnische*) *Front Bataillon 38*.
Frontkämpfer – Front-line soldier.
Führer – Leader; specifically, in the Second World War, referring to Adolf Hitler.
Führungshauptamt – Leadership Head Office.
Gau – The main territorial division of the Nazi Party. Germany was divided into forty-two *Gau*. The conquered territories also had this system.
Gauleiter – The highest-ranking Nazi Party official in a *Gau*. The *Gauleiter* was responsible for all political and economic activity, mobilization of labour and civil defence in his area.

Gefreiter – Enlisted rank, senior to the rank of private, but not considered an NCO.

Geheimfeldpolizei – Secret Field Police of the *Heer* (Army).

Geheimstaatspolizei (*Gestapo*) – State Secret Police. Formerly *Amt IV* (Department IV) of the *Reichssicherheitshauptamt* (*RSHA*), the Reich Main Security Office.

Gemeindepolizei – Municipal police.

Gendarmerie – The rural police, including motorized units for traffic control.

Generalgouvernement – The General Government, i.e., German-occupied Poland administered by a German civilian governor with its headquarters in the city of Cracow. It was classed as an appended territory (*Nebenland*, meaning outlying) of the Reich.

Generalkommando – General command. Refers to a corps-sized unit in the military.

Generalleutnant – Lieutenant general.

Genesenden – Convalescent. Example: *Genesendenbataillon* (convalescent battalion).

Gestapo – see *Geheimstaatspolizei.*

Goldfassanen – Golden Pheasants. Pejorative reference to the representatives of Alfred Rosenberg's Office for the Eastern Occupied Territories, who wore the Nazi Party brown uniform with gold epaulets (shoulder insignia). The term was derogatory and implied Nazi opportunists who sought their fortune by exploiting the captured eastern territories, with no regard for the people they ruled.

Grenadier – Elite infantrymen of the seventeenth and eighteenth centuries. In 1943 Hitler redesignated most of his infantry units as 'Grenadier', thus elevating them to the status of elite troops, if only in name.

Grenzpolizei – Border police.

Grenzschutz – Frontier or border.

Gruppenführer – The SS equivalent to *Generalleutnant* (lieutenant general).

Gulag – Soviet penal camp for political dissidents and others considered to be enemies of the state. Such camps were usually located in Siberia. Very few ever left these camps. For example, when the German 6th Army surrendered at Stalingrad, the Red Army captured approximately 91,000 soldiers. They were force-marched to Siberian gulags and many died along the way. From these camps only about 3,000 survived to return to Germany between 1953 and 1956.

Hauptamt – Main office.

Hauptmann – Captain.

Hauptmann der Polizei – Captain of the police.

Hauptsturmführer – The SS rank equivalent to captain.

Heer – Army.

Heeresgebiet – Army region. It usually referred to an army's rear area.
Heeresgruppe – Army group.
Heimat – Homeland.
Heimatwehr – The uncapitalized version of home guard.
Heimwehr – Home Guard (capitalized).
Hilfsdienst – Auxiliary service.
Hilfswilliger – Helper or assistant.
Höhere SS und Polizeiführer (HSSPF) – Higher SS and Police Commander. Also referred to as Senior SS and Police Commander. These staffs represented *Reichsführer SS* Heinrich Himmler's personal representatives in the Reich military districts and in the occupied territories.
Hundertschaft – Century, equivalent to a company or more of men.
im Dienst – In service.
Infanterie – Infantry.
Inspekteur – Inspector.
Iwan – Ivan, German slang term used to denote a Red Army soldier.
Jagdkommando – Hunting commando. In Second World War terms, a German anti-partisan unit between a platoon and company in size.
Jagdpanzer – Tank destroyer.
Jäger – Hunter; in military terms it meant light infantry.
Kaukasische – Caucasian. In the Second World War the Germans recruited Caucasian volunteers from the Caucasus mountains in southern Russia.
Kavallerie – Cavalry.
KdO – see *Kommandeur der Ordnungspolizei.*
KdS – see *Kommandeur der Sicherheitspolizei.*
kollektive Gewaltmassnahmen – Collective violence, but meaning 'collective punishment'.
Kommandeur – Commander.
Kommandeur der Ordnungspolizei (*KdO*) – Commander of the uniformed police. A subordinate command to the *BdO.*
Kommandeur der Sicherheitspolizei (*KdS*) – Commander of the security police. A subordinate command to the *BdS.*
Kommandeur des Rückwartige Heeresgebiete (*Korück*) – Commander of the Army Rear Area.
Kommissarbefehl – Commissar Order – the infamous command which ordered that all Red Army political officers were to be shot, even if they surrendered.
Kompanieführer – Company commander.
Konzentrationslager (*KZL*) – Concentration camp.
Korporal – Corporal.
Korps – Corps.
Korpsabteilung – Army detachment.

Kriegsgefangener – Prisoner of war (pl. *Kriegsgefangene*).

Kriegsmarine – The German Navy, as it was referred to between 1935 and 1945 (the Third Reich era).

Krim – Crimea.

Kriminalpolizei – Criminal police.

Krimtatar – Crimean Tartar. A Turkic people that live in the Crimea.

Landesschützen – The literal translation is 'provincial shooters', but in the Nazi period it meant older-age men who were members of regional defence battalions. Like the Army security forces, these battalions were employed behind the German lines. They guarded important geographical structures, like bridges and rail lines, and physical structures vital to the war effort. They also took part in anti-partisan drives.

Landkreis – A rural administrative district.

Landrat – A district administrator.

Lebensraum – Living space. The Nazi belief that Germans needed land upon which to grow and expand.

Lebensunwertes Leben – Life unworthy of life. In Nazi thinking, a person who does not deserve to exist.

Leichte – Light.

Lettische (*lett.*) – Latvian.

Leutnant – Lieutenant.

Litauische (*lit.*) – Lithuanian.

Luftwaffe – The German Air Force, as it was referred to between 1935 and 1945 (the Third Reich era).

Major – Major, a rank between captain and colonel.

Massenmörder – Mass murder.

Militär – Military.

Mitte – Centre, as in *Heeresgruppe Mitte* (Army Group Centre).

Mörser – Mortar.

Nachricht or *Nachrichten* – Communication, signals or even intelligence.

Nachrichtendienst – Intelligence service.

Nachschub – Supply.

Nationalsozialisten Kraftfahrkorps (*NSKK*) – National Socialist Motor Corps.

Nebelwerfer – Rocket artillery.

Nord – North.

NSKK – see *Nationalsozialisten Kraftfahrkorps*.

Oberbaustab – The higher military construction staff. This headquarters usually controlled several construction regiments.

Oberbürgermeister – Lord mayor.

Oberführer – SS rank below *Brigadeführer*. There was no equivalent rank in the British or US Armies.

Obergruppenführer – SS rank equivalent to lieutenant general.

Oberkommando des Heeres – Army High Command.

Oberkommando der Wehrmacht – Armed Forces High Command.

Oberstgruppenführer – Like *Obergruppenführer*, the *SS* rank equivalent to lieutenant general.

Oberstleutnant – Lieutenant colonel. Example: *Oberstleutnant der Polizei* (Lieutenant Colonel of the Police).

Obersturmbannführer – SS rank equivalent to lieutenant colonel.

OKH – see *Oberkommando des Heeres.*

OKW – see *Oberkommando der Wehrmacht.*

Omakaitse – Estonian term meaning 'self-defence'.

Ordnungsdienst – Auxiliary service, made up of foreign volunteers, that assisted the German police.

Ordnungspolizei – Order police.

Organization Todt – This was a semi-military Nazi government agency established in 1933 and used mainly for the construction of strategic highways and military fortifications and installations.

Ortskommandantur – Local command: local army headquarters below the *Feldkommandantur*.

Ost – East.

Ostbataillon – A battalion of foreign volunteers from eastern Europe, including the USSR.

Ostfront – Eastern Front.

Ostheer – 'Eastern Army': the German Army fighting on the Eastern Front.

Ostland German name for the Baltic region encompassing the Baltic countries of Lithuania, Latvia and Estonia, and part of Belarus (Belarusia, or White Russia).

Ostministerium – The (Nazi) Ministry for the Occupied Eastern Territories.

Osttruppen – Eastern troops who served in either the *Heer*, *SS* or Police forces of the Third Reich.

Ostvolker – Eastern people.

Panzer – Armoured.

Panzerfaust – Literally 'armoured fist'. It was a disposable, hand-held, one-shot, anti-tank weapon.

Panzerschreck – German name for Bazooka, a hand-held, reusable, anti-tank weapon.

Partisan – Partisan (pl. *Partisanen*).

Partisanenjäger – Partisan hunter.

Partisanhelfer – Partisan helper.

Pferd – Horse.

Pionier – Engineer.

Pleskau – German spelling for the Russian city of Pskov.

Polizei – Police.

Prepjet-Sümpfe – German spelling for the Pinsk (Pripyat) Marshes. In English the spelling is Pripet.
Putsch – An internal uprising against an existing government, like a *coup d'etat.*
Quartiërmeister – Quartermaster.
RAD – see *Reichsarbeitsdienst.*
Radfahr – Bicycle.
Regiment – Regiment.
Reich – Nation.
Reichsarbeitsdienst (*RAD*) – (Nazi) National Labour Service.
Reichsführer SS – National Leader of the SS.
Reichskommissar – National Commissioner.
Reichskommissariat Ostland – The civilian occupation government in the Baltic states, led by Hinrich Lohse.
Reichskommissariat Ukraine – The civilian occupation government in Ukraine, headed by Erich Koch.
Reichsministerium für die besetzten Ostgebiete – Reich Ministry for the Occupied Eastern Territories.
Reichssicherheitshauptamt – Reich Security Main Office.
Reiter – Horse, cavalryman.
Reserve – Reserve.
Reval – German spelling for the Estonian capital of Tallinn.
RSHA – see *Reichssicherheitshauptamt.*
Rückwärtig – Behind, as in the rear of the front lines.
Russische (*russ.*) – Russian.
SA – see *Sturmabteilung.*
Schlachtfliegerstaffel – Attack squadron.
Schule – School.
Schutzmannschaft (*Schuma*) – Self Defence Guard. These men, organized into battalions, assisted the SS and Police.
Schutzstaffel – The *SS* originated as a small core of bodyguards for Adolf Hitler, while he travelled the countryside giving speeches. This paramilitary branch of the Nazi Party expanded exponentially beginning in 1933, creating numerous separate departments, in much the same way that an octopus has many tentacles. They included such branches as the *Allgemeine SS*, *Waffen SS* and *SS Totenkopfverbände.*
Selbstschutz – Self-defence. Referring to eastern-raised militia units of volunteers from the USSR and other eastern countries. It was originally to have consisted of ethnic Germans from these territories, but also included large numbers of non-ethnic German people.
Sicherheitsdienst – SS Security Service.
Sicherheitspolizei – Security Police.
Sicherung – Security.

Sipo – see *Sicherheitspolizei.*

Sonder – Special. In Third Reich terminology, it could refer to a special detachment or even a penal formation.

Sonderdienst – Special Service. This organization was part of the German occupation force in Poland. It was made up of ethnic German Poles serving as guards.

Sonderkommando – Sub-group detachment of the *Einsatzkommando.*

Sonderstab – Special staff.

SS – see *Schutzstaffel.*

SS und Polizeiführer (*SSPF*) – SS and Police Leader.

SSPF – see *SS und Polizeiführer.*

SS Waffengruppe – An armed group, usually of regimental or brigade size, serving in the *Waffen SS.*

Stabsoffizier – Staff officer.

Staffeln Flieger Gruppe – Squadron Air Group.

Stamm – Cadre.

Standarte – Basically another way to say regiment. The formation so named was equivalent to a regiment in size.

Standartenführer – SS colonel.

Strafe – Penal, referring to a penal (punishment) formation, such as *Strafbataillon* (penal battalion).

Sturmabteilung – Storm detachment. The militarized members of the Nazi Party.

Sturmbannführer – SS major.

Sturmkompanie – Assault company.

Süd – South.

Technische Nothilfe (*TN*) – The Technical Emergency Corps, an auxiliary police force of the ORPO consisting of engineers, technicians and specialists concerned with communications, construction work, public utilities, salvage and recovery, etc. Each police regiment that entered the USSR in 1941 had one TN company attached. Later on, these companies were detached and expanded into battalions.

Teilkommando – A sub-unit of a special force, such as a *Teilkommando* of an *SS Sonderkommando.*

Totenkopfstandarte – Any one of a series of SS Death's Head (*Totenkopfstandarte*) regiments.

Truppenübungslager – Troop Training Camp.

Truppenübungsplatz – Troop Training Ground.

Ukrainische (*ukr.*) – Ukrainian.

Und (*u.*) – And.

Verband – Formation. Could also mean a military unit of brigade size.

Verbindungsoffizier – Liaison officer.

Vernichtungskrieg – War of extermination.
Vernichtungslager – Extermination camp.
V1 or *V2* – Designations for two types of rocket-propelled jet bombs used by the Nazis, mainly against the city of London.
Wach – Guard.
Wachbataillon – Guard battalion.
Waffen SS – Armed SS. SS ground combat formations that fought in the field.
Wehrkreis – A German military district.
Wehrmachtbefehlshaber – The Armed Forces Commander for a military region or area. Example: *Wehrmachtbefehlshaber der Rückwärtig Heeresgebiet* (Armed Forces Commander of the Army Rear Area).
Weissruthenische – White Russian. Properly spelled using the *eszett*: *Weißruthenische*. It refers to Belarus.
Weltanschauungskrieg – Ideological war.
Wolga – Volga.
zbV – see *zur besondere Verwendung*.
Zug – Platoon.
Zugführer – Platoon leader.
zur besondere Verwendung (*zbV*) – For special use, or special employment.

Notes

Author's note

1. https://freedomhouse.org/report/freedom-world/2022/global-expansion-authoritarian-rule, accessed 13 June 2022.
2. Sebastian Ullrich, *Der Weimar-Komplex. Das Scheitern der ersten deutschen Demokratie und die politische Kultur der fruhen Bundesrepublik 1945–1959.* Göttingen: Wallstein Verlag, 2009, p. 120.
3. In 1926 Marshal Józef Pilsudski established a dictatorship in Poland. Pilsudski claimed that he was doing this for the good of the nation. However, it is no coincidence that the political party he helped to create won all four of the next national elections (1928, 1930, 1935 and 1938). Most historians agree that the elections were rigged. Therefore, Czechoslovakia was the only nation in central Europe which remained a true democracy by 1938.
4. There were many instances between 1934 and September 1938 when Hitler broke the Treaty of Versailles and the democracies of the West did nothing.
5. Putin wanted this *Oblast*, which belonged to Georgia, because it has vast deposits of oil.

Introduction

1. The term literally translates as 'collective violence', but it meant 'collective punishment'.
2. Christopher Browning, *Ordinary Men: Reserve Police Battalion 101 and the Final Solution in Poland.* New York: Harper Collins, 1992, p. 182.
3. Christian Streit, 'Wehrmacht, *Einsatzgruppen*, Soviet POWs and Anti-Bolshevism in the Emergence of the Final Solution', *The Final Solution. Origins and Implementation*, ed. David Cesarani. London: Routledge, 1994, p. 110.
4. For our purposes, the term USSR refers to those lands that in 1941 encompassed the Baltic States, European Russia, Belarus (White Russia) and Ukraine. European Russia covers an area roughly 3,960,000km^2. Its eastern border is defined by the Ural Mountains, and in the south by the border with Kazakhstan. The Caucasus mountains and the region bordering Turkey and Persia define the southernmost boundary, while the northern edge covers the border area with Finland and Norway.
5. *Ostheer*: Eastern Army, the German military forces fighting on the Russian Front.
6. International Military Tribunal, *Trial of the Major War Criminals before the International Military Tribunal*, 42 vols. Nuremberg: Secretary of the Tribunal, vol. 7, p. 59.
7. Matthew Cooper, *The Nazi War Against Soviet Partisans 1941–1944.* New York: Stein & Day, 1979, pp. 171–2.
8. Ben Shepperd, *War in the Wild East: The German Army and Partisans.* Cambridge: Harvard University Press, 2004, p. 130.
9. Shepperd, *War in the Wild East*, p. 233.
10. The American edition of this book was released a year later, in 1957.
11. Although a bit dated, the book is still considered essential reading for anyone interested in the topic of the German occupation of the East.

12. Alexander Dallin, *German Rule in Russia 1941–1945: A Study of Occupation Policies*. London: MacMillan & Co. Ltd, 1957, p. 30.
13. Yitzhak Arad, 'The Holocaust of Soviet Jewry in the Occupied Territories of the Soviet Union', *Yad Vashem Studies XXI*, No. 21 (1991), p. 6.
14. Gerald Reitlinger, *The House Built on Sand: The Conflicts of German Policy in Russia*. New York: Viking Press, 1960, p. 81.
15. Reitlinger, *The House Built on Sand*, p. 81.
16. *Landser* is the German equivalent of G.I.
17. Omer Bartov, *The Eastern Front 1941–45: German Troops and the Barbarization of Warfare*. New York: St Martin's Press, 1986, p. 68.
18. Theo J. Schulte, *The German Army and Nazi Policies in Occupied Russia*. Oxford: Berg Publishers, 1989, p. 284.
19. Michael Geyer, 'Traditional Elites and National Socialist Leadership', in Charles S. Maier and Andrew Gould, eds, *The Rise of the Nazi Regime: Historical Reassessments*. Boulder: Westview Press, 1986, p. 71.
20. Edward Davies and Ronald Smelser, *The Myth of the Eastern Front: The Nazi-Soviet War in American Popular Culture*. New York: Cambridge University Press, 2007, pp. 22–4.
21. Davies & Smelser, *The Myth of the Eastern Front*, p. 24.
22. Paul Kohl, *Der Krieg der deutschen Wehrmacht und der Polizei 1941–1944*. Frankfurt am Main: Fischer Taschenbuch Verlag, 1995, p. 333.
23. Walter Manoschek, ed., *Die Wehrmacht im Rassenkrieg: Der Vernichtungskrieg Hinter der Front*. Vienna: Picus Verlag, 1996, p. 142.
24. Willi Dreßen, 'The Role of the Wehrmacht and the Police in the Annihilation of the Jews, the Prosecution of Postwar Careers of Perpetrators in the Police Force of the Federal Republic of Germany', *Yad Vashem Studies XXIII* (1993), pp. 295–319.
25. 'War of Annihilation: Crimes of the [German] Armed Forces 1941 to 1944'.
26. Hannes Heer and Klaus Naumann, *Vernichtungskrieg: Verbrechen der Wehrmacht 1941 bis 1944*. Hamburg: Hamburger Edition, 1995, p. 14.
27. Hannes Heer and Klaus Naumann, *War of Extermination: The German Military in World War II, 1941–1944*. New York: Berghahn Books, 2000, p. 4.
28. Wolfram Wette, *The Wehrmacht: History, Myth, Reality*. Cambridge: Harvard University Press, 2006, p. 296.
29. 'Crimes of the Armed Forces: Dimensions of the War of Extermination'.
30. Hamburg Institute for Social Research.
31. Wolfram Wette, *Die Wehrmacht: Feindbilder, Vernichtungskrieg, Legenden*. Frankfurt am Main: S. Fischer Verlag, 2002.
32. Wette, *The Wehrmacht*, p. 296.
33. Ibid., p. 297.
34. Daniel J. Goldhagen, *Hitler's Willing Executioners: Ordinary Germans and the Holocaust*. New York: Alfred A. Knopf, 1996, pp. 23–4.
35. Julius Schoeps, ed., *Ein Volk von Mordern? Die Dokumentation zur Goldhagen-Kontroverse um die Rolle der Deutschen im Holocaust*. Hamburg: Hoffmann & Campe, 1996, pp. 1–5.
36. Dr Fritz Stern, 'Book Review: *Hitler's Willing Executioners: Ordinary Germans and the Holocaust*', *Foreign Affairs*, vol. 75, No. 6 (November–December 1996), pp. 640–4.
37. Geoffrey P. Megargee, *War of Annihilation: Combat and Genocide on the Eastern Front, 1941*. New York: Rowman & Littlefield Publishers Inc., 2006, p. 151.
38. S.R.G.G. 1203 (c) v. 6. Mai 1945, PRO WO 208/4170 *Generalleutnant* SIRY171 (Comd., 347ID), Captured Friedrichsroda 10 April 1945 *Generalstabsintendant* PAUER172 (Formerly of the OKH), Captured Kleinrinderfeld, 7 April 1945.

39. Sönke Neitzel, *Abgehort: Deutsche Generale in britischer Kriegsgefangenschaft 1942–1945*. Berlin: List-Ullstein Verlag, 2007, p. 231.
40. Timothy Snyder, *Bloodlands: Europe Between Hitler and Stalin*. New York: Basic Books, 2010.
41. Mark Mazower, *Hitler's Empire: How the Nazis Ruled Europe*. New York: Penguin Books, 2008.

Chapter 1: German preparations for invading and occupying the USSR

1. Von Hardesty and Ilya Grinberg, *Red Phoenix Rising: The Soviet Air Force in World War II*. Lawrence: University Press of Kansas, 2012. A comment Adolf Hitler made during a military conference about how easy it would be to destroy the Soviet Union.
2. Adolf Hitler, *Mein Kampf*. New York: Reynal & Hitchcock, 1939, p. 951.
3. Hitler, *Mein Kampf*, p. 949.
4. Adolf Hitler, *My New Order*, ed. with commentary by Raoul de Roussy de Sales (New York: Reynal & Hitchcock, 1941), pp. 208–9, 373, 439.
5. *Trial of the Major War Criminals before the International Military Tribunal, Nuremberg, 14 November, 1945–1 October, 1946* (42 vol. Nuremberg, 1947), vol. X, pp. 124, 310. [Hereafter cited as *TMWC*.]
6. *Nazi Conspiracy and Aggression*, 10 volumes. Office of the United States Chief of Counsel for Prosecution of Axis Criminality (Washington, DC: Government Printing Office, 1946), vol. VIII, p. 646. [Hereafter cited as *NCA*.]
7. Franz Halder, *The Private War Journal of Generaloberst Franz Halder, Chief of the General Staff of the Supreme Command of the German Army*. 7 vols. Nuremberg: Office of Chief of Counsel for War Crimes, 1946), vol. VI, p. 42.
8. *Generalplan Ost. Richtlinien für die Wirtschaftsführung in den neu besetzten Ostgebieten, 1. Juni '41*, TMWC, VIII, p. 23.
9. Ibid.
10. *Generalplan Ost*, TMWC, VIII, p. 455.
11. Adolf Hitler, *Hitler's Secret Conversations, 1941–1944*, ed. H.R. Trevor-Roper. New York: Ferrar, Straus & Cudahy Inc., 1953, p. 501.
12. A poster in the Russian language addressed to the people of the occupied Eastern territories, found in the files of 9th Army, dated July 1941. Wi/ID 2.2960, GCRA.
13. This was a reference to Friedrich I, known more commonly as Friedrich Barbarossa, one of the more notable Holy Roman Emperors. He lived in the twelfth century and died in 1190 trying to cross a river in Anatolia, on his way to take part in the Third Crusade.
14. TMWC, vol. V, p. 35.
15. The German Army of the Second World War moved using horses. Nearly 3 million horses were employed by the German Army, of which about 750,000 died in the conflict. Shortly before the invasion of the Soviet Union, Hitler was able increase his tank force from 10 to 20 panzer divisions. He was able to do this by simply reducing the number of tanks per division from 300 to 150. The additional support units for these new panzer divisions were either drawn from non-armoured formations or created outright. So in spite of the belief held by some that the German Army of the Second World War was completely motorized, this could not be further from the truth.
16. Alex Alexiev, *Soviet Nationalities in German Wartime Strategy, 1941–1945*. Santa Monica: Rand Corporation, 1982, p. 10.
17. MS No. P-033, *German Military Government*. Office of Chief of Military History, Department of the Army, Washington, DC, vol. I, p. 10.
18. The Führer is quoted by Soviet historians in *Istoriia Velikoi Otechestvennoi Voiny Sovietskogo Soiuza, 1941–1945* [History of the Great Fatherland War of the Soviet Union, 1941–1945],

comp. Institute MarkizmaLininizma Pri Tzk KPSS (6 vols, Moscow, Voenizdat, 1960–1964), vol. I, p. 354. Hereafter referred to as *Istoriia Velikoi.*

19. Hungary took part in the initial invasion and later in the occupation of Yugoslavia. The Bulgarians did not initially invade Yugoslavia, but later they occupied the Yugoslav province of Macedonia and the Greek province of Thrace. Hungary had become part of the Axis on 20 November 1940. The Tripartite Pact had initially been signed in Berlin by Germany, Italy and Japan on 27 September 1940. The Pact was subsequently joined by Hungary (20 November 1940), Romania (23 November 1940), Slovakia (24 November 1940) and Bulgaria (1 March 1941).
20. *Istoriia Velikoi*, vol. II, p. 72.
21. John Erickson, *The Soviet High Command.* New York: St Martin's Press, 1962, pp. 837, 846–7, 843–4.
22. The muddy season, but the literal translation is 'season of bad roads'. Another similar term is 'bezdorizhzhia.'
23. *Istoriia Velikoi*, vol. II, pp. 107, 224.
24. Paul Carell, *Hitler Moves East 1941–1943.* Boston: Little, Brown & Company, 1963, p. 173.
25. E.P. Schramm, *Kriegstagebuch des Oberkommandos der Wehrmacht*, 8 vols. Munich: Bernard & Graefe Verlag, 1982, vol. 2, pp. 819–20.
26. MS No. P-033, *German Military Government*, vol. II (Appendices), p. 32.
27. A *muzjik* was a Russian peasant, especially before 1917. Other terms used to describe the Russian peasants are *moujik* and *krestianin.*
28. MS No. P-033, vol. II (Appendices), p. 31.
29. Quoted from a comment by Toppe in Wolfram Wette, *The Wehrmacht: History, Myth, Reality.* Cambridge: Harvard University Press, 2006, p. 296.
30. *Istoriia Velikoi*, vol. II, p. 53.
31. Ibid., p. 54.
32. NCA. Top Secret memorandum, Berlin, 25 October 1942, by Brautigam, vol. III, p. 243.
33. 'The well-being of the defeated is to not hope for much more well-being'.
34. Jürgen Thorwald, *The Illusion: Soviet Soldiers in Hitler's Armies.* New York: Harcourt Brace Jovanovich, 1974, pp. 29-30.
35. Alexander Pronin, *Guerrilla Warfare in the German Occupied Soviet Territories 1941–1945.* Georgetown University Graduate School: Georgetown, 1965, p. 172.
36. Eastern European volunteers included the various peoples who made up the Soviet Union, including Ukrainians, Belarusians, Russians, Armenians, Georgians, Azerbaijanis, Siberians, Kalmucks, Cossacks, men from Turkistan, Caucasians, Circassians, etc.
37. Alexiev, *Soviet Nationalities*, p. 27.
38. Korück = *Kommandeur für das Rückwärtige Heeresgebiet* (Commander for the Army Rear Area).
39. Pronin, *Guerrilla Warfare*, pp. 171–2.
40. This Korück command was established in February 1942, but the numerical designation 532 was not given until April 1942.
41. This Korück command was established in October 1942. From 12 January 1943 Korück 593 was made subordinate to Army Detachment Hollidt. In April 1943 Korück 585 was assigned to Panzer Group 4 (which from January 1942 was called 4th Panzer Army).
42. Dallin, *German Rule in Russia*, p. 537.
43. BA MA RH 26-113/13. *Divisionsbefehl* (Ia Nr. 693/42 geh.).
44. Veit Scherzer, '*Die Aermelabzeichen der russischen Freiwilligen im Bereichs der 113. Infanterie-Division*', in *Militaria.* Norderstedt: Militär-Verlag Klaus D. Patzwall, vol. 18, no. 4 (July–August, 1996), p. 102.

45. Prisoner of War Engineer Company, 113th Engineer Battalion.
46. Thorwald, *The Illusion*, p. 53.

Chapter 2: The *Ostland* (Baltic) and Belarus regions

1. Adolf Hitler had initially forbidden the creation of eastern volunteer units larger than a battalion in size. In order to get around this rule, many German divisional commanders would simply assign two or sometimes three battalions to one established Field Post Number, which every German unit needed to have. For example, 454th Security Division had been allocated the numerical listing of 454th Eastern Cavalry Battalion plus its corresponding Field Post Number. However, it had two battalions of Cossack volunteers, so the units were referred to as I. Battalion, 454th Eastern Cavalry Battalion, while its sister battalion was called II. Battalion, 454th Eastern Cavalry Battalion. In this way, German commanders were able to circumvent Hitler's order that eastern volunteer units could never be larger than a battalion in size.
2. Heer & Naumann, *Vernichtungskrieg Verbrecken der Wehrmacht*, p. 346.
3. The term and the region referred to as Belarus, White Ruthenia and White Russia are one and the same.
4. Stephen Darril, *M.I.6*. London: Fourth Estate Publishing Ltd, 2000, p. 215.
5. Commander of the Rear Army Area of Army Group Centre.
6. Antonio Muñoz, *Hitler's Eastern Legions. Vol. I: The Baltic Schutzmannschaft 1941–1945*. New York: Europa Books, 1998, 2nd revised and expanded edition, p. 58.
7. For communication purposes, these three Higher SS and Police commands were numbered as follows: 101 (North), 102 (Centre) and 103 (South). The initial leaders in 1941 were Hans Adolf Prützmann (101), von dem Bach (102) and Friedrich Jeckeln (103).
8. Prützmann held this post from 29 June until 1 November 1941, when SS Lieutenant General and General of the Police Friedrich Jeckeln took over the command and held it until 30 January 1945. Thereafter SS Lieutenant General and General of the Police Dr Hermann Behrends assumed actual control while Jeckeln served in the Waffen SS.
9. Orpo: abbreviation for *Ordnungspolizei* (Order Police).
10. It was not until April 1943 that control of Belarus was actually transferred to the Higher SS and Police Command Central Russia. At that time the HQ was renamed Higher SS and Police Leader in Central Russia and White Ruthenia, after Belarus was transferred from the control of the Higher SS and Police Leader in Eastland and North Russia HQ.
11. On 24 May 1944 Jäger was appointed acting police chief of Reichenberg in the *Reichsgau Sudetenland*.
12. *Oberst der Schutzpolizei*.
13. SS Colonel and Police Colonel.
14. SS Lieutenant Colonel and Police Colonel.
15. Police Lieutenant Colonel.
16. Police Colonel.
17. SS Lieutenant General and Lieutenant General of the Police.
18. SS Brigadier General and Major General of the Police.
19. SS Lieutenant Colonel and Police Colonel.
20. John Mendelsohn, ed., *The Holocaust. Selected Documents in Eighteen Volumes*. New York: Garland Publishing, 1982, p. 199.
21. Horst Boog et al., *Germany and the Second World War. Volume IV: The Attack on the Soviet Union*. Oxford: Clarenden Press, 1998, p. 1,203.
22. The Organization Todt was the official Nazi Party national labour force, organized on a military basis and employed as construction battalions.

23. Bernd Diroll, *Personen-Lexicon der NSDAP. Band 1–SS Führer A–B.* Norderstedt: Verlag Klaus D. Patzwall, 1998, p. 10.
24. French L MacLean, *The Field Men: The SS Officers Who Led the Einsatzkommandos* – the Nazi Mobile Killing Units. Atglen: Schiffer Military History, 1999, p. 36.
25. Helmut Krausnick, *Hitlers Einsatzgruppen*: Die Truppen des Weltanschauungskrieges 1938–1942. Fischer Taschenbuch Verlag: Frankfurt am Main: 1989, p. 156.
26. White Ruthenia: Belarus.
27. Tessin et al., *Waffen SS und Ordnungspolizei*, p. 219.
28. Boog et al., *Germany and the Second World War*, vol. IV, p. 1,218.
29. Edward B. Westermann, *Hitler's Police Battalions: Enforcing Racial War in the East.* Lawrence: University Press of Kansas, pp. 323–24.
30. Werner Regenberg, *Panzerfahrzeuge und Panzereinheiten der Ordnungspolizei 1936–1945.* Podzun Pallas Verlag: Friedberg, 1996, p. 43.
31. Westermann, *Hitler's Police Battalions*, p. 321.
32. Ibid., p. 320.
33. Tessin, *Verbände und Truppen*, vol. 1, p. 291.
34. Tessin, *Verbände und Truppen*, vol. 8, p. 104.
35. Dr Martin Gilbert, *Atlas of the Holocaust.* London: Lester Publishing Ltd, 1988, revised edition, 1993, p. 75.
36. Boog et al., *Germany and the Second World War*, vol. IV, p. 1,220.
37. Mark C. Yerger, *Riding East. The SS Cavalry Brigade in Poland and Russia 1939–1942.* Atglen: Schiffer Publishers, 1996, p. 128.
38. Earl F. Ziemke, *Stalingrad to Berlin: The German Defeat in the East.* Washington, DC: Center of Military History, United States Army, 1968, p. 207.
39. Tessin, *Verbände und Truppen*, vol. 12, p. 156.
40. Raul Hilberg, *Perpetrators, Victims, Bystanders. The Jewish Catastrophe 1933–1945.* New York: Harper Collins Publishers, 1992, p. 62.
41. Erich Hesse, *Der Sowietrussische Partisanenkrieg 1941 bis 1944.* Göttingen: Musterschmidt Verlag, 1969, p. 81.
42. Gerald Reitlinger, *The Final Solution.* New York: Thomas Yeseloff, 1961, p. 237.
43. Leonid D. Grenkevich and David M. Glantz, *The Soviet Partisan Movement, 1941–1944: A Critical Historiographical Analysis.* London: Frank Cass Publishers, 1999, p. 75. Excerpt from the conference between Hitler and the Army High Command, held in Rastenburg, Hitler's East Prussian headquarters, on 16 July 1941. This was shortly after Joseph Stalin had called for the establishment of partisan forces.
44. Hilberg, *Perpetrators, Victims, Bystanders*, p. 63.
45. Boog et al., *Germany and the Second World War*, vol. IV, p. 1,218.
46. *General der Flieger a. D.* Karl Drum, *Airpower and Russian Partisan Warfare.* New York: Arno Press: 1968, pp. 7–9.
47. Drum, *Airpower and Russian Partisan Warfare*, p. 14.

Chapter 3: The SS command in the Baltic States and North Russia ...

1. The title was later changed to Higher SS and Police Leader Ostland and White Ruthenia, when the Bialystok District was added to the Ostland command.
2. SS Brigadier General Walter Schimana, von Gottberg's second in command, would assume the post whenever von Gottberg was ill, on vacation or away at a meeting.
3. Ehrlinger was promoted to SS colonel on 1 September 1943 and to police colonel on 27 June 1944.
4. At its maximum this command had 28,987 men.

5. Dr KG Klietmann, *Die Waffen SS eine Dokumentation*. Osnabrück: Verlag 'Der Freiwillige' GmbH., 1965, p. 395.
6. Rolf Michaelis, *Die Kavallerie-Divisionen der Waffen SS*. Erlangen: Privately published, 1993, p. 32.
7. NARA Microfilm T175, Roll 16, Frames 2519158–98.
8. Browning, *Ordinary Men*, p. 11.
9. The Escort Battalion of the National Leader of the SS would form the basis for the Assault Brigade National Leader of the SS in 1943, and later the 16th SS Armoured Infantry Division National Leader of the SS in 1944.
10. NARA Microfilm T-175, Roll 16, Frames 2519158–251998.
11. Westermann, *Hitler's Police Battalions*, p. 324.
12. Tessin et al., *Waffen SS und Ordnungspolizei*, p. 631.
13. Ibid., p. 581.
14. *Bundesdarchiv Militärarchiv Frieburg*. BA-MA, RH 22-271.
15. Hans-Heinrich Wilhelm, *Die Einsatzgruppe* A: der Sicherheitspolizei und des SD 1941/42. Frankfurt am Main: Peter Lang Verlag GmbH, 1996, p. 13.
16. Known formally as *Sonderbataillon zur Verfügung des Kommandostab Reichsführer SS* (Battalion for Special Employment of the Command Staff of the National-SS Leader).
17. Helmut Krausnick et al., *Anatomy of the SS State*. New York: Walker & Company, 1968, p. 564.
18. Wilhelm, *Die Einsatzgruppe* A, p. 11.
19. Heinz Höhne, *The Order of the Death's Head. The Story of Hitler's SS*. New York: Coward-McCann, Inc., 1970, p. 358.
20. Krausnick, *Hitlers Einsatzgruppen*, p. 128.
21. Prechtl, *Unsere Ehre Heisst Treue*, p. 244.
22. Harald Buhlan and Werner Jung, eds, *Wessen Freund und wessen Helfer? Die Kölner Polizei im Nationalsozialismus*. Köln: Emons Verlag, 2000, pp. 285–6.
23. Antonio Muñoz, *Göring's Grenadiers: The Luftwaffe Field Divisions, 1942–1945*. New York: Europa Books, 2002, pp. 339–43.
24. Westermann, *Hitler's Police Battalions*, p. 324.
25. The Order Police was nominally under the control of the Nazi Interior Ministry, but its executive operations rested with the SS command.
26. The five companies of the 69th Reserve Police Battalion Todt were used individually. The 5th Company was employed in the siege of Leningrad and also performed security duty for Organization Todt construction sites in Pleskau and Luga. The 4th Company took part in the shooting of Jews in Vilnius, Luninecz, Lachva and Radiszkoeicze. In November 1941 it served in Slonim (Belarus), where 9,000 Jews were eventually killed. The 3rd Company was absorbed into SS *Einsatzgruppe* 7c, which was operating in the region of Army Group Centre. The 2nd Company was sent to Ukraine and used in Kiev, Kharkiv and Poltava. Finally, the 1st Company was absorbed into SS *Einsatzgruppe* D and used near Nikolayev and Vinnitsa in Ukraine.
27. Police Regiment 9 was merely a redesignation of Police Regiment North.
28. Wilhelm, *Die Einsatzgruppe* A, p. 162.
29. Apparently, Police Major Schallert took over as Commander of the Order Police Estonia sometime after Heinrich Möller left.
30. There is no rank equivalent to *Oberführer* in the British or American military rank structure. It is a rank between full colonel and brigadier general.
31. Erich Stockhorst, *5000 Köpfe: Wer War Was Im Dritten Reich*. Kiel: Arndt Verlag, 2000, p. 456.
32. Stockhorst, *5000 Köpfe*, p. 367.

33. The *Gestapo* – abbreviation for *Geheimstaatspolizei* (State Secret Police).
34. Prützmann was tasked with combating the growing partisan threat in Ukraine and southern Russia, but in early 1942 he was tasked with securing forced labour for the *Durchgangsstrasse IV*, a large project to build a road from Lemberg (Lviv) to Stalino (now Donetsk).
35. MacLean, *The Field Men*, p. 228.
36. Latvian Thunder Cross Party.
37. Jurs et al., *Estonian Freedom Fighters in World War II*, p. 32.
38. Wilhelm, *Die Einsatzgruppe* A, p. 206.
39. Email from Estonian researcher, Andrus Ojamaa, dated 17 June 1998.
40. Tessin et al., *Waffen SS und Ordnungspolizei*, p. 583.
41. Tessin, *Waffen SS und Ordnungspolizei*, vol. 7, pp. 181–234.
42. Muñoz, *Hitler's Eastern Legions*, p. 52.
43. This battalion was quickly redesignated the 18th Latvian Self-Defence Battalion in November 1941. Behms led the unit from its creation in September 1941 until 16 December 1941, when Colonel Karlis Lobe assumed command. Lobe's control was brief, however, as he gave up control of the battalion later in the same month. Colonel Arvids Kurze was then the commander, but on 21 February 1942 Major Fridrichs Rubenis took over from Kurze.
44. This battalion was used as the basis for the 20th Latvian Self-Defence Battalion, created in Abrene on 9 May 1942. It was simply a redesignation of the Latvian Engineer Security Battalion Abrene. A month later it became the 270th Latvian Engineer Self-Defence Battalion. It was employed in the region of Army Group South.
45. This officer did not assume command of the battalion until 18 May 1942.
46. This Latvian self-defence battalion was created in just three days in Riga between 19 and 21 December 1941. Major Skrauja led the unit until 21 July 1942. Thereafter Captain J. Nikans led the battalion up until May 1943.
47. Between November and December 1939 Gendarmerie Captain Espey (his rank at the time) was Company Chief of the 4th Company, 121st Police Battalion. From 1942 until his appointment as Commander of the Rural Police in Riga, he worked for the Reich Main Security Office.
48. NARA Microfilm T-78, Roll 413, Frame 966 – *Anlage 1 zu O.K.H./Gen.St.d.H./Org.Abt. (II) Nr. 4971/42 g.Kdos. v. 17. Okt.42. Landeseigene Verbände - Heeresgruppe Nord Stand 1. Okt. 42.*
49. Redesignated the 5th Lithuanian Self-Defence Battalion in November 1941.
50. This guard company was created in the autumn of 1941, but was disbanded one year later in the autumn of 1942.
51. This company was created in the autumn of 1941 and was disbanded in the autumn of 1943.
52. Employed as a guard unit in the German Army.
53. Friedrich Husemann, *Die guten Glaubens waren. Geschichte der SS Polizei Division*, 2 vols, Osnabrück: Munin-Verlag, 1984, vol. I, pp. 210–12.
54. German cadre staff and Norwegian SS volunteers.
55. The 306th Police Battalion was added to the kampfgruppe on 19 February 1942, but was withdrawn in order to serve alongside 223rd Infantry Division from 7 April 1942.

Chapter 4: Controlling the rear areas of Army Group North

1. Werner Haupt, *Army Group North*. Schiffer Military Publishing: Atglen, 1997, p. 366.
2. Wilhelm, *Die Einsatzgruppe* A, pp. 277–8.
3. From 1942 to 1943 this division would also employ a company of captured tanks (285th Tank Company) as well as the 285th Eastern Cavalry Battalion, comprising four eastern volunteer cavalry squadrons. On 10 October 1943 the 285th Eastern Cavalry Battalion was transferred to France. In February 1942 the 236th Regional Defence Battalion (Major Döring) and the 853rd Regional Defence Battalion (Captain Günzel) were attached to the

division. The III. Battalion, 322nd Infantry Regiment was actually motorized and was initially held back as an Army High Command reserve unit, but was reattached in July 1941. This security division was dissolved in November 1944, with some of its component parts transferred to the 207th and 281st Security Divisions.

4. Renamed the 113th Security Regiment on 15 October 1943.
5. The 853rd, 941st and 972nd Regional Defence battalions were all renamed as security battalions on 1 June 1942.
6. Because Kriegsheim made comments critical of the regime, he was replaced as Chief of Staff, Rear Army Area North, in May 1942 and was dismissed first from the SS and later from the *Wehrmacht*.
7. Josef von Gise had previously been the commander of 605th Security Regiment from 17 March 1943.
8. Haselmayr was born in 1879 and died in 1965. He was a member of the political wing of the Nazi Party. He was a lieutenant general in the German Army and an SA major-general. Until 26 December 1941 Haselmayr was in command of the 569th Field Command, then he served as commander of the 579th Field Command. *See also* a letter sent from Munich by retired Lieutenant General Haselmayr to Mr Stephen Bumball dated 19 July 1960, and its description by Alexander Historical Auctions, sale at auction, Lot 58, 29 May 2022 at: https://www.alexautographs.com/auction-lot/friedrich-haselmayr_7D1452C870 (accessed 25 October 2023).
9. Muñoz et al., *Hitler's Eastern Legions*, vol. 1, p. 15.
10. 4th Armoured Group was transferred to Army Group Centre on 24 September 1941. It was later redesignated 4th Panzer Army.
11. Andris J. Kursietis, *The Wehrmacht at War 1939–1945*. Aspekt Publishers: Soesterber, 1999, p. 158.
12. Bayer was replaced by Lieutenant General Theodor Scherer on 1 October 1941.
13. Tessin, *Verbände und Truppen*, vol. 18, pt III, p. 258. On 10 October 1941 the 579th Field Command was renamed the 579th Senior Field Command. Initially, 579th Field Command had been in charge of the territory in the region of Volilynia-Podolia in northwestern Ukraine.
14. Goldhagen, *Hitler's Willing Executioners*, p. 191.
15. Tessin, *Verbände und Truppen*, vol. 6, p. 252.
16. *Befehlshaber der Rückwärtigen Heeresgebiet Nord, Ia Tgb. – Nr. 62O/41 geh., nicht unterzeichneter Entwurf.*
17. The large number of captured or apprehended people was due to an operation being conducted in the area of Luga. Of this number apparently 140 people were apprehended near Wyritza.
18. Haupt, *Army Group North*, p. 305.
19. Ibid., p. 307.
20. Ibid., p. 308.
21. Aschenauer, Rudolf. *Abgehört. Deutsche Generäle in britischer Kriegsgefangenschaft 1942–1945*. Munich: Druffel-Verlag, 1982, p. 133.
22. Kursietis, *The Wehrmacht at War*, p. 77.
23. Dr Samuel W. Mitcham Jr, *Hitler's Legions: The German Army Order of Battle, World War II*. New York: Dorset Press, 1985, p. 42.
24. Tessin, *Verbände und Truppen*, vol. 1, p. 20.
25. Alexander Werth, *Russia at War 1941–1945*. New York: E.P. Dutton, 1964, p. 716.
26. Joachim Hoffman, *Stalin's War of Extermination 1941–1945*. Capshaw: Thesis and Dissertations Press, 2001, p. 135.

27. L.V. Richard, *Partisanen: Kämpfer hinter den Fronten*. Rastatt: Verlag Arthur Moewig GmbH, 1986, p. 74.
28. Hoffman, *Stalin's War of Extermination*, p. 135.
29. David M. Glantz, *The Battle for Leningrad, 1941–1944*. Lawrence: University Press of Kansas, 2002, p. 146.
30. Richard, *Partisanen*, p. 79.
31. Carell, *Hitler Moves East*, p. 139.
32. Kohl, *Der Krieg der deutschen Wehrmacht und der Polizei*, p. 199.
33. Muñoz et al., *Hitler's White Russians*, p. 159.
34. Kohl, *Der Krieg der deutschen Wehrmacht und der Polizei*, p. 201.
35. Wilhelm, *Die Einsatzgruppe* A, p. 265.
36. Krausnick, *Hitlers Einsatzgruppen*, p. 233.
37. Supplementary interrogation of Yevgeniy Kozlov, *GFP* 727, *No. 336/41 Geheim, Okt. 1, '41, BA-MA RH 22/271.*
38. Anthony Beevor, *Stalingrad: The Fateful Siege, 1942–1943*. New York: Penguin Books, 1999, p. 37.
39. Richard, *Partisanen*, p. 78.
40. Ibid., p. 79.
41. Grenkevich and Glantz, *The Soviet Partisan Movement*, p. 204.
42. Glantz, *Battle for Leningrad*, p. 251.
43. Aschenauer, op. cit., p. 146.
44. Alexander Hill, *The War Behind the Eastern Front: The Soviet Partisan Movement in North-West Russia, 1941–44*. New York: Frank Cass, 2005, p. 25.
45. The *Aussenkommando Sonderrat R* (Foreign Command Special Council R) was created to interrogate all German POWs who had returned from Russian captivity bearing sealed letters from the Russian-sponsored National Committee 'Freies Deutschland', which was led by the captured German general Seydlitz.
46. National Archives, Kew, Richmond, Surrey, C.S.D.I.C. (U.K.) S.I.R. 1675, 24 May 1945. 'Notes on the GFP and Other Security Services in the Area of Army Group North (later Kurland), 1942–1 Jan. 1945', p. 1.
47. National Archives, 'Notes on the GFP and Other Security Services', p. 2.
48. Johannes Hürter, '*Die Wehrmacht vor Leningrad: Krieg und Besatzungspolitik der 18. Armee im Herbst und Winter 1941/42*', in Oldenbourg: Institut für Zeitgeschichte, Jahrgang 49, 2001, p. 387.

Chapter 5: The start of the war behind the lines

1. Created principally from the two SS Death's Head cavalry regiments that were under the Command Staff of the National Leader of the SS.
2. Those German Army units which took part in the operation included the 162nd and 252nd Infantry Divisions.
3. Police Regiment Centre.
4. MI-14 was a department of British Military Intelligence that worked for the War Office and specialized in Germany.
5. F.H. Hinsley, *British Intelligence in the Second World War*. London: HMSO, 1984, vol. 3, pt I, p. 671.
6. Ibid.
7. Yerger, *Riding East*, p. 104.
8. Hesse, *Der Sowietrussische Partisanenkrieg*, p. 57.
9. Ibid., p. 59.

10. Ibid., p. 60.
11. Jack Nussan Porter, *Jewish Partisans. A Documentary of Jewish Resistance in the Soviet Union During World War II.* Washington DC: University Press of America, 1982, p. 52.
12. Ziemke, *Stalingrad to Berlin*, p. 209.
13. Ibid.
14. Boog et al., *Germany and the Second World War*, vol. IV, p. 1201.
15. Ibid.
16. Tessin, *Verbände und Truppen*, vol. 8, p. 219.
17. Hans Pottgeiser, *Die Reichsbahn in Ostfeldzug*. Neckargemünd: Kurt Vowinckel Verlag, 1960, pp. 33–40.
18. Alan Clark, *Barbarossa. The Russo-German Conflict, 1941–45*. New York: William Morrow & Co., 1965, p. 154.
19. Ibid., p. 153.
20. Ibid., p. 79.

Chapter 6: Collaboration in Belarus and central Russia, 1941–1942

1. Browning, *Ordinary Men*, p. 24.
2. Clark, *Barbarossa*, p. 154.
3. For guarding air installations, the *Luftwaffe* had security troops but often they were insufficient.
4. Martin Gilbert, *The Holocaust: A History of the Jews of Europe During the Second World War*. New York: Henry Holt & Co., 1985, p. 300.
5. Bernhard Chiari, *Alltag Hinter der Front: Besatzung, Kollaboration und Wiederstand in Weissrussland 1941–1944*. Neckargemund: Droste Verlag, 1998, p. 163.
6. Ibid., p. 185.
7. Krausnick, *Hitlers Einsatzgruppen*, p. 236.
8. David Littlejohn, *The Patriotic Traitors: The History of Collaboration in German-Occupied Europe, 1940–45*. New York: Doubleday & Co. Inc., 1972, p. 364.
9. Sven Steenberg, *Vlasov*. New York: Alfred A. Knopf, 1970, p. 71.
10. Tessin et al., *Waffen SS und Ordnungspolizei*, p. 591.
11. Westermann, *Hitler's Police Battalions*, pp. 324–5.
12. Chiari, *Alltag Hinter der Front*, p. 164.
13. George Fischer, *Soviet Opposition to Stalin. A Case Study in World War II.* Cambridge: Harvard University Press, 1952, p. 43.
14. Ibid.
15. Thorwald, *The Illusion*, p. 96.
16. Cooper, *The Nazi War Against Soviet Partisans*, p. 121.
17. Thorwald, *The Illusion*, p. 97.
18. Waitman W. Beorn, 'A Calculus of Complicity: The Wehrmacht, the Anti-Partisan War, and the Final Solution in White Russia, 1941–1942', *Central European History*, 44, 2011, pp. 308–37.
19. *Sonderanweisungen zum Kampf gegen Partisanenbanden*. Berlin: *Gedruckt in der Reichsdruckerei*, 1941, p. 7.

Chapter 7: The war against the Jews and the partisans resurgent

1. Mary Soames testimony, on a comment made by Joseph Stalin to her father, Winston Churchill.
2. Memel is the German name for the city of Klaipėda, on the Baltic coast of Lithuania.
3. Wilhelm, *Die Polizei im NS Staat*, p. 203.

4. Wolfgang Benz, Konrad Kwiet and Jürgen Matthäus, *Einsatz im 'Reichskommissariat Ostland'. Dokumente zum Völkermord im Baltikum und in Weibrussland 1941–1944*. Berlin: Metropol Verlag, 1998, p. 73.
5. Ibid., p. 75.
6. Wilhelm, *Die Einsatzgruppe* A, p. 68.
7. Ibid.
8. Muñoz et al., *Hitler's White Russians*, p. 154.
9. Gilbert, *The Holocaust*, p. 234.
10. Wilhelm, *Die Einsatzgruppe* A, p. 67.
11. Benz, Kwiet and Matthäus, *Einsatz im 'Reichskommissariat Ostland'*, pp. 96, 105.
12. Minutes from Jeckeln's interrogation on 14 December 1945 (Major Zwetajew, interrogator; Sergeant Suur, interpreter), pp. 8–13, Historical State Archives, Riga, Latvia.
13. Max Knecht was the commander of the municipal police in Latvia.
14. To Himmler's Hochwald headquarters in Lötzen.
15. Dated 25 January 1942, 11:30a.m.–1:00p.m., per National leader of the SS appointment book, NS-19 DC/vorl. 12, Bundesdarchiv, Koblenz.
16. We now know that the actual number of Jews killed in the Baltic States was somewhere in the neighbourhood of over 223,000.
17. Riga Trial, transcripts from 26 January–3 February 1946: Friedrich Jeckeln.
18. Boog et al., *Germany and the Second World War*, vol. IV, p. 1,224.
19. Westermann, *Hitler's Police Battalions*, p. 325.
20. Muñoz, *Göring's Grenadiers*, p. 339.
21. Regenberg, *Panzerfahrzeuge und Panzereinheiten*, p. 42.
22. Grenkevich and Glantz, *The Soviet Partisan Movement*, p. 206.
23. Hermann Pottgiesser, *Die Reichsbahn im Ostfeldzug*. Neckargemünd: Kurt Vowinckel Verlag, 1960, pp. 176–7.
24. Westermann, *Hitler's Police Battalions*, p. 327.
25. John A. Armstrong (ed.), *Soviet Partisans in World War II*. Madison: University of Wisconsin Press, 1964, p. 151.
26. Ziemke, *Stalingrad to Berlin*, p. 202.
27. Grenkevich and Glantz, *The Soviet Partisan Movement*, p. 130.
28. Ziemke, *Stalingrad to Berlin*, p. 243.
29. Hesse, *Der Sowietrussische Partisanenkrieg*, p. 135.
30. Armstrong, *Soviet Partisans*, p. 189.
31. Regenberg, *Panzerfahrzeuge und Panzereinheiten*, p. 58.
32. Lucy S. Dawidowicz, *The War Against the Jews 1933–1945*. New York: Holt, Reinhard & Winston, 1975, p. 403.
33. MacLean, *The Field Men*, pp. 18–19.
34. Browning, *Ordinary Men*, p. 13.
35. Ibid., p. 15.
36. Raul Hilberg, comments attributed to Professor Hilberg.
37. The town commissioner meant the Lithuanian police auxiliaries.
38. *Trial of Major War Criminals before the International Military Tribunal*. International Military Tribunal: Nuremberg, 1948, vol. 1, p. 66.
39. Westermann, *Hitler's Police Battalions*, p. 321.
40. Dawidowicz, *The War Against the Jews*, p. 403; Gilbert, *Atlas of the Holocaust*, p. 244.
41. David J. Hogan, (ed.), *The Holocaust Chronicle: A History in Words and Pictures*. Lincolnwood: Publications International Ltd, 2002, p. 286.

42. Gilbert, *Atlas of the Holocaust*, p. 74; this included the deaths of Jews from the following towns and cities: Riga, Jelgava, Siauliai, Jekabpils, Virbalis, Vandziogala, Mariampole and Vilnius.
43. For purposes of simplification, Belarus here includes territories taken from northeastern Poland and parts of what would be considered central Russia bordering eastern Belarus.
44. Dawidowicz, *The War Against the Jews*, p. 403.
45. *Einsatzgruppe* A recorded the following numbers of Jews killed in their report for 1941: 963 killed in Estonia, 35,238 in Latvia, 136,421 in Lithuania and 41,828 in White Russia.
46. MacLean, *The Field Men*, p. 23.
47. Hogan, *Holocaust Chronicle*, p. 234.
48. Armstrong, *Soviet Partisans*, pp. 75–84.
49. Grenkevich and Glantz, *The Soviet Partisan Movement*, pp. 127.
50. Ibid., p. 166.
51. Armstrong, *Soviet Partisans*, p. 22.
52. Earl F. Ziemke and Magna E. Bauer, *Moscow to Stalingrad: Decision in the East.* Washington, DC: Center of Military History, United States Army, 1987, p. 204.
53. Ibid.
54. Pronin, *Guerrilla Warfare*, pp. 112–13.

Chapter 8: Rear area security in Ukraine and southern Russia

1. Michael Hanusiak, *Lest We Forget*. Toronto: Progress Books, 1976, p. 10.
2. The term *Landser* (pl. *Landsers*) is the German equivalent of the American 'G.I.'
3. Armstrong, *Soviet Partisans*, p. 86.
4. Hesse, *Der Sowietrussische Partisanenkrieg*, p. 59.
5. Ibid., p. 81.
6. The Abwehr was the German Army's military intelligence branch.
7. John Mendelsohn, ed., *Covert Warfare: Intelligence, Counterintelligence, and Military Deception During the World War II Era*, 18 volumes, vol. 13: *The Final Solution of the Abwehr*. New York: Garland Publishing, Inc., 1988, Section 7, pp. 5–6.
8. NARA Microfilm T-315, Roll 2214, Frame 1050.
9. John A. Armstrong, *Ukrainian Nationalism*. Englewood: Ukrainian Academic Press, 1990, p. 100.
10. NARA Microfilm T-315, Roll 2214, Frame 1052.
11. Armstrong, *Ukrainian Nationalism*, p. 95.
12. Oleksii Federov, *Partisans d'Ukraine: Operations Contre la Wehrmacht*. Paris: Ěditions J'ai Lu, 1951, pp. 12–13.
13. Ibid., p. 85.
14. NARA Microfilm T-315, Roll 2214, Frame 1051.
15. Tessin et al., *Waffen SS und Ordnungspolizei*, p. 594.
16. Klietmann, *Die Waffen SS eine Dokumentation*, p. 194.
17. Wendy Lower, *Nazi Empire-Building and the Holocaust in Ukraine*. Chapel Hill: University of North Carolina Press, 2005, p. 53.
18. Westermann, *Hitler's Police Battalions*, p. 318.
19. NARA Microfilm T-315, Roll 2214, Frame 1169.
20. Historians believe that the origin of Europe's Romany people lies in the northwest region of the Indian subcontinent, where there lived an Indian tribe, whose members were known for their squabbling, banditry and fierce independence. They proved to be particularly troublesome to the local Gupta rulers, who wished to get rid of them. Sometime around AD 500 the tribe was ordered to leave its ancestral home and head west as 'ambassadors'. The truth is that they were expelled by force by the Gupta rulers, who considered them too

difficult and troublesome to handle. Another story has them leaving on account of the invasion of the Indian subcontinent by the Huns. In any event, they wandered westward through Afghanistan, Iran, Mesopotamia and other regions of the Near East. By the time of the Middle Ages, they had reached the Balkans. In order to be more readily accepted by the people whom they encountered there, they claimed to be Christian pilgrims from Egypt – hence the term 'Gypsies' (Egyptians). When they mixed with the population of the Balkans, they became the Romany people of today, with their particular customs and ways. The Romany have been the subject of persecution and hatred for hundreds of years. Even as late as the 1970s numerous German municipalities still had laws on their books which made discrimination against *Zigeuner* (Gypsies) legal.

21. Hilberg, *The Destruction of the European Jews*, vol. 1, pp. 384–5.
22. Ibid.
23. NARA Microfilm T-315, Roll 2213, Frame 746.
24. Ibid., Frame 786.
25. Ibid., Frame 803.
26. Ibid., Frame 804.
27. The strength of these three groups was as follows: GFP-711 had 7 officials, 15 NCOs and 63 enlisted men; GFP-720 had 7 officials, 9 NCOs and 76 enlisted men; GFP-726 had 7 officials, 9 NCOs and 74 enlisted men. Therefore, the combined total secret field police strength for the 444th Security Division at this time was 267 officials, NCOs and men.
28. Werner Haupt, *Army Group South: The Wehrmacht in Russia 1941–1945*. Atglen: Schiffer Military History, 1998, p. 395.
29. NARA Microfilm T-315, Roll 2213, Frame 825.
30. Nechama Tec, *The Bielski Partisans*. Oxford: Oxford University Press, 1993, p. 197.
31. For example, of the estimated 91,000 German POWs taken after the defeat and surrender of the 6th Army at Stalingrad on 3 February 1943, only 3,000 returned to Germany in 1955.
32. Rüdiger Overmans, *Deutsche militärische Verluste im Zweiten Weltkrieg*. Munich: R. Oldenbourg Verlag, 1999, p. 282.
33. Megargee, *War of Annihilation*, p. 118.
34. Heer & Naumann, *Vernichtungskrieg Verbrecken der Wehrmacht*, pp. 96–7.
35. Ibid.
36. NARA Microfilm T-315, Roll 2213, Frame 829.
37. The 444th Security Division temporarily absorbed the 90th Romanian Infantry Regiment, as well as taking on several more regional defence battalions and other support units. The 46th Regional Defence Regiment was renamed the 46th Security Regiment on 1 June 1942. At this time the regiment comprised two battalions: the 286th Volunteer Battalion and the 416th Security Battalion. In November 1942 the II. Battalion, Police Regiment 6, was also attached.
38. Cooper, *The Nazi War Against Soviet Partisans*, p. 169.
39. Ibid., pp. 169–70.
40. Ibid., pp. 171–2.
41. Author's translation.
42. This parenthetic remark was included in the order, so women were to be shot alongside the men.
43. NARA T-315, Roll 2216, Frame 72.
44. Cooper, *The Nazi War Against Soviet Partisans*, p. 180.
45. Andrej Angrick, *Besatzungspolitik und Massenmord: Die Einsatzgruppe* D in der südlichen Sowjetunion 1941–1943. Hamburg: Hamburger Edition, 2003, p. 487.
46. Author's translation; Angrick, *Besatzungspolitik und Massenmord*, pp. 489–90.
47. Gilbert, *Atlas of the Holocaust*, p. 87.

48. Angrick, *Besatzungspolitik und Massenmord*, p. 487.
49. Boog et al., *Germany and the Second World War*, vol. IV, p. 511.
50. Criminal actions by front-line units have also been established by prior authors and some cases are documented in this work.
51. Robert Kirchubel, *Hitler's Panzer Armies on the Eastern Front*. London: Pen & Sword, 2009, p. 34.
52. NARA Microfilm T-175, Roll 233, Frame 27291.
53. Paeffgen's SS membership number was 324971, while his Nazi Party membership number was 3965964.
54. Dr Boyd C. Shafer, ed., *Records of the Reich Leader of the SS and Chief of the German Police*, No. 39, 3 parts. Washington, DC: National Archives and Records Service General Services Administration, 1963, pt III, p. 20.
55. Jens Banach, *Heydrichs Elite: Das Führerkorps der Sicherheitspolizei und des SD 1936–1945*. Paderborn: Ferdinand Schönigh, 1998, p. 244.
56. Michael Wildt, *Generation des Unbedingten: Das Führungkorps des Reichssicherheitshauptamtes*. Hamburg, Hamburger Edition, 2003, p. 942.
57. Tokmak lies near the southern Russian city of Stalino.
58. Angrick, *Besatzungspolitik und Massenmord*, p. 320.
59. Ibid.
60. Ibid., p. 323n.
61. Vaad Leumi, ed., *The Black Book: The Nazi Crime Against the Jewish People*. New York: Jewish Black Book Committee, 1946, p. 101.
62. Heer & Naumann, *War of Extermination*, p. 159.
63. Tessin, *Verbände und Truppen*, vol. 7, p. 140.
64. Truman Anderson, 'Incident at Baranivka: German Reprisals and the Soviet Partisan Movement in Ukraine, October-December 1941.' *The Journal of Modern History*, Chicago: The University of Chicago Press, 1999, p. 616.
65. Ibid., p. 618. On 24 December 1941 this unit was renamed the 202nd Security Brigade.
66. This order was issued on 13 May 1941.
67. NARA Microfilm T-315, Roll 2213, Frame 698.
68. 837th Garrison Command Headquarters.
69. Tessin, *Verbände und Truppen*, vol. 13, p. 46.
70. NARA Microfilm T-315, Roll 2213, Frame 747.
71. Klaus-Michael Mallmann, Volker Rieß and Wolfram Pyta, *Deutscher Osten 1939–1945: Das Weltanschaungskrieg in Photos und Texten*. Stuttgart: Wissenschaftliche Buchgesellschaft, 2003, p. 159.
72. NARA Microfilm T-315, Roll 2215, Frame 512.
73. Mallmann et al., *Deutscher Osten 1939–1945*, p. 159.
74. Stephen Campbell, *Police Battalions of the Third Reich*. Atglen: Schiffer Publishers, 2007, p. 125.
75. NARA Microfilm T-315, Roll 2213, Frame 705.
76. German losses in this anti-guerrilla drive totalled a paltry nine men killed, as follows: 1st Company, 246th Construction Battalion, stationed in Snamenka since 10 December 1941, lost two men; the 311th Police Battalion lost one man; and the 3rd Company, 531st Construction Battalion, also lost one man. The 3rd Company, 414th Regional Defence Battalion, stationed in Volynoye since 21 December 1941, lost five men. The volunteer Cossack cavalry squadron also took part in this operation but suffered no losses. On 24 December 1941 it was stationed in Vassilyevka. The 720th Secret Field Police Group, which also participated, was stationed in Budyenni, where it processed the prisoners taken during the drive.

77. Its commander was Benjamin Shakhnovich, a Russian Jew, but we do not know exactly how many men out of the 500 partisans were Jews. Shakhnovich was killed on 24 December 1941 during the anti-partisan operation, along with a sizeable portion of his guerrilla unit.
78. Shmuel Spector, 'Jews in the Resistance and Partisan Movements in the Soviet Ukraine', *Yad Vashem Studies XXIII*; Aharon Weiss, ed., 'Jerusalem: Yad Vashem – The Holocaust Martyrs' and Heroes' Remembrance Authority', 1993, 131.
79. Martin Dean, *Collaboration in the Holocaust: Crimes of the Local Police in Belarusia and Ukraine, 1941–1944*. New York: St Martin's Press, 2000, p. 170.
80. NARA Microfilm T-315, Roll 2213, Frame 704.

Chapter 9: German security divisions in Ukraine and southern Russia

1. Lieutenant General Helge Auleb temporarily assumed control of the division from February to March 1942. Then Major General (later promoted to Lieutenant General) Adalbert Mikulicz assumed command, and led the division from March 1942 until it was disbanded in May 1944.
2. NARA Microfilm T-315, Roll, 2215, Frame 396.
3. Ibid., Frame 399.
4. Ibid., Frame 400.
5. Ebert would be promoted to major in the Order Police later in the summer.
6. Gilbert, *Atlas of the Holocaust*, p. 31.
7. NARA Microfilm T-315, Roll 2215, Frame 406.
8. Ibid., Frame 408.
9. Haupt, *Army Group South*, p. 24.
10. NARA Microfilm T-315, Roll 2215, Frame 414.
11. Reitlinger, *The Final Solution*, p. 218.
12. Kampe et al., *Die Einsatzgruppen*, p. 74.
13. Hilberg, *The Destruction of the European Jews*, vol. 1, p. 300.
14. Angrick, *Besatzungspolitik und Massenmord*, pp. 168n, 169n.
15. Gilbert, *Atlas of the Holocaust*, p. 68.
16. Ibid, p. 76.
17. Ibid, p. 68.
18. Ehrenburg & Grossman, *Black Book*, p. 17.
19. Gilbert, *Atlas of the Holocaust*, p. 76.
20. Hamburg Institute for Social Research, *The German Army and Genocide: Crimes Against War Prisoners, Jews, and Other Civilians in the East, 1939–1944*. New York: New Press, 1999, pp. 84–7.
21. Ibid., p. 84.
22. NARA Microfilm T-315, Roll 2215, Frame 416.
23. NARA Microfilm T-315, Roll 2215, Frame 420.
24. Ibid., Frames 420–1.
25. Ibid., Frames 400–60.
26. Ibid., Frame 422.
27. Ibid., Frames 422–3.
28. Ibid., Frame 428. Translation: 'These bands were cleansed', although the more proper form would be: *Diese Banditen wurden beseitigt* ('These bandits have been eliminated') – author's translation.
29. Ibid., Frames 431–2.
30. Ibid., Frame 435.
31. Ibid., Frame 439.
32. Ibid., Frame 446.

33. Ibid., Frames 443–4.
34. Klaus Geßner, *Geheime Feldpolizei: Die Gestapo der Wehrmacht*. Berlin: Militärverlag, 2010, p. 159.
35. NARA Microfilm T-315, Roll 2215, Frame 146.
36. Ibid., Frame 465.
37. The regiment had been created on 25 April 1943, as a result of the reorganization of the 454th Security Division.
38. NARA Microfilm T-315, Roll 2215, Frames 464–5.
39. Ibid., Frame 465.
40. On 3 October the 13th Company, 375th Infantry Regiment, supported by the 987th Regional Defence Battalion and Slovak troops, was sweeping the railway line between Zhitomir and Fastov. After discussion with Major Vessely, commander of the Slovak Fast Division, the 13th Company was withdrawn and ordered to rejoin its parent regiment for an operation in the southeastern outskirts of the Pripet marshes region.
41. Tessin, *Verbände und Truppen*, vol. 6, p. 186.
42. Ibid., vol. 14, p. 221.
43. Klietmann, *Die Waffen SS eine Dokumentation*, p. 309.
44. Martin Cüppers, *Wegbereiter der Shoah: Die Waffen SS, der Kommandostab Reichsführer-SS und die Judenvernichtung 1939–1945*. Darmstadt: Wissenschaftliche Buchgesellschaft, 2005, p. 172.
45. Ibid., p. 206.
46. NARA Microfilm T-315, Roll 2215, Frame 468.
47. Ibid., Frame 471.
48. Ibid., Frame 485.
49. Ibid., Frame 474.

Conclusions

1. Albert Seaton, *The Russo-German War 1941–1945*. Westport: Praeger Publishers, 1971, p. 172.
2. Field Marshal Walther von Brauchitsch would be relieved from this command by Adolf Hitler on 19 November 1941 and was blamed for the failure of Operation Barbarossa. Thereafter Hitler assumed direct command of the *Ostheer*.
3. These were the so-called *Front Bataillone* (front battalions) which differed from the rear area *Schutzmannschaft* and *Selbstschutz*. These front battalions were intended for service, as the name implies, on the front lines.

Appendix: Russian volunteer formations in the East, 1941–1942

1. The Brandenburgers were the field commandos of the *Abwehr* – the German Armed Forces Intelligence Service.
2. 50 men is more akin to a reinforced platoon than a company, but if you add on the 25–30 German soldiers attached to each Russian unit, then you get a figure of 75–80 men – roughly a half-company. No doubt the hope was to gather more volunteers and increase the size of each company to about 125–150 men.

Bibliography

Primary Sources

Belarus Central State Archives, Minsk, Records 1941–1949

Belarusian State Minsk Archives, USHMM RG-53.002M (1993.A.0082), Folder 1262 and 1265.

Grodno Oblast Archive Records, 1940–1944. Records Group RG-53.004M, Reel 5.

Grodno Oblast Archive Records, 1940–1944. RG-53.004M. Reel 2, Fond 1, Section 100 – Grodno Amtskommissar correspondence.

Records Group RG-53.002M, Reels 3, 5, 11, and 13.

Military Historical Institute (Prague), Records 1941–1944

Records Group RG-48.004M, Reels 1, 2, 3, 4, and 6.

RG-48.004M (1993.A.0019), Reel 3 – *1. SS Infanterie-Brigade (mot.) – 29.11.42, 'Aufmarsch Glebokie'.*

Bundesarchiv, Koblenz

BAK-N756/214a, *SS Kampfgruppe von Gottberg: Band Zwei. Vgl. BArch Bestand RS 4 Brigaden, Legionen, Standarten sowie Kampfgruppen und Einheiten der Waffen SS; Verschiedene Sperrverbände und Eingreifgruppen Fotografie von SS Hauptsturmführer Robert Ancans.*

BAK-NS19-03, *Reichssicherheitshauptamt Nachrichten Uebermittlung*, NR 162/42 (G) AUS 160 ZWEI/42. pp. 12–13.

BAK-NS19-11. 470.

BAK-NS19-13, *Reichsführer-SS Meldung an der Führer über Bandenbekämpfung. Feldkommandostelle*, 8.10.1942. Neldung Nr. 23.

Bandenkampf Unternehmen – Folio: NS19/1, 1500, 1671, 1463, 2661, 2835, 3140, and 3695.

Meldung vom 06.06.1943 über die Personalstärke der landeseigenen Verbände (BA-MA, RH 21-2/509, Bl. 78 und 78r). Vgl. Tabelle im Anhang auf Seite 405f. Der Arbeit. Operations Abteilung, No. 5645/42, Heeresgruppe Mitte. 15.07.42.

RH 22-229. Berück, Kriegstagebuch 07.04.42.

Bundesarchiv, Freiburg

Heeresgruppe Mitte, Ia. Nr.14550/43 g.Kdos., 8.XII.43., Anlage zur Kriegstagebuch, Heeresgruppe Mitte, Führungsabteilung, Akte XXIII, Heft 12, 1.X.-31.XII.43. 65002/24. Bundesarchiv, Frieburg. Chef der Sicherungstruppen–Rückwartigen Heeresgebiet 102, Operationsabteilung Nr.272/43, 25.1.43. 23.

Reichssicherheitshauptamt. Höhere SS und Polizeiführer Ostland. 7.8.42. BAF, NS–19/1, 1500, 1671, 1463, 2661, 2835, 3140 and 3645.

Bundesarchiv/Militärarchiv Berlin-Lichterfelde

BA-MA RH 19 VII/2, Bl. 2.

BA-MA RH 19 XI/37, *Bericht des GFP-Angehörigen Georg Koch*, 37.

BA-MA RH 22/31, *Meldung Direktor GFP, Mai 1942.*

BA-MA RH 22/60, *Bericht GFP für Heeresgebiet B, August 1942.*

BA-MA RH 22/86, 27.

BA-MA RH 22/173, *Meldung Direktor GFP, Juli 1942.*

BA-MA RH 22/199 *Befehlshaber rückwärtiger Heeresgebiete Tätigkeitsberichte der Geheimen Feldpolizeigruppen* 1, 708, 719, 725, 730, 739, 721. – *Stärkemeldungen Laufzeit: Jan.–Aug. 1942.*

BA-MA RH 22/200 *Befehlshaber rückwärtiger Heeresgebiete Tätigkeitsberichte der Geheimen Feldpolizeigruppen 1, 708, 719, 725, 730, 739, 721. - Stärkemeldungen Laufzeit: Sept.–Dez. 1942.*

BA-MA RH 23-25, *'Befehl Nr. 1 für Unternehmen 'Dreieck,' 11 September 1942'.*

BA-MA RH 23-25, 'Gefechtsbericht über Unternehmen "Dreieck" und "Viereck" vom 17.9-2.10.1942, 19 October 1942'.

BA/MA RH 24-22/21, folio 88–9.

BA-MA RH 24-22/23, *Jäger – Gen.Kdo.22 AK, 14 May 1944, Ic – Aussenstelle Korfu - Korpsgruppe Joannina / Ic, 25 April 1944.*

BA-MA RH 24-23/24.

BA-MA RH 26, 117/16.

BA-MA RH 48 *Dienststellen und Einheiten der Ordnungstruppen, der Geheimen Feldpolizei, der Betreuungs und Streifendienste des Heeres. RW 40/170: Fester Platz Kreta, Sept. 1944 RW 40/172: Tätigkeitsbericht, Juli - Aug. 1944; Bundesarchiv.*

BA-MA RH 40, 10.

BA-MA RH 40, 11.

BA-MA WF 01/2151, Bl. 816.

BA-MA WF 03/15831, *Feldpolizeidirektor beim Befehlshaber Heeresgebiet 103.*

National Archives, College Park, Maryland

NARS Microfilm T-78 Rolls 413, 645.

NARS Microfilm T-175 Rolls 16, 111, 129, 140, 141, 174, 191, 225, 233.

NARS Microfilm T-315, Rolls 1665, 1687, 2213, 2214, 2215, 2216.

NARS Microfilm T-580 Roll 88.

NARA RG-238 Working Conference on 23 April 1940, Service Diary of Governor General Hans Frank, vol. 9.

National Archives, Kew, Richmond, Surrey, United Kingdom

CSDIC (UK) SIR (Special Interrogation Report) 730 (8 Aug 1944) 'Geheime Feldpolizei Gruppe 644.'

CSDIC (UK) SIR (Special Interrogation Report) 818 (20 Aug 1944) 'Geheime Feldpolizei in Greece 1942.'

CSDIC (UK) SIR (Special Interrogation Report) 1675 (24 May 1945) 'Notes on the GFP and Other Security Services in the Area of Army Group Nord (Later Kurland) 1942–1 Jan 45.'

CSDIC (UK) SIR (Special Interrogation Report) 1676 (24 May 1945) 'Notes on the GFP and Other Security Services in the West 1939–42.' CAB/129/28, *Kommandobefehl, den 18 Okt. 1942.*

German Armed Forces War Diary

Schramm, Percy. *Kriegstagebuch Des Oberkommandos Der Wehrmacht 1939–1945*, 8 vols. Herrsching: Manfred Pawlak, 1982.

Supreme Headquarters Allied Expeditionary Force, Office of Assistant Chief of Staff G-2, Counterintelligence Sub-Division Evaluation and Dissemination Section

EDS Report No. 15 – *Geheime Feldpolizei* (Secret Field Police) January 8, 1945, Supreme Headquarters Allied Expeditionary Force, Office of Assistant Chief of Staff G-2, Counterintelligence Sub-Division Evaluation and Dissemination Section.

Geheime Feldpolizei (GFP) Vol. I XE 019650 Par 43, SR 380-20-10. General Staff, U.S. Army G2 Central Records Facility, Fort Holabird, Baltimore 19, Maryland.

Geheime Feldpolizei – EI (GFP) G-2 Department of the Army, Volume II, XE 019650.

Office of Strategic Services Research and Analysis Branch, R and A N, 2500.15, 'German Military Government Over Europe: Economic Controls in Occupied Europe,' Washington DC, 28 August 1945.

Records of the Army Staff (Record Group 319) – CIC Collection - Declassified Files

Box No. 4 – No. XE003923 German Police System in Occupied Czechoslovakia.

Box No. 5 – NND 881019, File No. XE019650 *Geheime Feldpolizei* (GFP) vols I and II.

Military Intelligence Service Centre/US Forces European Theater CI

Final Interrogation Report No. 98 (14 Mar 1946) 'Reg.-u.Krim.Dir. Philipp GREINER, Leitender FP Direktor, Mil.Befh. Frankreich.'

7th Army Interrogation Centre

Final Interrogation Report No. 20 (8 Aug 1945) 'Secret Military Police Unit 712.'

French Army Military Archive, Paris

Ordre De Bataille II – A – Etat-Major de la 30ěme Division d'Infanterie des Waffen-SS (Russe Nr. 2) (plustard): Stab Waffen Grenadier Brigade der SS (Weissruthenien).

Legal Court Cases

Innsbruck Court Case: GG Innsbruck 10 Nr. 415170-23 10 H 7170: 1–43.

Nuremberg Trial: NOKW 1382, Directive of the Quartermaster of the *Kommandant rückwärtiges Armeegebiet* 560 (Army Groups A, Twelfth Army, 560th Army Rear Area Security Command), 21 May 1941.

The Minister of Canadian Citizenship and Immigration vs. Vladimir Katriuk Court transcripts, Docket No.: T-2409-96. Date: 1999/01/29.

Court transcripts: *The Canadian Government vs. Vladimir Katriuk*. Docket No. T-2409-96, Date: 1999.01.29.

Nazi Conspiracy and Aggression (Washington, DC: Government Printing Office, 1946), 8:205–8. R-135.

Trials of War Criminals before the Nuremberg Military Tribunals under Control Council Law No. 10, October 1946–April 1949 (Washington, DC: Government Printing Office, 1949), 13:516-22. NO-3028.

Court Trial Testimonials

Testimony of Heinz Hermann Schubert, Office of Chief of Counsel for War Crimes. APO 696 A, US Army, Document No. 4816, pp. 3–4, 18).

Testimony of Private Albert Rodenbusch, Grenadier (Feldausbildungs) Regiment 635, given during court proceedings of the Minsk war crimes trials held in 1946 and 1947. Belarusian SSR, 15–19 January 1946 (Minsk Trial), Minsk (1947), pp. 262–3.

Testimony of Erich von dem Bach-Zelewski at the Nuremberg War Crimes Trials: The Trial of German Major War Criminals. London: HMSO, 1946–1952. 24 volumes.

The Trial of Major War Criminals. London: HMSO, 1946–1952. 23 volumes.

Other Primary Sources

Krüger to Gunst, 14 November 1939, W. Gunst SS Officer file (formerly Berlin Document Centre), RGp-242, A3343/SSO/043A/321, NARA; judgment in proceedings against Friedrich Paulus, 26 May 1977, p. 6, file 4 Ks 1/74, State Prosecutor's Office in Frankfurt am Main.

Meyer, Brünn. *Dienstalterliste der Waffen-SS: SS Obergruppenführer bis SS Hauptsturmführer; Stand vom 1 Juli 1944*. Osnabrück Biblio Verlag: 1987.

Telex: General Löhr to the *Befehlshaber Südost*, dated October 1, 1944-RH 19 VII/37, Part 1, Annex 12.

'*Generalkommando LIV.A.K., Abt.Ic/A.O. vom 2.8.41, An den Führer des Sonderkommandos* XIa Herrn SS Sturmbannführer Zapp.,' MAP, microfilm 56748, fr. 954; '*Geheime Feldpolizei 647, Koat II beim LIV.A.K., Tgb.-Nr. 77/41 vom 2.8.1941, An den Stab der Geheimen Feldpolizei 647 beim A.O.K. 11.*,' Ibid, fr. 945.

'*Der Beauftragte des Chefs der Sicherheitspolizei und des SD beim Befehlshaber des rückwartigen Heeresgebiet Süd, Sonderkommando* 11a, Tgb. 83/41 vom4.8.1941, Betrifft: Bericht über die Tätigkeit des *Sonderkommandos* in der Zeit vom 17. Juli bis 3. August und die Einsatzplanung für die erste Augusthalfte 1941.' On the concentration of Jews in labour camps in Bessarabia, see '*Die Gesandschaft in Bukarest an das Auswartige Amt*,' 6 August 1941, Nuremberg Doc. NO-2067, reproduced in ADAP, Series D, vol. XIII/1, 238–9.

Roosevelt, Franklin D. 'No Peace with Hitler: Eight Common Principles for a Better World,' in *Vital Speeches of the Day*. vol. 7, issue 22 (1 September 1941).

'Central Registry of War Criminals and Security Suspects' (CROCASS Allied Control Authority, Part 1 and 2, US Army, APO 742, 1947).

Publications by the Third Reich Printing Office, Berlin

Der Reichsführer SS und Chef der Deutschen Polizei, Banden-bekämpfung. Berlin: Gedruckt im Reichssicherheitshauptamt, 1. Ausgabe, September 1942.

Dienstalterliste der Schutzstafel der NSDAP (SS Obergruppenführer bis SS Standartenführer) Stand vom 30. Januar 1942. Herausgegeben vom Personalhauptamt. Berlin: Gedruckt in der Reichsdruckerei, 1942.

Dienstalterliste der Schutzstafel der NSDAP (SS Obersturmbannführer und SS Sturmbannführer) Stand vom 1. Oktober 1944. Herausgegeben vom Personalhauptamt. Berlin: Gedruckt in der Reichsdruckerei, 1944.

Dienstalterliste der Schutzstafel der NSDAP (SS Obergruppenführer bis SS Standartenführer) Stand vom 1. Oktober 1944. Herausgegeben vom Personalhauptamt. Berlin: Gedruckt in der Reichsdruckerei, 1944.

Befehlsblatt des Chefs der Sicherheitspolizei und der SD, Nr. 14/44 Berlin, 1. April 1944. Herausgegeben vom Reichssicherheitshaupt-amt. Berlin: Gedruckt in der Reichsdruckerei, 1944.

Dienstalterliste der Schutzstaffel der NSDAP, Stand vom 1. Oktober 1934. Berlin: Gedruckt in der Reichsdruckerei, 1934.

Dienstalterliste der Schutzstafel der NSDAP, stand vom 30 Januar 1942. Berlin: Gedruckt in der Reichsdruckerei, 1942.

Dienstalterliste der Schutzstafel der NSDAP, stand vom Oktober/November 1944. Berlin: Gedruckt in der Reichsdruckerei, 1944. *Wi. Kdo. Witebsk, 'Monatsbericht,' 23 November 1942 (GMDS, Wi/ID 2.779)*

Dienstalterliste der Schutzstafel der NSDAP, stand vom 1 Juli 1944. Berlin: Gedruckt in der Reichsdruckerei, 1944.

Secondary Sources

Doctorate of Philosophy Works Cited

Birn, Ruth Bettina. *Die Höheren SS und Polizeiführer: Himmlers Vertreter im Reichs und in den besetzten Gebieten*. Droste Verlag, 1986.

Gordon, Gary Howard. *Soviet Partisan Warfare, 1941–1944. The German Perspective*. University Microfilms: Ann Arbor, 1972.

Porter, Jack Nusam. *Jewish Partisans: A Documentary of Jewish Resistance in the Soviet Union during World War II*. Volume II. University Press of America, Inc.: Washington DC, 1982.

Pronin, Alexander. *Guerrilla Warfare in the German Occupied Soviet Territories 1941–1945*. Georgetown: Georgetown University Graduate School, 1965.

Sheppard, Ben. *German Army Security Units in Russia, 1941–1943: A Case Study*. A thesis submitted to the Faculty of Social Science and Commerce of the University of Birmingham for the degree of Doctor of Philosophy, Institute for German Studies Faculty of Social Science and Commerce: University of Birmingham, June 2000.

Pamphlets and journals

German Anti-Guerrilla Operations in the Balkans, 1941–1944. DA Pamphlet 20-243, August 1954, Washington, DC: Centre of Military History, US Army.

Krichbaum, Wilhelm. *The Secret Field Police*. MS# C-029, ed. George Vanderstadt, trans. M. Franke. Washington, DC: Centre for Military History, US Army Historical Division, 18 May 1947.

The Case Against General Heusinger. Documents Illustrating the Charges of the USSR Against Former Lieutenant General Adolf Heusinger, Former Operations Chief of the Wehrmacht High Command. Soviet Government. New York: TransWorld Publishers, 1961.

Kowalska, Magdalena. *A Polish heart in a feldgrau uniform – complicated journeys from the Wehrmacht to the Polish Army in Exile* in 'Polish Scientific Society Abroad in London'. Poznań: Adam Mickiewicz University, Humanities Education No. 2 (33), 2015.

Internet

Grabowski, Jan. *The Polish Police: Collaboration in the Holocaust*. US Holocaust Memorial Museum: Washington, DC. https://www.ushmm.org/m/pdfs/20170502-Grabowski_OP.pdf (2017).

Published works

Adair, Paul. *Hitler's Greatest Defeat. The Collapse of Army Group Centre*. New York: Sterling Publishing, 1994.

Albrecht-Carrié, René. *A Diplomatic History of Europe Since the Congress of Vienna*. New York: Harper & Row, 1958.

Anders, Wladyslaw. *Hitler's Defeat in Russia*. Chicago: Henry Regnery Company, 1953.

Anders, Wladyslaw. *Russian Volunteers in Hitler's Army, 1941–1945*. New York: Europa Books. 1997.

Andrew, Christopher. *Defend the Realm: The Authorized History of MI5*. New York: Knopf Doubleday, 2009.

Andreyev, Catherine. *Vlasov and the Russian Liberation Movement. Soviet Reality and Émigré Theories*. Cambridge: Cambridge University Press, 1987.

Angolia, Lieutenant Colonel J.R. *Cloth Insignia of the SS*. San Jose: R. James Bender Publishing, 1983. 2nd (updated) edn.

Angrick, Andrej. *Besatzungspolitik und Massenmord: Die Einsatzgruppe D in der Sowjetunion 1941–1943*. Hamburg: Hamburger Edition, 2003.

Applebaum, Ann. *Red Famine: Stalin's War on Ukraine*. New York: Doubleday, 2018.

Arad, Yitzhak. 'The Holocaust of Soviet Jewry in the Occupied Territories of the Soviet Union', in Aharon Weiss (ed.), *Yad Vashem Studies XXI*, Jerusalem: The Holocaust Martyrs' and Heroes' Remembrance Authority, 1991.

Arico, Massimo. *Ordnungspolizei Volume 1: Encyclopedia of the German Police Battalions September 1939–July 1942*. Stockholm: Leandoer & Co. Forlag, 2016.

Armstrong, John A. (ed.) *Soviet Partisans in World War II*. Madison: University of Wisconsin Press, 1964.

Armstrong, John A. *Ukrainian Nationalism*. Englewood: Ukrainian Academic Press, 1990.

Aschenauer, Rudolf. *Abgehört. Deutsche Generäle in britischer Kriegsgefangenschaft 1941–1945*. Munich: Druffel-Verlag, 1982.

Axworthy, Mark W.A. *Axis Slovakia: Hitler's Slavic Wedge, 1938–1945*. New York: Europa Books, 2002.

Baker, Gabriel. *Spare No One: Mass Violence in Roman Warfare*. New York: Rowman & Littlefield, 2021.

Banach, Jens. *Heydrichs Elite: Das Führerkorps der Sicherheitspolizei und des SD 1936–1945*. Paderborn: Ferdinand Schöningh, 1998.

Bartov, Omer. *The Eastern Front 1941–1945: German Troops and the Barbarization of Warfare*. New York: St. Martin's Press, 1986.

Bartov, Omer, *Hitler's Army: Soldiers, Nazis, and War in the Third Reichs*. Oxford: Oxford University Press, 1992.

Bartov, Omer. *Mirrors of Destruction: War, Genocide, and Modern Identity*. Oxford: Oxford University Press, 2000.

Bartov, Omer. *Germany's War and the Holocaust: Disputed Histories*. Cornell: Cornell University Press, 2003.

Bauer, Eddy. *The History of World War II*. London: Galley Press, 1984.

Bayer, Hanns. *Die Kavallerie Der Waffen SS*. Heidelberg: Selbstverlag der Truppenkameradenschaft der SS Kavallerie Divisionen, 1980.

Bayer, Hanns. *Kavallerie Divisionen der Waffen-SS im Bild*. Osnabrück: Munin Verlag, 1982.

Becker, Hans. *Devil on My Shoulder*. London: Jarrolds Publishers, 1955.

Beevor, Anthony. *Crete: The Battle and the Resistance*. New York: Penguin Books, 2014.

Bennett, Rab. *Under the Shadow of the Swastika: The Moral Dilemmas of Resistance and Collaboration in Hitler's Europe*. New York: New York University Press, 1999.

Bergen, Doris L. *War and Genocide: A Concise History of the Holocaust*. New York: Rowman & Littlefield, 2009.

Berthel, Hans Dieter. *Die Feldgendarmerie im Zweiten Weltkrieg und ihre Teilnahme an völkerrechtswidrigen Aktionen 1939–1945*. Norderstedt: Herstellung & Verlag, 2006.

Bethell, Nicholas. *The Last Secret. The Delivery to Stalin of Over Two Million Russians by Britain and the United States*. New York: Basic Books Inc., 1974.

Birn, Ruth Bettina. *Die Sicherheitspolizei in Estland, 1941–1944: Eine Studie zur Kollaboration im Osten*. Paderborn: Ferdinand Schöningh, 2006.

Bischof, Günther, Plasser, Fritz and Maltschnig, Eva (eds). *Austrian Lives: Contemporary Austrian Studies Vol. 21*. New Orleans: University of New Orleans Press, 2012.

Blood, Philip W. *Hitler's Bandit Hunters: The SS and the Nazi Occupation of Europe*. Washington DC: Potomak Books Inc., 2006.

Bonn, Keith E. (ed.) *Slaughterhouse: The Handbook of the Eastern Front*. Bedford: Aberjona Press, 2005.

Boog, Horst et al. *Germany and the Second World War. Vol. IV, the Attack on the Soviet Union*. Oxford: Clarenden Press, 1998.

Boshyk, Yury (ed.) *Ukraine during World War II: History and its Aftermath*. Edmonton: Canadian Institute of Ukrainian Studies, 1986.

Brandon, Ray and Lower, Wendy. *Shoah in Ukraine: History, Testimony, Memorialization*. Bloomington: Indiana University Press, 2008.

Browning, Christopher. *Ordinary Men: Reserve Police Battalion 101 and the Final Solution in Poland*. New York: Harper Collins, 1992.

Browning, Christopher. *The Origins of the Final Solution: The Evolution of Nazi Jewish Policy, September 1939–March 1942*. Lincoln: University of Nebraska Press, 2004.

Browning, Christopher R. *Project Muse. Nikolaev and Dnepropetrovsk Regions*. The United States Holocaust Memorial Museum Encyclopedia of Camps and Ghettos, 1933–1945, vol. II: Ghettos in German-Occupied Eastern Europe. Indiana University Press, 2012.

Bruns, Friedrich. *Die Brücke von Neuenburg: Eine Dokumentation über den Endkampf der 19 Armee in Elsaß 1945*. Celle: Self Published, 1990.

Buchanan, Patrick J. *Churchill, Hitler, and The Unnecessary War: How Britain Lost Its Empire and the West Lost the World*. New York: Crown Press, 2008.

Buchner, Alex. *Ostfront: The German Defensive Battles on the Russian Front 1944*. West Chester: Schiffer Military History, 1991.

Campbell, Bruce. *The SA Generals and the Rise of Nazism*. Lexington: University Press of Kentucky, 1998.

Campbell, Stephen. *Police Battalions of the Third Reich*. Atglen: Schiffer Publishers, 2007.

Carell, Paul. *Hitler Moves East, 1941–1943*. Boston: Little, Brown & Company, 1964.

Carell, Paul. *Scorched Earth. The Russo-German War 1943–1944*. Boston: Little, Brown & Company, 1970.

Carnier, Pier Arrigo. *L'Armata Cosaca in Italia 1944–1945*. Milan: Mursia Editoriale, 1990.

Caroe, Olaf. *Soviet Empire. The Turks of Central Asia and Stalinism*. New York: MacMillan & Co. Ltd, 1954.

Chiari, Bernhard. *Alltag Hinter Der Front: Besatzung, Kollaboration und Widerstand in Weissrussland, 1941–1944*. Düsseldorf: Droste Verlag, 1998.

Cholawsky, Shalom. *The Jews of Belarusia during World War II*. Amsterdam: Harwood Academic Publishers, 1998.

Citino, Robert M. *The German Way of War: From the Thirty Years' War to the Third Reichs*. Lawrence: University Press of Kansas, 2005.

Clark, Alan. *Barbarossa. The Russo-German Conflict, 1941–45*. New York: William Morrow & Co., 1965.

Clarke, Jeffrey J. and Ross Smith, Robert. *United States Army in World War II. The European Theater of Operations: Riviera to the Rhine*. Washington DC: Centre of Military History, 1993.

Cooper, Matthew. *The Nazi War Against Soviet Partisans, 1941–1944*. New York: Stein & Day, 1979.

Conquest, Robert. *Harvest of Sorrow: Soviet Collectivization Methods and the Terror-Famine*. New York: Oxford, 1986.

Costantini, Colonel Aimé. *L'Union Soviétique En Guerre (1941–1945)*. Paris: Imprimerie Nationale, 1968, 3 vols.

Coudry, Georges. *Les Camps Sovietiques Les Russes Livres a Stalin en 1945*. Paris: Albin Michel, 1997.

Crankshaw, Edward. *Gestapo: Instrument of Tyranny*. London: Greenhill Books, 1990.

Cüppers, Martin. *Wegbereiter der Shoah: Die Waffen SS, der Kommandostab Reichsführer-SS und die Judenvernichtung 1939–1945*. Darmstadt: Wissenschaftliche Buchgesellschaft, 2005.

Curilla, Wolfgang. *Die deutsche Ordnungspolizei und der Holocaust im Baltikum und im Weißrußland, 1941–1944*. Paderborn: Verlag Ferdinand Schöningh GmbH, 2006.

Dallin, Alexander. *German Rule in Russia 1941–1945, A study of Occupation Policies*. London: MacMillan & Co. Ltd, 1957.

Dasnoy, Philippe and Leon Charles, Jean. *Les dossiers secrets de la police allemande en Belgique. La Geheime Feldpolizei en Belgique et dans le Nord de la France, Vols. 1 and 2*. Brüssel: Arts et Voyages/Lucien De Meyer, 1972.

Dawidowicz, Lucy S. *The War against the Jews 1933–1945*. New York: Holt, Reinhart & Winston, 1975.

Dean, Martin. *Collaboration in the Holocaust: Crimes of the Local Police in Belarusia and Ukraine, 1941–1944*. New York: St. Martin's Press, 2000.

Dixon, Brigadier C. Aubrey and Heilbrunn, Otto. *Communist Guerrilla Warfare*. New York: Frederick A. Praeger, 1954.

Dorril, Stephen. *M.I.6*. London: Fourth Estate, 2000.

Dreßen, Willi. 'The Role of the Wehrmacht and the Police in the Annihilation of the Jews; the Prosecution of Postwar Careers of Perpetrators in the Police Force of the Federal Republic of Germany.' *Yad Vashem Studies XXIII*, 1993: 295–319.

Drum, D. Karl et al. *Airpower in Russian Partisan Warfare*. USAF Historical Study No. 177. New York: Arno Press, 1968.

Dunnigan, James F. et al. (eds). *War in the East: The Russo-German Conflict, 1941–45*. New York: Simulations, 1977.

Eckmann, Lester, and Lazar, Chaim. *The Jewish Resistance: The History of the Jewish Partisans in Lithuania and White Russia during the Nazi Occupation 1940–1945*. New York: Shengold Publishers, 1977.

Ehrenburg, Ilya, and Grossman, Vasily. *The Black Book*. New York: Holocaust Library, 1981.

Erickson, John. *The Road to Berlin. Stalin's War with Germany*. London: Weidenfeld & Nicolson, 1983.

Evans, Richard J. *The Third Reich in Power*. New York: Penguin, 2005.

Evans, Richard J. *The Third Reich at War*. London: Penguin Books Ltd., 2008.

Ezergailis, Andrew. *The Holocaust in Latvia 1941–44*. Washington DC: United States Holocaust Memorial Museum, 1996.

Faber, David. *Munich 1938: Appeasement and World War Two*. New York: Simon & Schuster, 2010.

Federov, Alexander. *Partisans d'Ukraine – 2. operations contre la Wehrmacht*. Paris: Editions J'ai Lu, 1951.

Fischer, George. *Soviet Opposition to Stalin: A Case Study in World War II*. Cambridge: Harvard University Press, 1952.

Fontaine, Thomas. 'Chronology of Repression and Persecution in Occupied France, 1940–44', in *The Encyclopedia of Mass Violence* (Philadelphia: Running Press, 2004).

Förster, Jürgen. 'The German Army and the Ideological War against the Soviet Union', in *The Policies of Genocide: Jews and Soviet Prisoners of War in Nazi Germany*, 15–29, ed. Gerhard Hirschfeld (London: Allen & Unwin, 1986).

Franz, Hermann. *Gebirgsjäger der Polizei: Polizei-Gebirgsjäger-Regiment 18 und Polizei-Gebirgs-Artillerieabteilung 1942*. Bad Nauheim: Verlag Hans Henning, 1963.

Frei, Norbert. *Vergangenheitspolotik*. Einbeck: AHA-Buch GmbH, 1996.

Geldmacher, Thomas. *Wir als Wiener waren ja bei der Bevölkerung beliebt: Östtereichsische Schutzpolizisten und die Judenvernichtung in Ostgalizien 1941–1944*. Vienna: Mandelbaum Verlag, 2002.

Gellermann, Guenther W. *Moskau ruft Heeresgruppe Mitte. Was nicht im Wehrmachtbericht stand: Die Einsätze des geheimen Kampfgeschwaders 200 im Zweiten Weltkrieg*. Koblenz: Bernard & Graefe Verlag, 1988.

Gerlach, Christian. *Kalkulierte Morde: Die deutsche Wirtschafts- und Vernichtungspolitik in Weißrußland, 1941 bis 1944*. Hamburg: Hamburger Edition HIS, 2013.

Gerlach, Christian. 'Men of 20 July and the War in the Soviet Union', in *War of Extermination: The German Military in World War Two 1941–1944*, ed. Hannes Heer and Klaus Naumann. New York: Berghahn Books, 2000.

Geßner, Klaus. *Geheime Feldpolizei*. Berlin: Militarverlag der Deutschen Demokratische Republik, 1986.

Geßner, Klaus. *Geheime Feldpolizei: Die Gestapo der Wehrmacht*. Berlin: Militärverlag, 2010.

Geyer, Michael, Maier, Charles S and Gould, Andrew (eds). 'Traditional Elites and National Socialist Leadership', 77–133, in *The Rise of the Nazi Regime: Historical Reassessments* (Boulder: Westview Press, 1986).

Gibson, Hugh, and Welles, Sumner (eds). *Ciano Diaries 1939–1943, Complete, Unabridged Diaries of Count Galeazzo. Italian Minister for Foreign Affairs 1936–1943.* New York: Doubleday & Co., 1946.

Gilbert, Dr Martin. *Atlas of the Holocaust.* London: Lester Publishing, 1988; rev. edn, 1993.

Gilbert, Dr Martin. *The Holocaust: A History of the Jews of Europe During the Second World War.* New York: Henry Holt & Co., 1985.

Gildea, Robert, Warring, Anette and Wieviorka, Olivier (eds). *Surviving Hitler and Mussolini: Daily Life in Occupied Europe.* New York: Bloomsbury Academic, 2006.

Glantz, David M. and Orenstein, Harold S. *Belarusia 1944: The Soviet General Staff Study.* London: Frank Cass, 2001.

Gogun, Alexander. *Stalin's Commandos. Ukrainian Partisan Forces on the Eastern Front.* London: I.B. Tauris, 2016.

Goldhagen, Daniel Jonah. *Hitler's Willing Executioners: Ordinary Germans and the Holocaust.* New York: Alfred A. Knopf, 1996.

Gooch, John. *Mussolini and His Generals: The Armed Forces and Fascist Foreign Policy, 1922–1940.* Cambridge: Cambridge University Press, 2007.

Görlitz, Walter, and David Irving (eds). *In the Service of the Reich.* New York: Stein & Day, 1979.

Grenkevich, Leonid. *The Soviet Partisan Movement 1941–1944.* London: Frank Cass, 1999.

Grundmann, Siegfried. *Die V-Leute des Gestapo-Kommissars Sattler.* Berlin: Hentrich & Hentrich Verlag, 2010.

Hamburger Institut für Sozialforschung (ed.) *Verbrechen der Wehrmacht: Dimensionen des Vernichtungskrieges 1941–1944.* Hamburg: Hamburger Edition HIS, 2002.

Hanusiak, Michael. *Lest We Forget.* Toronto: Progress Books, 1976.

Hartmann, Christian, Hürter, Johannes and Jureit, Ulrike. *Verbrechen der Wehrmacht: Bilanz einer Debatte.* Munich: Verlag C.H. Beck, 2005.

Hartmann, Christian et al. *Der deutsche Krieg in Osten 1941–1944: Faceten einer Grenzüberschreitung.* Oldenbourg: Wissentschaftsverlag, 2009.

Haupt, Werner. *Leningrad: Die 900 Tage Schlacht 1941–1944.* Friedberg: Podzun Pallas Verlag, 1980.

Haupt, Werner. *Die Schlachten Der Heeresgruppe Mitte 1941–1944.* Friedberg: Podzun Pallas Verlag, 1983.

Haupt, Werner. *Die Schlachten Der Heeresgruppe Süd. Aus der Sicht der Divisionen.* Friedberg: Podzun Pallas Verlag, 1985.

Haupt, Werner. *Die 8. Panzer Division im 2. Weltkrieg.* Friedberg: Podzun Pallas Verlag, 1987.

Haupt, Werner. *Die Deutschen Infanterie-Divisionen.* Friedberg: Podzun Pallas Verlag, 1991. 3 vols.

Haupt, Werner. *Army Group North. The Wehrmacht in Russia 1941–1945.* Atglen: Schiffer Publishers, 1997.

Haupt, Werner. *Army Group Centre. The Wehrmacht in Russia 1941–1945.* Atglen: Schiffer Publishing, 1997.

Haupt, Werner. *Army Group South. The Wehrmacht in Russia 1941–1945.* Atglen: Schiffer Publishers, 1997.

Hausser, Paul. *Soldaten Wie Andere Auch. Der Weg der Waffen SS.* Osnabrück: Munin Verlag GmbH, 1966.

Hechelhammer, Bodo, and Meinl, Susanne. *Geheimobjekt Pullach: Von der NS-Mustersiedlung zur Zentrale des BND.* Berlin: Christoph Links Verlag, 2014.

Heer, Hannes, and Naumann, Klaus. *Vernichtungskrieg: Verbrechen der Wehrmacht 1941–1944.* Hamburg: Hamburger Edition, 1995.

Heer, Hannes and Naumann, Klaus (eds). *The German Army and Genocide: Crimes Against War Prisoners, Jews, and Other Civilians in the East, 1939–1944.* New York: New Press, 1999.

Heer, Hannes and Naumann, Klaus (eds). *War of Extermination: the German Military in World War II–1944.* New York: Berghan Books, 2000.

Heer, Hannes and Naumann, Klaus (eds). *Verbrechen der Wehrmacht: Dimensionen des Vernichtungskrieges 1941–1944.* Hamburg: Hamburger Institut für Sozialforschung, 2002.

Herbert, Ulrich (ed.) *National Socialist Extermination Policies: Contemporary German Perspectives and Controversies.* New York: Berghan Books, 2000.

Herf, Jeffrey. *Reactionary Modernism: Technology, Culture, and Politics in the Third Reich.* New York: Cambridge University Press, 1984.

Hesse, Erich. *Der Sowietrussische Partisanenkrieg 1941 bis 1944.* Göttingen: Musterschmidt Verlag, 1969.

Hilberg, Raul. *Perpetrators, Victims, Bystanders: The Jewish Catastrophe 1933–1945.* New York: Harper Collins, 1992.

Hilberg, Raul. *The Destruction of the European Jews.* New Haven: Yale University Press, 2003, 3rd edn.

Hill, Alexander. *The War Behind the Eastern Front: The Soviet Partisan Movement in North-West Russia, 1941–44.* New York: Frank Cass, 2005, 3 vols.

Hinsley, F.H. *British Intelligence in the Second World War.* London: HMSO, 1984. Vol. 3, pt I.

Hinze, Rolf. *Der Zusammenbruch Der Heeresgruppe Mitte Im Osten 1944.* Stuttgart: Motorbuch Verlag, 1980.

Hinze, Rolf. *Das Ostfront-Drama 1944.* Stuttgart: Motorbuch Verlag, 1988.

Hinze, Rolf. *Rückzugskämpfe in der Ukraine 1943/44.* Meerbusch: Verlag Dr Rolf Hinze, 1991.

Hinze, Rolf. *East Front Drama 1944. The Withdrawal Battle of Army Group Centre.* Winnipeg: J.J. Fedorowicz, 1996.

Hoffmann, Joachim. *Die Geschichte Der Wlassow-Armee.* Frieburg: Rombach Verlag, 1986.

Hoffmann, Joachim. *Deutsche und Kalmyken 1942 bis 1945.* Frieburg: Rombach Verlag, 1986.

Hoffmann, Joachim. *Die Ostlegionen 1941–1943.* Frieburg: Rombach Verlag, 1986.

Hoffmann, Joachim. *Kaukasien 1942/43. Das deutsche Heer und die Orientvölker der Sowjetunion.* Frieburg: Rombach Verlag, 1991.

Hogan, David J. (ed.) *The Holocaust Chronicle: A History in Words and Pictures.* Lincolnwood: Publications International Ltd, 2002.

Höhne, Heinz. *Der Orden unter dem Totenkopf. Die Geschichte der SS.* Frankfurt am Main: Fischer Bücherei, 1969.

Höhne, Heinz. *The Order of the Death's Head. The Story of Hitler's SS.* New York: Coward McCann, Inc., 1970.

Höttl, Wilhelm. *The Secret Front: The Story of Nazi Political Espionage.* New York: Praeger, 1954.

Howell, Edgar M. et al. *The Soviet Partisan Movement 1941–1944.* Washington DC: Centre of Military History, US Army, 1956.

Hull, Isabel V. *Absolute Destruction: Military Culture and the Practices of War in Imperial Germany.* Ithaca: Cornell University Press, 2005.

Huxley-Blythe, Peter J. *The East Came West.* Caldwell: Caxton Printers Ltd, 1968.

Ignatov, P.K. *Partisans of the Kuban.* New York: Hutchinson & Co., 1944.

Ioanid, Radu. *The Holocaust in Romania: The Destruction of Jews and Gypsies under the Antonescu Regime, 1940–1944.* Chicago: Ivan R. Dee, 2008.

Jackson, Robert H. *Tyranny on Trial: The Evidence at Nuremberg.* Dallas: Southern Methodist University Press, 1954.

Jörgensen, Christer. *Hitler's Espionage Machine: The True Story Behind One of the World's Most Ruthless Spy Networks*. Guilford: Lyons Press, 2004.

Jurado, Carlos Caballero. *Rompiendo Las Cadenas: La Division Ucraniana De Las Waffen-SS*. Granada: Garcia Hispan, 1992.

Jurado, Carlos Caballero. *Commandos En El Caucaso: La Unidad Especial Bergmann, Voluntarios Caucasianos En El Ejercito Aleman, 1941–45*. Granada: Garcia Hispan, 1995.

Jurado, Carlos Caballero. *Breaking the Chains. 14. Waffen Grenadier Division der SS and Other Ukrainian Volunteer Formations, Eastern front, 1942–1945*. London: Shelf Books, 1998.

Jurado, Carlos Caballero and Thomas, Nigel. *Germany's Eastern Front Allies (2) Baltic Forces*. London: Osprey Men-at-Arms Series, Osprey Publishing, 2002.

Jurs, August (ed.) *Estonian Freedom Fighters in World War II*. Printed with a grant from the 'New Horizons Program.' Onatrio: Vôitleja Relief Foundation, n.d.

Kamenetsky, Ihor. *Hitler's Occupation of Ukraine (1941–1944). A Study of Totalitarian Imperialism*. Milwaukee: Marquette University Press, 1956.

Kampe, Norbert, Schleffler, Wolfgang and Schoenberger, Gerhard (eds). *Die Einsatzgruppen in der besetzten Sowjetunion 1941/42. Die Tätigkeits und Lageberichte des Chefs der Sicherheitspolizei und des SD*. Berlin: Edition Hentrich, 1997.

Karashuk, A. (ed.) *Russkiya Osvobodetelnya Armia 1939–1945* (Russian Liberation Army, 1939–1945). Moscow: Act Publishers, 1999.

Keegan, John. *The Second World War*. Toronto: Key Porter Books, 1989.

Keilig, Wolf. *Rangliste Des Deutschen Heeres 1944/45*. Friedberg: Podzun Pallas Verlag, n.d.

Kershaw, Ian. *Fateful Choices: Ten Decisions That Changed the World, 1940–1941*. New York: Penguin Press, 2007.

Kirchubel, Robert. *Operation Barbarossa 1941: Army Group South*. Westport: Praeger Illustrated Military History Series, 2004.

Kirchubel, Robert. *Hitler's Panzer Armies on the Eastern Front*. London: Pen & Sword, 2009.

Klausch, Hans Peter. *Antifaschisten in SS-Uniform*. Bremen: Edition Temmen, 1993.

Klee, Ernst, Dressen, Willi and Riess, Volker. *The Good Old Days*. Old Saybrook: Konecky & Konecky, 1991.

Kleitmann, Dr K.G. *Die Waffen SS: eine Dokumentation*. Osnabrück: Verlag 'Der Freiwillige' GmbH, 1965.

Kliment, Charles and Nakladal, Bretislav. *Germany's First Ally: Armed Forces of the Slovak State 1939–1945*. Atglen: Schiffer Publishing Ltd, 1997.

Knopp, Guido. *Die Wehrmacht – Eine Bilanz*. Munich: Wilhelm Goldmann Verlag, 2009.

Kohl, Paul. *Der Krieg der deutschen Wehrmacht und der Polizei 1941–1944*. Frankfurt am Main: Fischer Taschenbuch Verlag, 1995.

Krätschmer, Ernst-Günther. *Die Ritterkreuzträger der Waffen-SS*. Preussich Oldendorf: Verlag K.W. Schütz KG, 1955.

Krausnick, Helmut. *Hitlers Einsatzgruppen. Die Truppen des Weltanschauungskrieges 1938–1942*. Frankfurt am Main: Fischer Taschenbuch Verlag, 1985.

Krausnick, Helmut (ed.) *Anatomy of the SS State*. New York: Walker & Co., 1965.

Künrich, Heinz. *Der Partisanenkrieg in Europa 1939–1945*. Berlin: Dietz Verlag, 1968.

Kurowski, Franz. *Deadlock before Moscow: Army Group Centre 1942–1943*. Atglen: Schiffer Publishers, 1992.

Kurowski, Franz. *The Brandenburgers – Global Mission*. Winnipeg: J.J. Fedorowicz Publishing, 1997.

Kurowski, Franz. *The Brandenburger Commandos: Germany's Elite Warrior Spies in WWII*. Mechanicsburg: Stackpole Books, 2005.

Kursietis, Andris J. *The Fallen Generals: The Destruction of the German Officer Corps in World War II and Its Aftermath*. Osceola: Ark Publications Co., 1994.

Kursietis, Andris J. *The Wehrmacht at War 1939–1945. The Units and Commanders of the German Ground Forces during World War II.* Soesterberg: Aspekt, 1999.

Laar, Mart, *War in the Woods: Estonia's Struggle for Survival, 1944–1956.* Washington DC: Compass Press, 1992.

Landwehr, Richard. *Fighting for Freedom: The Ukrainian Volunteer Division of the Waffen SS.* Silver Spring: Bibliophile Legion Books, 1985.

Laqueur, Walter. *The Holocaust Encyclopedia.* New Haven: Yale University Press, 2001.

Laub, Thomas J. *After the Fall: German Policy in Occupied France, 1940–1944.* New York: Oxford University Press, 2010.

Leide, Henry. *NS-Verbrecher und Staatssicherheit: Die geheime Vergangenheitspolitik der DDR.* Göttingen: Vandenhoeck and Ruprecht GmbH and Co., 2007.

Lemkin, Raphael. *Axis Rule in Occupied Europe: Laws of Occupation, Analysis of Government. Proposals for Redress.* Washington DC: Carnegie Endowment for International Peace, 1944.

Le Tissier, Tony. *Zhukov at the Oder: The Decisive Battle for Berlin.* Westport: Praeger Publishing, 1996.

Le Tissier, Tony. *The Battle of Berlin 1945.* New York: St Martins Press, 1988.

Leumi, Vaad (ed.) *The Black Book: The Nazi Crime Against the Jewish People.* New York: The Jewish Black Book Committee, 1946.

Lichtenstein, Heiner. *Himmlers grüne Helfer: Die Schutz-und-Ordnungspolizei im Dritten Reich.* Bund Verlag: Berlin, 1996.

Lieb, Peter. *Konventioneller Krieg oder NS-Weltanschauungskrieg? Kriegfürung und Partisanenbekämpfung in Frankreich 1943/44.* Munich: R. Oldenbourg Verlag, 2007.

Lieb Peter: 'Täter aus Überzeugung? Oberst Carl von Andrian und die Judenmorde der 707. Infanteriedivision 1941/42,' in Hartmann/Hürter/Lieb/Pohl, *Der deutsche Krieg im Osten 1941–1944.* Oldenbourg: De Gruyter, 2009.

Linck, Stephan. *Der Ordnung verpflichtet: Deutsche Polizei 1933–1949.* Paderborn: Ferdinand Schöningh Verlag, 2000.

Littlejohn, David. *The Patriotic Traitors: The History of Collaboration in German Occupied Europe, 1940–45.* Garden City: Doubleday & Co., 1972.

Littlejohn, David. *Foreign Legions of the Third Reichs, Vol. IV – Poland, Ukraine, Bulgaria, Rumania, Free India, Estonia, Latvia, Lithuania, Finland and Russia.* San Jose: R. James Bender Publishing, 1987.

Littman, Sol. *Pure Soldiers or Sinister Legion: The Ukrainian 14th Waffen-SS Division.* Montreal: Black Rose Books, 2003.

Loftus, John. *The Belarus Secret.* New York: Alfred A. Knopf, 1982.

Logusz, Michael O. *Galicia Division: The Waffen SS 14th Grenadier Division 1943–1945.* Atglen: Schiffer Publishing Ltd, 1997.

Longhardt-Söntgen, Rainer. *Partisanen, Spione und Banditen: Abwehrtätigkeit in Oberitalien 1943–1945.* Neckargemünd: Kurt Vowinckel Verlag, 1961.

Lower, Wendy. *Nazi Empire-Building and the Holocaust in Ukraine.* Chapel Hill: University of North Carolina Press, 2005.

Lower, Wendy and Ray Brandon (eds). *The Shoah in Ukraine: History, Testimony, Memorialization.* Bloomington: Indiana University Press, 2008.

Lukas, Richard C. *The Forgotten Holocaust: The Poles under German Occupation 1939–1944.* Lexington: University Press of Kentucky, 1986.

Lumans, Valdis O. *Himmler's Auxiliaries: The Volksdeutsche Mittelstelle and the German National Minorities of Europe, 1933–1945.* Chapel Hill: University of North Carolina Press, 1993.

MacLean, French L. *The Cruel Hunters. SS Sonderkommando Dirlewanger. Hitler's Most Notorious Anti-Partisan Unit.* Atglen: Schiffer Publishers, 1998.

MacLean, French L. *The Field Men. The SS Officers Who Led the Einsatzkommandos – the Nazi Mobile Killing Units*. Atglen: Schiffer Publishers, 1999.

MacLean, French L. *The Camp Men: The SS Officers Who Ran the Nazi Concentration Camp System*. Atglen: Schiffer Military History, 1999.

Mallmann, Klaus-Michael, Rieb, Volker and Pyta, Wolfram. *Deutscher Osten 1939–1945: Der Weltanschauungskrieg in Photos und Texten*. Darmstadt: Wissenschaftliche Buchgesellschaft, 2003.

Malthäus, Jürgen. *War, Pacification, and Mass Murder, 1939: The Einsatzgruppen* in Poland. Lanham: Rowman & Littlefield, 2014.

Manoschek, Walter. *Die Wehrmacht Im Rassenkrieg: Der Vernichtungskrieg Hinter der Front*. Vienna: Picus Verlag, 1996.

Mayer, Hermann Frank. *Blutiges Edelweib: die 1. Gebirgsdivision im Zweiten Weltkrieg*. Berlin: Christoph Links Verlag GmbH, 2008.

Megargee, Geoffrey P. *War of Annihilation: Combat and Genocide on the Eastern Front, 1941*. New York: Rowman & Littlefield, 2006.

Mehner, Kurt. *Die Geheimen Tagesberichte Der Deutschen Wehrmachtführung Im Zweiten Weltkrieg 1939–1945*. Biblio Verlag: Osnabrück, 12 vol., 1989–1994.

Mehner, Kurt. *Die Waffen-SS und Polizei 1939–1945*. Norderstedt: Militair-Verlag Klaus D. Patzwall, 1995.

Mendelsohn, John (ed.) *The Holocaust. Selected Documents in Eighteen Volumes*. New York: Garland Publishing, 1982. 18 vols.

Mendelsohn, John (ed.) *Covert Warfare: Intelligence, Counterintelligence and Military Deception during the World War II Era*, 18 vols. Vol. 13: *The Final Solution of the Abwehr*. New York: Garland Publishing, Inc., 1988.

Messenger, David A. and Paehler, Katrin (eds). *A Nazi Past: Recasting German Identity in Postwar Europe*. Lexington: University Press of Kentucky, 2015.

Messerschmidt, Manfred. *Die Wehrmachtjustiz 1933–1945*. Paderborn: Ferdinand Schöningh Verlag, 2005.

Michaelis, Rolf. *Der Weg zur 36. Waffen Grenadier Division der SS*. Rodgau: Verlag fuer Militaerhistorische Zeitgeschichte, 1991.

Michaelis, Rolf. *Die Russische Volksbefreiungsarmee 'RONA' 1941–1944*. Erlangen: Selbstspubliziert, 1992.

Michaelis, Rolf. *Die Kavallerie Divisionen der Waffen SS*. Erlangen: Selbstpubliziert, 1993.

Michaelis, Rolf. *Ukrainer in der Waffen SS: Die 14. Waffen Grenadier Division der SS* (*ukrainische Nr. 1*). Berlin: Michaelis Verlag, 2000.

Michaelis, Rolf. *Russen in der Waffen SS*. Berlin: Michaelis Verlag, 2002.

Milton, Sybil, transl. *The Stroop Report*. New York: Pantheon Books, 1979.

Mitcham, Samuel W. *Hitler's Legions: the German Army Order of Battle, World War II*. New York: Dorset Press, 1985.

Mitcham, Samuel W. *Crumbling Empire: The German Defeat in the East, 1944*. Westport: Praeger Publishers, 2001.

Mitcham, Samuel W. *German Order of Battle, Vol. One: 1st–290th Infantry Divisions in WWII*. Mechanicsburg: Stackpole Books, 2007.

Mollo, Andrew. *Uniforms of the SS. Volume 5: Sicherheitsdienst und Sicherheitspolizei 1931–1945*. London: Windrow & Greene, 1992.

Müller, Norbert. *Deutsche Besatzungspolitik in der UdSSR 1941–1944*. Köln: Pahl-Rugenstein Verlag, 1980.

Müller, Rolf-Dieter and Ueberschaer, Gerd R. *Hitler's War in the East 1941–1945. A Critical Assessment*. Providence: Berghahn Books, 1997.

Müller, Rolf-Dieter, and Volkmann, Hans Erik. *Die Wehrmacht: Mythos und Realität.* Oldenbourg: Wissenschaftsverlag, 1999.

Mulligan, Patrick Timothy. *The Politics of Illusion and Empire. German Occupation Policy in the Soviet Union, 1942–1943.* New York: Praeger Publishers, 1988.

Muñoz, Antonio. *Forgotten Legions: Obscure Combat Formations of the Waffen SS, 1943–1945.* Boulder: Paladin Press, 1991.

Muñoz, Antonio. *Forgotten Legions Companion Booklet.* New York: Europa Books, 1995.

Muñoz, Antonio. *Hitler's Eastern Legions, Vol. I – The Baltic Schutzmannschaft 1941–1945.* New York: Europa Books, 1996.

Muñoz, Antonio. *The Kaminski Brigade: A History, 1941–1945.* New York: Europa Books, 1996.

Muñoz, Antonio. *For Croatia and Christ: The Croatian Army in World War II, 1941–1945.* New York: Europa Books, 1996.

Muñoz, Antonio. *Hitler's Eastern Legions, Vol. II – The Osttruppen.* New York: Europa Books, 1997.

Muñoz, Antonio (ed.) *The German Police.* Supreme Allied Headquarters, G-2 Section, prepared jointly with British MI-14(d). Washington DC: US Army War Office, April 1945. Reprinted in rev. and exp. format. New York: Europa Books, 1997.

Muñoz, Antonio. *The last Levy: Waffen SS Officer Roster, March 1st 1945.* New York: Europa Books, 2000.

Muñoz, Antonio. *The Druzhina SS Brigade: A History, 1941–1943.* New York: Europa Books, 2000.

Muñoz, Antonio (ed.) *The East Came West: Muslim, Hindu, and Buddhist Volunteers in the German Armed Forces, 1941–1945.* New York: Europa Books, 2002.

Muñoz, Antonio. *Göring's Grenadiers: The Luftwaffe Field Divisions 1942–1945.* New York: Europa Books, 2002.

Muñoz, Antonio. *The Kaminski Brigade: A History, 1941–1945.* New York: Europa Books, 2003, 2nd rev. and exp. edn.

Nafziger, George F. *The German Order of Battle. Waffen SS and Other Units in World War II.* Conshohocken: Combined Publishing, 2001.

Neufeldt, H.-J., Huck, J. and Tessin, Georg. *Zur Geschichte der Ordnungspolizei: Die Stabe und Truppeneinheiten der Ordnungspolizei, 1936–1945.* Koblenz: Als Manuskript gedruckt. Bundesarchiv, 1957.

Neulen, Hans Werner. *An Deutscher Seite: Internationale Freiwillige von Wehrmacht und Waffen SS.* München: Universitas Verlag, 1985.

Newland, Samuel J. *Cossacks in the German Army, 1941–1945.* London: Frank Cass & Co. Ltd, 1991.

Newton, Steven H. *German Battle Tactics on the Russian Front.* Atglen: Schiffer Publishing, 1994.

Newton, Steven H. *Retreat from Leningrad. Army Group North, 1944/1945.* Atglen: Schiffer Publishing, 1995.

Niehorster, Leo W.G. *The Royal Hungarian Army, 1920–1945.* New York: Europa Books, 1998.

Niepold, Gerd. *Battle for White Russia: The Destruction of Army Group Centre June 1944.* New York: Brassey's Defence Publishers, 1987.

Nirenstein, Albert. *A Tower from the Enemy: Contributions to a History of Jewish Resistance in Poland.* New York: Orion Press, 1959.

Overmans, Rüdiger. *Deutsche militärische Verluste im Zweiten Weltkrieg.* München: R. Oldenbourg Verlag, 1999.

Overy, Richard. *Russia's War: A History of the Soviet War Effort, 1941–1945.* New York: Penguin Putnam Inc., 1998.

Padfield, Peter. *Himmler.* New York: Henry Holt & Co., 1990.

Perro, Oskars. *Fortress Cholm.* Toronto: Kurland Publishing, 1981.

Person, Katarzyna. *Warsaw Ghetto Police: The Jewish Order Service during the Nazi Occupation.* Ithaca: Cornell University Press, 2021.

Piotrowski, Tadeusz. *Poland's Holocaust: Ethnic Strife, Collaboration with Occupying Forces and Genocide in the Second Republic, 1918–1947.* Jefferson: MacFarland & Co., 1998.

Pohl, Dieter et al., *Der deutsche Krieg im Osten 1941–1944.* Munich: De Gruytyer, 2009.

Pohl, Otto J. *Ethnic Cleansing in the USSR, 1937–1949.* Westport: Greenwood Press, 1999.

Poirier, Robert G. and Conner, Albert Z. *The Red Army Order of Battle in the Great Patriotic War.* Novato: Presidio Press, 1985.

Porter, Jack Nusan (ed.) *Jewish Partisans: A Documentary of Jewish Resistance in the Soviet Union During World War II.* Washington DC: University Press of America, 1982.

Pottgeiser, Hans. *Die Reichsbahn in Ostfeldzug.* Neckargemünd: Kurt Vowinckel Verlag, 1960.

Präg, Werner and Jacobson, Wolfgang. *Das Dienstagebuch des deutschen Generalgouverneurs in Polen 1939–1945.* Stuttgart: Deutsche Verlag Anstalt, 1975.

Prechtl, G.M. *Unsere Ehre Heisst Treue: Kriegstagebuch des Kommandostabes Reichsführer SS; Tätigkeitsberichte der 1. und 2. SS Infanterie-Brigade und von Sonderkommandos der SS.* Zürich: Europa Verlag, 1965.

Preradovich, Nikolaus von. *Die Generale der Waffen-SS.* Berg Am See: Kurt Vowinckel Verlag, 1985.

Ramme, Alwin. *Der Sicherheitsdienst Der SS.* Berlin: Deutscher Militärverlag der DDR, 1970.

Ready, J. Lee. *The Forgotten Axis: Germany's Partners and Foreign Volunteers in World War II.* Jefferson: MacFarland & Co., 1987.

Redcliffe, Alexander. *Lessons Learned from the Partisan War in Russia.* MS No. P055C, Washington DC: Office of the Chief of Military History, Department of the Army, 1947.

Redelis, Valdis. *Partisanenkrieg: Entstehung und Bekämpfung der Partisanen und Untergrundbewegung im Mittelabschnitt der Ostfront 1941 bis 1943.* Heidelberg: Scharnhorst Buchkameradenschaft, 1958.

Regenberg, Werner. *Panzerfahrzeuge und Panzereinheiten der Ordnungspolizei 1936–1945.* Friedberg: Podzun Pallas Verlag, 1996.

Regenberg, Werner. *Armored Vehicles and Units of the German Order Police (Ordnungspolizei) 1936–1945.* Atglen: Schiffer Military History, 2002.

Reinicke, Adolf. *Die 5. Jäger-Division 1939–1945.* Friedberg: Podzun Pallas Verlag GmbH, n.d.

Reitlinger, Gerald. *The SS, Alibi of a Nation, 1922–1945.* London: William Heinemann Ltd, 1956.

Reitlinger, Gerald. *The House Built on Sand: The Conflicts of German Policy in Russia, 1939–1945.* New York: Viking Press, 1960.

Reitlinger, Gerald. *The Final Solution. The Attempt to Exterminate the Jews of Europe 1939–1945.* South Brunswick: Thomas Yoseloff, 1961.

Richter, Hans. *Einsatz der Polizei bei den Polizei Bataillonen im Ost, Nord, und West.* Berlin: Zentralverlag der NSDAP, 1943.

Romanko, Oleg and Antonio Muñoz. *Hitler's White Russians: Collaboration, Extermination and Anti-Partisan Warfare in White Russia, 1941–1944.* New York: Europa Books, 2002.

Rossino, Alexander B. *Hitler Strikes Poland: Blitzkrieg, Ideology, and Atrocity* (Modern War Studies) Lawrence: University Press of Kansas, 2003.

Rürup, Dr Reinhard and Jahn, Dr Peter (eds). *Der Krieg gegen die Sowjetunion 1941–1945.* Berlin: Berliner Festspiele GmbH, 1991.

Ryan, Cornelius. *The Last Battle.* New York: Simon & Schuster, 1966.

Scheibert, Horst. *Die Träger Der Deutschen Kreuzes In Gold: Kriegsmarine, Luftwaffe, Waffen SS.* Friedberg: Podzun Pallas Verlag, n.d.

Scheibert, Horst. *Die Träger Der Ehrenblattspange Des Heeres Und Der Waffen SS.* Friedberg: Podzun Pallas Verlag, 1986.

Schellenberg, Walter. *The Labyrinth. The Memoirs of Hitler's Secret Service Chief.* New York: Harper & Brothers, 1956.

Schmitz, Peter and Thies, Klaus-Jürgen. *Die Truppenkennzeichen der Verbände und Einheiten der Deutschen Wehrmacht und Waffen SS und ihre Einsätze im Zweiten Weltkrieg 1939–1945.* Osnabrück: Biblio Verlag, 1987-1994. 4 vols.

Schneider, Jost W. *Verleihung Genehmigt! Eine Bild und Dokumentargeschichte Der Ritterkreuzträger Der Waffen SS und Polizei 1940–1945.* San Jose: R. James Bender Publishing, 1993.

Schülte, Theo. *The German Army and Nazi Policies In Occupied Russia 1941–1944.* New York: Berg Publishers, 1989.

Schumann, Wolfgang and Ludwig Nestler. *Nacht über Europa: Band II: Die faschistische Okkupationspolitik in Polen (1939–1945).* Köln: Pahl-Rugenstein Verlag GmbH, 1989.

Schuster, Peter and Tiede, Harald. *Die Uniformen und Abzeichen der Kosaken in der Deutschen Wehrmacht.* Norderstedt: Verlag Klaus D. Patzwall, 1999.

Seaton, Albert. *The Russo-German War 1941–45.* New York: Praeger Publishers, 1970.

Seewald, Dr Heinrich. *Das toenende Erz: Deutsche Propaganda gegen die Rote Armee im Zweiten Weltkrieg.* Stuttgart: Seewald Verlag, 1978.

Seidler, Franz W. *Deutscher Volkssturm: Das letzte Aufgebot, 1944–1945.* München: F. A. Herbig Verlag, 1989.

Seidler, Franz W. *Die Militaergerichtsbarfeit der Deutschen Wehrmacht 1939–1945.* Munich: Herbig Verlag, 1991.

Seidler, Franz W. *Die Kollaboration 1939–1945.* München: F.A. Herbig Verlagsbuchhandlung, 1995.

Silgailis, Arthur. *Latvian Legion.* San Jose: R. James Bender Publishing, 1986.

Snyder, Timothy. *Into the Bloodlands: Europe Between Hitler and Stalin.* New York: Basic Books, 2022.

Steenberg, Sven. *Vlasov.* New York: Alfred A. Knopf, 1970.

Stein, George H. *The Waffen SS: Hitler's Elite Guard at War 1939–1945.* Ithaca: Cornell University Press, 1966.

Stöber, Hans. *Die Flugabwehrverbände der Waffen SS.* Preussiche Oldendorf: Verlag K.W. Schütz KG, 1984.

Stöber, Hans. *Die 22. Panzer Division; 25. Panzer Division; 27. Panzer Division; und die 233. Reserve Panzer Division.* Friedberg: Podzun Pallas Verlag, 1985.

Stockhorst, Erich. *5000 Köpfe: Wer War Was Im Dritten Reich.* Kiel: Arndt Verlag, 2000.

Stoves, Rolf. *Die Gepanzerten und Motorizierten Deutschen Grossverbände 1935–1945.* Friedberg: Podzun Pallas Verlag, 1986.

Strik-Strikfeldt, Wilfried. *Against Stalin and Hitler. Memoir of the Russian Liberation Movement 1941–1945.* New York: John Day Co., 1973.

Tec, Nechama. *The Bielski Partisans.* Oxford: Oxford University Press, 1993.

Tessin, Georg. *Verbände und Truppen der deutschen Wehrmacht und Waffen SS 1939–1945.* Osnabrück: Biblio Verlag, 1975–2002. 18 vols.

Tessin, Georg, with Neufeldt, H.J. and Huck, J. *Zur Geschichte der Ordnungspolizei, 1936–1945.* Koblenz: Bundesarchiv, 1956.

Tessin, Georg, Kannapin, Norbert and Meyer, Brün. *Waffen-SS und Ordnungspolizei im Kriegseinsatz 1939–1945.* Biblio Verlag: Osnabruck, 2000.

Thomas, Nigel et al. *Partisan Warfare 1941–45.* London: Reed International Books Ltd, 1983.

Thomas, Nigel and Caballero Jurado, Carlos. *Wehrmacht Auxiliary Forces.* London: Osprey Publishing, 1992.

Thorwald, Juergen. *The Illusion: Soviet Soldiers in Hitler's Armies.* New York: Harcourt Brace Jovanovich, 1975.

Thurston, Robert W. and Bonwetsch, Bernd (eds). *The People's War: Responses to World War II in the Soviet Union*. New York: University of Illinois Press: Urbana, 2000.

Tieke, Wilhelm. *Das Ende Zwischen Oder Und Elbe: Der Kampf Um Berlin 1945*. Stuttgart: Motorbuch Verlag, 1994.

Tolstoy, Nikolai. *The Secret Betrayal 1944–1947*. New York: Charles Scribner's Sons, 1977.

Tys-Krokhmaliuk, Yuriy. *UPA Warfare in Ukraine: The Ukrainian Insurgent Army*. New York: Vantage Press, 1972.

Ullrich, Sebastian. *Der Weimar-Komplex. Das Scheitern der ersten deutschen Demokratie und die politische Kultur der frühen Bundesrepublik 1945–1959*. Göttingen: Wallstein Verlag, 2009,

Vakar, Nicholas P. *Belarusia: The Making of a Nation: A Case Study*. Cambridge: Harvard University Press, 1956.

Vizetelly, Frank H. (ed.). *Funk and Wagnall's New Standard Encyclopedia of Universal Knowledge*. New York: Funk & Wagnall's Company, 1931. Vol. 25.

Wegner, Bernd. *The Waffen-SS: Organization, Ideology and Function*. Oxford: Basil Blackwell, 1990.

Werbizky, George G. *Ostarbeiters: Belarusian, Russian and Ukrainian Forced Laborers in Nazi Germany – World War II*. Endwell: Self Published, 2002.

Westermann, Edward B. *Hitler's Police Battalions: Enforcing Racial War in the East*. Lawrence: University Press of Kansas.

Westwood, David. *The Waffen SS: Higher formations, Divisions, Brigades 1939–1945*. Derbyshire: Privately Published, n.d.

Wette, Wolfram. *The Wehrmacht: History, Myth, Reality*. Cambridge: Harvard University Press, 2007.

Wicziok, Wilhelm. *Die Armee Der Gerichteten. Zur besonderen Verwendung – Bewaehrungsbataillon 500*. Essen: Heitz & Hoeffkes Verlag, 1992.

Wilhelm, Hans-Heinrich. *Die Einsatzgruppe A: der Sicherheitspolizei und des SD 1941/42*. Frankfurt am Main: Peter Lang Verlag GmbH, 1996.

Witte, Hans Joachim and Peter Offermann. *Die Boeselagerschen Reiter: Das Kavallerie-Regiment Mitte die aus ihm hervorgegangene 3. Kavallerie-Brigade/Division*. München: Schild Verlag, 1998.

Witter, Robert E. *Chain Dogs: The German Army Military Police of World War II*. Missoula: Pictorial Histories Publishing Co., 1994.

Yelton, David K. *Hitler's Volkssturm: The Nazi Militia and the Fall of Germany, 1944–1945*. Lawrence: University Press of Kansas, 2002.

Yerger, Mark C. *Riding East. The SS Cavalry Brigade in Poland and Russia 1939–1942*. Atglen: Schiffer Publishers, 1996.

Yerger, Mark C. *Allgemeine SS*. Atglen: Schiffer Military Publishing, 1997.

Yerger, Mark C. *Waffen SS Commanders: Augsberger to Kreutz*. Atglen: Schiffer Military Publishing, 1997.

Yerger, Mark C. *Waffen SS Commanders: Krüger to Zimmermann*. Atglen: Schiffer Military Publishing, 1999.

Zaloga, Steven. *Bagration 1944: The Destruction of Army Group Centre*. London: Osprey Military, 1996.

Zawodny, J.K. *Nothing But Honor: The Story of the Warsaw Uprising, 1944*. Hoover Institution Press, 1978.

Ziemke, Earl F. and Bauer, Magna E. *Moscow to Stalingrad: Decision in the East*. Washington DC: Centre of Military History, US Army, 1987.

Index

Persons

Abraham, Walter, 46, 63
Achamer-Pifrader, Humbert, 51
Altrichter, Friedrich, 99
Amirov, G.S., 136
Andropov, Yuri, xii
Arad, Yitzhak, 6–7
Aräjs, Viktor, 80
Aschenbrandt, Heinrich, 94
Assad, Bashar al, x, xviii
Auleb, Lieutenant General Helge, 218
Axt, Gendarmerie Major, 86

Bach-Zelewski, Erich von dem, 38, 45, 107–8, 207
Baltin, First Lieutenant, 95
Barkhold, Police Major, 42, 70
Barrows, Robert H., 110
Barsukov, J.M., 137
Bartel, Albert, 167
Bartov, Omer, 4, 7, 178
Bassewitz-Behr, Georg Graf von, 46
Batz, Rudolph, 39, 69
Bayer, Friedrich, 96, 211
Bechtolsheim, Gustav Freiherr von Mauchenheim genannt von, 55, 57–8
Behms, Captain Karlis, 45, 84, 210
Behr, Karl, 48
Behrends, SS Lieutenant General and General of the Police Dr, 62, 207
Belov, Pavel, 136
Bendzko, Police Major, 42, 70
Berger, Gottlob, 78
Bergmann, Police Major, 43, 83
Blobel, Paul, 41
Blume, Walter, 39
Bock, Fedor von, 21, 158
Böhme, Hans-Joachim, 123
Bomhard, Adolf von, 48
Bonaparte, Napoleon, 19, 100–1
Bormann, Martin, 6
Both, Hans Kuno von, 92
Boyarsky, Vladimir, 119
Bradfisch, Otto, 40
Braschnevitz, Herbert, 70
Brauchitsch, Walter von, 19, 21, 188, 219
Braun, Werner von, 8
Braune, Werner, 163–4
Braunschweig, Police Major von, 46
Bredow, Gendarmerie Lt Colonel von, 48
Brenner, Karl, 48
Brezhnev, Leonid, xi–xii
Browning, Christopher, 1, 8
Budenny, Semyon Mikhailovich, 20
Burke, Edmund, xvii, xix
Bush Jr, George, xiii

Canaris, Wilhelm, 115
Chamberlain, Neville, xvii, xix
Chernenko, Konstantine, xii
Chlebtsov, V., 140
Churchill, Winston, xi, 213
Clark, Alan, 111, 113

Daladier, Édouard, xvii, xix
Dall, Police Captain, 49
Dallin, Alexander, 6–7
Daluege, Kurt, 36–7, 73, 75, 107, 138
Damerau, Helmut, 155
Danukalov, A.F., 137
Davies, Edward, 8
Deckert, Police Major, 49
Demelhuber, Karl, 38, 64
Demenkov, F.N., 136
Denicke, Wolfgang, 45
Diaz-Canel, Miguel, x
Dirlewanger, Oskar, 38, 64
Ditfurth, Wolfgang von, 56
Döring, Major, 210
Dreßen, Willi, 9
Dyatschkov, M.I., 137

Eberhardt, Friedrich-Georg, 57
Ebert, Police Captain/Major, 174, 180, 218
Ehrlinger, Erich, 39, 63, 69, 208
Eisenbach, Erich Wilhelm, 94
Erdoğan, Recep Tayyip, x
Espey, Gendarmerie Captain Oswald, 86, 210, 239

Fechner, Police Captain, 70
Federov, Oleksii, 155
Filbert, Alfred Karl, 40
Fischer, Kurt, 94
Fischer-Schweder, Bernhard, 123
Franz, Hermann, 49
Franz, Martin, 44
Frolov, V.M., 137
Fromm, Police Colonel Werner, 45
Fuchs, Wilhelm, 51, 131

Gänzer, Johannes, 155
Gärtner, Reinhold, 8
Geissler, Police Major, 42, 70
Geßner, Klaus, 180
Geyer, Michael, 7
Giesecke, Gustav, 73
Giesecke, Otto, 41
Gilbert, Martin, 164, 175
Ginckel, Oskar van, 91, 94
Gise, Freiherr Ernst August Karlimilian Josef von, 94, 211
Gnesdilov, F.D., 136
Goldhagen, Daniel J., 10–11
Gorbachev, Mikhail, xii
Göring, Hermann, 6, 22–3, 51, 131
Gottberg, Curt von, 63, 208
Graaf, Kurt, 52
Gray, John, x, xx
Gresser, Erwin, 48
Griese, Bernhard, 48
Grishin, Sergey, 136
Guderian, Heinz, 21, 149, 187–8
Günzel, Captain, 210

Haas, Lieutenant, 167
Hachte, Hans, 45
Hahn, Adolf, 49
Halder, Franz, 16, 18
Hallman, SS Major, 38, 64
Haltermann, Hans, 46
Hanner, August, 44, 70
Hannibal, Heinrich, 49
Harm, Hermann, 62
Hartmann, Ernst, 46
Haselmayr, Friedrich, 94, 211
Heer, Hannes, 8–9, 159
Heimburg, Erik von, 36, 46, 62
Helwes, Police Major, 42, 70
Helwig, Hans, 94
Hellwig, Otto, 45
Herf, Eberhard, 36, 46, 62, 76
Herff, Jeffrey, xvi
Herrmann, Günther, 41
Hersmann, Werner, 123
Hewelcke, Georg, 56
Heydrich, Reinhard, 35, 37, 73, 78, 125, 131, 174
Hilberg, Raul, 8, 157
Himmler, Heinrich, 35, 37–8, 52, 61, 63, 65, 75, 77–9, 117, 130–1, 138, 197, 214
Hirsch, Max, 48
Hitler, Adolf, x, xi, xii, xiv–xvii, xix–xx, 3, 6–8, 10–11, 13, 15–19, 21–2, 24–5, 30, 50, 53, 58, 79, 85, 109, 111, 115, 185–9, 195–6, 200, 203–5, 207–8, 219
Hornung, Ela, 8
Hubig, Hermann, 52
Hussein, Saddam, xiii

Iskaukas, Antanas, 80
Isselhorst, Erich, 52

Jaagund, Major, 82
Jaanson, Hugo, 82
Jäger, Karl, 36, 39, 51, 69, 125, 132, 207
Jeckeln, SS Lieutenant General and General of the Police Friedrich, 61–2, 79, 86–7, 130, 207, 214
Jedicke, Georg, 41, 73, 75
Jong-un, Kim, x
Jost, Heinz, 35, 51, 131

Kadirov, Ramzan, x
Kangro, Peeter, 82
Kapusta, F.F., 137
Karik, Alfred, 82
Karolus, SS Second Lieutenant, 91
Kasubski, V.V., 136
Kazalpov, Vasily, 103
Keitel, Wilhelm, 3–4, 6, 16, 25, 53, 161
Keuper, Hermann, 42, 70
Khrushchev, Nikita, xi
Kirpitsch, G.A., 137
Klaus, Police Major, 49
Kleffel, Phillipp, 99

Klepsch, Johann, 36, 46, 62–3
Klimaitis, Jonas, 79
Klingelhöfer, Woldemar, 40
Knecht, Karl, 88, 130
Knuth, Hans, 91, 94
Koch, Erich, 78–9, 200
Kochem, Thümmel, 94
Kohl, Paul, 8
Kohler, Kurt, 155
Koniev, Ivan, 103
Körgmaa, August, 82
Koronevski, I.F., 137
Korotkin, S.M., 137
Kövenig, Police Major J., 43
Kozmovich, Dimitri, 116, 120–1
Krenzki, Curt von, 94
Krichbaum, Wilhelm, 37
Kriegsheim, Arno Graf von, 92, 211
Kröger, Erhard, 41
Kromiadi, Konstantine, 118–19
Kunsberg, Eberhard von, 38, 64
Küpper, Hans Friedrich, 94
Kurg, Franz, 43, 83
Kusnyetzov, Alexey, 100
Kutschera, Franz, 46
Kutuzov, Prince Mikhail, 101

Lääne, Joosep, 82
Laden, Osama bin, xiv
Lammers, Hans Heinrich, 6
Lamsdorff, Grigory von, 118
Lange, Erwin Rudolf, 36, 44, 130–2
Lange, Fritz, 51
Lechthaler, Franz, 45, 70
Lenin, Vladimir, xi, 15
Lilleleht, Paul, 82
Limpere, Major K., 43, 83
Litvinenko, Alexander, xv
Lohse, Hinrich, 34, 50, 79, 130, 200
Lombard, Gustav, 38, 64
Lorge, Ernst, 48
Lower, Wendy, 151
Lukashenko, Aleksander, x
Lvova-Belova, Maria, xviii

Machanko, S.V., 137
Maduro, Nicolas, x
Magill, Franz, 38, 64, 142
Maiss, Captain, 95
Maliki, Nouri al, xiv
Mangulis, Colonel Gustavs, 44, 84
Manoschek, Walter, 8
Manstein, Erich von, 162
Mauchenheim, Gustav Freiherr von, 55, 57
Mazower, Mark, 13
Megargee, Geoffrey P., 11–12
Meier, Paulus, 42, 70
Melnikov, V.V., 137
Mere Ain Ervin, 39, 81
Merkulov, Vsevolod, 100
Messerschmidt, Manfred, 8
Mironenko, P.I., 137
Mikulicz, Lieutenant-General Adalbert, 218
Möller, First Lieutenant, 94
Möller, Heinrich (Hinrich), 35, 41, 62, 132, 209
Molotov, Vyacheslav, 18
Montua, Karl, 48
Montua, Max, 47
Müller, Colonel, 163–4
Müller, Heinrich, 35, 57
Mussolini, Benito, x–xi, xiii, xvii, xx

Nagel, Police Major, 48
Naumann, Klaus, 9
Navalny, Alexei, xv
Nebe, Arthur, 39
Neitzel, Sönke, 12
Nemtsov, Boris, xv
Nikans, Captain J., 210

Obama, Barak, xviii
Oelhafen, Otto von, 48
Ohrt, Hans-Detlef, 47
Orbán, Viktor, x
Ortega, Daniel, x
Osis, Robert, 130

Paeffgen, Theodor, 165
Panzinger, Friedrich, 51
Pauer, *Generalstabsintendant* Friedrich, 204
Paul, Johann, 82
Pavlovski, F.I., 137
Pechau, Manfred, 52
Peiker, Major J., 44
Perz, Bertrand, 8
Petersen, Police Major, 42, 70
Pfeffer-Wildenbruch, Karl von, 75
Pflugbeil, Johann, 56
Pfugradt, Curt, 94
Plotho, Wolfgang Baron von, 50, 96
Popov, Vasily, 100
Pori, Anton, 82
Porietis, Karlis, 84

Prudnikov, M., 140
Prützmann, Hans-Adolf, 35, 61–2, 79, 132, 207, 210
Putin, Vladimir, x–xx, 203

Rasch, Otto, 41
Raudmäe, Colonel J., 43, 83
Rausch, Günther, 39, 110
Rehberg, Richard, 86
Reich, Otto, 38
Reichenau, Walter von, 4, 161–2, 167–8
Reinhardt, Georg-Hans, 21
Reitlinger, Gerald, xi, 5–7, 58, 125, 174
Renter, Police Major, 43, 83
Ribbentrop, Joachim von, 18
Riesen, Abwehr Major, 162–3
Riipalu, Captain, 43, 83
Roch, Police Colonel Heinz, 45
Romanov, Czar Alexander Pavlovich I, 100–1
Rommel, Erwin, 188
Roques, Karl Franz von, 50, 92
Rosenberg, Alfred, 6, 50–1, 78–9, 196
Rosenow, SS First Lieutenant, 71
Rußwurm, Wilhelm, 56, 173

Sacharov, Andrei, 103
Safrian, Hans, 9
Saidra, Evald, 82
Sakharov, Igor, 119
Sandberger, Martin, 36, 39, 42, 51, 69
Sander, August, 82
Sarev, Lieutenant Colonel, 43, 83
Sauer, Major, 94
Saulite, Captain P., 84
Schäfer, Karl, 62–3
Schallert, Police Major Hermann, 36, 76, 209
Schellbach, Oskar, 53
Scherer, Theodor, 133, 211
Schiller, Police Major, 43, 83
Schimana, SS Brigadier General Walter, 208
Schkredo, R.V., 137
Schmyrev, Mihay Filipovich, 136–7
Schöngarth, Eberhard, 40
Schröder, Walter (Walther), 35, 44, 62, 76–7, 132
Schulte, Theo J., 7, 151
Schulz, Erwin, 41
Sedlezki, F.M., 137
Sehmsdorf, Johannes Ludwig, 94
Shcherbakov, Alexander, 103
Shek, Chiang Kai, xi
Shepperd, Ben, 4–5, 151
Shishik, I.K., 137
Shmyrev, Mihay Filipovich, 136
Sinka, Arnold, 82
Siry, *Generalleutnant* Maximilian, 12, 204
Six, Franz, 40
Skirpa, Kazys, 79
Skrauja, Alfons, 84
Skripal, Sergei, xv
Smelser, Ronald, 8
Snyder, Timothy, 13
Sobolev, Major, 43, 83
Sonnenburg, Richard, 70
Spemann, Kurt, 91, 94
Sporrenberg, Jakob, 63
Stäglich, Karl, 54
Stahlecker, Franz Walter, 39, 51, 69, 124–5, 132
Stalin, Joseph, xi–xii, 4, 6, 15, 18, 24–6, 30, 82, 88, 100, 118, 120, 123–4, 132, 148, 152, 187–8, 208, 213
Stolyarevitch, Partisan Leader, 58
Strauch, Eduard, 36, 46, 51
Streit, Christian, 2, 8
Subbotin, Mikhail, 100

Thaden, Wilhelm von, 36
Thomas, Georg, 110–11
Thomas, Max, 41
Tiedemann, Karl von, 95
Tiivel, August, 82
Timoshenko, Semyon Konstantinovich, 20
Traut, Karl, 52
Treuenfeld, Karl von, 38, 64

Ullrich, Sebastian, xvi

Vaska, Captain, 82
Vermet, Lieutenant Colonel, 43, 83
Viilip, Artur, 82
Vitushka, Mikhail, 120
Vogts, Lieutenant Colonel Josef, 44
Volkogonov, Dmitri Antonovich, 100
Vorontschenko, V.I., 136
Voroshilov, Kliment Yefremovich, 20, 100

Weber, Chief Court Martial Councillor Dr, 165
Weichs, Maximilian Freiherr von, 109
Weinhaus, Nat, 58
Weis, Ernst, 47
Westermann, Edward, 156
Wette, Wolfram, 9–10
Wilson, Woodrow, xvi
Wysocki, Lucian, 35, 45, 62, 76, 132

Xi Jinping, x–xi

Yeltsin, Boris, xii, xiv
Yerger, Mark, 108
Yudenkov, A.F., 136

Zakharov, Igor, 118
Zelensky, Volodymyr, xix
Zenner, Carl, 35, 45, 63, 121
Zhadanov, Andrei, 100
Zhukov, Georgy, 100, 103

Formations

Soviet Army

Soviet Fifth Army, 111
2nd Guard Cavalry Corps, 136
36th Cavalry Division, 107
37th Cavalry Division, 107
121st Rifle Division, 107

Soviet Partisan Units

1st Smolensk Partisan Division, 136
1st Belarusian Partisan Brigade, 136–7
2nd Belarusian Partisan Brigade, 137
'Alexey' Partisan Brigade, 137
'Batia' Partisan Brigade, 136
'Czechist' Partisan Brigade, 137
'Death to Fascism' Partisan Brigade, 137
'Dsershinski' Partisan Brigade
'Stschors' Partisan Brigade, 137
'Voroshilov' Partisan Brigade, 137
'24th Year' Partisan Regiment, 136
'Laso' Partisan Regiment, 136
'Grishin' Partisan Regiment, 134, 136
'Komarov' Partisan Battalion', 109
'Krasny October' Partisan Battalion, 109
'Victory or Death' Partisan Battalion, 108
'Shmyrev' Otriad, 136
'Chernigov' Partisan Band, 155
'Federov' Partisan Band, 155
'Gluchov' Partisan Band, 155
'Michailovka-Dimitrovsk' Partisan Band, 156

Nazi Party Organizations or Regions

Ministry for the Occupied Eastern Territories, 50, 78, 199–200
NSKK (National Socialist Motor Corps), 50, 76
Reich Main Security Office, 36, 52, 68, 73, 78, 196, 210
Arbeitsbereich Osten der NSDAP (East Working Area of the National Socialist German Workers' Party), 79
Organization Todt, 50, 137, 178, 199, 207, 209
Reich Kommissariat Ostland, 50, 61, 77, 82, 95, 104
Reichsgau Sudetenland, 207
Reichsbahn (German National Railway), 111
Volkssturm ('People's Assault', i.e. the German Home Guard), 116

German Army and Nazi Party Commands

Armed Forces High Command, 4, 16, 122, 161, 185, 199
German General Staff, 18
German Armed Forces Military Commander for the Ostland, 95
Rückwärtige Heeresgebiet Süd 103 (Rear Army Area South 103), 181
(German) Military District VIII, 173
(German) Military District XII, 191
Reichskommissariat Ostland, 32, 127–9, 200
Reichskommissariat Ukraine, 200
Reichskommissariat Weißruthenien, 34
Generalbezirk Bialystok (General District 'Bialystok'), 32
Generalbezirk Estland (General District 'Estonia'), 32
Generalbezirk Lettland (General District 'Latvia'), 32
Generalbezirk Litauen (General District 'Lithuania'), 32
Generalbezirk Weissruthenien (General District 'White Ruthenia'), 34
Wirtschaftsinspektion Süd (Economic Inspectorate South), 155
Heeresgruppe Mitte/Army Group Centre, 18, 20–1, 27, 32, 34–5, 40, 47, 53–4, 59, 63, 71, 97–8, 104–5, 107, 111, 120–2, 124, 140, 149, 186–7, 191–2, 198, 209, 211
Heeresgruppe Nord/Army Group North, 18–19, 32, 34–5, 38–9, 41, 43, 53, 59, 63, 68–9, 71, 73, 75, 77, 84–6, 91–2, 95–105, 157, 192, 212
Heeresgruppe Süd/Army Group South, 18, 20, 32, 34–5, 50, 57, 63, 71, 97, 104–5, 152, 155, 158, 160–1, 162, 168, 173, 186–7, 210
Army Detachment Hollidt, 206
2nd Army, 27, 53–4, 109–10, 155
4th Army, 27, 54
6th Army, 27, 161–2, 168, 174, 182–3, 196, 216

9th Army, 27, 53–4, 191, 205
11th Army, 27, 160, 162–3, 165–6, 177
16th Army, 27, 39, 44, 69, 85, 91, 94–5, 100, 105
17th Army, 28
18th Army, 28, 39, 41, 43, 69, 84–7, 91, 94–5, 98, 100, 105
Panzergruppe 1/1st Panzer Army, 28, 160, 177, 182
Panzergruppe 2/2nd Panzer Army, 28, 31, 192
Panzergruppe 3/3rd Panzer Army, 28
Panzergruppe 4/4th Panzer Army, 28, 95,192, 204, 206, 211
Befehlshaber des Rückwärtigen Heeres-gebietes der Heeresgruppe Mitte, 34
Korück: Kommandant Rückwärtiges Armeegebiet 101 (101st Army Rear Area Command), hereafter referred to as *Korück 101*, 39, 76
Korück 102, 76
Korück 103, 76, 181
Korück 531, 28
Korück 532, 28, 192
Korück 550, 28
Korück 553, 27
Korück 559, 27, 54
Korück 580, 27, 54
Korück 582, 27, 53–4, 191
Korück 583, 28, 43–4, 84, 91, 94
Korück 584, 27, 44, 91, 94–5, 102
Korück 585, 27, 206
Korück 590, 28
Korück 593, 28, 31, 206
Oberfeldkommandantur 392 (Minsk) (392nd Senior Field Command), 95
Oberfeldkommandantur 394 (Riga) (394th Senior Field Command), 95
Oberfeldkommandantur 396 (Kaunas) (396th Senior Field Command), 95
Oberfeldkommandantur 579 (579th Senior Field Command), 96
Feldkommandantur 181 (181st Field Command), 47
Feldkommandantur 182 (182nd Field Command), 94
Feldkommandantur 190 (190th Field Command), 96
Feldkommandantur 192 (192nd Field Command), 94
Feldkommandantur 195 (195th Field Command), 175–6
Feldkommandantur 197 (197th Field Command), 175–6
Feldkommandantur 198 (198th Field Command), 175–6
Feldkommandantur 238 (238th Field Command), 94
Feldkommandantur 270 (270th Field Command), 169
Feldkommandantur 286 (286th Field Command), 169
Feldkommandantur 561 (561st Field Command), 94
Feldkommandantur 569 (569th Field Command), 96, 211
Feldkommandantur 579 (579th Field Command), 94, 211
Feldkommandantur 611 (611th Field Command), 92, 94
Feldkommandantur 679 (679th Field Command), 157, 173, 177
Feldkommandantur 774 (774th Field Command), 157, 160, 177
Feldkommandantur 811 (811th Field Command), 175–6
Feldkommandantur 817 (817th Field Command), 92, 94–5
Feldkommandantur 818 (818th Field Command), 92, 94–5
Feldkommandantur 819 (819th Field Command), 92, 94–5
Feldkommandantur 820 (820th Field Command), 92, 96
Feldkommandantur 821 (821st Field Command), 92, 96
Feldkommandantur 822 (822nd Field Command), 92, 96
Feldkommandantur 829 (829th Field Command), 169
Feldkommandantur 835 (835th Field Command), 169
Feldkommandantur 837 (837th Field Command), 169
Ortskommandantur 270 (270th Local Command), 173, 177
Ortskommandantur 272 (272nd Local Command), 173, 177
Ortskommandantur 283 (283rd Local Command) (Haapsalu), 94
Ortskommandantur 286 (286th Local Command), 173, 177
Ortskommandantur 308 (308th Local Command), 175–6
Ortskommandantur 318 (318th Local Command), 175–6

Ortskommandantur 320 (320th Local Command), 96
Ortskommandantur I./322 (I./322nd Local Command), 94
Ortskommandantur 325 (325th Local Command), 175–6
Ortskommandantur 327 (327th Local Command), 175–6
Ortskommandantur 328 (328th Local Command), 160, 175–7
Ortskommandantur 330 (330th Local Command), 175–6
Ortskommandantur 332 (332nd Local Command), 94
Ortskommandantur 338 (338th Local Command), 175–6
Ortskommandantur 348 (348th Local Command), 175–6
Ortskommandantur 358 (358th Local Command), 175–6
Ortskommandantur 360 (360th Local Command), 94
Ortskommandantur II./362 (II./362nd Local Command), 94
Ortskommandantur 366 (366th Local Command), 94
Ortskommandantur 367 (367th Local Command), 175–6
Ortskommandantur 368 (368th Local Command), 175–7
Ortskommandantur II./371 (II./371st Local Command), 94
Ortskommandantur II./565 (II./565th Local Command), 95
Ortskommandantur I./574 (I./574th Local Command), 94
Ortskommandantur I./629 (I./629th Local Command), 94
Ortskommandantur II./658 (II./658th Local Command), 95
Ortskommandantur 679 (679th Local Command), 169
Ortskommandantur 746 (746th Local Command), 160, 177
Ortskommandantur 829 (829th Local Command), 173, 177
Ortskommandantur 835 (835th Local Command), 173, 177
Ortskommandantur 837 (837th Local Command), 170, 173, 177
Ortskommandantur 852 (852nd Local Command), 92, 95
Ortskommandantur 854 (854th Local Command), 92, 95
Ortskommandantur 858 (858th Local Command), 92, 95
Ortskommandantur 859 (859th Local Command), 92, 95
Ortskommandantur 860 (860th Local Command), 92, 95
Ortskommandantur 861 (861st Local Command), 92, 96
Ortskommandantur 862 (862nd Local Command), 92, 96
Ortskommandantur 863 (863rd Local Command), 92, 96
Ortskommandantur 864 (864th Local Command), 92, 96
Ortskommandantur 865 (865th Local Command), 92, 96
Ortskommandantur I./882 (I./882 Local Command), 156–7, 160
Ortskommandantur 882 (882nd Local Command), 177

German Code Names

Operation Barbarossa, 6–7, 19–20, 65, 123, 173, 185–6, 188–9, 193, 205, 219
Operation Typhoon, 21, 102, 186

German Regular Army Units

Ostheer (the German Army in the USSR), 2, 4–6, 12, 19, 22–3, 25, 29, 32, 61, 77, 86, 164–5, 187–8, 199, 203, 219

Corps

VI Army Corps, 191
X Army Corps, 134
XI Army Corps, 160, 177
XIII Army Corps, 110
XLIII Army Corps, 133

Divisions

1st Panzer Division, 102
1st Infantry Division, 98–9
6th Infantry Division, 191
15th Infantry Division, 133
19th Panzer Division, 133
58th Infantry Division, 87
62nd Infantry Division, 168–9
84th Infantry Division, 134
113th Infantry Division, 29
134th Infantry Division, 28
158th Infantry Division, 87

162nd Infantry Division, 212
207th Security Division, 71, 76, 92–3, 95, 97–8, 211
212th Infantry Division, 87
213th Security Division, 76, 154, 165, 169–73, 181–2
221st Security Division, 53–5, 56, 76
252nd Infantry Division, 110, 212
281st Security Division, 76, 92–3, 96–8, 102, 135, 211
285th Security Division, 50, 71, 76, 92, 96–8
286th Security Division, 57, 76
309th Infantry Division, 55
339th (Static) Infantry Division, 56, 122
347th Infantry Division, 204
403rd Security Division, 56–7, 76, 133
444th Security Division, 76, 157–8, 160, 171, 173–4, 181, 216
454th Security Division, 76, 173–6, 178, 180–1, 207
707th Infantry Division, 55, 57, 59

Regiments or *kampfgruppen*

800th Special Purpose Brandenburg Regiment, 191
Cavalry Regiment North, 93
3rd Security Regiment, 92
50th Infantry Regiment, 56
46th Regional Defence Regiment, 173, 177, 216
46th Security Regiment, 216
61st Regional Defence Regiment, 57
75th Regional Defence Regiment, 92, 95
94th Regional Defence Regiment, 95
Landesschützen Regiment 102 (102nd Regional Defence Regiment), 175–6
107th Regional Defence Regiment, 92, 96
113th Regional Defence Regiment, 92
113th Security Regiment (formerly 113th Regional Defence Regiment), 96
122nd Regional Defence Regiment, 57
177th Regional Defence Regiment, 56
Artillery Regiment 158, 87
Artillerie Regiment 221 (221st Artillery Regiment), 175–6
290th Infantry Regiment, 47
322nd Infantry Regiment (reinforced), 96–7
360th *Jäger* (Light) Infantry Regiment (ex-360th Infantry Regiment), 173, 177
105th Infantry Regiment, 163
162nd Artillery Regiment, 171
329th Infantry Regiment, 87
354th Infantry Regiment, 57
Jäger Regiment 375 (ex-375th Infantry Regiment), 175–6, 178–9, 181–2
406th Infantry Regiment, 56
409th Infantry Regiment, 87
691st Infantry Regiment, 122
727th Infantry Regiment, 55, 57
747th Infantry Regiment, 55, 57

Battalions

I.–III. Battalions/50th Infantry Regiment, 56
II. Battalion, 164th Infantry Regiment, 168
III. Battalion, 190th Infantry Regiment, 168
I. Battalion, 207th Artillery Regiment, 95
II. Battalion, 207th Artillery Regiment, 96
III. Battalion, 207th Artillery Regiment, 96–7
II. Battalion, 213th Artillery Regiment, 57
III. Battalion, 213th Artillery Regiment, 56
I. Battalion/221st Artillery Regiment, 56
III. Battalion/221st Artillery Regiment, 182
I.–III. Battalions, 322nd Infantry Regiment, 96
III. Battalion, 322nd Infantry Regiment, 211
339th Artillery Battalion, 56
I.–III. Battalions/354th Infantry Regiment, 57
I.–III. Battalion, 375th Infantry Regiment, 179
III. Battalion, 375th Infantry Regiment, 180
I.–III. Battalions/406th Infantry Regiment, 56
207th Cavalry Battalion, 95, 192
70th Engineer Battalion, 163
207th Engineer Battalion, 92
246th Construction Battalion, 171
281st Eastern Cavalry Battalion, 96
285th Russian Cavalry Battalion (from 285th Cavalry Squadron), 97, 210
531st Guard Battalion, 94
531st Construction Battalion, 171
619th Bicycle Guard Battalion, 92
620th Bicycle Guard Battalion, 92
657th Artillery Battalion, 55, 57
694th Security Battalion, 89
571st Guard Battalion, 94
701st Guard Battalion, 55–6
704th Guard Battalion, 57
705th Guard Battalion, 56
706th Guard Battalion, 92, 95
707th Guard Battalion, 92, 96
708th Guard Battalion, 157, 160, 173, 176–7
821st Signals Battalion, 95
822nd Signals Battalion, 96
823rd Signals Battalion, 96–7
826th Signal Battalion, 56
(leichte) Flak Abteilung 828, 173, 177

416th Security Battalion, 216
493rd Security Battalion, 95
853rd Security Battalion, 96
865th Security Battalion, 95
868th Security Battalion, 95
941st Security Battalion, 96
972nd Security Battalion, 96
236th Regional Defence Battalion, 210
258th Regional Defence Battalion, 160, 173, 177
264th Regional Defence Battalion, 173, 177
266th Regional Defence Battalion, 92, 95
286th Regional Defence Battalion, 160, 173, 175, 177
414th Regional Defence Battalion, 169–71, 177, 217
415th Regional Defence Battalion, 175–6
416th Regional Defence Battalion, 175–6
418th Regional Defence Battalion, 175
566th Regional Defence Battalion, 175–6, 180
853rd Regional Defence Battalion, 92, 95, 210–11
859th Regional Defence Battalion, 92, 95
860th Regional Defence Battalion, 95
865th Regional Defence Battalion, 92, 96
868th Regional Defence Battalion, 92, 96
869th Regional Defence Battalion, 92, 96
901st Regional Defence Battalion, 170, 177
920th Regional Defence Battalion, 92
941st Regional Defence Battalion, 92, 211
960th Regional Defence Battalion, 92, 96
972nd Regional Defence Battalion, 92, 211
987th Regional Defence Battalion, 175–6, 182, 219

Military Field Police

521st Military Field Police Battalion, 95
531st Military Field Police Battalion, 32
541st Military Field Police Battalion, 32
561st Military Field Police Battalion, 32, 91, 95
571st Military Field Police Battalion, 32
591st Military Field Police Battalion, 32
682nd Military Field Police Battalion, 32
683rd Military Field Police Battalion, 32, 166
685th Military Field Police Battalion, 32
689th Military Field Police Battalion, 32, 94–5
690th Military Field Police Battalion, 32
691st Military Field Police Battalion, 32, 95
692nd Military Field Police Battalion, 32
693rd Military Field Police Battalion, 32
694th Military Field Police Battalion, 32
695th Military Field Police Battalion, 32
696th Military Field Police Battalion, 32
697th Military Field Police Battalion, 32
698th Military Field Police Battalion, 32

Companies

4th Technical Emergency Company, 174
9th Company, 18th Infantry Regiment, 191
207th Bicycle Reconnaissance Squadron, 92
213th Cossack Cavalry Squadron, 169–70
1st Company, 246th Construction Battalion, 171
285th Tank Company, 210
285th Cavalry Squadron (Russian), 97
286th Signals Company, 57
286th Cavalry Squadron, 57
339th Signals Company, 56
339th Engineer Company, 56
368th Engineer Company, 96
374th Engineer Company, 95
403rd Engineer Company, 56
444th Cossack Cavalry Squadron, 169–71
Panzer Kompanie 445, 173
Turkic Caucasian Volunteer Company, 173
3rd Company, 531st Construction Battalion, 171, 217
637th Propaganda Company, 176, 178
707th Engineer Company, 57
707th Engineer Company, 57
13th Company, 375th Infantry Regiment, 219
14th Company, 375th Infantry Regiment, 178
3rd Company, 691st Infantry Regiment, 122
1st Company/694th Security Battalion, 89
3rd Company, 414th Regional Defence Battalion, 217
4th Company/901st Regional Defence Battalion, 169–70

Secret Field Police Groups

GFP-501, 105
GFP-520, 105
GFP-523, 105
GFP-580, 102
GFP-640, 147
GFP-705, 104
GFP-708, 174–6, 180, 182
GFP-709, 143
GFP-711, 158, 169–70, 173, 177, 216
GFP-713, 104–5
GFP-714, 104
GFP-715, 104
GFP-720, 158, 169–71, 173, 177, 216–17
GFP-721, 174–6, 180, 182–3

GFP-722, 104
GFP-725, 157, 169–70
GFP-726, 157–8, 173, 177, 216
GFP-727, 104
GFP-728, 104
GFP-730, 174–6, 182–3
GFP-744 (L), 105
GFP-774, 157

Armoured Trains

[Note: The *Ostheer* employed twenty-one armoured trains for the 1941 campaign.]
Armoured Train No. 30, 94

POW Camps

Stalag 350, 26
Stalag XX (20), 192
101st Prisoner of War Transit Camp, 92, 95
102nd Prisoner of War Transit Camp, 92, 95
110th Prisoner of War Transit Camp, 92, 96
134th Prisoner of War Transit Camp, 92, 96
152nd Prisoner of War Transit Camp, 173, 177
162nd Prisoner of War Transit Camp, 173, 177
170th Prisoner of War Transit Camp, 175–6
182nd Prisoner of War Transit Camp, 173, 177
201st Prisoner of War Transit Camp, 175–6
205th Prisoner of War Transit Camp, 175–6
320th Prisoner of War Transit Camp, 96

German Army Training and Replacement

202nd Replacement Brigade, 169

German Air Force Formations

Flak Platoon Hatje, 89

SS and Police Commands

Reichssicherheitshauptamt (Reich Security Main Office), 35–6, 196, 200
Kommandostab Reichsführer SS, 35,38, 209
Höhere SS und Polizeiführer Ostland (Higher SS and Police Leader Ostland), 35, 61–2, 66, 71, 208
Höhere SS und Polizeiführer Ostland und Weißruthenien (Higher SS and Police Leader Ostland and White Ruthenia), 208
Höhere SS und Polizeiführer Russland Mitte und Weißrussland (Higher SS and Police Leader Central Russia and White Russia), 45, 62–3, 108, 207
Höhere SS und Polizeiführer zur besondere Verwendung (Higher SS and Police Leader for Special Employment), 49
SS und Polizeiführer Białystok (SS and Police Leader Bialystok), 45
SS und Polizeiführer Estland (SS and Police Leader Estonia), 35, 41, 62
SS und Polizeiführer Lettland (SS and Police Leader Latvia), 35, 44, 62, 77
SS und Polizeiführer Litauen (SS and Police Leader Lithuania), 35, 45, 62
SS und Polizeiführer Lublin (SS and Police Leader Lublin), 44
SS und Polizeiführer Mogilev (SS and Police Leader Mogilev), 46
SS und Polizeiführer Weißruthenien (SS and Police Leader White Ruthenia), 35, 45, 121
SS and Police Station Post Baranovichi, 46
SS and Police Station Post Dorpat (Tartu), 42
SS and Police Station Post Mogilev, 46
SS and Police Station Post Pleskau (Pskov), 42
SS and Police Station Post Smolensk, 46
SS and Police Station Post Vilna (Vilnius), 45
SS and Police Station Post Vitebsk, 46
SS and Police Leader Pripet, 46
Leader of the Order Police and Gendarmerie Reval (Tallinn), 42
BdS Ostland – Befehlshaber der Sicherheitspolizei und Sicherheitsdienst Ostland (Commander of the Security Police and Security Service Eastern land), 52
KdS Estland/(Commander of the Security Police and Security Service Estonia), 36, 39, 52
KdS Lettland/(Commander of the Security Police and Security Service Latvia), 36, 39, 52
KdS Litauen/(Commander of the Security Police and Security Service Lithuania), 36, 39, 52
KdS Weissruthenien/(Commander of the Security Police and Security Service White Ruthenia), 36, 39, 46, 52
KdO Estland - Kommandeur der Ordnungspolizei Estland (Commander of the Order Police Estonia), 41
KdO Lettland - Kommandeur der Ordnungspolizei Lettland (Commander of the Order Police Latvia), 36
KdO Litauen - Kommandeur der Ordnungspolizei Litauen (Commander of the Order Police Lithuania), 45
KdO Ukraine - (Commander of the Order Police Ukraine), 48
Polizeiführer, KdO und Gendarmerie Chernigov (Police Leader and Commander of the Order Police and Gendarmerie in Chernigov), 48

Polizeiführer, KdO und Gendarmerie Nikolayev (Police Leader and Commander of the Order Police and Gendarmerie Nikolayev), 48
Polizeiführer, KdO und Gendarmerie Charkow (Police Leader and Commander of the Order Police and Gendarmerie Kharkov), 48
Kommandant der Staatsschutzpolizei Kertsch (Commander of the State Protection Police Kerch), 48
Polizeistelle Posten Cherson (Police Station Post Kherson), 49
Polizeistelle Posten Dnjepropetrovsk (Police Station Post Dnepropetrovsk), 49
Polizeistelle Posten Kirowograd (Police Station Post Kirovograd), 48, 49
Polizeistelle Posten Kremenchug (Police Station Post Kremenchug), 49
Polizeistelle Posten Melitopol (Police Station Post Melitopol), 49
Polizeistelle Posten Nikopol (Police Station Post Nikopol), 49
Polizeistelle Posten Poltawa (Police Station Post Poltava), 49
Polizeistelle Posten Sumy (Police Station Post Sumy), 49
Polizeistelle Posten Zaporhye (Police Station Post Zaporizhzhia), 49

Murder Commandos

Einsatzgruppe A, 35, 39, 51, 68–9, 71, 73, 80–1, 84, 123–5, 132, 139–41, 146, 215
Einsatzgruppe B, 35, 40, 124, 140, 146
Einsatzgruppe C, 35, 44, 124–5, 174–5
Einsatzgruppe D, 35, 37, 124, 166, 209
Sonderkommando 1a, 39, 51–2, 69, 80–1, 146
Sonderkommando 1b, 39–40, 52, 69, 79, 91, 146
Sonderkommando 1c, 52
Sonderkommando 4a, 41, 165
Sonderkommando 7a, 146
Sonderkommando 7b, 110, 143, 146
Sonderkommando 7c, 40, 209
Sonderkommando 8, 142
Sonderkommando 11b, 163–4
Einsatzgruppe Reval, 39
Einsatzkommando 1a, 82, 124
Einsatzkommando 1b, 124
Einsatzkommando 2, 51, 69, 124, 146
Einsatzkommando 3, 39, 52, 69, 124, 146
Einsatzkommando 4, 41
Einsatzkommando 4a, 174
Einsatzkommando 6, 167
Einsatzkommando 7a, 40
Einsatzkommando 7b, 40
Einsatzkommando 8, 40, 115, 146
Einsatzkommando 9, 40, 146
Einsatzkommando 10b, 37
Einsatzkommando *12*, 166–7
Teilkommando 3, 71
Teilkommando 4, 41
Arājs Kommando, 80
Vorkommando Moskau, 40
For the *Einsatzgruppen:* 1–12 Estonian Auxiliary Police Companies, 39
For the *Einsatzgruppen:* 1st–5th Lithuanian Auxiliary Police Companies, 40

Police

Police Regiment Centre, 47–8, 54, 56, 138–9, 142, 146–7, 212
III. Battalion/Police Regiment Centre, 138
Police Regiment North, 42, 47, 70–1, 73–4, 134, 147, 209
Police Regiment South, 47, 49, 174
Police Regiment for Special Employment, 47
II. Battalion, Police Regiment 6, 216
Police Regiment 9, 75, 209
III. Battalion/Police Regiment 12, 75
Police Regiment 15, 75
Police Regiment 16, 75
Police Regiment 17, 75
III. Battalion/Police Regiment 27, 42, 70
Police Regiment 28 Todt, 42
1st Police Cavalry Battalion, 49
3rd Police Battalion, 68
6th Police Battalion, 48
7. *Technische Nothilfe Bataillon* (7th Technical Emergency Battalion), 94
9th Police Battalion, 68
11th Reserve Police Battalion, 40, 45, 58, 70, 73–4, 79–80, 138, 143, 146–7
22nd Reserve Police Battalion, 145, 147
32nd Police Battalion, 46
33rd Reserve Police Battalion, 44, 70, 74
42nd Police Battalion, 75
53rd Police Battalion, 70
56th Police Battalion, 75, 87
61st Police Battalion, 42, 66, 70, 75–6, 92
65th Police Battalion, 42, 70–1, 96, 133
66th Reserve Police Battalion, 75
69th Reserve Police Battalion Todt, 42, 66, 70, 75, 209
74th Police Battalion, 75
82nd Police Battalion, 76, 174–6, 178–81
85th Police Battalion, 48

91st Police Battalion, 56, 76
102nd Police Battalion, 75, 87
105th Police Battalion, 42, 70, 75, 94
111th Police Battalion, 76
112th Police Battalion, 42, 66, 70, 75–6
121st Police Battalion, 75, 87
131st Police Battalion, 47, 54, 133
132nd Police Battalion, 42, 66, 70, 75–6
134th Police Battalion, 76
254th Police Battalion, 42, 70
301st Police Battalion, 48
304th Police Battalion, 42, 49
305th Police Battalion, 75
306th Police Battalion, 75, 87, 210
307th Police Battalion, 47, 53–4, 56, 133
308th Police Battalion, 48
309th Police Battalion, 47, 53–4, 138
310th Police Battalion, 75, 87
311th Police Battalion, 47, 76, 157–8, 160, 169–71, 173–4, 177
315th Police Battalion, 42, 49
316th Police Battalion, 48, 138, 144, 146–7
317th Police Battalion, 48, 54, 56
318th Police Battalion, 76, 171
319th Police Battalion, 42, 70–1, 74
320th Police Battalion, 42, 49
321st Police Battalion, 42, 70, 74
322nd Police Battalion, 48, 138, 144, 147
323rd Police Battalion, 48
Reserve Polizei Bataillon Ostland (Reserve Police Battalion Eastland), 44, 70, 74–5
10th Police Signals Company, 64
631st Police Communications Company, 46
33rd Police Signals Company, 66–7
82nd Police Communications Company, 45, 68
1st Company/Waffen-SS Battalion for Special Employment, 40
3rd Company/Waffen-SS Battalion for Special Employment, 41
Polizei Technische Nothilfe Kompanie der Polizei Regiment Nord (Police Technical Emergency Company of Police Regiment North), 70
Polizei Technische Nothilfe Kompanie der Polizei Regiment Süd (Police Technical Emergency Company of Police Regiment South), 49
10th Gendarmerie Platoon (motorized), 88
4th Company, 121st Police Battalion, 210
3rd Company, 322nd Police Battalion, 138
Police Economic Warehouse Bialystok, 47
Police Economic Camp Bialystok, 47
Police Economic Camp Vinnitsa, 49
Police Supply Camp Bialystok, 47
Police Supply Warehouse Bialystok, 47

SA (Sturmabteilung)

73rd SA Brigade, 76
134th SA Regiment, 76
171st SA Regiment, 76

Waffen-SS

SS Police Division, 87
16th SS Armoured Infantry Division 'National Leader of the SS', 209
I.–III. Artillery Battalions of the SS Police Division, 87
SS Cavalry Brigade, 37, 55, 63, 65–6, 107–8, 142
SS Cavalry Regiment 1, 37, 63–4
SS Cavalry Regiment 2, 37, 63–4
SS Infantry Brigade 1, 63–4, 66, 181
SS Infantry Brigade 2, 64, 66, 133
3rd Estonian SS Volunteer Brigade, 93
1. Battery, 51st SS Artillery Battalion, 181–2
8th SS Infantry Regiment, 181
10th SS Infantry Regiment, 181–2
III. Battalion, 10th SS Infantry Regiment, 179
8th and 9th Flak Batteries from 51st Flak Company, 182
SS Flak Battalion I, 63, 65
SS Flak Battalion II, 64–5
SS Flak Battalion *Ost* (East), 64–6
SS Escort Battalion *Reichsführer SS*, 64–5, 209
SS Volunteer Regiment Northwest, 64
SS Volunteer Legion Flanders, 65
SS Volunteer Legion Netherlands, 65
SS Volunteer Legion Norway, 87
Battalion of the Waffen-SS for Special Employment, 64, 68
1st Company/Battalion of the Waffen-SS for Special Employment, 71
SS Geological Battalion, 65–6
SS Supply Battalion/*Kommando Stab Reichsführer-SS*, 65–6
Veterinary Battalion/*Kommando Stab Reichsführer-SS*, 65–6
V. Battalion, SS Adolf Hitler Bodyguard Regiment, 87
SS Sonderkommando Dirlewanger, 64
SS Kampfgruppe von Gottberg, 63
SS Kampfgruppe Jeckeln, 86–7

Volunteer Formations

Russian Liberation Army/Russian Army of Liberation, 30

1st Prisoner-of-War Labour Battalion, 192
246th Eastern Construction Battalion, 192
Special Staff Hohlfeld, 192
Special Staff Knoth, 192
Eastern Combat Battalion Dnieper, 192
Graukopf Verbände, 118–19
286th Volunteer Battalion, 216
617th Eastern Battalion, 192
Ukrainische Hundertschaft Feldgendarmerie Trupp 113 (Ukrainian Hunter Field Police Company 113), 29
Intervention Group Tietjen, 191
Defence Operation Tiger B, 191
Kommandeur der Osttruppen 582 (582nd Eastern Troops Command), 191
3rd Prisoner-of-War Labour Engineer Battalion, 191
582nd Eastern Artillery Battery, 191
Kriegsgefangen Kompanie der Pionier Bataillon 113, 29
1st Eastern Guard Company, 31
454th Eastern Cavalry Battalion, 207
I. Battalion/454th Eastern Cavalry Battalion, 31, 207
II. Battalion/454th Eastern Cavalry Battalion, 207
583rd Cossack Infantry Battalion, 31
783rd Turkestani Infantry Battalion, 31
802nd North Caucasian Infantry Battalion, 31
36. Kosaken Kavallerie Kompanie, (36th Cossack Cavalry Company), 94
38. Kosaken Kavallerie Kompanie (38th Cossack Cavalry Company), 94

***Schutzmannschaft* Battalions**

Lithuanian

Lithuanian Guard Company Dno, 45, 86
Lithuanian Guard Company Toropets, 45, 86
Lithuanian Security Battalion Kaunas, 86
650th Lithuanian Eastern Guard Company, 86
651st Lithuanian Eastern Guard Company, 86
5th Lithuanian Self-Defence Battalion, 45, 210
Lithuanian Self-Defence Guard Battalion Kaunas, 86
250th Lithuanian Self-Defence Battalion, 86

Latvian

267th Latvian Self-Defence Guard Battalion, 95
276th Latvian Self-Defence Battalion, 88
277th Latvian Self-Defence Battalion, 88
278th Latvian Self-Defence Battalion, 88
279th Latvian Self-Defence Battalion, 88
321st Latvian Police Battalion, 89
652nd Latvian Eastern Guard Company, 86
Latvian Security Battalion Riga, 45
16th Latvian Self-Defence Battalion, 44, 84, 133, 135
4th Company/17th Latvian Self-Defence Battalion, 86
18th Latvian Self-Defence Battalion, 45, 210

Estonian

Estonian Security Battalion Pleskau (Pskov), 83
Estonian Self-Defence Cadre Battalion, 43
19th Latvian Self-Defence Battalion, 45
Estonian Self-Defence Battalion Dorpat (Tartu), 43
Estonian Self-Defence Battalion Fellin (Viljandi), 43
Estonian Self-Defence Battalion Pihkva, 43
Estonian Self-Defence Battalion Poltsama (Põltsamaa), 43
Estonian Self-Defence Construction Battalion, 43
Estonian Self-Defence Front Battalion 36, 43, 83
37th Estonian Self-Defence Front Battalion, 43, 83
38th Estonian Self-Defence Front Battalion, 43
39th Estonian Security Battalion, 43, 83
40th Estonian Self-Defence Front Battalion, 43
41st Estonian Self-Defence Front Battalion, 43, 83
42nd Estonian Engineer Self-Defence Battalion, 43, 83
181st–186th Estonian Security Battalions (later redesignated 658th–665th Estonian Eastern Battalions), 43

Estonian *Omakaitse* Battalions

Estonian Self-Defence Cadre Battalion, 83
Estonian Self-Defence Battalion Dorpat, 83
Estonian Self-Defence Battalion Fellin, 83
Estonian Self-Defence Battalion Poltsama, 83
Self-Defence Tallinn, 82
Self-Defence Harju County, 82
Self-Defence Järva County, 82
Self-Defence Lääne County, 82

Self-Defence Viru County, 82
Self-Defence Narva, 82
Self-Defence Pärnu, 82
Self-Defence Petseri, 82
Self-Defence Saaremaa, 82
Self Defence Sakala, 82
Self-Defence Tartu, 82
Self-Defence Valga, 82
Self-Defence Võru, 82
Self-Defence School (battalion in size), 82

Eastern and Front-line Security Battalions

Estonian
181st Estonian Security Battalion, 43, 84
182nd Estonian Security Battalion, 43, 84
183rd Estonian Security Battalion, 43, 84
184th Estonian Security Battalion, 43, 84
185th Estonian Security Battalion, 43, 84
186th Estonian Security Battalion, 43, 84
657th Estonian Eastern Battalion, 43, 84
658th Estonian Eastern Battalion, 43, 84, 94
659th Estonian Eastern Battalion, 43, 84, 94
660th Estonian Eastern Battalion, 43, 84, 94
661st Russian Eastern Battalion, 84
662nd Russian Eastern Battalion, 84
663rd Russian Eastern Battalion, 84
666th Estonian Eastern Battalion, 94

Russian
667th Russian Eastern Battalion, 95
668th Russian Eastern Battalion, 95

Finnish
664th Finnish Eastern Battalion, 94

Axis Allied Axis Units

Romanian 90th *Jäger* (Light) Regiment, 160, 166, 170, 177
Slovak Fast Division, 181